Madhu Jain was educated at Connecticut College in the United States, following which she did her masters in literature from Delhi University and studied French literature at the Sorbonne in Paris. In the 1970s she worked as a reporter for the *Statesman*, moving towards the end of the decade to *Sunday* magazine to write on politics, foreign affairs and culture. She was also the New Delhi correspondent with the French national daily, *La Croix*, for a decade before she joined *India Today* in 1986, where she remained until 2000. Since then she has written for several publications, including *Outlook* and the *Hindu*, on contemporary life, art and cinema. She has curated two art exhibitions—Kitsch Kitsch Hota Hai on kitsch and the contemporary imagination and the other on the painter Viswanadhan.

Madhu Jain lives in Delhi with her physicist husband Krishna Jain. They have two children.

PRAISE FOR THE BOOK

'Extremely engrossing and eminently readable...a treat for all cinema lovers'—*Tribune*

'It's amazing that a book on the first family of Hindi cinema took so long in coming...Jain's book is a compelling account of a family consumed by passion...'—*Sunday Mid-day*

'Madhu Jain's exhaustive and epic biography of the Kapoors is, all at once, a meticulous history of the "first family of Indian cinema", a study of the development of cinema and performance in post-independent Inida, and, most grippingly, a romantic saga of the lives of a proud and powerful *khandaan*...'—*Osian Cinemaya*

'Well-written [and] well-researched...the section on Raj Kapoor is fascinating'—*Hindustan Times*

'[Madhu Jain's] style is chatty...[The] book is like an entertaining masala movie—it has action, drama and romance...full of anecdotes, historical tidbits and movie lore'—*Tehelka*

The Kapoors

The First Family of Indian Cinema

REVISED EDITION

MADHU JAIN

PENGUIN BOOKS

PENGUIN BOOKS
Published by the Penguin Group
Penguin Books India Pvt. Ltd, 11 Community Centre, Panchsheel Park, New Delhi 110 017, India
Penguin Group (USA) Inc., 375 Hudson Street, New York, New York 10014, USA
Penguin Group (Canada), 90 Eglinton Avenue East, Suite 700, Toronto, Ontario, M4P 2Y3, Canada (a division of Pearson Penguin Canada Inc.)
Penguin Books Ltd, 80 Strand, London WC2R 0RL, England
Penguin Ireland, 25 St Stephen's Green, Dublin 2, Ireland (a division of Penguin Books Ltd)
Penguin Group (Australia), 250 Camberwell Road, Camberwell, Victoria 3124, Australia (a division of Pearson Australia Group Pty Ltd)
Penguin Group (NZ), 67 Apollo Drive, Rosedale, North Shore 0632, New Zealand (a division of Pearson New Zealand Ltd)
Penguin Group (South Africa) (Pty) Ltd, 24 Sturdee Avenue, Rosebank, Johannesburg 2196, South Africa

Penguin Books Ltd, Registered Offices: 80 Strand, London WC2R 0RL, England

First published in Viking by Penguin Books India 2005
Published in Penguin Books 2009

10 9 8 7 6 5 4 3 2 1

ISBN 9780143065890

Typeset in *Sabon Roman* by SÜRYA, New Delhi
Printed at Gopsons Papers Ltd, Noida

To my parents
the late Lakhpat Rai and Padma Sethi
For giving me everything and more

Contents

Acknowledgements

I am grateful to all those who in their interviews and reminiscences gave so unstintingly of their time, and of themselves. Their conversations with me have been included in the book as far as possible in their own voices. The list of those I would like to thank is unending. I have mentioned many from the Kapoor family and circle of friends in the introductory chapter. There are numerous others.

From the world of cinema: Tinnu Anand, Tanuja, Nadira, Amit Khanna, Lekh Tandon, Yograj Tandon, Dara Singh, Shyam Benegal, Govind Nihalani, Ramesh Sippy, Sudhir Mishra, Amitabh Bachchan, Sharmila Tagore, Shakti Samanta, Nanda, Ali Raza, Nimmi, Zul Vellani, Sanjay Leela Bhansali, Prem Chopra, B.R. Chopra, the late Yash Johar, Yash Chopra, Zohra Segal, B.M. Vyas, Vishwamitra Mehra 'Mamaji', Dev Anand, Simi Garewal, Ramanand Sagar, Kumar Shahani, Vyjanthimala and James Ivory. I owe special thanks to the late Ismail Merchant, a friend who encouraged me from the outset: I deeply regret the fact that he is no longer with us to read this book, and tell me what more I could have done. The contribution of P.K. Nair, a walking encyclopaedia of cinema, is invaluable. As is that of Bunny Reuben, who was not only generous in sharing his knowledge of the Kapoors, but whose biography of and articles about Raj Kapoor were immensely important in my research. Ritu Nanda's book on her father was studded with nuggets of information about the rest of the Kapoors. She and Shashi Kapoor have very generously provided a large number of the photographs used in this book.

Friends have been pillars of support, and a few of them like

Rashmi Shankar and Madhu Malik shed some new light on Raj Kapoor. The contribution of Bina Ramani, a close friend of many of the Kapoors, is considerable. I am also grateful to Rupika Chawla for the trip to Loni, Raj Kapoor's farm: she was researching a book on Raja Ravi Varma not far from there at Karla Caves. I would also like to thank her for our many conversations about the Kapoor films, and the challenge of getting under the skin of the respective subjects of our inquiry. I would also like to thank fellow journalists and film writers for the insights they shared with me: Khalid Mohammed, Suresh Kohli, Sunil Sethi, Nasreen Munni Kabir, Nina Arora, Anupama Chopra, Dinesh Raheja, Namrata Joshi, Deepa Gahlot and Lata Khubchandani.

This book would not be possible without the generous hospitality of Anuradha and Udayan Patel in Mumbai: their home was my home while researching there. I am grateful to Udayan for the endless conversations we had over the years which gave me a deeper understanding of the Kapoors and their films.

Special thanks to my editors at Penguin: Ravi Singh, whose gentle pressure spurred me through what at times seemed an impossible task over the long years, and Sumitra Srinivasan and Shantanu Ray Chaudhuri who stepped up the required pressure. It was fun working with them. I would also like to thank David Davidar and Karthika at Penguin.

Lastly, but most importantly, I would like to thank my family. My sister, Nina, and her husband Ranjit Puri have always been very supportive. My husband, Krishna, has not only encouraged me but more importantly, all but locked me into the study to write. I could not have written this book without his prodding or understanding. Or without the moral and loving support of our two children, Sonali Jain-Chandra and Siddharth Jain, and son-in-law Rinku Chandra.

Kapoor Family Tree

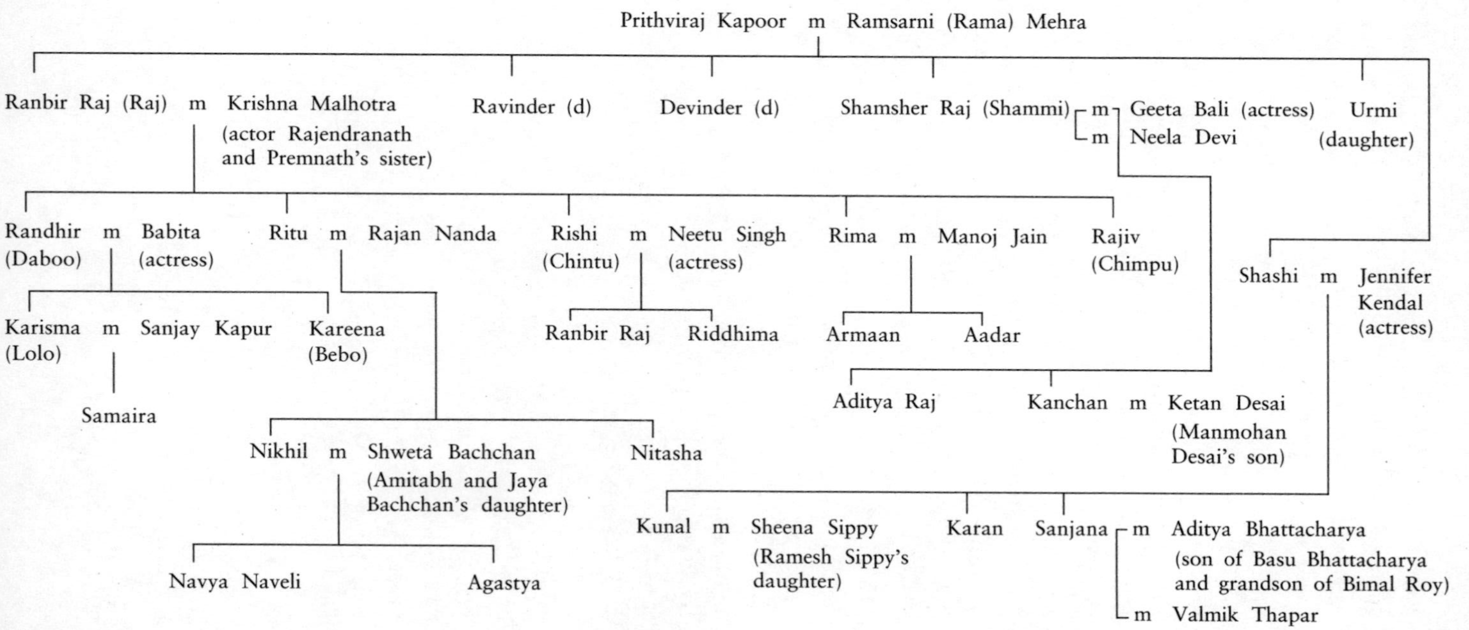

Introduction

Darkness had settled in on the way to Khandala. The narrow road curved into oblivion, the street lights slanting feebly on it. Three of us were driving down from Bombay on a winter day in 1969 to this charming hill station in the Western Ghats. We wanted to surprise an actor-friend on a film shoot here. The road was deserted, and we were hopelessly lost, until we saw a tall man walking down the road, the mist playing hide and seek with this figure in a white kurta pyjama. I rolled down the car window a few inches to ask for directions, not quite making the effort to look the stranger in the eye. In impeccable, pucca-sahib English he obliged. There was something familiar about his voice. Curious, I rolled the window down further to stick my head out: the bemused, smiling face of Shashi Kapoor came into view. And then that face with its trademark smile—one that has launched a million crushes—disappeared into the night.

Shashi Kapoor has this habit of going up to people and saying, 'I am Shashi Kapoor. Haven't we met before?' It sounds like a 'line', but he actually means it when he says it. The actor has a phenomenal memory, rarely forgetting a face and the name that goes with it. A few years later, while lunching at Ginza, a popular Chinese restaurant in New Delhi, I spotted Shashi Kapoor at another table. He was lunching with a common friend, who introduced us. And out came the trademark line, 'Haven't we met before?' I smiled vaguely and, tongue-tied, mumbled something about seeing him at various film festivals. 'No, it was in Khandala,' he said, grinning mischievously.

I was a reporter with the *Statesman* through much of the seventies. Occasionally asked to write about films I often turned to my 'Khandala friend' for help, continuing to do so through the next two decades when I shifted to *Sunday* magazine and later to *India Today*. Shashi was never less than generous in sharing his perceptive insights into and anecdotes about Indian cinema. He even tried to help arrange an interview with a recalcitrant Amitabh Bachchan. The eyes of most actors glaze over when you talk about other actors, or something other than themselves. Shashi Kapoor, however, seldom speaks about himself, preferring to tell fascinating stories about his father, his wife Jennifer Kendal and his brother Raj Kapoor.

Almost a decade ago a publisher suggested I write an authorized biography of Shashi Kapoor. When I asked him, he didn't take more than a second to refuse. Nor did he want to write an autobiography. 'There are things about myself,' he told me, 'that even I don't want to know.' What he was keen on, however, was a biography of Prithvi Theatres—to record for posterity the contribution of Prithviraj Kapoor in its first avatar, and that of Jennifer and his two children Sanjana and Kunal in its second. (The book he had in mind was eventually published in 2004 as *Prithviwallahs*.)

So, I shelved the idea of a Shashi Kapoor biography. I realized that I had missed the wood for the trees. The biography that was waiting to be written was not of a particular Kapoor but of the Kapoors en masse, the Kapoor *khandaan* (dynasty). The Kapoor family is unique in the history of cinema, Indian or international. In the first decade of the new millennium, the fourth generation of Kapoors continues to be on the cinema marquees. Or, one can say the fifth generation if you include Bashesharnath Kapoor, Prithviraj Kapoor's father: he played the judge in *Awara*. In his review of *Bobby* in the *New York Times*, Bernard Weintraub described the Kapoors as the 'Redgraves of Indian cinema'. It was an understatement then, and even more so now. You can count the Redgraves on your hands, as you can other film dynasties like the Hustons and the Barrymores. You would need two sets of hands and more to count the number of actors and directors in the Kapoor family tree. In quantifiable terms no film dynasty even begins to approach the Kapoors. The only dynasty (excluding monarchies) comparable to the Kapoors in this respect is a political one—the Kennedys.

It would have been a dream alliance—a merger between the first family of Indian politics and the first family of Indian cinema. Sometime in the mid-sixties, Indira Gandhi was looking for a suitable Indian bride for her elder son, Rajiv. And, apparently, she thought she had found her in Ritu Kapoor, Raj and Krishna Kapoor's blue-eyed daughter. But the dream alliance was not to be: Rajiv, away at Cambridge, was by then deeply in love with Sonia Maino, and the two were married in 1967 in New Delhi.

Mrs Gandhi wasn't star-struck. In fact, we may even assume that Bollywood was an unusual place for her to look for a daughter-in-law. But the appeal of the Kapoors lay beyond the fact that they were India's premier film family, and that Raj Kapoor was almost a household name in the erstwhile Soviet Union, parts of China and North Africa, and even Israel. It had to do with family pedigree. Prithviraj Kapoor, the founder of the Kapoor film dynasty, was a close associate of Jawaharlal Nehru. He also knew Jawaharlal Nehru's father, Motilal Nehru. A Rajya Sabha member of Parliament for five years, Prithviraj had been a staunch Congressman. Jawaharlal and he were roughly the same age, and shared more or less the same ideals. While the charismatic politician played out his vision of socialism and a secular society on the political stage, the imposing thespian transported a similar vision in his productions for Prithvi Theatres, staging the plays in remote corners of the country.

Raj Kapoor, too, like his father, was an admirer of Nehru and knew him well. He almost put Nehru on screen. According to Vishwa Mehra, Raj Kapoor's relative, shadow and Man Friday at R.K. Films, Nehru had agreed to appear in *Ab Dilli Door Nahin*, a film produced by Raj Kapoor. 'Rajji had met Panditji. The film was about a boy who goes to see Chacha Nehru with a letter for him, hoping to get his innocent father released from jail. The episode was to be shot in Teen Murti. But then others advised the prime minister not to appear in a film.'

Nevertheless, Nehru was an unseen presence in Raj Kapoor's early films that celebrated his socialist, old-world idealism.

Convinced about the importance of cultural diplomacy, Nehru even sent Prithviraj to South East Asia on a mission. In fact, the prime minister wanted him to travel extensively, representing India in international forums. Nor was he unaware of Raj Kapoor's popularity in the erstwhile Soviet Union. Apparently, when Nehru was in Moscow, Stalin asked him who this Kapoor was about whom he had been hearing so much.

At some level, this close connection appears natural; its absence might even surprise us. The Nehru-Gandhis and the Kapoors are two dynasties that rule the nation's popular imagination. Generations of the two families have nourished it through much of the last century, and continue to do so in this one. While the political family impinges on our public lives, the show business originals inveigle themselves into our intimate lives and fantasies, feeding our notions of romance, and even our notions of history. Akbar, historians tell us, was barely five feet tall, but after K. Asif's 1960 epic *Mughal-e-Azam*, many people began to believe that the great Mughal was tall and imposing, with a booming voice—like Prithviraj Kapoor who played him so memorably in the film.

The progenitors of both the clans made the blueprints, laying the foundation for their heirs. And successive generations have adapted the legacy to their time and zeitgeist. Indira Gandhi was as different from her father as Raj Kapoor and his brothers Shammi and Shashi were from theirs. Idealism had lost some of its shine by the time they took up the reins. By the time the Gandhis were represented by Rajiv and Sanjay Gandhi, and the Kapoors by Randhir and Rishi Kapoor, the heroic was no longer in vogue, nor were patriarchs. It was the time for pragmatism. The current generation of both families has more of an individualistic streak and inherent noblesse oblige. Whether it is the savvy Priyanka Gandhi Vadra and the outspoken Rahul Gandhi or Randhir Kapoor's spunky daughters Karisma and Kareena Kapoor, their names are their fortunes. The clans live on.

A family of professional actors and film-makers, the Kapoor khandaan spans almost a century of Indian cinema—from the time of the silent movies to the present. Prithviraj joined films when Indian cinema was in its infancy, starring in the first full-length talkie *Alam Ara* (1931). On the eve of the new millennium, his great-granddaughter Kareena made waves with her very first film, *Refugee*. Her elder sister, Karisma, the first daughter of the clan to become a star, was already a veteran by this time, straddling both commercial and middle-of-the-road cinema. As this book goes to press, Rishi Kapoor's son Ranbir Raj is waiting in the wings.

There is no other film family quite like the Kapoors. Each decade in the history of Indian cinema has had at least one Kapoor—if not more—playing a large part in defining it. Prithviraj Kapoor's three sons—Raj Kapoor, Shammi Kapoor and Shashi Kapoor (each separated by seven years)—have earned secure and distinct places in the celluloid pantheon. The three brothers represent three different styles, according to director Govind Nihalani, who has worked with Shashi Kapoor. 'Raj Kapoor inherited his father's acting talent as well as his humanist and leftist ideology, apparent especially in his earlier films. Even when it was pure entertainment, he highlighted the social aspects of his characters. Shammi brought a new colour to Indian cinema with his sense of exuberance and expression. Shashi had a different kind of sensibility because of his long association with Prithvi Theatres, Shakespeareana and his wife Jennifer. His sensibility is more Western and modern. Charm, understatement and restraint define him. He also had a contemporary way of expressing emotions.'

Through the fifties and sixties, the three brothers dominated Hindi cinema. And through the next decade and a half, Shashi Kapoor, with his nephews Randhir and Rishi Kapoor, especially the latter, survived the Amitabh Bachchan-spawned age of the angry, fist-flinging hero, playing romantic leads. Later, just when it looked like the first family of Indian cinema was finally in decline, Karisma and Kareena put it right back in the lead.

Surf the channels on the small screen on any given day and there is likely to be a Kapoor popping up. If not a Kapoor by birth, the star you see could well a Kapoor by marriage. If you are even moderately interested in Hindi cinema, the 'spot-the-Kapoor-connection' game becomes far more intricate and interesting. The Kapoors have married other film personalities or into other film families. Apart from marital connections, there are many actors who are associated with the family as friends.

The tentacles of the Kapoor 'family' spread wide and deep into the Indian film industry (see family tree). Geeta Bali (Shammi Kapoor's first wife) was an actress; Neetu Singh (Rishi's wife) was his leading lady in several box-office hits; Babita (married to Randhir Kapoor) was also an actress; even Jennifer Kendal (Shashi Kapoor's wife), arguably the finest actress of her time, acted in a couple of Hindi films. Actors Premnath and Rajendranath are not only Raj Kapoor's cousins, they are also the brothers of his wife, Krishna. Actor–director Tinnu Anand is a cousin. The 'other' Kapoors (Boney, Anil and Sanjay) belong to the larger Kapoor clan from Peshawar. Actor Prem Chopra is married to one of Krishna Kapoor's half-sisters. There are several marital alliances with the scions of Bollywood luminaries: Shammi Kapoor's daughter Kanchan is married to Manmohan Desai's son Ketan Desai; Shashi Kapoor's elder son Kunal is married to Sheena Sippy, Ramesh Sippy's daughter; while Shashi's daughter Sanjana was married to film-maker Aditya Bhattacharya, Basu Bhattacharya's son, whose maternal grandfather was Bimal Roy.[1]

There are also, of course, the much talked about might-have-been marital mergers between the Kapoors and the Bachchans. Harivansh Rai and Teji Bachchan, it is said, had asked for the hand of Raj Kapoor's daughter Ritu for their son Amitabh, but horoscopes came in the way. The two families had to wait decades for another alliance: Bachchan's daughter Shweta married Ritu's son Nikhil Nanda. Raj Kapoor's granddaughter Karisma Kapoor was engaged to Amitabh Bachchan's son Abhishek. This time something other than horoscopes—no one outside the families quite knows what—prevented the union.

The Kapoors consider themselves Hindu Pathans[2] from Peshawar, which is located in the North West Frontier Province and borders Afghanistan. Displacement, migration—just moving away—make life's journey unpredictable, and usually more uphill.

There are, however, compensations, like the opportunity to reinvent oneself. Once transplanted to new soil, this branch of the Peshawar Kapoors rapidly grew another set of roots. Fair skin, light eyes, an exaggerated notion of hospitality, a soupçon of macho swagger, a love for food—these are a few of the vestiges of the Pathan character that survived the move to Bombay from the Frontier outpost. The family used these imported kernels to create a fantasy of what being a Kapoor meant. The migrant Pathans from a solid middle-class background reinvented themselves as the royals of tinsel town. Old snobberies gave way to new, extravagant ones. The Kapoors are after all, if nothing else, masters of myth making.

In creating a sense of home in this new city, Prithviraj Kapoor formed Prithvi Theatres—a moving tower of Babel comprising about 160 theatre professionals from various regions of the country spouting different languages—in the image of the city of Bombay itself, which was a sound kaleidoscope of many tongues, a rich brew of languages. His repertory was his larger family, one always on the move. Yet, it would almost seem that the more the family wandered, the further they went from 'home', the more the rituals and customs from a distant homeland surfaced—and predominated—with a vengeance. It was almost as if Prithviraj was trying to recreate the world of the Pathans which he had given up. He took the Pathan virtue of hospitality to an extreme: the Kapoor home in Matunga was like a dharamsala, and the man himself a paterfamilias to those who worked for him in Prithvi Theatres—and anybody else who turned up at the door for help. Among his peers, his gestures were the grandest, his voice and laughter the loudest.

Raj Kapoor did it differently. He rarely moved out of his famous cottage in R.K. Films in Chembur, spending most of his waking hours there with his colleagues, friends and hangers-on; but like his father, all of them were from different parts of the country. And for Raj Kapoor, home was a bit of Punjab grafted on to Bombay. In Kapoor tradition, conversation is punctuated with *ji*s. Countless *peri pena*s (feet touching) are a visual refrain in family gatherings. Robust *jhappi*s (hugs) are the ubiquitous form of greeting—perhaps an atavistic inkling of tribal bonding.

'We are actually deep-rooted Punjabis,' says Randhir. 'We follow all the customs at weddings. Even in life, we are old-fashioned.' Ramesh Sippy based some of his characterizations and mannerisms in *Buniyad*, his epic saga on television of a Punjabi family, on the Kapoors. 'A lot of *Buniyad*—the feet-touching, all the chaijis, papajis, baujis came from my impressions of the Kapoor clan...they came closest to my idea of the story of a Punjabi family.' This is hardly surprising, for the Kapoor vision of life tends to be refracted through the world of cinema. It defines their lives. For them, the line between art and life is blurred. Fantasies of the screen materialize in the real world and vice versa. Who better then than the Kapoors as inspiration for a soap opera?

Prithviraj was a man of simple tastes. For the next generation however everything had to be the biggest and the best: whether it was clothes, jewels or cars. Raj Kapoor blew it out of all proportion with his Gatsbyesque parties where everything imaginable was on offer—from a smorgasbord of kebabs and canapés to Scotch. There were stalls for diverse kinds of food—Indian, Continental and Chinese (long before five-star hotels cottoned on to the multiple-choice concept)—and even live lobsters. Every kind of liqueur was also on offer. Like Jay Gatsby, Raj Kapoor wanted to serve his guests the best and the most expensive the world had to offer, without really partaking of any himself. He did love his food and his drink, more than was good for him, but was happiest in the role of an observer, watching his guests enjoy his hospitality.

When the Kapoors ran out of customs and rituals, they invented them. The family began to envelop itself in an imagined lore: new rites and celebrations evolved, all burgeoning into a still-expanding Kapooriana. Social and family events, premieres and birthdays were routinely transformed into elaborate productions. Raj became the original showman of Hindi cinema. He celebrated his birthday as Worker's Day: on this day there were traffic jams on the roads leading to R.K. Films. Not only were there games and an abundance of food, but also extravagant presents for the workers: bicycles, watches or radios. Shashi emulated his brother when he could. After the premiere of a film he had produced, he would throw a party. All the technicians and workers were invited, and he gave them transistor radios and watches when his bank balance allowed it. Raj Kapoor's Holi and Diwali parties became annual landmark events for the film community in Bombay, a red-letter day on filmdom's social register. The R.K. Holi parties, in particular, had the entire film industry turning up, and most of the guests ended up in a large pond filled with coloured water. Raj even celebrated his daughter Ritu's doll's wedding in grand style: the *barat* came in an old Studebaker and Shammi Kapoor took an 8mm movie of the wedding. Years later, when Ritu herself was married, Raj Kapoor unleashed a week-long extravaganza. The groom's family was flown down in a chartered plane, Shankar–Jaikishen composed the music, and there was food from all corners of the country and the finest liqueurs at an elegant sit-down dinner for thousands. A decade later, Rishi Kapoor and Neetu Singh's wedding went on for almost three weeks. Since the guest list went into thousands, the wedding reception took place in the Chembur golf course. For the latest Kapoor wedding—Karisma's—over a thousand guests were invited to Devnar Cottage, and again there was food from all corners of the country and the finest from abroad.

Generation Y may not host lavish parties or give away presents, but the love for the good things in life, especially food, still sets the Kapoors apart. In a television chat show, the youngest Kapoor star, Kareena Kapoor, went ecstatic talking about tandoori food. Her father, Randhir Kapoor, announces proudly, 'She is like me...She's a Kapoor all right. As a family we are fond of the better things in life. Good food, good booze, good living—our life revolves around this.' This great love has spawned a few family rites. At regular intervals the senior Kapoors—Shammi and Shashi—still take the entire clan out to a Chinese restaurant: Nanking (before it closed down), Kamlin and China Garden. (Many restaurants in Mumbai stock monogrammed chopsticks for the Kapoors.) Or, they meet at Devnar Cottage.

Nothing succeeds like excess for the Kapoors. And nothing destroys quite like it either. The flip side of the eat-drink-and-be-merry philosophy of life has been obesity, alcoholism, the occasional streak of wildness and a bouquet of maladies, among which diabetes has been most persistent. Wherever the gene for alcoholism may have originally come from, it became progressively more pronounced as it made its way down the family tree. Shammi Kapoor describes it as the 'family curse'. It is probably the most prominent tragic flaw of the Kapoors. While Prithviraj Kapoor drank only moderately, his sons have had their dark passages with liquor. Raj's three sons have been devastated by alcohol and have struggled with its demons.

If you look at the Kapoor family today, scattered all over the city, they seem quite sealed into their nuclear family unit; those in the case of Randhir and his wife Babita are further split. However, there is strong sense of family binding them all, like invisible glue. The ritual is clearly about the entire clan staying together, for the Kapoors have an exaggerated sense of family. Randhir, or Daboo as he is popularly known, likes to compare his family to the Italian mafia: 'We are our own individual personalities. We are brought up like individual thinking men; we don't meddle in each other's lives. But we are like Sicilians: when you need us, we gang up. We are like the Corleones in *The Godfather*. We flock together when there is a crisis.' Daboo's similies are endless: he compares his clan to a 'fire brigade—when needed, they are there'. This was amply displayed when Randhir Kapoor underwent heart surgery at Escorts Hospital in Delhi in 2003. The entire clan flew down from Mumbai to be with him. His uncles, Shammi and Shashi, his mother, his brothers, his sisters, their husbands, even his estranged wife and daughters, cousins and friends transformed the hospital into Kapoor country. The 'Sicilians' also kept vigil in Breach Candy Hospital in Mumbai when Shammi Kapoor was seriously ill the same year. There is an unstated protocol here. 'In sickness,' says Shashi Kapoor, 'all the Kapoors come together.'

Looking back, it seems improbable that this banyan-tree spread, this huge, larger-than-life, hyperbolic image of the Kapoors has developed over just seven-and-a-half decades—it was only in 1928, after all, that Prithviraj Kapoor left the rather rough terrain of the North West Frontier and moved to the fledgling metropolis of Bombay to carve a new life for himself.

It is almost as if the Kapoors scripted their lives. Self-invention and self-promotion went hand in hand in the carnival world of show business. The Kapoors have always been both actors and stars, and most of them have led their lives trapped in their cinematic images. Randhir says of his father's image: 'You see, any normal person cannot become Raj Kapoor unless he is larger than life.' Talking of his father's death, Randhir says, 'He could not have died in his sleep...It was fated that he would go as he did. From 1 May to 2 June he created a big climax to his life. When he got his attack in Siri Fort Auditorium, the president himself walked up to him to give him the Dadasaheb Phalke Award. Raj Kapoor was a great showman—going into a coma at the ceremony, the president's ambulance taking him to the hospital. Every film has a climax. Raj Kapoor's life, too, had a climax.'

Raj Kapoor has even left behind a cinematic symbol of his life: the black granite samadhi he shares with his parents, Prithviraj and Ramsarni Kapoor, in Raj Bagh, his farm in Loni a little outside Pune. When Sohanlal, the caretaker who was once Raj Kapoor's cook, takes me on a tour of the great showman's retreat, the place almost comes to life. He shows us the room in which *Bobby*'s evergreen song sequence 'Hum tum ek kamre mein band hon' was filmed. He takes us to the river Mora Mutha, towards the end of the farm, where *Satyam Shivam Sundaram*'s dramatic sequence of floods was filmed. Images of Raj Kapoor sitting on the curved veranda, working on his scripts late into the night, flash before my eyes.

This 100-acre farm where many of the R.K. films were partially made (*Satyam Shivam Sundaram*, *Bobby*, *Prem Rog* and *Prem Granth*) has now been sold to the Maharashtra Education Institute Training College. All that is left of the great showman's retreat is the rectangular samadhi, his house and the two-storeyed tower-like stone-and-wood office. And the hundreds of Gulmohar trees that sway gently in the breeze the late winter afternoon I am there. A few flowers left by an anonymous fan lie on the smooth surface of the samadhi. The Kapoors don't come here any more. Shashi Kapoor used to visit the samadhi of his parents and his brother. But he hasn't visited since the farm was sold.

The subsequent generation of Kapoors is different. As Randhir Kapoor likes to repeat, they are 'urbans', people of the city, of

Bombay, not Pathans from the Frontier. The cinematic torch of this 'traditional, old-fashioned family' is being carried forward by two women, Karisma and Kareena (while their cousin Ranbir gets ready to make his acting debut). Only one thing remains unchanged: there will always be another Kapoor waiting in the wings as one fades out, for when it comes to the Kapoors there will always be an encore.

This book is largely based on hundreds of interviews conducted over the last seven years. Countless interviews with Shashi Kapoor yielded a goldmine of information. His photographic memory made his reminiscing all the more valuable. He also opened many doors, even unmarked ones, into the universe of India's first family of cinema: from family, to friends, colleagues and the many forgotten actors, actresses and cineastes who had once played an important role in the life and work of the older Kapoors. Raj Kapoor was no longer alive when I started researching this book. Fortunately, I had met him a couple of times in his beloved cottage in R.K. Films while working on feature articles. Several members of the family opened their respective bags of memories. Shammi Kapoor, reluctant at first but more forthcoming later, was delightfully frank and at times quite theatrical. He often read out from the personal diary he writes on his computer. Ritu Nanda related interesting anecdotes from her childhood. Randhir Kapoor opened up both the studio as well as their Chembur home for me, and was very generous with his time. 'Mamaji', the studio's living memory bank, was a fund of information about life in Peshawar and R.K. Films. Both Rishi and Neetu Kapoor were candid beyond expectation, as were their two children. As also the children of the other Kapoors, particularly Sanjana Kapoor.

In writing this book, what interested me was the life behind the work of the Kapoors. I wanted to explore the terrain between gossip and academic analysis, essentially steering clear of both. The screen personas of this 'dynasty' are in our collective memory. Biography deals with events that throw light on a character.

What goes into the forging of a character, however, tends to remain elusive. Since childhood, and even adolescence, are said to hold the key to the character of a person, it was essential to go beyond the small circle of immediate family to the larger clan, and to friends and neighbours who had grown up with them.

Recollections about Prithviraj Kapoor come wrapped in hagiographic epithets. He was by all accounts an exceptional man, pioneering and larger-than-life. But what made him tick? What was he like as a child, a son, husband, father, and friend? What made this Kapoor—for me the most intriguing and adventurous of the family—leave the North West Frontier Province in the twenties and head to Bombay to become an actor, abandoning his semi-bourgeois background and the path to a legal career laid out for him? What explains Raj Kapoor's all-consuming, at times self-destructive passion for cinema? What demons plagued him? What was it like for the other Kapoors growing up in the shadow of their overwhelming father and elder brother?

A few of the answers came from the inhabitants of 'Hollywood Lane', the little lane in Matunga called College Back Road that was home to the Kapoors for most of the growing-up years of Prithviraj Kapoor's children. Mrs Jagat Singh Ahuja (known as Lachcha masi) was Ramsarni Kapoor's closest friend, and shed light on the quotidian life of the family. Her son Vinny Ahuja, a close friend of Raj and Shashi Kapoor, was very generous with his time and refreshingly frank about the Kapoors in a series of interviews. As was screenwriter and director Prayag Raaj: he did not live in the Kapoor home but close by, and started working in Prithvi Theatres as a child. His observations are invaluable.

It would have been impossible to reconstruct the Frontier days and the respective childhoods of Prithviraj and Raj Kapoor had it not been for Mrs Seth, the elder Kapoor's cousin. Prithviraj Kapoor was raised by his grandfather. He spent much of his childhood with Mrs Seth's mother in Peshawar and Murree: she was the closest he had to a mother, and loaned him the crucial two hundred rupees when he set out from Peshawar to Bombay to become an actor. Raj Kapoor spent most of his holidays in these cities, and Mrs Seth's brother, Colonel Khanna, shared many fond memories of Raj Kapoor's prank-filled childhood.

Chance encounters filled the blanks, leading to interesting digressions into this family's story. Intrigued by the number of DVDs of films I was buying in which various Kapoors have acted, the owner of the shop on Janpath told me that his father used to wrestle, desi style, with Prithviraj Kapoor. When I asked to meet his father, he said that it would be better to go down Janpath to Whitehouse, a shop selling cloth. It belonged to a cousin of Krishna Kapoor, and fortunately Mr Malhotra, who was also related to Raj Kapoor, had his share of anecdotes to relate about the family.

Perhaps Shashi Kapoor will write his autobiography one day, waiting for the time when he will be able to confront what he half-jokingly refers to as secrets about himself that even he does not want to know. His advice to me when I set out to write this book was that I be 'honest', which I suppose in some way was a carte blanche to look at the less flattering side of the Kapoors as well as their achievements. I hope I have been able to do justice to that.

PART 1

The Patriarch

1

The Socialist from Peshawar: Prithviraj Kapoor

It was one of those muggy, post-monsoon days when the quiet of the Arabian Sea and the heavy, still air over Bombay could dampen the spirits of even the most optimistic. Prithviraj Kapoor, not quite twenty-three, and fresh despite two days and nights (third class) on the Frontier Mail from Peshawar, stepped off the train at the terminal in Colaba, which was located next to the Cooperage playground at the time, and hailed a Victoria. '*Mujhe samundar dekhna hai*,' he told the Victoriawalla in that booming, stagey voice of his. He had never seen the sea, and could not wait to get to the Gateway of India. Once there, he looked up at the sky and pledged: 'God, I have come here to become an actor. If you don't make me one here, I will cross the seven seas and go to Hollywood.'

God listened. But he didn't make it easy. All Prithviraj Kapoor had with him that day in 1928 was a hockey stick, a small trunk, a felt cap and seventy-five rupees in his pocket. Had it not been for a generous and adoring aunt his pockets would have been empty. His father, Bashesharnath, a ruddy bon vivant Pathan with a walrus moustache and an ample girth, had become purple with rage when his son had told him about his plans to become an actor. '*Kanjar*[1]—is that what you want to become?' he exploded.

Bashesharnath was in the police. Prithviraj's grandfather, the rather stately Dewan Keshavmal Kapoor, had been the tehsildar of Samundari in Lyallpur district (now in Pakistan). Young Prithviraj had already received his Bachelor of Arts degree from King Edwards College in Peshawar and was studying to be a lawyer at the College of Law in Lahore. For this Hindu Pathan family, actors belonged to the 'debauched' world of wandering street performers and nautanki groups, people outside the pale of society.

Actors were bad news in the macho world that was Peshawar. No wonder Dilip Kumar, who spent much of his childhood in Peshawar, didn't dare tell his father, Sarwar Khan, when he first became an actor. His first film *Jwar Bhata* was made in 1944. Fear of being found out is one the reasons he changed his name from Yusuf Khan to Dilip Kumar. He obviously knew that for his father acting was a fate worse than death. Sarwar Khan used to tease Prithviraj by calling him a *kanjar ka puttar* after he became a popular actor. He didn't spare Prithviraj's father either. The Kapoors and the Khans were friends from Peshawar, and continued to meet in Bombay. Dilip Kumar recounts an interesting anecdote about the friendly sparring between Bashesharnath and his father. 'My father used to say to him [Bashesharnath] that after letting his son join films he could not afford to keep his moustaches elevated and would taunt him, "*Unko neeche karo.*"'[2] Ironically, and not without a measure of revengeful glee, Prithviraj's father broke the news of Sarwar Khan's son's profession to him. A fruit merchant, Sarwar Khan had a shop in Crawford Market in Bombay. While visiting him one day, Bashesharnath pointed to a poster of *Jwar Bhata*. Sarwar Khan looked up and remarked that one of the actors on the poster did indeed look like his son Yusuf. Bashesharnath was happy to dispel his friend's illusion. '*Yeh Yusuf jaisa nahin, Yusuf hi hai. Aab tu bhi kanjar da puttar ho gaya hai.*'

Acting most certainly was not in Prithviraj Kapoor's genes. He was breaking the family mould when he set off for Bombay to become an actor, leaving behind his wife Ramsarni (Rama) and their three children—Raj, the eldest, and two younger boys, Ravinder (Bindi) and Devinder (Devi). Raj Kapoor was nearly five at the time. (Bindi and Devi subsequently died within a fortnight of each other in Bombay when Ramsarni was pregnant with Shammi—one of them ate rat poison, the other died of pneumonia.)

Failure has persistently prodded each of the Kapoors to acting and has often been the turning point in their scripted lives. Prithviraj failed his first-year law exams. Raj Kapoor failed his matriculation exam as well as an entrance exam for the navy: his ambition was to become an admiral and ride the seas in a spanking white uniform. Rishi Kapoor failed his English paper during his final year in school and could not get into college. Other Kapoors have followed much the same pattern: acting was the only the thing they could do. But we are getting ahead of our story here.

After Prithviraj Kapoor made his pact with god at the Gateway of India, he asked the Victoriawalla to take him to a hotel. He did not know a soul in this city, nor did he have a single address. The driver left him at Kashmir Hotel, opposite Metro cinema, where he got a room for five rupees a night. The next morning he asked the manager of the hotel where the nearest film studio was. Aware by now that his seventy-five rupees would not last very long, he walked to Imperial Studios on Kennedy Bridge, near the Royal Opera House. The studio belonged to the legendary Ardeshir Irani, who made India's first talkie *Alam Ara* in 1931.

The imposing gates of the studio would have deterred a lesser mortal. Prithviraj just stood there. He might have had to stand a long time had the gateman of the studio not been a Pathan. Prithvi spoke to him in Pashto. The guard, Behramshah, happy to discover a fellow Pathan, let him in and advised him to stand in line with the extras. Prithvi returned there every morning. He worked as an extra for the first few days in the silent film *Challenge* (1929). On the third day, Ermeline, a Jewess star-heroine, passing by the line of extras, stopped in her tracks when she saw Prithviraj. She was immediately struck by the extraordinary looks of this tall, fair, strapping man with the head of a Greek god, a Roman nose and good legs. The gamine actress was the leading lady of *Cinema Girl*, a film then being made by the Imperial Film Company. And like a princess inspecting a line-up of men to choose a husband during a *swayamvara*, she picked Prithviraj to play the male lead opposite her in the film.

So, thanks to Ermeline, this charismatic Pathan from Peshawar never had to stand in line as an extra again. And this was the beginning of a career in films which spanned more than four decades—from the silent era to Technicolor and 70mm.

Prithviraj—or 'Prithee' as his family called him—was born on 3 November 1906 in Samundari, a village in Lyallpur district located between Peshawar and Rawalpindi. Unfortunately, Prithviraj never got to know his mother. She died when he was three. Prithviraj's grandfather, Dewan Keshavmal, took it upon himself to bring him up. He was afraid that his own son, Bashesharnath, would remarry, and he did not want his grandson to be brought up by a stepmother.

A young Prithviraj (extreme left) with his grandfather and siblings

Bashesharnath Kapoor was a gregarious man with a healthy appetite for life and its pleasures. He soon remarried. Perhaps the infamous glad eye for women many of the Kapoor men have—particularly Raj and Shammi Kapoor—is a legacy from their paternal grandfather. 'His [Prithviraj's] father was a playboy. He married again and had several friends. We often used to hear *philani naal* [with such and such woman]. He was in the police and left it, and lived on his father's money,' says Mrs Dharam Chand Seth, Prithviraj's cousin. Whenever he visited his friend Sarwar Khan, the women of the Khan household would scoot, warning each other, '*Hai ni, parda dal lo. Luchche chacha aa gaye.*' (Run away, that shameless uncle has come.)

Prithviraj thus grew up in Samundari without parents. A simple and upright man, as well as a strict disciplinarian, Dewan Keshavmal was both mother and father to him. No doubt this dignified gentleman was the most important influence during his formative years. Life in Samundari was simple: there were fields all around, and not much else. A buffalo shed was probably his first stage, where he acted out bits and pieces of the Ramayana and Mahabharata. In Samundari, Prithee acquired his extraordinary generosity and unflinching sense of justice. In most middle-class homes of the time, and even indeed today, the worlds of masters and servants are kept apart. But in Samundari servants did not need to 'know their place'. And the masters learned to behave themselves. Prithviraj's grandfather made sure that he played kabbadi and other games with the children of the domestic servants. The sweeper's son was a frequent playmate. Every time Prithviraj left the house or returned, he touched the feet of Sajjanmal, an elderly servant employed by his grandfather.

Dewan Keshavmal

Nor could he play the little lord of the manor. He had to—metaphorically and even literally—dirty his hands. There is an oft-told tale about the young Prithviraj. One day at 5 p.m., when the sun was seeing itself out of the sky, a visitor to the Kapoor khandaan saw him running around frantically. When asked why he was in such a great hurry, the young boy, breathless, continued to run, shouting that he had work to do. 'It is my duty to light all the lamps of the house and clean the chimneys before dark.' The guest could not understand why the *ladla puttar* of Dewan Keshavmal had to do this 'menial' task when there were so many servants around. The grandfather then explained to his grandson, in front of the guest: '*Chimneyan di kalak laanda hain, usi taran duniya di kalak laanda.*' (Just as you removed the black and the dirt from chimneys, you will remove the dirt from the world.)

Perhaps the act of cleaning a chimney was a metaphor for a bit of self-cleansing as well. Years later, Prithviraj tried to instill similar discipline in his children: he made each of his sons start at the bottom of the ladder in Prithvi Theatres. There were no silver spoons for them, no fast lanes. Raj swept the floors of the theatre; it was only after several years that his father made him the art director of Prithvi Theatres. The two younger sons were also made to do just about everything at Prithvi Theatres.

Prithviraj adored his grandfather but he still craved a mother. He found one in his father's cousin, Kaushalya Khanna. He called her mataji and remained devoted to her all his life. The young Prithvi did a lot of his growing up in the Khanna household. As a child he often slept in his aunt's bed when his grandfather left him in her care in Peshawar. Her daughter, Mrs Dharam Chand Seth, grew up with Prithviraj. 'My mother loved him as if he were her own son. When he wet the bed, she used to put a chunni over the part of the sheet which had become wet and place him on the other side of her.'

If there was a fairy godmother in his life, it was she. Kaushalya Khanna understood his dreams and helped him realize them, particularly when he wanted to become an actor. She was the one who gave him two hundred rupees for his expenses, when, a bit like Dick Whittington, Prithviraj left Peshawar for Bombay. She also arranged to give him seventy-five rupees a month so that his wife and three children, whom he had had to leave behind in Peshawar, were taken care of, since his father had washed his hands off him.

The Khannas were the rich relatives. While the Kapoor home in Bhola Ram di Gali in Peshawar was respectably large, with four floors and a retinue of servants, it was an outhouse compared to the Khanna home. The Khanna house, called Dubgari Gate, had one hundred and twenty rooms. When the Prince of Wales came to Peshawar, the government borrowed the Khannas' horse and carriage with the silver harness for the bodyguard. Mrs Seth's grandfather, Bhaiya Mal Khanna, was a contractor and supplied ammunition for the Afghan war.

Describing their home Mrs Seth says: 'It was like a fortress on all four sides, and there were turrets for the guards. There were stables and servants' quarters. The horses came from Lyallpur, where my grandfather had 4000 acres. Four big families lived in the house: each of them had their own apartments. The fifth apartment was *dadiyan da veda* [grandmothers' courtyard]. We had three of them. My grandfather married twice, so we had two dadis and one great dadi.'

The Khanna home plays a significant role in the story of both Prithviraj and his eldest son Raj. As a chubby, round-faced boy with apple-red cheeks, Raj spent many holidays with the Khannas, both in Peshawar and in their summer home, Ashley Hall, in Murree, a quaint hill station 14 miles from Rawalpindi. This was Raj's peek into the rarefied world of the very rich, and the goings-on in the Khanna mansion left deep imprints in his memory bank of images and sensations, some of which would surface in his films years later. (The huge feudal home with its courtyards and series of endless rooms in his film *Prem Rog* is apparently modelled on Dubgari Gate.)

Prithviraj moved into the underbelly of the metropolis. Kashmir Hotel, an intriguing-looking building, stands at a busy intersection of the city, next to the famed Metro cinema and a stone's throw from St Xavier's College. Curving slightly and with myriad small windows on its many floors, it looks like a ship. The hotel is on the edge of the city's red light area. The aspiring actor took a room on the fourth floor, and often went to a small restaurant opposite the hotel to eat. However, one day he hurt his foot and couldn't walk down the dilapidated stairs. Prithviraj went hungry for three days. He would have continued to do so for much longer had a young prostitute, who used to see him eating at the restaurant, not come up to see what was wrong. She brought him food that day but hesitated to serve him because she was afraid he would not eat anything touched by a 'fallen' woman. Shashi Kapoor recalls: 'Papaji asked her to tie a rakhi on him and then feed him.' Thus, duly anointed as his sister, she brought food till he was able to walk again.

Prithviraj started as an extra (mostly unpaid) in three silent films in 1929—*Challenge*, *Wedding Night* and *Dao Pech*—in Ardeshir Irani's Imperial Film Company. Irani's Imperial Studio was established in the mid-twenties near Kennedy Bridge to produce silent films. B.P. Mishra directed several of these films, including *Alibaba* and *Alladin*. Stars on the studio rolls were Gauhar, Ermeline and Sulochana (also know as Ruby Meyers who acted in *Wild Cat of Bombay*). It could have been a long haul had Ermeline, the exquisitely beautiful Jewish star, not spotted him waiting in the line of extras. Described as India's Clara Bow, the actress who was later to work for Prithviraj in Prithvi Theatres, anointed him her leading man in *Cinema Girl* in 1930.

The silent movies being churned out by the studios in Bombay were the original quickies: nearly hundred were made between 1929 and 1930. It took anywhere between a week and six weeks to make a film. One film was even completed in two days! Mythologicals, stories about Rajput valour or Oriental fantasies were staple fare. However, producers began to explore more contemporary issues. Hollywood dominated cinema halls in India in the twenties. The British in India wanted to see them, as did the Indian elite. Kohinoor Film Company produced films with English titles—*Gun Sundari* (*Why Husbands Go Astray*) (1925), *Typist Girl* (1926), *Telephone Girl* (1927). English titles were logical according to authors Erik Barnouw and S. Krishnaswamy: '...the drama lay in the transfer to an Indian world of elements of Western life—more accurately, of the Western film.' Only the titles were in English. There was an obvious shift towards telling the modern Indian story. Such films put 'the Indian social on a footing with the mythological—at least, as far as the urban Indian was concerned'.[3]

The Pathan with a mesmerizing presence and empty pockets soon graduated to hero status, with a monthly salary of seventy rupees. But life was still tough: he lived in an 8 feet by 12 feet room in Tardeo in central Bombay with his wife and children who had by now joined him in the city. Not a princely amount, the salary stretched just enough to feed the family. A few months later, impressed by him, the company raised his salary to two hundred rupees a month.

Prithviraj was perfect for playing, quite literally, the strong, silent type. He had a good body and a manly jaw. Action films predominated in the silent era, and a muscular body was a primary requirement for the silent hero. Size, not voice, mattered. Not surprisingly many actors came from a wrestling background in an era when the demand was for action heroes. Some had even been *pahalwan*s. The circus was another catchment area for our first action heroes. Prithviraj was a natural: he was into bodybuilding and Indian wrestling and, in those pre-gym days, 'worked out' in Hanuman *akhara*s. In fact, Shashi Kapoor's first memory of his father is seeing him lifting weights on the terrace of their flat in Matunga.

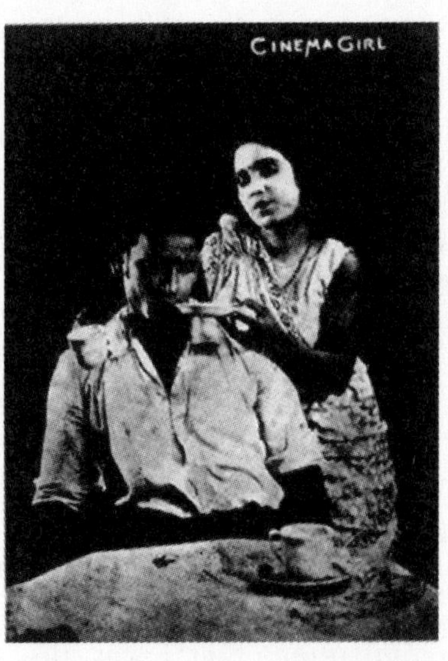

Prithviraj Kapoor with Ermeline in his first film Cinema Girl *(1929) (Photo courtesy Roli Books)*

Ermeline wasn't the only one to be bowled over by him. There was something about Prithviraj. His beauty—yes, there is no other word—seems to have had a staggering impact on both the sexes. It was not just the handsome, almost impossibly handsome, face framed by the abundant hair that often fell in cherubic locks on his high forehead when he was young. It was not just those penetrating eyes brimming over with warmth and compassion. Nor was it just his sculpted body, perfect for the heroic, frequently shirtless roles in costume dramas and mytho-historical films like *Sikandar* and *Sher-e-Arab*—long before the biceped Salman Khan made topless males a cinematic cliché. Prithviraj owed his good body to his *kushti* days and long hours in akharas, where he wrestled, Indian-style, for several years. A keen sportsman, Prithvi had also played a lot of hockey and tennis in college.

Rather, it was the aura that enveloped him. He possessed more than his share of what in today's fashionable currency is called 'energy', at times a euphemism for vitality and sexual energy, and the preserve of rock stars. He was often compared to Ramon Navarro,[4] an American actor of the forties with a perfect profile who had the female half of the American nation in love with him. Says actress Zohra Segal who worked in Prithvi Theatres: 'I first saw him in the play *Shakuntala* in Bombay. My sister Uzra was the leading lady. Papaji was very, very handsome. Actually, he had a lovely physique at that.'

While women might have swooned, men, too, were left in near-swoon conditions. In a few cases, encounters with Prithviraj proved life changing. The actor Premnath was so struck by his appearance when he saw him in the film *Daku Mansoor* as a schoolboy in Nagpur that he decided to become an actor. 'The hero inspired me so much that then and there I told my companions that I was also going to become an actor like him. His handsome face, his marvellous physique haunted me,' Premnath wrote in a commemoration volume felicitating the thespian.

What Premnath didn't know then was that Prithviraj was his father's cousin. Nor could he imagine that his sister Krishna would marry Raj Kapoor years later. From that day on all Premnath thought of was going to Bombay and becoming an actor, to 'swim or drown' in the Arabian Sea. Like Prithviraj's father, Premnath's father, Raisaheb Kartar Nath, too, was a policeman—an inspector general of the Central Provinces in fact. And like Prithviraj, Premnath had also studied law. When Premnath mustered up enough courage to tell his father that he wanted to become an actor like their illustrious relative, his father was furious and packed him off to the Indian States Forces Military Training School at Indore. Nine months later he ran away to become an actor, boarded a train full of jawans going to Bombay and reached the Kapoor household on College Back Road in Matunga. He had a hundred rupees in his pocket, twenty-five more than what Prithviraj had when he first arrived in the city by the Arabian Sea.

It was also awe at first sight for the brilliant writer K.A. Abbas, who was later to write the screenplay for *Awara* with Prithviraj in mind. Abbas was a schoolboy when he first set eyes on Prithviraj on a railway platform in Delhi. He saw a tall, fair, athletic figure in khaki shirt, shorts and Pathani chappals. A few years later, when he saw Prithviraj shirtless as Rama in Debaki Bose's classic *Seeta*, he found the actor even more compelling: 'To our youthful imaginations he presented the acme of perfection. What a perfect figure, like a sculptured Greek god come to life.'[5] Longhaired pahalwans with side-whiskers were the matinee idols of those days in the 'tinselly mythologicals' which were then being made. Prithviraj must have seemed to them like a being who had literally descended from the heavens in a chariot.

Many years later, Abbas spotted Prithviraj—again at a railway station. This time it spurred him to a decision about his own life. Recounts Shashi Kapoor: 'Abbas sahib once told me that he was going to leave Bombay—he was on a platform at the railway station and he saw a crowd, and wondered who was attracting so much attention. Then he saw this gorgeous-looking man in white. He told himself that he would go back to Bombay and write for him. He used to often tell me, "Shashi, be a chip of the old block." Even today when I see *Sikandar* I can't get over the beauty.' Shashi, who looks uncannily like his father (more so as he grows older), was often asked 'to do a Sikandar'. But he refused: there could never be another Sikandar as far he is concerned.

Prithviraj's resonant voice had to wait for the first full-length Indian talkie (*Alam Ara*) to enthrall audiences. Prithviraj Kapoor played heroine Zubeida's father in this costume fantasy. Master Vithal, a popular star of the silent era was the film's main hero. By this time Prithviraj had acted in nine silent films, including *Children of the Storm*. He also acted in *Draupadi* in 1931 and in *Dagabaz Ashiq* the following year. Most of these films were costume dramas: his transition to the talkies was through mythologicals or historicals. And his salary jumped once his vocal chords came into play.

Prithviraj became restless after less than two years at the Imperial Film Company. His first love—theatre—called, and in 1932 he joined the Grant Anderson Theatrical Company, a touring company with English and Indian actors put together by British theatre director J. Grant Anderson. David, the veteran character actor of many Hindi movies, and the legendary actress Durga Khote were also part of this wandering company which performed plays by Shakespeare and George Bernard Shaw, and Indian classics like *Mrichhakatika* in English. Shakespeare and Shaw were the staple fare. Prithviraj played Laertes in *Hamlet*, Romeo in *Romeo and Juliet*, Cassius in *Julius Caesar* and Charudatta, the infatuated young man in love with the sensuous courtesan Vasantasena, in *Mrichhakatika*.

This was the only time Prithviraj was not his own boss in theatre. Life was tough with the Grant Anderson Company. It was uphill all the way for the troupe members: there were days in their theatrical tours when they had nothing to eat but parched gram. Eventually, the money ran out, and Anderson disbanded the group in Calcutta. Many actors went back to England; Prithviraj stayed on in Calcutta. However, the year with the travelling theatre company ensured that the old bard of Stratford had gotten under his skin.

In later years, whenever he took part in charity shows to raise money for a cause he would always recite from Shakespeare. 'Today the stars jump like monkeys. There were no filmy numbers in those days. Only performers like Sitara Devi or Lacchu Maharaj danced during these shows. The stars spoke. My father would appear for a cause, and he would recite Shakespeare. He liked doing Shylock from *The Merchant of Venice*, the "To be or not to be" soliloquy from *Hamlet* or Marc Anthony's "Friends, Romans, countrymen" speech in *Julius Caesar*,' remembers Shashi Kapoor.

Shylock was obviously his forte. K.A. Abbas describes an evening when Prithviraj enacted a few scenes from *The Merchant of Venice* before two visiting Russians, the director V.I. Pudovkin and the well-known actor Nikolai Cherkasov, 'in his usual flowing toga-like white khaddar dress. When he finished, exhausted by the intensity of the performance, Pudovkin had tears in his eyes and Cherkasov was embracing and kissing the Indian actor.'

It is difficult to imagine how a Pathan who grew up in the hinterland of Samundari could have become so obsessed with Western theatre.

Prithviraj joined New Theatres in Calcutta when he decided

to stay on in the city after the Grant Anderson Company was disbanded there. Calcutta was rapidly becoming a hub for good cinema: a more meaningful and socially relevant cinema emerged from directors like Debaki Bose, Nitin Bose, P.C. Barua, Hemchandra and A.R. Kardar. These directors were able to exploit the thespian's histrionic skills beyond his good looks and physique that had been his trademark in his Bombay movies. Moreover, New Theatres with Birendra Nath Sircar at the helm soon became a 'film-maker's haven'. Sircar set up the studio in 1932 with the help of an American engineer, Wilford Denning. Soon, it began to attract some of the best creative talent in the country. Unlike many of the Hollywood moghuls, Sircar gave the directors on his rolls artistic freedom. He was probably India's first creative executive producer.

Debaki Bose mined legends and myths for his films and directed Prithviraj in some of his more memorable roles in the thirties. Under Bose's directorial baton the actor brought more emotional resonance to his roles. Bose's oeuvre occupies a significant place in the history of Indian cinema. *Seeta*, made while the director was on loan to East India Films in 1933, was not only the first Indian film to be shown at the Venice Festival, it is also considered the best mythological film made in India. Bose's films were essentially historical costume dramas. Yet, his legendary characters were palpably human, inevitably involved in the complexity of human relationships. Critical success, however, was to come later. In *Vidyapati* (1937), Prithviraj plays Shiva Singha, a fourteenth-century king of Mithila whose wife is in love with the Vaishnava poet–saint Vidyapati enacted by Pahadi Sanyal. Considered the most accomplished of Bose's films, it seamlessly wove songs into the narrative.

The heroines were centre stage in these essentially romantic films: the heroes were more like actors in supporting roles. For instance, Kanan Bala, the leading lady of Bengali cinema at the time, was the star of *Vidyapati*. Durga Khote was the main protagonist of *Seeta*. Based on the *Uttara-kand* (a sort of postscript to the epic Ramayana), this is Seeta's story: the film begins after the heroics are over and Rama, doubtful about his wife's chastity, sends her into exile. Bare-bodied Prithviraj was a muscular

Rama—unlike many of the effeminate heroes of the time. However, the stronger character of the film is the heroine. 'Bose typically contrasts a strong Seeta with a weak Rama, otherwise the most perfect of mortals to the Hindus,' writes B.D. Garga in *So Many Cinemas*. Similarly, *Rajrani Meera* (1933) is heroine-centric: the film is based on the life of a sixteenth-century poetess queen, played by a forceful Durga Khote, who becomes an ascetic and writes Bhakti poetry in praise of Lord Krishna.

Prithviraj was paired with many leading ladies in his long career in films—amongst others Durga Khote, Kanan Bala, Sitara Devi, Jamuna and Sadhana Bose. In 1952, some years before Geeta Bali became his daughter-in-law, she acted with him in *Anandmath*. Directed by Hemen Gupta, the film explored the first uprising by militant monks against colonial rule. In fact, Prithviraj even acted in a film with Nargis in 1957—*Pardesi*. An Indo–Soviet production co-directed by K.A. Abbas and Vassili Pronin, the film also had Balraj Sahni in its cast and was about a trader, Afanassiev, who came to India in the fifteenth century. (Abbas also directed him in the award-winning film *Asman Mahal* in 1965.) Among his many heroines, he shared a special screen chemistry with Vanmala and Lila Desai, both of whom remained close friends until the end.[6]

Calcutta proved to be an important interlude in the thespian's film career, giving him the opportunity to expand his acting vocabulary and go beyond playing virile, seductive men. During his six years in Calcutta he acted in about a dozen films, many of which became popular and won him acclaim. New Theatres offered him a break from historical, bewigged figures. Although Debaki Bose's films were situated in a distant past, Nitin Bose placed his characters in a contemporary context. Prithviraj acted in both *President* (1936) and *Dushman* (1939). Based on literary works, the first unfolds against the background of a textile mill, the second in a sanatorium for the terminally ill. Barua did the same in his popular film *Manzil* (1936). Based on Saratchandra Chattopadhyay's novel *Grihadah*, the film is a tragic love story about a man in love with his friend's wife (played by the actress Jamuna). While the director plays the stoic husband, Prithviraj brings a measure of flamboyance to his role as the infatuated lover who abducts his friend's wife.

The actor also explored the darker side of the human character in *Manzil*. It's not just romantic dreamy love he feels for Jamuna; it is unequivocally lust. He invests his character with a bit of the caveman—very unlike the image of the tragic hero being incarnated by Saigal and Barua in films like *Devdas*. He is more like the playboy character he was to create for his son Shammi in the play *Kalakar*. The dark side really surfaces in his performance in A.R. Kardar's film *Pagal* (1940). In this film, Prithviraj plays a psychotic doctor in charge of a lunatic asylum—decades before *One Flew Over the Cuckoo's Nest*. Forced to marry the sister of the girl he really wanted to marry, he keeps his wife in the asylum, injecting her to make her appear insane.

The sojourn in Calcutta was responsible for more than the growth of Prithviraj as an actor. He also learned a way of life. At New Theatres he realized that rigid hierarchies actually come in the way of creativity—lessons he was to apply years later when he started Prithvi Theatres.

Meanwhile, Bombay had become a dynamic centre for films. Studios like Ranjit Movietone, Kohinoor Film Company, Minerva Movietone, Wadia Movietone and others were churning out films. Once again Bombay beckoned Prithviraj. So, in 1939, when Raj Kapoor was fifteen, Shammi eight and Shashi barely a year old, he returned to Bombay. It wasn't too long on his return to Bombay before Prithviraj joined Chandulal Shah's Ranjit Movietone. The forties were glory days for the actor as well as for studios. Prithviraj worked like a busybee. He was the first major actor to abandon the studio system of stars on the rolls and freelance, moving from studio to studio, making films like *Sikandar*, *Raj Nartaki* and *Ujala*.

The film that Prithviraj is most remembered for is *Sikandar*, a lavish historical saga made by Sohrab Modi for his studio Minerva Movietone. Made in 1940 with the élan of a Cecil B. de Mille production, and released the following year, the film focuses on the encounter between Alexander of Macedon (played by a glorious Greek-godlike Kapoor in his matinee-idol prime with his kiss curls and enviable physique) and the Indian king Porus (played by the equally stentorian-voiced Modi).

Anybody dropping in on the sets of the film could well

imagine that they had walked into an akhara, observes Garga in *So Many Cinemas*. They would spot Prithviraj flexing his muscles, clad just in shorts. Garga writes in his book: 'So particular was Modi about details, that while shooting for *Sikandar* he had even discovered the actual weight of the historical figure of Sikandar...Every alternate day, the actors had to strip down to their underwear and stand on the weighing scales, closely scrutinized by the director. Then the cast was subjected to a strict regimen of diet and exercises.'

Half a century before gym-toned and souped-up bodies became the trend, Prithviraj was adding muscle to his. A few months before shooting for *Sikandar* was to begin, the actor sent his family to Peshawar so that he could get in shape, both physically and mentally, for the title role. He used to go to akharas or lift weights on the roof of his Matunga home. Long before method acting became part of the vocabulary, and actors talked about getting under the skin of their characters, Prithviraj Kapoor was doing it. He *became* Alexander/Sikandar. Shashi Kapoor recounts an incident in his book *Prithviwallahs*, about Modi walking in one day while Prithviraj was in costume. Prithviraj remained seated. Nor did he wish the actor–director, as was customary. 'When Modi asked him why...Prithviraj replied: "Sikandar does not know Sohrab Modi." Modi saluted his Sikandar and said, "But I know Sikandar."'

Compared to the best of Hollywood, *Sikandar* was even talked about in the same breath as D.W. Griffith's path-breaking *The Birth of a Nation*. The film created ripples. The war in Europe was at its peak and Gandhi's call to civil disobedience made the British censors nervous about a film that showed the mutiny of Alexander's soldiers: the parallels between British rule and Alexander's were obvious. Showing the retreat of the invading foreigner was not palatable for the British: they were not ready to pack up their bags. Consequently, the film was banned from some theatres, particularly those near army cantonments.

Prithviraj became a matinee idol nonetheless. Wherever he went people used to say, 'There goes Sikandar', much like what happened with Raj Kapoor after *Awara* in the erstwhile Soviet Union where bands began playing 'Awara hoon' as soon as he entered a restaurant. The blue-eyed actress Vanmala who starred with Prithviraj in *Sikandar* used to tease him about his total absorption in his role. In *I Go South with Prithviraj*, Jai Dyal, Prithviraj's college professor, writes: 'Prithviraj used to sit before a large mirror, fully dressed for the part, and would gaze at himself—trying to get into the character he was playing. Vanmala saw him like this on the sets of *Sikandar* and one day could not help crying out Narcissus, and he retorted with Echo.'

If Prithviraj believed he was Alexander, so did thousands of school-children. Apparently, after the film became a huge success, textbooks used his photograph when they wanted to show Alexander the Great. Shashi Kapoor recalls his embarrassment when he came across his father's photograph in his history book when he was a student at Don Bosco. It was the same with Akbar: the emperor's face bore Prithviraj's features.

The cameras kept rolling. It was a whirl of mythologicals and historicals: through Pune, Kolhapur, and the proliferating studios in Bombay. Yet, the actor brought the same kind of commitment to cinema as he did to theatre—even, at times, an over-the-top earnestness which could have been dangerous. For instance, while shooting for *Valmiki* near Kolhapur, Prithviraj had to swim across a river clad in a dhoti, deer skin, wig and beard. The water was cold, his dhoti twisted round his legs, making it almost impossible for him to swim. He almost didn't make it to the other side.

Prithviraj Kapoor didn't believe in cinematic tricks. If he had to show pain on-screen, he had to feel it first. When they were filming *Mughal-e-Azam* in Rajasthan, the director, K. Asif, asked him to put on chappals for Akbar's famous walk-in-the-desert scene. The director offered to place the camera in such a way that the audience would not see his feet. But Prithviraj refused and walked barefoot on the burning sand. The pain the audience sees on his face in that scene is real.

In one of the more memorably resonant clash-of-will scenes between the Emperor Akbar and his son Salim in the same movie, Prithviraj Kapoor has his back to the audience. Apparently when he requested Asif to film that particular scene without showing his face, the cynics tittered that the elder thespian feared he would not be able match the histrionics of the younger actor and fellow Pathan, Dilip Kumar. Prithviraj Kapoor incarnated the old theatrical school of acting; Dilip Kumar with his quiet voice and understated acting was clearly a creature of the cinema.

Prithviraj Kapoor had begun to lose his voice during the making of this celluloid epic. Acting without respite day after day for fourteen years for Prithvi Theatres had taken its toll: he refused to use mikes or an understudy through those long, arduous years. He was also burning the candle at both ends: he used to shoot at night while producing and acting in plays for Prithvi Theatres during the day. Others claimed that Kapoor could do more with just his back than Dilip Kumar with his face. Dilip Kumar, it seems, was uncomfortable with his screen father's theatrical style. But in the end, despite the camera zeroing in on the verbal duel from behind Prithviraj Kapoor's bewigged back, his Akbar carried the day. His back emoted superbly. Rather, his hands did: he clenched and unclenched them with such telling effect, upping the tension.

Acting was so great an obsession for Prithviraj that he seldom switched off. He was always trying to enhance his own acting skills. Even the zoo became an acting class for him. Prithviraj used to spend a long time observing lions. He was fascinated by the way the caged king of the jungle moved and roared: he wanted to roar like a lion on stage. Writer Esther David recounts an interesting story her father Reuben David, the founder of the Ahmedabad Zoo, told her. 'My father asked him to accompany him into the lion's cage. Prithviraj stayed outside, observing intently, while my father went in. Later, he told my father that he often went to the beach in Bombay and roared at the sea like a lion.' It must have been quite a sight on Juhu Beach: this magnificent hulk of a man talking to the Arabian Sea, loudly. For Prithviraj it was a form of *riyaaz*: he wanted to throw his voice the way a lion does, the rumble coming from deep within the belly. A right royal roar like the MGM lion.

'What a difference, watching him [Prithviraj] on the stage and then on the sets. I told him it was like having seen a lion in a jungle and then watching him perform tricks in a circus.'

—Uzra Mumtaz

The theatre actress had dropped in, unannounced, on the sets of V. Shantaram's film *Dahej*. It was 1949, a time when Prithviraj shuttled between theatre and cinema, using his screen earnings to subsidize his theatre. Amused by the remark, he said: 'I really feel that way. When I go on the sets, I put my tail between my legs and jump into the cage.'[7]

Prithviraj made almost 130 films in that gilded cage, a hundred of them between 1930 and 1960. Theatre was Prithviraj's first love and abiding passion. But films were his bread and butter. Eventually, they became a necessary evil for him. He acted in indifferent and even B-grade films to pay for his theatre, not to speak of the innumerable charities and individuals he supported. The last play he produced, *Paisa*, was a relatively successful stage production for Prithvi Theatres. But it almost financially crippled the thespian when he made it into a film.

After *Mughal-e-Azam* in 1960, Prithviraj's film career slid into an impasse. Producers were not exactly lining up outside his door with proposals. Shashi Kapoor believes that his father's performance was so overwhelming, despite being pitted against the actor's actor Dilip Kumar, that producers were afraid to cast him in their films. The less generous maintain that the thespian was too stagey: he failed to tone down the theatricality of his days in Prithvi Theatres.

Neither Sohrab Modi nor he could adjust to the camera. Both had done the trajectory from stage to film. The two had been Shakespearean actors with travelling groups. The theatrical training, as Garga puts it, veered them towards 'spectacular oratory, grand gestures and literary flourish'. They failed to make the transition to more nuanced and natural acting, so important for cinema where the camera picks up every gesture and amplifies it. It was but a small step from being theatrical to being a ham.

Prithviraj's voice had also lost some of its timbre and elasticity by now. Years of theatre had taken their toll. According to Ali Raza, the scriptwriter of *Mughal-e-Azam*, K. Asif was not too happy with the way Prithviraj had spoken his lines in the film. 'Asif asked Prithviraj to do the dubbing again [as] he was not pleased with his dialogue delivery. Prithviraj Kapoor said he wouldn't. An irritated Asif told him that had he liked the way he had done it why would he ask him to dub again. Prithviraj then began to sweat. Nobody had ever talked to him like that.'

Lance Dane, photographer and collector of Indian erotica, who happened to stray on to the sets of *Mughal-e-Azam* in Mehboob Studios, recalls seeing the difficult time the actor had remembering a line in a scene. 'Prithviraj kept having to do take after take. He could not remember a particular line. I think he did nineteen takes for one scene. I counted.'

It must have been difficult for the man who was like a god at Prithvi Theatres to 'perform' for younger directors, and alongside actors with huge egos and young enough to be his son. Dilip Kumar was the superstar of *Mughal-e-Azam*. When a particular shot was ready, Asif sent his assistant to see if Prithviraj was ready, to hurry him up as it were. The actor was getting his make-up done, and answered: '*Prithviraj hazir hai, Akbar abhi nahin aya*.' (Prithviraj is ready, but Akbar is not.) 'And when he walked out it was not Prithviraj but Akbar,' says Ali Raza. 'He had become Akbar.' In the first advertisement for the film the billing placed the older actor before the younger. When Dilip Kumar complained about the order of the names, Asif said: 'I am making *Mughal-e-Azam*, not Salim.'

Later, Prithviraj faced the same problem with another Pathan; this time it was his middle son Shammi Kapoor. Father and son were acting in the film *Rajkumar*. Once again top billing was going to the older actor. An upset Shammi complained to the director K. Shankar, pointing out that he, and not his father, was the star of the film. When Shankar informed Prithviraj about this 'request', he said, '*Pagal ho*? He is my son, he's a star. Who is happier than me if he gets first billing.'[8]

Unlike many other actors, Prithviraj was able to laugh at himself. One day on the sets of a film he called the sprightly actress Tanuja aside, and after offering her a Ganesh bidi (his brand), asked her listen to a 'funny story'. 'It was about the time when he had decided to become thin. He went on a diet and did exercises and then reported on the sets of *Mughal-e-Azam*. Asif took one look at him and said, "*Yeh kaun hai? Agar Salim ka role karna hai*, you should have done so earlier. But now go and get fat and put on weight for Akbar,"' recalls Tanuja.

The tragedy of the last phase of the thespian's screen career was that he couldn't play Mr Common Man. Prithviraj was all right as long as he was a king, a god or a patriarch with a big mansion as his backdrop. Costume dramas—historicals or mythologicals—suited him. He was best talking at, not talking to, unlike his son Raj, the quintessential common man. The elder Kapoor was always dominating. He was the power at the centre of the film; others fell in line round him.

Awara in 1952 marked his transition to a character actor, according to P.K. Nair, former head of the National Film Archive in Pune. 'In this film, he wore real clothes and was contemporary. You first see him in real-life costumes.' Prithviraj had now stepped into the era of drawing rooms—alongside, of course, his jungles and battlefields. Nevertheless, he could *not* be anything but centre stage. You could not put him in a meek role: neither his physique nor his growly voice would allow it.

This formula worked for a few of his later films like K.A. Abbas's *Asman Mahal* in 1965. In this film about the decline of feudalism written by Inder Raj Anand, Prithviraj portrays a nawab who refuses to let his mansion become a hotel. In his book, *I Am Not an Island*, Abbas writes: 'Prithviraj was tall, heavybodied, with a leonine face...He was the obvious choice to play the central role of the feudal lord...He really *lived* the role of the doomed nawab.'

Prithviraj gave one of his finest screen performances in *Asman Mahal*. He even won an acting award at the Karlovy Vary film festival in 1965 for his effort. Abbas describes Prithviraj as their 'trump card' in Karlovy Vary. 'With his *chadar* slung over his kurta and churidars he created quite an impression. I gave a cocktail party...we selected bottles by designs and colours. But the main topic was his performance, and the Academy of Art gave him an award.' Yet, back home in India, the audience was not impressed. In fact, his screen intensity evoked the opposite reaction. 'Some of the highly emotional scenes of Prithviraj

Kapoor were received with loud guffaws! I was heartbroken and slunk out of the darkened cinema hall,' writes Abbas.

Such criticism didn't get Prithviraj down. He soldiered on, accepting any role that came his way. Sunset Boulevard was certainly not scripted into his life. While the sixties saw his three sons move towards the respective zeniths of their film careers, the decade also witnessed his twilight and fade-out. He had come full circle: back to the costume dramas and B-grade action films, to low-flying banners. Prithviraj Kapoor acted because he enjoyed acting, and because he needed the money for the various charities and people he supported. Generous to a fault, he could never say no: anybody who came to him for help went away a few rupees richer. You could describe him as the indigenous Santa Claus of the one-rupee note: young and old got one each time he saw them. Those old notes now form part of the memorabilia of all those who came within rupee-receiving distance—his sons, grandchildren, family at large, colleagues.

But he was a proud man, and never accepted any money from his sons. In fact, before he died, he had cleared all his hospital bills, paid his income tax and left his sons Unit Trust shares.

When he was out of work it was Dara Singh who came to his 'rescue'. Prithviraj acted in about fourteen films with him, including films like *Lutera*, *Insaaf* and *Daku Mangal Singh*. The former pahalwan and vanquisher of the world champ wrestler King Kong even directed him in a film, *Nanak Dukhiya Sab Sansar*, in 1970. It is ironic that the actor who had reached some sort of screen epiphany with *Sikandar* in 1941 was now, nearly three decades later, playing Porus to Dara Singh's Sikandar in *Sikandar-e-Azam*. Both actors were well past their prime.

After the forties Prithviraj could not really control either his voice or figure. Nor was he good at variety. Nevertheless, Prithviraj brought the same earnestness to these films, much as he had done to everything else. He gave them all he had. And sometimes, it was too much, particularly in the fencing scenes. Recalls Dara Singh: 'Papaji would come into real *josh* while fencing. He had no control. It was as if he was doing it for real. I could not bring myself to tell him *ahista maro*. It was like a real fight for him because he got carried away. Once while filming *Sikandar-e-Azam*—he was on an elephant, I was on a horse—my hand got injured several times. The fight masters would tell us when to hold back, but he and Premnath never did. I remember that some actors refused to fight with him. They used duplicates. I didn't. I respected Papaji too much to do that.'

In their films together they played father and son, brothers, dacoit and cop, king and subject. *Lutera*, a swashbuckler about pirates, made by Raj Kumar Kohli, was probably the best known film from this period of his life. 'We played two brothers in love with the same girl. The actress Nishi was the girl. There was romance in the film. Papaji had a black beard and the public accepted his young man ki acting.' (Nishi later married Raj Kumar Kohli.)

Prithviraj continued to play guru as well. He still carried the baggage of Prithvi Theatres with him. When he was not playing a sitar during the lunch break on location, he used to give Dara Singh acting lessons. 'He would tell me, when you leave home and sit in your car, you should prepare three kinds of scenes: loud, middle and soft. Then, you should rehearse them in your mind in three speeds: fast, medium and slow. Don't waste time.'

Nor could Prithviraj help rewriting scripts. In the dialogue Dara Singh had written for *Nanak Dukhiya Sab Sansar*, he had made a distinction between Hindus and Sikhs. 'Papaji told me to change this. Hindus and Sikhs were not two, but one, he said. The krantidars from Hinduism became Sikhs. So, I changed the dialogue.'

Prithviraj's film career did not stop with Dara Singh; he also acted in films in the south, including a Gemini production in which he played the head of a joint family. He kept going, almost until his last breath, even after he had been diagnosed with Hodgkin's disease in 1971. It shows in *Kal Aaj Aur Kal*—his last film and his grandson Randhir Kapoor's first. The once-glorious voice is muffled. (His voice was actually dubbed for one of the last films he acted in, *Teen Bahuraniyan*.) He is all hyperbole: his gestures are exaggerated, almost as if he were doing mime. The viewer realizes that Prithviraj is pushing himself beyond endurance. But *Kal Aaj Aur Kal* was one for the Kapoor khandaan, a parting shot for his first grandson.

The photographs of two striking-looking women stood side by side in a little niche in a wall in Prithviraj Kapoor's *jhompra* (cottage) in Juhu (opposite Prithvi Theatre today) where he spent the last ten years of his life. Each morning after he bathed, he used to light two agarbattis and circle them around the two portraits, mumbling a few words to himself as he did so. He seldom left the house without this brief, private ritual. One of the portraits was of his mother; the other was of Mrs Norah Richards, the wife of his professor at King Edwards College in Peshawar. One could say that she was the mother of his creative being, the English muse for his theatrical ambitions.

Norah Richards had encouraged the young Prithvi during his undergraduate years in Peshawar, and later over the years—even after she had settled in Andretta in Himachal Pradesh. 'Norah nourished his dream about a theatre of his own. She initiated him into the world of Western plays,' writes Zohra Segal in her autobiography *Stages*. The correspondence[9] between Prithviraj and Norah reveals the great bond between the two. She was like a distant fairy godmother, always feeding his love of theatre and encouraging him to be creative. In fact, she asked Jai Dyal—who had taught Prithviraj at King Edwards—to write a diary of the few months he spent travelling with Prithvi Theatres in south India in 1940.

Norah Richards later edited the diary and gave it its final shape as a book. Titled *I Go South with Prithviraj and His Prithvi Theatres*, the book, despite its passages of purple prose and lachrymose hyperbole, is insightful about Prithviraj and his touring company. In the foreword she writes: 'I am deeply interested in Prithvi Theatres, a theatre in a theatreless land. Fellow-feeling makes us wondrous kin and I too am that sort of "man" in a land where there is no theatre. He is a theatre architect but the building of an actual theatre of bricks and mortar is beyond his financial resources...he is [a] vagabond actor, not into savings.' Norah used to refer to Prithviraj as her 'beloved vagabond' and addressed him thus in her many letters to him. Perhaps that word lodged itself in Raj's subconscious, only to resurface when he made *Awara*.

Prithviraj studied at the Anglo-Vernacular District Board

Middle School in Samundari. The acting bug was born in him here: he played Laxman at the age of eight in a school performance of the Ramayana. However, it was not until he went to King Edwards College that theatre became an obsession, so much so that he failed his first year.

Mentors were a refrain in his life. Jai Dyal also played a key role in instilling a love of theatre in the adolescent Prithviraj. Bashesharnath had asked Professor Dyal to guide the fifteen-year-old Prithee. Head of the college's Dramatics Society, Dyal saw in his 'chubby, handsome face' a great actor. He immediately cast him in three one-act plays: *Dina Ki Baraat* (an original play by R.L. Sahni), Lady Gregory's *Spreading the News*, and Synge's *Riders to the Sea*. The enthusiastic professor made him play a female role on stage. 'Had he been born a girl, his face would have been his fortune. He had a personality, too. I utilized his face and figure by making him play a lady's role onstage,' writes Professor Dyal in his book. Prithviraj soon became the secretary of the college's Amateur Dramatic Club, and obviously the lodestar of the college. 'He forgot himself in the person that he was impersonating. He left Prithee behind him in the green room. He had become Dina himself or Mrs Fallon or Norah,' continues Dyal. Later, the budding thespian was to relish his Shakespearean interlude with the Grant Anderson Company.

Shylock may have been his favourite role onstage, but what Prithviraj appeared to be enacting offstage (rather backstage at Prithvi Theatres) was Prospero, among the most magnetic characters Shakespeare created. Prithvi Theatres, a travelling theatre repertory company Prithviraj set up in 1944, was not unlike the self-contained island Prospero conjures up in *The Tempest*. Both played god in the microcosmic worlds of their creation. Prospero had his daughter Miranda; Prithviraj had his three sons, all of whom were part of his nomadic company. Not only was his father on board but cousins and other family members were also part of the repertoire—Kamal and Ravinder Kapoor, Premnath and Rajendranath, Nand Kishore Kapoor, Harkishen Kapoor (Tiger) and Prannath Khanna. Prithvi Theatres became a gigantic family on the move.

According to Geoffrey Kendal, Prithviraj was a 'throwback to the old-time English actor-managers'. In his book, *The Shakespearewallah*, he writes: 'He loved it all—being a father figure, a great actor, the idol of all and sundry. He did everything in a big way and he acted all the time, onstage and off.' The father figure also played the role of teacher offstage. His troupe became a travelling university. The cast and crew of Prithvi Theatres came to work even when they were not touring. And when they were not rehearsing, Prithviraj used to deliver impromptu lectures on all sorts of topics—from theatre to life. He was an avid reader of biographies of stage actors, and admired John Gielgud.

The thespian was obsessive about not dispelling the illusion of reality onstage. When part of the stage fell on him during a performance in Indore, he refused to move. Prithviraj was supposed to be dead in that scene, and when asked later why he hadn't moved, he replied: 'Dead people don't move.'[10] Prithviraj also introduced a more naturalistic style of acting to Hindi theatre. Unlike most of the actors at the time, he made his own rules. Nor, according to Kendal, did he 'come to the footlights to address the audience. He was the first to stand with his back to the audience, then speak and be heard...He broke the rules of Corinthian theatre prevalent then.'

Talking of the significant role Prithviraj played in the history of contemporary theatre in India, Shyam Benegal says: 'I consider him to be the one with vision, a vision about what he thought theatre should do, and what he did. The period he lived in was a watershed—both colonial India and independent India. He combined both. His theatre work had socio-political underpinnings. He brought together a huge number of people—actors, writers, directors—who became crucial in Indian cinema. All of his sons were part of his theatre.'

It was an accidental beginning. Prithviraj started Prithvi Theatres on 15 January 1944 as a favour to a friend. Prithviraj could never say no, particularly to the down and out. Betabji, a dejected poet, asked Prithviraj to help him. He had been commissioned by film director V. Shantaram to write a simplified version of the classic *Shakuntala*. Shantaram rejected his effort and asked another writer. Prithviraj gave the author money for the play and set about trying to mount a production in Bombay. (Shantaram made *Shakuntala* under his new banner, Rajkamal Kalamandir, with wife Jayshree and actor Chandramohan. Apparently, Prithviraj was disappointed that his rival had been chosen to play the screen Dushyant; it may have spurred him on to enact an even better Dushyant on stage.)

Prithviraj turned to K.A. Abbas, who was at that time writing plays for IPTA (Indian People's Theatre Association). It took a year before Prithviraj and his team were ready. It was not easy. The first task was to find an actress to play Shakuntala. Prithviraj's first choice was Vanmala, a blue-eyed beauty from Mathura who had acted in many pre-Independence-era films. She said yes, but soon married and dropped out. Abbas then took Prithviraj to see a play starring the charismatic Damayanti Sahni (actor Balraj Sahni's first wife). Damayanti Sahni, however, had other acting commitments, including films. But there was another sprightly young actress in *Zubeida*, an IPTA play written by Abbas. Uzra Mumtaz, a Pathan from the Rampur family, played the title role. Impressed by her, Prithviraj gave her the script and insisted that she do it. And that was that: she remained Prithviraj's leading lady and intimate friend for sixteen years. Her sister, the actress Zohra Segal, joined the company later.

Uzra Mumtaz
(Photo courtesy Roli Books)

Raj Kapoor, not quite twenty, was waiting in the wings. An underpaid assistant in Kidar Sharma's Ranjit Studios, he doubled up as art director in Prithvi Theatres. The young Kapoor designed a heavy darbar set with huge pillars for *Shakuntala*. The first show, a press show, did not go down very well. The second scene was in an ashram and the sets were heavy, like film sets. Changing the sets for different scenes was a nightmare for the stagehands. The props were clunky and cumbersome, and there was too much noise. 'Unlike the Parsi theatre sets that could be folded, these were going *thap, thap*,' says Yograj Tandon, whose father F.C. Tandon was Prithviraj's childhood friend. (The two had taken an oath of brotherhood as students.) 'Papaji's father was there, watching. He became red with anger and scolded everybody. He told his son to find a theatre company that made theatre sets.'

Apparently, Bashesharnath had been impressed by the sets of Parsi Theatre, particularly a play in which the set itself had moved forward towards the audience and Hanuman appeared flying on a wire. He met Shanji Shah of Parsi Theatre and ordered foldable sets. *Shakuntala* opened on 9 March 1945: there were 112 performances before the curtain came down on this play for the last time. Prithviraj lost one lakh rupees in his debut production; yet despite the considerable loss the large-hearted Prithviraj gave his cast and crew two months' bonus.

Prithviraj could ill-afford the financial setback. But what was important was that Prithvi Theatres had been born. The unique institution endured for sixteen years: 2662 performances across over hundred cities, many in dusty corners of the country so remote that trains did not stop there. The repertoire had eight plays, seven of them specially written for Prithvi Theatres. The grand patriarch himself played the lead in all the plays. He never missed a performance, not even when he was reeling with a fever of 104 degrees, despite varicose veins, heart problems, not even when his voice had given way. Not surprisingly, he never had an understudy for his roles—the others did.

Prithvi Theatres came at the right time, for theatre and for Prithviraj. Theatre was his first and abiding, and initially thwarted, love. It was a childhood love sparked by his theatrical debut at the age of eight in a school play in Lyallpur. A schoolteacher, Lala Narayandas Dua, whom he addressed as Guruji, first nurtured his histrionic talent. Before each stage performance, Prithviraj bowed his head in memory of his guru. He continued to do the same on movie sets, at the start of each shooting shift.

The thirties and forties were a barren landscape for Indian theatre. The choice was limited to adaptations of Western plays by amateur societies, schools or colleges. Or to folk theatre inspired by the epics and interspersed with religious songs as well as long declamatory passages from myths and legends. As a young child, Prithviraj used to watch the Corinthian Company perform Agha Hashar's plays. Intended to be modern Urdu plays, these were largely based on Western classics. But the young Prithviraj was not comfortable with this kind of theatre. Heroes would get up minutes after their stage death and sing an encore. 'Even the extravagant melodramas of the Parsi theatrical companies had fizzled out with the advent of cinema. With the exception of Bengal and Maharashtra, professional theatre was non-existent,' explains Zohra Segal. Prithviraj's vision was different: he wanted a national theatre, in a language that could be understood all over the country.

After a kind of false start with *Shakuntala*, Prithviraj went on to stage original dramas with a message. The response to this classic was lukewarm. It is not surprising that the subject of this romantic play based on Kalidas's classic about King Dushyant and Shakuntala failed to capture the imagination of the audience. These were restless times: the nationalist movement was at its peak and communal tension uncomfortably palpable. The Second World War was over. And the British had let it be known that the sun had begun to set over their Empire: it was getting close to pack-up time. The Quit India movement had by then become a mini juggernaut, grist to the intellectuals' mill.

Prithviraj immediately realized the need to stage plays that depicted the realities of the new, breaking day. Just as his son Raj Kapoor was to do later with cinema, Prithviraj broke new ground by being courageously contemporary. He also had an agenda. At heart he was an idealist and a nationalist with a strong sense of justice. His plays were vehicles to get across his ideas of equality and compassion. 'Beneath the showman's mask...there is a sensitive face of a real artist, a genuine idealist, who is concerned to serve his fellow beings through the medium of his art,' writes Abbas.

Prithviraj's in-house team wrote the seven plays of Prithvi Theatres' repertoire—*Deewar* (1945), *Pathan* (1947), *Gaddaar* (1948), *Ahooti* (1949), *Kalakar* (1951), *Paisa* (1953) and *Kisan* (1956). On board were Abbas, Inder Raj Anand, Lalchand Bilal and even Ramanand Sagar, who would later become the chronicler of epics like the Ramayana on television—idealistic men who were also closely associated with IPTA. The writers focussed on the traumatic events of the eventful decade of the forties.

Deewar emerged out of a discussion between Inder Raj Anand and Prithviraj. Recalls the writer's son, film-maker–actor Tinnu Anand, 'There was censorship then. You could not show anything anti-British. Papaji wanted to project Britain as a villain and not get caught. So you have this British woman who walks into this happy, united family, and soon the two brothers, who were close, are separated by a wall.' The play was essentially about two brothers who live together in harmony until a British woman comes into their lives. The brothers could symbolize Jinnah and Nehru or India and Pakistan, the wall between them the border between the two countries. Prithviraj was vehemently against Jinnah's two-nation theory. The play ends on a positive note: the brothers unite, and peasants, with the help of women, break the wall. The socialist underpinnings of the theme are clear.

According to Zohra Segal, who played the British vamp in *Deewar*, the impact of the play was stunning and instantaneous. It certainly had a life-changing impact on the actress herself. She wanted nothing more than to join Prithvi Theatres, where her sister Uzra Mumtaz was the leading lady. Until then she had pooh-poohed *Shakuntala*, the maiden production of the group. 'Here was a play that was fresh, topical and original, that inspired spectators to immediate action as it dealt with the approaching partition of India, the wall between Hindu and Muslim unity. To hell with all the films, this is what I have always wanted to do, I told my husband.'

There was no looking back after this play. The play was a success despite the fact that the speeches of Mahatma Gandhi, Jinnah and even Macaulay had been grafted onto the dialogues. *Deewar*'s appeal went beyond the country's borders. It was translated into Russian. (Later, Raj Kapoor unintentionally emulated his father when his films like *Awara* and *Shree 420* won over the Soviet Union.) Prithviraj had to struggle to get his play past the British censors. He needed police permission. He wanted to stage this play at any cost, even if he had to use subterfuge.

The British government had refused to give permission without a prior green signal from the Muslim League.

Driven and determined to raise the curtain on his play, Prithviraj held a secret meeting with the Muslim League in Bhendi Bazaar. According to Yograj Tandon, he pleaded his case for forty minutes before its working committee members. 'But at the end of it the Muslim League members told Papaji and my father that they would not allow him to stage *Deewar*. They told him, "What you have said is true, but what have you got against our Pakistan ideal? We want it." Papaji pleaded to be allowed to stage just one show before Jinnah and if he said no, it was no. The Muslim League members did not want Jinnah to see the play, saying, "He is very emotional." So they returned, very disappointed.'

But the thespian was not one to give up so easily. It is said that the loss of a parent in childhood often inspires unusual ambition, and Prithviraj was no exception. Yograj Tandon accompanied him to the Grant Road police station to find out if permission for staging the play had arrived. 'He went in with the chaprasi. The file was there; permission had not been given. But that "No" was on a separate paper, not on the file. Papaji removed the paper and gave the file to the censor. They concluded that no remarks meant it was okay. And that is how *Deewar* was staged in 1945,' says Yograj.

Prithviraj, the artist–patriot, later regretted his subterfuge. It wasn't that he had lied. He had just not been generous with the truth. The importance of staging *Deewar* for him lay in the play's ability to assuage communal feelings. It was a cri de cœur against the impending partition. The purpose of the three-act play was to break down the wall of misunderstandings between communities. The curtain came down with the dialogue, '*Hum ek thay, hum ek hain, hum ek rahenge*.' (We were, are and shall remain one.)

Prithviraj was keen to stage the play before the Congress Working Committee. After seeing the play, a visibly moved Sardar Patel told him that Prithvi Theatres had done with just one show what the Congress Party hadn't been able to do for two years. The Sardar, according to Professor Dyal, 'sat through the play, though he had merely come to put in an official appearance'.

The play had a curious epilogue on this occasion: Patel's unexpected half-hour speech, the result of which was exemption of entertainment tax for Prithvi Theatres.

The next production, *Pathan*, arguably the most critically acclaimed play staged by Prithvi Theatres, was an impassioned plea for communal harmony. Written by Bilal, the play focuses on the friendship between two families—one Muslim, the other Hindu, in the North West Frontier Province. The Muslim Khan sacrifices the life of his only son to save the life of his Hindu friend Dewan's son. Prithviraj's performance as Sher Khan, the Pathan who hands over his son to enemies, and to certain death, left not a single dry eye in the audience. The fact that one of his sons (Raj or Shammi) always played the sacrificed son added to the poignancy of the play.

Abbas describes Prithviraj's portrayal of Sher Khan as 'a piece of great acting'—a character he had imbued with much of his own personality. 'He put into it the tenderest memories of his childhood, the flavour of all the tales and legends of Pathan chivalry that he had ever heard, the patriotic feeling of a Pathan for his people and their noble qualities, and the idealist's passion to make the play a vehicle for the theme of unity.' Secularism was a subject particularly close to his heart. For Prithviraj, secularism was not just a word being tossed around by the Congress Party and Jawaharlal Nehru: it was a way of life.

Prithviraj's third play *Gaddaar* tackles the delicate subject of the dilemma of the Muslims during the freedom struggle. Written by Inder Raj Anand, and first performed in 1948, the play depicts Muslim society in the United Provinces caught between the Muslim League and the Congress. Its protagonist, Ashraf, a freedom fighter and a Congressman who is against the division of the nation, is temporarily won over by the Muslim League. Eventually, horrified by the carnage of partition—on both sides of the rapidly emerging cantankerous border—the protagonist comes to the conclusion that Pakistan was really the demand of a few opportunist leaders, and stays on in India.

Gaddaar, like most other Prithvi Theatres productions, was a vehicle for Prithviraj's beliefs: his mission was to tackle the burning issues of the day. *Ahooti*, first staged in 1949, was equally complex—and controversial. Set against the backdrop of the partition riots, this tragic play has the fate of an abducted young Hindu girl as its theme. Rescued from her kidnappers by a Muslim, she is rejected by the family of the man she is engaged to. Even her father, played by Prithviraj, is momentarily swayed by his social milieu and refuses to take his daughter back. There are obvious echoes of Sita's story in the Ramayana here.

Interestingly, Raj Kapoor picks up a similar thread in his film *Awara*. The eminent lawyer Raghunath (played by Prithviraj) refuses to take back his pregnant wife who has been kidnapped by a dacoit. He doubts the paternity of the child in her womb. In quite a casting coup, Raj Kapoor plays the young man this child grows up to be, thereby imparting a resonance to the on-screen tension between Raghunath and Raju, Raj's alter-ego in the film. The fate of women who were abducted and raped—both Hindu and Muslim—was a concern of the writers of the time. Sadat Hasan Manto's powerful and moving work *Khol Do* looks at the tragic fate of a young woman who becomes insane after being repeatedly raped.

The remaining three productions of Prithvi Theatres— *Kalakar*, *Paisa* and *Kisan*—are not among Prithviraj's more memorable plays. But they do reflect his missionary zeal for social reforms. *Kisan* glorifies the noble farmer, contrasting him with the wily zamindar. Indian cinema exploited this theme for decades. *Paisa* follows the graph of an individual's descent into corruption—Prithviraj plays the aptly named Shantilal, a bank manager whose pursuit of wealth changes his relationship with his family and friends, and in the end robs him of his peace of mind. The only Prithvi Theatres production to be filmed, the play was a dismal flop in its screen avatar. *Kalakar* is about the loss of innocence and of purity. The importance of this play lies in the fact that it contains the prototype of the trademark 'yahoo' persona of Prithviraj's second son Shammi. A rich city slicker, he turns the head of an innocent and naïve beauty from the hills. Ramanand Sagar wrote the play, but Prithviraj changed the third act and created the flamboyant character Shammi Kapoor plays. Prayag Raaj, who was part of the Prithvi Theatres family for years, describes the elder Kapoor enacting the role before his son. 'It

Still from Paisa

was all there, the rebellious yahoo character. Papaji changed his hairstyle and then showed him how to walk with a swagger. He did all those crazy movements.'

Prithvi Theatres was a collective workshop. Normally it took a year or two to produce a play. Once it was written, it was read to the entire cast and technicians. Every member had the right to point out the mistakes in its theme, plot and characterization. Actors often improvised their own lines, which were later incorporated into the play.

Prithvi Theatres had its own team of writers. But the man guiding the various pens was the patriarch himself. 'All the plays were inspired by Prithviraj, partly dictated, sometimes written, mostly added to in the form of extempore dialogue by him,' writes Balwant Gargi, novelist and a habitué of Prithvi Theatres, in the commemoration volume. Sometimes, he just coaxed the writers, practically midwifing their creative efforts. For instance, the play *Kalakar* came out of a conversation with Ramanand Sagar, who was a struggling writer at the time.

Recounts Sagar: 'I had promised to write a play for him. Papaji told me that he wanted a romantic play. So I said, okay Prithee but I can't write for two months because I am halfway through my novel *Ek Aur Insan*. One day the artist Sajjan just came and took me to Malad. We went by train, third class. It cost one and half a paise, and we walked the rest of the way. He put the bedding in the veranda, and gave me the agreement. Papaji had typed it and kept it ready. There were four lines: You will write a play for Prithvi Theatres. You will complete it whenever you want. You don't have to attend office. You will be paid three thousand rupees. The next morning I went to him. His staff was not happy: other writers had taken money and not written anything. I asked Papaji to give me three hundred rupees for ten months. I sent two hundred rupees home and kept hundred for myself.'

The plays, however, did not begin and end with the performances. In press conferences, in late-night discussions that often followed the performances (at times beyond midnight), or on diverse platforms, Prithviraj seldom lost an opportunity to declare his views. Describing a press conference in Hyderabad during the course of which the Muslim League press objected to the play *Gaddaar*, Professor Dyal writes that these objections were 'as a red rag to the bull. Prithvi gored them right and left. Muslims, he said, glorified in the title of iconoclast but they themselves had now become idol-worshippers. For sophisticates to worship a living idol was worse...than for the ignorant and the superstitious to worship the images of clay. They had made a god of Jinnah and in this and all their disintegrating acts they were un-Islamic.' He also lectured them on the evils of the two-nation theory. 'The India of tomorrow has to be shaped by Indians, not by Hindus or Muslims.'

Sometimes he got carried away by his own rhetoric offstage. In a sense the world became his stage. Once at Khandala Station, Prithviraj scolded Golwalkar, then head of the RSS who had just been released from jail and was travelling around the country. Golwalkar's followers were shouting vociferous slogans at every stop. Prithviraj entered his compartment and gave him a lecture on the need to control his men: 'There is only one chair and so many want to sit in it. There is such a scramble for it that not only will many bones be broken but also the chair itself will be smashed. In politics, discipline is absolutely essential and yet our crowds are witness to the utter lack of it.'[11]

The thespian's didactical strain got the better of him occasionally. In his critique of the play *Pathan*, Balwant Gargi writes: 'The first act where he [Prithviraj] buttonholes the teacher and harangues him breathlessly for twenty minutes on all subjects—education, foreign rule, politics, white man's intrigues, national language and Hindu-Muslim, etc—could have easily been cut short. The Muslim teacher is only a peg on which Prithviraj hangs the heavy robes of his sermons.'

Often, Prithviraj or his ideas form the kernel around which the plays are written, like a grain of sand which triggers the pearl-making process in an oyster. This makes it easy for the playwright, much like today's screenplay writers in popular Hindi cinema who create a story around a bestselling star. For instance, in *Pathan*, the lead role was really like a second skin for the author: it was he. However, this centrality, being such a centrifugal force, can also be quite a disadvantage. Gargi was convinced that the characters in many of the plays were 'sacrificed to the towering Prithviraj playing the lead. When he is on the stage he seldom leaves Prithviraj behind. Sometimes one wonders if the tribal chief in *Pathan*, the elder brother in *Deewar*, the artist in *Kalakar*, the bank manager in *Paisa* and the farmer in *Kisan* are not playing the role of Prithviraj.'

It wasn't as if Prithviraj wanted his actors to be his clones. During rehearsals when an actor floundered, he would clap. Everything would stop and complete silence follow. He would then ask the actor in 'dulcet tones', as Professor Dyal puts it, to try again. 'He asks him to be himself in the part—not Prithvi. The last thing he wants is mimicry; he wants an actor to feel the part.' But Dyal's former student had a 'terrible aspect'. 'At rehearsals he does not come down on the heads of individual actors like a sledgehammer, rather he woos them—cooing as gently as a dove; but woe betide the transgressor on the stage—

to whom Prithvi has been known to hiss from the wings, "Blast ye". Offstage he is the loving and beloved chief, but on the stage he is the inexorable presiding deity, beyond himself as a human.'

In Matunga lane, years later in Janaki Kutir, and backstage and offstage with his travelling company, real life and theatre life kept bumping into each other. What was real became theatrical and what was drama became real. The towering presence on the screen or stage was no less so in reality. There were many tense moments during the peregrinations of Prithvi Theatres in the forties. Had it not been for the presence of mind and imposing personality of Prithviraj, it could have ended in real-life tragedy. Once, a crowd had gathered when *Pathan* was about to be staged. Fanatics threatened to stop the performance because there were Muslim actors in the cast. Prithviraj kept his calm, asking the agitated men 'to pick out the Muslims' when the members of the group walked past them. '"For me they are all *kalakar*s, you pick out the Muslims," he said. 'They found no Muslims, all looked Hindu,' recounts Zohra Segal. Zohra also remembers an incident when a few fanatics threatened to kill Prithviraj because she and her sister were Muslims.

The Prithvi Theatres family was like a travelling joint family, with Prithviraj playing both papa and mama. 'Though in the form of man, he mothers his troupe. Both man and woman are in his spiritual make-up,' writes Professor Dyal. British theatre actress Felicity Kendal, sister of Shashi Kapoor's wife Jennifer, contrasts the nomadic life of Prithvi Theatres and her parents' famous travelling theatrical company Shakespeareana in her book *White Cargo*. 'Prithviraj Kapoor...had his own itinerant theatre company, very similar to my father's, except that he travelled with enormous scenery, a cast of hundreds, cooks, cleaners, wives and children. When they went by rail, they hired most of the train, whereas we were lucky to get two compartments.'

The caravan comprised about sixty actors and an additional fifty members that included technicians, tailors, make-up men—and whoever happened to drop in. Like a true Frontiersman, Prithviraj preferred to sit on the floor and eat. Everybody sat in rows on the floor to eat. And everybody ate the same food. The only exception was Prithviraj's father who had become a part of

Prithvi Theatres: he often ate food cooked specially for him. Ironically, the man who had shunned his son when he chose to become an actor, was to later spend most of his time with him, even moving next door to Prithviraj in Juhu.

On the road Prithviraj abhorred any kind of hierarchy: everybody had to be treated the same. Nor could he ever say no, not even to a dacoit. Jagga,[12] a real bandit, accompanied the troupe on two tours. 'He came to Papaji and said he wanted to act. Actually he sang quite well. And Papaji just could not say no,' says Zohra. Perhaps, it was a Pathan thing. Perhaps it was his instinctive communist inclinations. You could even say that Prithvi Theatres was like a circus on the move.

This democracy of the road often caused problems in life away from the arc lights. Ayahs were also part of the caravan. Prithviraj did not distinguish between them and the memsahibs when it came to food. Recalls Zohra, 'Everybody, including our ayahs, got the same treatment. Two eggs for breakfast, puri-aloo for the veggies. But when we went home, our ayahs turned up their noses; they wanted eggs and toast. We were not going to give them toast and eggs. So three of us, Uzra, Sati Devi and I, went in a deputation to Papaji and told him that we could not afford to give our ayahs even one egg, let alone two. So he said, "Achcha, shall I start with you...no eggs from tomorrow." Well, we quietly slunk out, and never complained again.'

There was no first amongst equals—not even among the progeny of the Kapoor khandaan. Everybody had to line up for food with his or her thali and katoris, and no asking for more. Apparently, on one occasion Shammi Kapoor came back for seconds of yoghurt. Shortly after, B.M. Vyas, a tall, well-built actor from Rajasthan, wanted his share. He was refused because Prithviraj's middle son had just gulped down the last spoonful of yoghurt. Angry, he complained about Shammi's second helping. Prithviraj heard about the incident the next morning and was furious, declaring in his stentorian voice: '*Ghar me mera beta hai, yaha nahin.* (He is my son at home, not here.) If anybody asks, there are no seconds.'[13] There was no *laad-pyaar* on the sets.

Not even for his nephews. Premnath lived with the Kapoors for a year. Prithviraj gave him seventy-five rupees a month as pocket money, and he in turn worked in the theatre as an apprentice and an extra. 'Whenever we took it easy, he used to remind us that we were not jagirdars but mazdoors,' Premnath wrote in the commemoration volume.

The most endearing, enduring image of this grand man of the theatre is of him standing there in front of the theatre hall, larger than life, in his kurta, the kurta cupped into a cloth donation box. Prithviraj used to bow his head and hold out his jholi after each performance to raise money for various causes. At times his managers also stood with him, when there was more to be collected during calamities. There is a mistaken impression that the donations were for his theatre, even though it was perennially short of funds. He used his silver screen earnings to support his theatre. The trademark jholi was exclusively for charities. Prithviraj raised money to help widows, lepers, the victims of famine, and other causes, including the Indian National Army (INA). (Subhash Chandra Bose was one of his heroes.)

If Prithviraj appeared larger than life onstage, he was even more so off it. The curtain never really came down after a show. The histrionics, as in the case of many great actors, carried over into his personal life. His gestures, manner and speech were no less theatrical—he lived life melodramatically, at full volume. Nobody else could have scripted his life. There was a certain over-the-topness about the way he lived it. For instance, if you dropped in on him at home in his jhompra, you were likely to spot him sitting under a tree in the courtyard. He would continue sitting even when it rained. The joke was that he was Shiva, and the Ganga was flowing through his hair. Shiva was also the family deity.

Theatre and life kept criss-crossing each other throughout his life: moving from the theatre to the theatrical was second nature to him. 'It would be difficult for a psychoanalyst to determine where Prithviraj the man ends and Prithviraj the artist begins,' explains Balwant Gargi. 'There is an element of drama and showmanship in the simplest and sincerest actions of his life—

with bowed head standing with his jholi at the theatre collecting donations for charity, beating the drums of unity in a peace brigade procession in riot-torn Bombay, or dancing alfresco on the streets to celebrate the advent of freedom!'

The street was also his stage. Ramanand Sagar, a close friend, narrates some interesting street dramas. The two first met in Pune when Sagar was an impoverished journalist and Prithviraj a film star. 'I met him during a lunch break, and we were still talking at one the next morning. We roamed the lonely streets of Pune, exchanging our romantic experiences, reciting *sher*s, talking about life and philosophy.'

The next street encounter, in Bombay, was even more dramatic. Sagar was jobless and homeless. When Prithviraj learned about his predicament, he sent for him. After dinner he accompanied him to the bus stop near his Matunga flat. 'He suddenly took out a bundle of notes, but I refused the money. I could not bear it. I took out two ten-rupee notes from my pocket and told him that I have twenty rupees. When they finish I will take it from you. He understood. He knelt on his knees on the road, that six-foot-tall man, and caught my feet and said, "Sagar, I am not doing this to insult you." We hugged each other and cried on the road. And then he said, "Tell me, we are friends. If I came like this, a refugee, wouldn't it be your *farz* to help a friend?" I was crying and I said that I would do the same.'

Perhaps his greatest role is the one he wrote for himself on the larger stage of the real world. Who else could have invented Prithviraj, the man. His drawing room in Bombay had a huge slab of black Kota stone—that was his sofa. Yet another slab of stone in his bedroom served as his bed. Prithviraj had no use for normal beds, a habit his eldest son Raj Kapoor shared with him. Both made the floor their bed. However, the elder Kapoor was even more eccentric than the younger one.

His bedroom was his library, with quite original cataloguing. Stacks of books encircled the 'bed'. Each of the four sides had a different set of books as well as a lamp next to it. Prithviraj didn't do anything as humdrum as picking up a book and bringing it back to bed to read. He simply leaned over to whichever side had the book he fancied, and read it in that position, belly side down, switching on the lamp on that particular side. His cousin, Mrs Seth, a frequent visitor to his jhompra, describes his reading habits. 'One pile of books had the Guru Granth Sahib. Papaji would read it while smoking a bidi. Often, he used his cigarette box as a bookmark. When anybody questioned his smoking while reading the Granth Sahib, he would say, "Now, tell me where it is written in the Granth Sahib or in the Koran that you cannot smoke."'

Prithviraj's furniture for his inner sanctum resembled theatre props. He had a few blackboards with scribblings in different languages on them, in addition to the gaddis on top of his infamous slabs of stone and chowkis. While one blackboard might have had Tamil writing on it, another could have Pashto. Perhaps he was a budding linguist. But that was not the entire picture: this was Prithviraj playing the role of saviour. He could never refuse anyone in need, or anybody who came to him for help, yet he didn't believe in giving money without making the person he was giving it to feel that he had earned it, that it wasn't just charity.

Whenever anyone came to him for financial help he asked: What can you do? Once, when he asked the same question of a middle-aged man who had come for help, the man replied that he could teach him Tamil. Prithviraj asked him to return the following morning and start teaching him Tamil. Similarly, a Pathan who had fallen on bad days ended up teaching Prithviraj Pashto. Eventually, he had five to six 'masters' a day. The roster of 'teachers' gradually became varied and longer: a tabla master, a harmonium teacher and a masseur joined the Tamil and Pashto masters. He used to give each master two hundred rupees a month. Mrs Seth recalls an incident when she was visiting her cousin. 'One day, a very poor man, who was illiterate, came for help. Papaji asked him what he could do. The man said, "Nothing. I can do nothing." Papaji then asked him if he could do *maalish*. He said yes, and he too began to come there every day to massage him.'

Sanskrit and Gurumukhi teachers continued the lifelong education of Prithviraj Kapoor. He also learned to play the sitar, the tabla and the harmonium, as well as dance Bharatnatyam.

Strangely enough, a typist came regularly to teach him typing. Generosity, though second nature to him, was not the only reason for all these lessons. It had to do with self-preservation: imbued with the wisdom of the sages he was giving himself the antidote to post-retirement blues. Puzzled by the strange extracurricular activities of his father, Shashi asked him why he was doing all this. 'My father told me to learn to play a musical instrument. "Kya hai, when you are old, it will be your companion in old age. These will be your only friends, not people." He bought a piano in the sixties—a Yamaha,' recalls Shashi.

There was another beloved companion: his old Opel. He remained faithful to it for much of his life, driving it everywhere, even when he, grown large and bulky, could barely get into it. While his sons bought progressively bigger cars—Buicks, Chevys, Mercedeses—he clung to his little Opel. He drove himself, except towards the end when his driver Prati did. Shashi held on to the Opel as a memento of his father for quite some time. 'It was turning to dust and was garaged in Prithvi Theatre. The Opel lived there for many years before it was finally taken away by the *raddiwalla*,' says Shashi.

Politics is the other stage his life played out on. A Congressman, Prithviraj was nominated to the Rajya Sabha and moved to Princess Park in New Delhi for much of his tenure. Not content to be an armchair man of the public, he was also the president of the Central Railway Workers' Union for four years. During his years as a member of the Rajya Sabha, Prithviraj Kapoor worked hard to improve the working conditions of stage actors. He was able to get a 75 per cent rail concession for performing artists. 'Till today we are able to travel throughout the country for 25 per cent of the cost because of my grandfather,' says Sanjana Kapoor, adding, 'We couldn't have survived otherwise.' Prithviraj also established Rabindra Natya Mandirs in several cities.

But he did not forget his 'theatre people'. Mrs Seth happened to be in his home when Pandit Nehru sent his secretary to invite Prithviraj for dinner. 'Papaji told him, "*Mein haath jodta hoon*, but my theatre people are here. I will not go alone." Panditji called the next day and asked him to bring all of them for tea. There were nearly sixty of them. So, all the carpenters, cooks, tabalchis and actors went for tea to Teen Murti house, in the private dining room. The prime minister showed us the museum and all the gifts.'

There appears to have been a special bond between the prime minister and Prithviraj. He wanted the thespian to spend more time with him, according to Mrs Seth. 'I overheard Panditji telling Papaji, "When you walk with me you give me strength."' In fact, the prime minister often asked him to lead cultural delegations abroad. In her book, Segal writes: 'Prithviji had to refuse on account of an impending tour. Panditji chided him for not having an understudy for his roles. "I know someone else who is without an understudy," apologized Prithviraj. "Who?" asked Panditji. "You!" responded the actor.'

Prithviraj Kapoor was also the man for all solutions. When Shashi Kapoor was reluctant to 'really' kiss a particular leading lady for a Bollywood film, his father devised a perfect solution. 'He showed me how to appear to be kissing without actually doing so,' remembers Shashi. The lesson was quite simple. All he had to do was to place his thumbs on his lips: they became a buffer between the two pairs of lips apparently coming together on the screen.

Prithviraj never did really hang up his boots. Even in the late autumn of his life, when roles in B-grade films came intermittently, he would sit down every Sunday, like a people's maharaja, in the garden in his jhompra. 'A long line of people would form in front of him, with each person coming up to him one by one to tell his story,' says Mrs Seth. 'Papaji would write cheque after cheque. Sometimes, he would ask his secretary to take the cheques from the account books of his three sons. They don't give *daan*, so take it from their accounts, is what he used to say.'

Prithviraj may have left Peshawar when he moved to Bombay, but the Pathan in him remained. Peshawar and Punjab occupied a lot of his mental baggage; more significantly, his love of tradition and rituals. He had imbibed the adventurous, almost foolhardy, spirit of the Frontier. What else would have made him leave his secure existence, wife and three children to follow a whim?

His years in Peshawar and in Samundari instilled in Prithviraj an acute sense of family that he was deprived of when he lost his mother as a child. The warmth of the Khanna family, with its vast cast of aunts, uncles and cousins, left an enduring impression on him. As did the idea of a large joint family rooted in tradition, with elements of both Pathaniyat and Punjabiyat. Incipient was a strong sense of heritage, even if it was the result of subsequent accretions.

An unshakable belief in friendship is an enduring Pathan trait. There is something almost mythical about male bonding amongst Pathans. They are also true to their word: once you make a friend, you give your life for that friend. It was this feature of Pathaniyat that Prithviraj took most seriously. His play *Pathan* is based upon this idea. The thespian wanted to portray the legends of Pathan chivalry and courage as well as to demonstrate the strong feelings a Pathan had for his people.

For the Hindus, friendship was also critical as a means of survival: almost 90 per cent of the population in the areas bordering Afghanistan comprised Muslim Pathans. The rest were either Hindus or Sikhs. There had to be, as producer Surinder Kapoor[14] puts it, 'pyar mohabat' between the Hindus and Muslims. '*Agar sab pishaab karte, hum doob jaate.*' (If all the Muslim Pathans pissed collectively, we would have drowned.) Traditionally, the two communities exchanged food. The Hindus adopted many of the customs of the Pathans. Recalls Mrs Seth: 'Since there were so few Hindus, we had to fall in line with the Muslims. So, we celebrated Eid with more gusto than Diwali.'

The Kapoor tradition of accommodating or appropriating diverse religions for survival continues even today. Cinema is a tricky, risky business. So, the Kapoors like to please or appease different gods. It is the 'Amar, Akbar, Anthony' approach to life. They visit mosques, churches and temples. They celebrate Eid, Holi and Christmas. 'When my father and my grandfather died, we read from the Bible, Guru Granth Sahib and the Koran,' explains Randhir Kapoor. His daughters Karisma and Kareena often go to church. 'My daughters go to mass at Mount St Mary's on Christmas night, and they are young and with it.'

Prithviraj also brought along with him a bit of the machismo of the men of the Frontier: there is often an air of a swagger about the Pathans. There was a perceptible physicality about Prithviraj, which manifested itself in his preoccupation with bodybuilding and wrestling. Prithviraj had a good physique, obviously a matter of pride for him as it was for many young men in those days. There appears to have been a cult of the beautiful body: bare-chested actors like Jagdish Sethi and David were bodybuilders as well. David, who was also part of Prithvi Theatres, was even involved with an international bodybuilding group. Shashi's earliest memory of his father is of 'a giant of a man lifting dumb-bells. We were all scared of him. He was six feet tall and had a loud, roaring voice. I had to look up and keep looking up a long way. We used to have a terrace, a huge one, and what I first remember about him is his doing exercises there. He had these Indian dumb-bells that he'd hold over his head. I couldn't even lift one of them; he would lift two. He used to go to the Hanuman akharas, and once I went with him to the Matunga akhara for kushti.'

The ruggedness of these men did not exclude a slight touch of narcissism. Prithviraj was conscious of his looks, especially of his luxuriant head of hair that dazzled the nation in *Sikandar*. Mrs Seth remembers the thespian's preoccupation with his hair. 'Papaji was afraid of going bald. His father was bald. He used to run both his hands through his hair and pull it with great gusto. He used to tell us that this was the best thing for growth. And yes, he never did go bald.'

The spirit of the Wild West clung to the Pathans. The landscape of the Frontier is wild and beautiful at the same time, as are the Pathans. 'The stage on which the Pathan lived out his life was at the same time magnificent and harsh—and the Pathan was like his background,' said Olaf Caroe, former governor of the NWFP. 'I remember Lord Ronaldshay saying: "The life of a Frontiersman is hard and treads daily on the brink of eternity."'[15] Blood feuds at the time accounted for about 300 murders a year. There was a hint of the risqué about the Frontier. Writing about the area in 1929, a nurse, Irene Edwards, describes Peshawar as the 'city of a thousand and one sins'.

Pathans are known to be a strange mixture of the tough and the kind, probably because life in the North West Frontier had a frisson of danger about it. It was close to a violent border, and those who lived there never knew when the men from the hills would descend in their baggy salwars with rifles slung across their shoulders. In fact, it took quite a lot to tame some of the Pathans even after many years of living in the concrete jungle of Bombay. Vishwa Mehra, or Mamaji as everybody in R.K. Films calls him, is Raj Kapoor's mother's cousin, and was a sort of Man Friday to him (as he is today for Randhir Kapoor). It took much persuasion and long years before he discarded the long knife he carried, tucked into his baggy Pathani salwar. 'We had to tell him that nobody was going to attack him in Bombay,' jokes Randhir Kapoor.

Prithviraj also had flashes of the Pathan temper in him. Zohra Segal recalls an incident when young men whistled at some of the women from their troupe when they were getting off a train. 'Papaji just caught hold of their heads and crushed them together. He was really very angry, and very strong.' He obviously shared the fearlessness of the Pathan as well.

When Prithvi Theatres planned to stage a special show of *Deewar* for the Congress Working Committee in Jodhpur, some Congressmen warned Prithviraj that there would be trouble. Yograj Tandon recalls that one of them actually threatened Prithviraj by saying, 'You are going into politics, and that too with girls. What if somebody abducts one of them?' A furious Prithviraj replied, 'In that case it will have to be my body first. *Meri lash gire gi.*'

He had obviously imbibed the spirit of the Frontier, a taste for adventure and risk. How else could one explain his setting off from Peshawar to an unknown Bombay, penniless and without any letters of reference? Prithviraj must have believed in Manifest Destiny. Referring to his father on his web site, Shammi Kapoor writes: 'The spirit of pioneering manifests in the urge, the obsession, and the overall aim to shape your destiny and what could only be termed as deranged thinking, as many then thought.'

Another personality trait the man from Peshawar brought

with him was his simplicity and transparency of intent: he did not have the artifice of the more circumambulating city dwellers. Describing the nature of the men of the Frontier, Lord Rathenhouay wrote: 'There was among the Pathans something that called to the Englishman or the Scotsman—partly that the people looked you straight in the eye, that there was no equivocation and that you couldn't browbeat them.'[16]

According to Professor Dyal, Prithviraj's father also embodied several of the salient characteristics of the Pathan: 'A Pathan is both Muslim and Hindu, and yet he is neither—he is simply and solely a Pathan, personified for us at the moment off the stage, yet within its charmed circle, by DBN [Dewan Bashesharnath] whose build, searching eyes, commanding voice and martial gait bespeak his origin. He can be suave—has polished manners like a courtier, and his hospitality, characteristically unbounded.'

Hospitality was almost a religion with the Pathans, as it was indeed with Prithviraj and his sons. A colourful Punjabi phrase encapsulates this: *Gadi vi tyar tay roti vi tyar hai* (If you want to go back, the car is ready to take you and food is also ready). The Kapoor home in Bombay became a mini-Punjab after partition. College Back Road, or R.P. Masani Road as it is now called, in Parsi Colony near Matunga metamorphosed into a mini Mecca for refugees from the other side of the border. The Punjabi invasion of the film industry had, in fact, begun earlier when singer K.L. Saigal, actor Jagdish Sethi, F.C. Mehra and B.R. Chopra and other families from West Punjab had made Bombay their home. After partition, the busy neighbourhood began to attract other homeless and jobless migrants from Punjab. But the only house that had an endless stream of them in front of its door was the Kapoor home. 'I remember after partition, for three years, there used to be a line of people outside our house in Matunga. The street had many other families from north India but it was full of people coming to only one house,' says Shashi Kapoor.

Like Mother Hubbard's shoe, the Matunga flat overflowed with people. Grandfather Kapoor, several uncles (on a separate floor) made this five-bedroom flat their home. While a large number of them were relatives, especially refugees from across the border, many were friends of friends, or from Peshawar. Clansman Surinder Kapoor came for a week in 1951, and stayed two years. Premnath lived for a year. Others who stayed on were strangers. Like the mysterious young man who turned up one afternoon looking for a job. The Kapoors offered him lunch. He had lunch and stayed on for dinner—and eternity. It was only many years later when a member of the family asked who the stranger was that they discovered nobody knew him. His face had become so familiar that he had become part of the furniture of the house.

Anybody who visited had to eat, even if they didn't want to. Tinnu Anand describes a night when, as a young man, he had gone to Prithviraj's home to deliver an urgent message. 'One evening I had to rush to Matunga with a message which had to be given personally to Papaji. It was 9.30 at night. I touched his feet and told him that I had come from the Khanna household with a message for him. He said, "*Baad mein*, first eat." The dining table was huge and long and laden with the most delicious food. There were fourteen people at the table. The table took over the house. After that we got up, washed our hands and said goodbye. Later my friend told me as we were leaving the house, "Thank god we were not sitting on the table, he would have eaten us too."' The Kapoor dining table was low: people sat on the floor round the table.

Sometimes the trademark Kapoor hospitality verges on caricature, especially in the case of Indian cinema's original and quintessential showman, Raj Kapoor. His famous table groaned with food; his banquets were legendary, the stuff gatecrashers' dreams are made of. Prithviraj's hospitality, on the other hand, was more of the earth: it had more to do with generosity and sharing and less to do with showmanship, or one-upmanship.

It also had to do with a Pathan's sense of community, his tradition of communal eating. Eating was a collective affair. The poor and rich supped from the same plate; literally in the case of Pathans, figuratively with the elder Kapoor. Shashi recalls during the first few years after partition how '[the] house in Matunga was always full of people. All the rooms had families from Pakistan and food was always cooked for at least forty people for every meal.' The fires of the kitchen were almost always burning in his home—for everybody and anybody who dropped in. No wonder the inmates called the Kapoor home an 'ashram'.

In a way Prithviraj was a curious amalgam: part communist, part Pathan and part Gandhian. When Premnath, impressionable and young, lived there, he discarded trousers for a kurta, churidar and a Jawahar jacket; the young actor also gave up smoking and drinking. 'Every evening Papaji, Chaiji, Raj, Shammi, Shashi and all of us sat down to sing bhajans,' writes Premnath.

Peshawar *has* to be responsible for the gargantuan appetite of the Kapoors. Peshawar was a gourmand's heaven on earth: in this land of plenty even the poor ate paranthas. Needless to say, its bracing climate helped. The air of the Frontier is invigorating and its water sweet. Peshawaris get misty-eyed when they talk about the quality of the water of the city they have left behind. You could eat anything and any amount, and would be ready for a refill a few hours later. Like a boa constrictor a Pathan could ingest anything. 'The water was so good that you could eat anything and digest it. *Lakar vi hazam, pathar vi hazam* (You could digest wood and stones),' says Mohan Sahni, who grew up in Peshawar. His family owned a chain of cinema theatres in Peshawar and Murree.

The word cholesterol did not exist in anybody's vocabulary: anything that moved found itself in a tandoor. Vendors called *naanbhai*s did brisk business all day long selling tandoori food. Prithviraj was particularly fond of red meat: burra kababs disappeared into his mouth the fastest. Recalls Mrs Seth: 'At tea time we often had a roti and two seekh kababs or eggs fried in batter. People ate fried quails. The shops in Peshawar even sold sparrows fried in batter.' Tea also came with different kinds of bread like Peshawari kulcha and rogini roti, often gulped down with gulabi or lal chai.[17] Breakfast at the Kapoors often included paaya, kababs or paranthas with fried eggs.

The Kapoor family lived in a four-storeyed house in Bhola Ram di Gali. Prithviraj's wife Ramsarni grew up in Lahoriyan di

Gali in the neighbourhood. Most of the houses were cheek by jowl: you could jump from one roof to the other. Winters were bitterly cold. If you left water out overnight on the roof, it became ice. But the sun shone warmly during the day. So, life in winter vacillated between the roof and the street. The kitchen moved to the roof. Food, however, also called out from below. Peshawar was full of vendors who moved through the galis with carts selling all kinds of street food. The hungry and lazy used to lower a basket tied to a rope all the way down to the street and pull up the food. Firm and round double-decker paneer cakes were among the favourite dishes being carried up in those baskets.

Peshawar was like an unspoiled Garden of Eden laden with all kinds of fruit, which were abundant and cheap: Kabul's fabled luscious grapes cost six annas a kilogram. Sarada melons from Central Asia, pale yellow, delicately veined, oblong and indescribably aromatic, were as ubiquitous as potatoes in the mandis of India today. There was the even sweeter garma melon, its fragrance as intoxicating as perfume. Dry fruit flooded the market, spilling out of the jute bags containing them. Peshawaris didn't peck at the pine nuts, pistachios or almonds; they ate fistfuls at a time. It was the popcorn of the day.

Of Prithviraj's three sons, Peshawar's gastronomical delights lingered the longest in Raj's memory, and on his palate. Raj spent a large part of his childhood in the Frontier. His love of fruit is a 'Peshawar thing'. Raj liked to buy his own fruit and he always knew the cost. He often stalked the markets of whichever city he might be in for good fruit. Shashi's son Kunal recalls the time Raj was in London with them. He had come when Shashi's wife Jennifer was very ill, and had stayed on a week after the funeral. 'He would go out and buy fruit. He kept it by his bed. Fruit was the last thing he ate at night.'

Dubgari Gate was the place where the Kapoor khandaan's, especially Raj's, infamous love of 'good' food was born. The Khannas had two liveried khansamas: a Goan for continental food and another for Indian food. Raj got his first taste of angrezi cuisine here. It was the beginning of a beautiful—and long—affair with food. Says his son Rishi Kapoor: 'When my father was very young, they were not rich; they were actually a bit humble. They had rich relatives in Peshawar whose table always had good food, and a variety of dishes. They had a butler with white gloves. *Angrezon ka zamana tha*. My father ate caramel custard for the first time in their home. He craved for caramel custard each night after that. Do you know that it was made in our house every day? There was a standing order that there had to be caramel custard, whether Raj Kapoor ate at home or not. We were *haath ke khane wale log*. Forget caramel custard, the Kapoors did not even have custard. Funnily enough my son Ranbir also has a passion for it.' The Kapoor genes are stubborn.

Prithviraj was more gourmand than gourmet: it was the quantity of food rather than its quality and sophistication that mattered to him. A simple daal was as close to heaven for him as was the Kapoor house specialty, yakhni pulao—not to forget burra kababs and jungli gosht and paaya. 'He was ruthless when it came to eating, according to my father,' says Yograj Tandon.

Food for Prithviraj had to find its way, fast, to his stomach. Nor did food have any protocol: anything went with anything. Director Lekh Tandon, who worked in Prithvi Theatres and later with Raj Kapoor at R.K. Films, recalls: 'During a wedding dinner, Papaji poured raita over his halwa and ate it with great relish. Once, a fly fell into something. He just took it out and continued to eat. He also had a sweet tooth and loved halwa. Papaji went to gurudwaras often just to eat some of the prasad. He would put the prasad in my father's pocket; this way he could take some more.'

The actress Nadira, whose memorably vampish number 'Mur mur ke naa dekh' in Raj Kapoor's *Shree 420* has become one of Indian cinema's unforgettable moments, acted in a couple of what she calls 'farcical films' with Prithviraj—*Insaaf Ka Mandir* and *Ek Nannhi Munni Ladki Thi*. She obviously spent a lot of her time on location observing Prithviraj's eating habits. 'Being a Peshawari, his idea of eating was wringing a neck, breaking a chicken. If he were on a diet, he would eat what the doctor ordered. Once he had gobbled it down, he would look around and say, "I have had the diet food, now let me eat some real food." He used to put a *gowtakiya* on the floor and lie over it. Somebody would be pressing his legs while he ate. I used to wonder where he kept his tummy while he did all this. And then he'd put his head on the same pillow, close his eyes and sleep. But if you dangled a kakri or kheera in front of his closed eyes, he'd suddenly wake up, and eat. Once while returning from location shooting, we had to wait at a railway level crossing. There was a man selling snacks near the crossing. You should have seen the look of glee on Papaji's face. His eyes lit up. "*Bhajia lao*, bring whatever is ready." And he would devour, mind you, not eat, but devour it all.'

Food was something that had to be gulped down, almost as if there was a huge void inside him crying out to be filled. His was a hunger that went beyond food. It was a lust for life, for all that life had to offer. And he went about it as if he was making up for lost time, looking for something permanently lost or elusive. If there was a Tantalus, it had to be in some form of food. Analysts, particularly Freudians, would probably say that the loss of his mother at an early age was responsible for his insatiable appetite and his intense relationship with food.

Their infamous love of food is jokingly called a Kapoor *bimari* (malady). Food stories about them abound. Professor Dyal writes about a rainy day when the troupe found shelter in Hamilton Hotel, near Lonavala a few hours from Bombay. His clothes barely dry, Prithviraj sat down for breakfast. The thespian had neither time nor concern for table etiquette. 'Prithvi is a real Frontier man where eating goes. He made short work of the jar of honey.'

It is something Prithviraj shares with his first-born. Little Raj Kapoor's food tales in Peshawar are also legendary. Round faced, podgy and pink, Raj was always on the prowl for food—and always playing. He would often run in to snatch some food from the table and run out again. If it was honey for the father, it was tomato ketchup for his eldest son. As a boy, Raj frequently visited the Khanna house in Murree. Lintot Café was the highlight of his holiday sojourn here. However, for the owners of this little restaurant with bright red check tablecloths, Raj must have seemed like a Pathani version of Dennis the Menace. Whenever the waiter spotted him coming towards the restaurant, he'd quickly remove the tablecloth and empty half the bottle of ketchup into another container. Raj used to go to the restaurant with his cousin and friend Colonel Ram Khanna. He always ordered a plate of chips: among the cheaper dishes on the menu for the customer, but expensive for the restaurant's owner if the customer happened to be ten-year-old Raj Kapoor. He invariably doused the chips with an entire bottle of tomato sauce and gobbled them up. Finally, when there was not a crumb in sight, he would wipe his ketchup-stained hands on the clean tablecloth with great relish.[18]

The truant in him always surfaced when it came to food. And the Peshawar habit continued in Bombay. As a teenager Raj often went to Marosa, a small restaurant owned by a Goan in the Fort area of Bombay. Its renowned chicken patties and samosas drew him there. His pockets, however, were always shallower than his hunger. Raj inevitably ordered chicken patties. The restaurant always served a plate of patties but billed the customers for only the number of patties consumed from that plate. Raj would eat one, remove the upper crust from the rest of them, scoop out the chicken in the middle and then replace the crusts. Of course, he only paid for one.

Raj's first real love was a young, rich and pretty Sardarni. They were both sixteen, and they used to meet at Marosa (presumably he paid for two chicken patties on those occasions) before her parents found out and the affair came to an end. But the Marosa habit continued for the rest of his life. The place became an adda for Raj and his entourage, which consisted of those working with him at R.K. Films—Abbas, Inder Raj Anand, V.P. Sathe, Shankar, Jaikishen, Mamaji, Radhu Karmakar, amongst others. They ate and talked cinema.

Travelling long distances for a meal is a Kapoor habit. Randhir does it even today. Shammi used to: he would think nothing of hopping into his car with his first wife Geeta Bali and driving to Tijola, a hour from Malabar Hill where they lived. The patriarch Prithviraj certainly passed his passion for food down the Kapoor line.

Food became so integral a part of the Kapoors that feasting

and filming went together like, well, rajma and chawal. Actors soon realize that a film with the R.K. banner means unwanted additional inches around the waist. 'Even if there was one dish they would say, *loji*, *loji*. If nobody wanted to eat it, they would say, okay then, we will eat it,' recounts Surinder Kapoor. Om Puri recalls the conversations around the dining table the week he spent during the filming of Rajiv Kapoor's *Prem Granth* at Loni farm, Raj Kapoor's retreat outside Pune. 'Breakfast was big, lunch bigger, tea was big and dinner even bigger, the biggest. Even the terms they used for food were from cinema. One day the long table on which the banquet was held had bharta in addition to all the chicken and yakhni pulao. Nobody touched the vegetables. They joked about it: *Iski delivery nahin uthi*.' The colourful phrase from the ever-expanding lexicon of Bollywood-speak is used when a distributor has not picked up a film. Of course, the chicken disappeared before you could say, well, Kapoor.

'Women were crazy about Papaji. He was like a Greek god...'

—Shashi Kapoor

There is no doubt, Prithviraj's looks could kill. There was an unearthly beauty about the man—he looked like an Apollo dropped down from the skies, with a heavenly buzz about him. Ermeline, who picked him up from the line of extras because of his good looks, was just the beginning. Many actresses fancied him, often letting him know how they felt. 'Women really threw themselves at him,' says Lekh Tandon.

You can't blame the ladies. It wasn't just his perfect beauty or his powerful voice that could both charm and intimidate. Prithviraj had the rare ability to make each individual believe that he or she was special to him. It must not have been easy for this man who was twenty-three and a father of three when he first stepped off the train in Bombay to become an actor. His leading ladies were stunning and intelligent—Vanmala, with her beautiful singing voice, and Durga Khote with her charismatic presence were women of substance. But the actor had a nice Indian remedy to deflect Cupid's arrows. When any heroine came along, he would ask her to tie a rakhi on him and make her his sister.

End of story? Well, almost. Cupid did win, eventually. 'You do know, of course, about my sister Uzra and Papaji?' asks Zohra Segal, the mischievous twinkle in her eyes dimming for an instant. I quickly suppress my surprised reaction and nod. It wasn't love at first sight, the stuff of Shakespearean romances and Persian poetry that was the compost of the romantic imagination of the youth at that time. This chronicle of a love story foretold onstage between Uzra Mumtaz and Prithviraj Kapoor had a slow, back-burner quality to it.

'The two were a godly pair,' says Zohra. The newly formed stage jodi endured for much of the sixteen years of the existence of Prithvi Theatres. In an interview to Deepa Gahlot for *Prithviwallahs*, Uzra says: 'I can't say what attracted Prithviraj Kapoor to me or why he preferred me for the role of Shakuntala. He didn't say anything. After landing up a few times at the hall where we were rehearsing for *Zubeida*, he used to send me the car and say, "Please come and watch my rehearsals."'

The romance must have come much later. The two were partners in their shared world of theatre and ideas. When they first met she was twenty-seven and married to Hamid Butt, an actor and writer involved with films in Pune. Prithviraj was nearly forty, and devoted to his wife Ramsarni, whom everybody called Chaiji. The relationship matured in the late summer of the thespian's life, according to Lekh Tandon. 'I gave Papaji a book of short stories by Guy de Maupassant on his birthday. I had inscribed it with something like "Too much a man or an angel". When he read it, a look of sadness suddenly came upon his face. "You had to give me this today," he said to me rather quietly. I realized later why he said what he did. He had fallen in love with another woman. I also realized then that the greatest of men could be vulnerable. He fell in love in his fifties. He wasn't even the sort of man who looked at other women. He was like a brother to them.'

What happened? For a man so engrossed in his work, so in love with his wife, and so much the paterfamilias of the repertory of Prithvi Theatres, Cupid must have had to work overtime and over decades. The world of theatre often becomes a *huis clos*, a world in which what is played out on the stage becomes as real as life itself. The world outside often seems less real. On the road, thrown together for hours and days and nights, colleagues become family, friends become lovers.

Also, the talented Uzra was not like the others: there was something of the muse about her. She did not fit into any of the stereotypes. Professor Dyal writes: 'She was both emotional and intellectual, with a certain dreaminess and a faint lisp. By no means goody-goody, she is good...there is something manly about her in spite of her charming feminity. She is rationalistic in outlook, so her words are well-weighed—not over-talkative in society as are so many emancipated Indian women. She possesses an ease and a poise that is often absent in the transition of woman *confined* to woman *free*...' Sometimes, what others imagine also triggers relationships. 'Chaiji pushed him into my sister's arms. She was jealous because they were a romantic pair in the plays. But there was nothing until she started suspecting them. He loved his wife,' says Zohra.

'He loved his wife' is a common refrain when people talk about Mr and Mrs Prithviraj Kapoor—whether it is strangers, intimate friends or family. There was a special bond between the two. His first encounter with her was in Peshawar, and it was like a scene out of a Shakespearean play. Prithviraj was all of seventeen—tall, thin and incredibly handsome. She was sixteen—short, thin and incredibly beautiful with light eyes and perfect features. (Raj Kapoor gets his blue eyes from her side of the family.) It was Lohri, the Punjabi festival that marks the onset of winter and the signal to harvest crops. Describing the moment, Shashi says: 'Lohri was taken seriously. Old things were not re-used. There were many bonfires with *revri*s. *Ganna* (sugarcane) was roasted. And that's where he first saw her, peeping from the balcony, like Juliet. Both fell in love. He told his stepmother and she arranged it. They were married in 1923; it was a three-day wedding.'

There was something else they shared: a motherless childhood. Both had lost their mothers when they were about three, and their respective fathers were not involved in their upbringing. Loneliness must have been at the core of their growing-up days in the Frontier. Prithviraj was only a little over a year older than her, yet he played her mentor, wise far beyond his years. 'My father wanted her to study and kept a tutor for her,' says Shashi. 'There used to be padri from St Joseph's school. At times there would be a nun.' She had been taken out of school in Peshawar because she was very good-looking. The Ramayana and the Granth Sahib were all she knew. But she was a good student. An indulgent husband, Prithviraj used to tease his wife when she started speaking English. 'In the fifties, Nehru sent him on a cultural delegation to South-East Asia—Singapore, Malaysia. My parents went to a reception and Chaiji spoke in English. My father was really amused. He used to say: "The British left Singapore *aram naal* and look at her, she is speaking angrezi,"' recounts an amused Shashi.

Prithviraj even learned to read the Devnagari script just so that he could read his wife's letters to him while he was away in Lahore studying law after their marriage. Men in the Punjab and Frontier spoke and wrote Farsi, Urdu and English, while the women learned Hindi. Prithviraj taught himself Hindi because he did not want anybody else to read her letters to him. Recalls Shashi: 'When my mother wrote to my father in Hindi and Punjabi she would make me write the address in English. I would say, "*Kisko?*" (To whom?), and she would say, "*Tere pyo nou.*" (To your father.) I would ask her, "*Na ki hai?*" (What's his name?) She would not take his name and simply say, "*Inna noon.*" (To him.) She used to call him Chanji and would address him as "Suno ji".'

Prithviraj loved to pamper his wife. He had been in Calcutta for six months, working for New Theatres in 1932, when he asked his wife to join him there. The day she was to come, he spent the entire morning cooking. Manmohan Malhotra,[19] who was staying with him at the time, says that he made some lobiya and then went out to buy bread before going to the station to fetch her. 'He brought her home and told her, Rama, come and eat, and he looked on tenderly as she ate,' says Malhotra. Cooking was, it seems, not quite her forte when she was a young bride. Prithviraj, however, never let on that this was so, according to Zohra Segal. 'He really loved his wife. When he was in films, he had a small little salary and lived in a *kholi*. Chaiji did not know how to cook; she'd make *jali-kachchi roti* (half-cooked, half-burnt rotis). And when she would ask him how it was, he'd say, "*Theekh hai ji, bahut swad hai.*" (It's fine, it is delicious.)'

Prithviraj Kapoor may not have played Othello on stage but he was no stranger to jealousy. Ramsarni, petite and with perfect features, loved fine clothes and jewellery; she was also quite a beauty. Shashi has this anecdote to narrate: 'My mother used to like Surendranath, the actor who sang beautifully. Papaji discovered that Chaiji was a fan of his. One day he came home and broke all his records. He was very possessive. My sister Urmi told me about this incident. My father's good friend Jagdish Sethi was not allowed to see my mother for two or three years after my parents were married.'

Chaiji may have appeared fragile, with her small frame, delicate features and her perfect bow-shaped mouth. But she had an inner strength and a strong will. She also had to evolve into the sacrificing sort: it was always 'family go slow' in the Kapoor household. Her husband's generosity, which seemed as endless as the Arabian Sea he so loved, placed its demands on her. Even in those early years in Calcutta. Soon after she joined him there with her two sons, Raj and Shammi (Shashi was born in Calcutta), Prithviraj called his father's family from Peshawar to join him. 'My grandfather had retired from the police and he came with his second wife and children,' says Shashi. 'My mother never complained. Even though they had a joint kitchen and my father's stepmother ruled the kitchen. Rajji and Shammiji were sent the *bacha kacha* (leftovers). I never knew this. My mother's dharam sister, Lachcha masiji, told me this. They lived with them until the end in 1956.'

Lachcha masi lived down the road from the Kapoors in Matunga. She was Ramsarni's best friend and confidante. Later, the Ahujas lived next to Raj Kapoor's home in Chembur. According to her friend, Rama loved playing cards. She also loved the finer things of life. Perhaps the famed Kapoorian love of the best in everything—clothes, jewellery and food—came from her. 'When she was ill—just four days before she died in fact—she ordered two silk salwar kameez ensembles, one blue, the other pink,' remembers Mrs Ahuja. She also liked to keep a tight control over her home. 'Rama never gave her keys to anybody.'

Prithviraj began to do well in the movies in the late thirties. He bought his first car in 1939, his famed Opel, when he was thirty-three years old. He bought a car for his wife as late as 1956, long after he had presented an Ambassador to his father and stepmother. It was the same with a home: only after he had got one for his parents in Matunga did he buy one for himself. Being the proverbial good son, the two homes faced each other.

Chaiji often accompanied her husband's touring company. However, unlike him, she kept her distance from the others. 'Chaiji was devoted to him. Petite and a little vain, she loved to wear good clothes and jewellery. When she went on tours, there was a *bai* to take care of all her needs,' says Zohra. Chaiji was certainly no shrinking violet. Contrary to her frail image, she lived life to the full, and was a good sport. 'Chaiji used to eat paan masala and tobacco. She would smoke a couple of cigarettes after dinner. Once in a while she would tell me, "Come here and let's have a *soota*,"' says Manmohan Malhotra.

Professor Dyal describes her as 'the unseen support of Prithvi's throne'. Interestingly, after he mentions the actresses Begum Uzra Hameed and Pushpa, he adds, 'Mrs Prithvi accompanies him on his tours alleviating the sting of venomous tongues and sharing the players' vagabondage.' Later in the book, he writes: 'She often sits in the wing, frail, on her chair, alert for any emergency...This frail creature is Prithvi's mainstay.' Prithviraj's temporary Boswell also insinuates that all this was a strain on her.

During the last decade of their lives the couple lived apart for much of the time. She in their old Matunga flat where the Kapoor children had grown up, he in what he called his jhompra in Janaki Kutir in Juhu, opposite where Prithvi Theatre stands today. (Prithvi Theatre was built by Shashi and his wife in Prithviraj Kapoor's memory and was opened on 5 November 1978.) Why did Prithviraj move to Juhu? Of course he liked being near the sea. He spoke to it, raged at it, roared like a lion while practising the art of throwing his voice on its shores, and walked into it, to immerse the amputated leg of his aunt Kaushalya who had been like a mother to him.

Juhu was a natural habitat for him. Several intellectuals and artists had moved here: old friends from IPTA, like Kaifi and Shaukat Azmi, Chetan Anand and those who had worked with him in Prithvi Theatres. He had closed down Prithvi Theatres in 1960 and was now acting in B-grade films.

The land belonged to the Ram Kishan Bajaj family. The Kapoor sons felt that the ten-year lease that their father had signed in 1962 was too expensive, something he could ill-afford. 'At that time we told him that he should not pay so much for the lease,' says Shashi. 'Papaji replied: "*Apni apni aayashi. Aap log Scotch pite ho, mein Solan whiskey. Aap log foreign cigarette pite ho, mein bidi. Yeh mere liye Scotch hai.*" (Each one has his own pleasures. You drink Scotch, I drink Solan whiskey. You smoke foreign cigarettes, I smoke bidis. This is my Scotch.)' Strangely enough, Prithviraj's words to Shashi proved to be prophetic. 'He told me, "*Puttar*, ten years *bahut honda hai.*" (Ten years is a lot.) The lease was from 1962 to 1972. When the lease expired, he expired.'

The jhompra became the final resting place for his beloved Prithvi Theatres. The bungalow was stuffed with three wagonloads of sets, costumes, jewellery, lights and props of Prithvi Theatres. 'He would let it out to friends for weddings,' says Shashi. Like the Matunga home, this too became a dharamsala for those who had no roof over their heads. Mrs Seth remembers visiting him there. 'His generosity knew no bounds. When Prithvi Theatres closed down, he asked those who did not have a place to live with him. The house had a long hall with *gadda*s, where he had put the sets and costumes. On the anniversary of the theatre, the players would stage a play here. He used to hold meetings as well, and there would be song and dance.'

While Chaiji held fort in Matunga, visiting the jhompra from time to time, and watched over the growing Kapoor clan, Prithviraj mingled with those in the world of the arts as well as the inhabitants of the kholis in Juhu, including the fishermen and

Prithviraj Kapoor (centre) in an early silent costumer, *Sher-e-Arab* (1930), a.k.a. *Arabian Knights*.

Cover of programme booklet for *Sikandar* (1939), which starred Prithviraj Kapoor in one of his most memorable roles as the Macedonian conqueror Alexander.

Still from *Ek Raat* (1942). Note how closely Prithviraj Kapoor resembles Shammi Kapoor in his 'yahoo' persona.

Prithviraj Kapoor (extreme right) in a scene from the Prithvi Theatres play *Gaddaar.*

Lunch at Prithvi Theatres was a communal affair with every member of the repertoire sitting on the floor and sharing the same food. Seen here at one such gathering are Prithviraj Kapoor (second from right) with father Bashesharnath Kapoor (extreme left) and co-artiste Uzra Mumtaz.

Prithviraj Kapoor (seated second from left) with father Basheshamath Kapoor (seated centre) and wife Ramsarni (seated second from right).

Prithviraj Kapoor supported a number of causes and individuals in his lifetime. Here, he is seen with his jholi at the theatre, collecting donations for charity—a familiar sight after a Prithvi Theatres performance.

Rishi Kapoor and Randhir Kapoor in Prithvi Theatres only film *Paisa*.

Raj Kapoor in a Prithvi Theatres play.

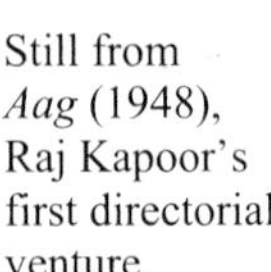

Still from *Aag* (1948), Raj Kapoor's first directorial venture.

Prithviraj Kapoor in K.A. Abbas's *Asman Mahal* (1965). Prithviraj's portrayal of the doomed nawab won an award at Karlovy Vary.

Prithviraj Kapoor as part of a cultural delegation to South East Asia, 1955.

Cover of programme booklet for *Boy Friend* (1961).

women. Separate lives, yes, but Prithviraj could not do without his wife.

Lekh Tandon narrates a moving but strange story about the last few weeks in their lives, a story which demonstrates the extraordinary will the thespian possessed and the depth of his love for his wife. Both were terminally ill: Chaiji had cancer and he was suffering from Hodgkin's disease. 'One day, while Papaji was in the Tata Memorial the doctor took Raj Kapoor out of the room and told him that his father had Hodgkin's disease. My father overheard him and must have looked distressed. Papaji already knew about it, though pretended not to. When my father, who was his closest friend, started to cry, he asked him why he was crying. "I will live until I have read the Koran and remembered it all," he said. Just then Dr Praful Desai told him that he could give him another four years. Papaji then said to my father, "Faqir, I told you I would beat death."

'But then Chaiji was wheeled in for blood transfusion. The doctor examined her and told Prithviraj that she did not have very long to live. Papaji told my father that he feared she would die before him. He did not want her to go first. He told my father that they would go to her room. He wanted to know if any other patient would be there that day because he wanted to be alone with her. "Okay, let's go to Rama," he told my father. And then the two of them, husband and wife, sat together and talked about their children. They began remembering their childhood. After a while he told my father: "It is late now, let me sleep. Faqir you go home." He then proceeded to his room and went into a coma, before which he asked us to call Shashi.'

Shashi was in England at the time: he had gone there to dub for Conrad Rook's film *Siddhartha*. But before he left he had told his father he would not go if he 'did anything naughty while he was away'. 'Papaji was just waiting for Shashi to come before he died,' says Tandon. 'The nurse brought in some tea. Papaji was in a coma, yet he suddenly said, pointing to my father, "My brother takes sugar." And then he went back into coma. A little later he asked if Shashi had come. When he arrived, Papaji hugged him, pressed him to his chest and died a little later.' The doctors had already removed the life-support systems.

He was clearly waiting for his youngest son. There is a moving account of Prithviraj's last few minutes by Shashi in *Prithviwallahs*. 'When Papaji heard the door open, he quickly turned...Rajji later told me that he had been unable to move for a while now. But when he sensed my presence, he managed to move his head. He had a faint smile on his face. I sat by his side, held his hand...a couple of hours later he was gone. The night before, the doctors told the family that it was all over, but he had survived the whole night when Rajji whispered in his ear that Shashi is coming...Shashilala is what Papaji always called me.'

The family took his body past the Matunga house. Raj Kapoor told his mother, '*Papaji aa gaye.*' But she refused to see the body: she did not want a darshan. She wanted to remember him alive. Later, when her sons were about to go to Haridwar with the remains of her husband, she asked the younger two to stay behind. She knew they would have to make another trip very soon.

She died sixteen days later.

PART 2

The Consolidators

2

The Showman and the Joker: Raj Kapoor

Chisto usually missed. But one summer day in Murree he fires his pellet gun at some birds in a tree and a little bulbul falls, with a gentle thud, near his feet. The look of triumph on his pudgy fair face with clownish red cheeks and startling blue eyes soon metamorphoses into one of sadness. He scoops out some mud with his plump hands and makes a tiny grave, into which he gently places the dead bird. He puts a stone over it and covers it with flowers. He makes quite a production of it, scurrying about looking for flowers and shrubs. He forces his cousin to do the same. Then, after a few minutes of silence, Chisto begins to describe in detail, and with great flourish, the gradual ascension of the bulbul's soul to heaven—to his audience of one.

Not quite twelve, Ranbir Raj Kapoor (nicknamed Chisto[1]) was already a seasoned storyteller. He had his mise en scène down pat, his imagination soaring like the dead bird's soul. Colonel Ram Khanna, his audience of one that day and younger by a few years, had to sit through many such impromptu 'stagings' by his cousin. The stage was usually the living room in the imposing Khanna family home.

It wasn't just the Khannas the budding schoolboy thespian wanted to impress. He would put on a play at the drop of a hat, or rather, at the sight of a pretty girl. The teenaged Georgie Porgie of Peshawar and Murree may not have kissed the girls and made them cry. But, according to the Colonel, the boy Pathan veered pretty close. 'Chisto always had a glad eye. He fell in love with every pretty girl. He would pay her special attention and make her act in the plays he staged for the family. He used to put his arm round the girl he fancied and show her what she had to do. We all knew what he was up to.' There are scores of pretty Peshawari and Punjabi women of a certain age who recall his romantic daredevilry.

Fast-forward five decades to his famed 'cottage' in R.K. Films in Chembur. It is the summer of 1987, and I am researching a story on romance in Indian cinema. Raj Kapoor sits cross-legged on the floor, his ample stomach pushing against the low table. There are cushions all over the place. I sit down next to him, and glance up. He follows my gaze, a quiet half-smile playing upon his face, which appears tired, puffy and lined—he won't quite last the year. There on the wall, high up and frozen in their prime, in black and white, are his famous women in white: Nargis, Vyjanthimala, Padmini.

The cottage is his chamber of creativity, and his laboratory of love. There is no film on the sets at the time. So that particular afternoon it seems more like a mausoleum for his lady-loves. Or perhaps Raj Kapoor's memories of them: two of them are still alive, but long since out of his working and personal life. Here, the strains of the tanpura, which Lata Mangeshkar played while she sang—often through the night—to her audience of one, must still resonate for him. There were 'moments of magic', of creativity during those musical soirées a deux, says Bina Ramani, who was a close friend of Raj Kapoor. 'The two were emotionally very close.' She may have even loved him, say those who know them both.

Love, star-crossed love, being in love with the idea of love, passion and lust—he takes me through his personal repertoire of romance, his voice soft, if a bit gruff on the edges. Asthma has taken its toll: he fights for each breath. Yet, beneath that mass of white flesh and in those fabled blue eyes that have almost creased to a line, you can catch glimpses of the naughty Chisto—the schoolboy who was always falling in love, the pubescent prankster storyteller who was always fabulating, the fledgling tubby gourmand who was always eating.

Like his father, Raj Kapoor spent much of his childhood in Peshawar. Born in Samundari on 14 December 1924 he was the only one of Prithviraj's children to speak Pashto and imbibe Pathan culture directly. When his father went to Bombay to become an actor, Raj lived with his mother and two younger brothers in Peshawar until Prithviraj called his family to Bombay. When Prithviraj set off on his quest to become an actor, Raj was about five. Here was a defiant Prithviraj who had abandoned his studies in law and was going against his father's wishes. His young family must have borne the brunt of this decision, left behind as they were with Prithviraj's father and stepmother and their children. His father's long absences thrust a burden of responsibility when Raj was but a child. He saw hard times, and in a way became his mother's protector while his father was lost in the world of theatre. No wonder there was something of an adult–child about him.

The Kapoor family shuttled between Peshawar and wherever—whenever—the wandering player put down some temporary roots. Prithviraj sent his family back to Peshawar when he toured with the Grant Anderson Company from 1930 to 1931. The Kapoors led a gypsy-like existence, desi bohemian you could say. Young Raj was frequently uprooted. As the family moved from one city to the next, he was yanked out of one school after another: Colonel Brown's School in Dehradun, a Bengali-medium school in Calcutta, and in Bombay, a Marathi-language municipal school in Girgaum and Antonio de Souza School in Byculla. The first school he attended was New Era Boys' School on Hughes Road in Bombay.

The only constant was change.

Food was the other constant—and a security blanket. Raj Kapoor started his love affair with food very early. For him it wasn't just something you put in your mouth, something to keep the stomach quiet. The importance of food in his life can't be overstated: it was young Raj's very raison d'etre. His intense love and lifetime pursuit of good food may have been a Peshawar thing. But it was something more as well. Compensation? Perhaps. His father was away for long stretches, filming, when Raj was a child. The Kapoors did not have much money. Life was fairly spartan and uncertain. His mother, orphaned as a child, had married young, and was not interested in cooking.

Raj tapped his considerable imagination to devise ways of getting what he lusted after. Naturally, the kilos piled up. He spent much of his boyhood in a fat body. Those magnificent blue eyes are hardly visible in the photographs of him as a child: the eyes move automatically to the ample cheeks and his podgy hands. His blazer, as he sits with four huge silver cups in the foreground of the picture, doesn't hide his extra kilos.

People, especially other children, can be cruel to fat children. He acknowledged as much with great self-awareness. 'My childhood memories are pitted with indelible scars of experience. I was a fatty. Every sort of practical joke was played on me. Apart from some vivid patches of happiness, my childhood days were quite miserable. These patches of happiness were occasions when I fell in love...I soon picked up the most natural defence mechanism—the one used by all the great jokers of the world. I learned that the more one resisted being a target, the more one suffered. So, instead, I put on the mask of a joker by reacting as though I thoroughly enjoyed being made the butt of practical jokes. Indeed, I even took this a step further by inventing jokes on myself, which would make my colleagues laugh. You see, I was seeking that which every schoolboy seeks—the love, affection and esteem of others. I wanted to be liked.'[2]

The clowning, self-mocking persona preceded Raj Kapoor's adoption of Chaplin's tramp. Many introverts, especially the creative, crack jokes about themselves to pre-empt others doing it. Conscious about being chubby and a bit awkward, Raj sought ways to seek attention or to make himself popular—and thereby loved. Making himself the butt of jokes was one way; sports was the other. Sports has always been the shortest route to popularity in school, and becoming known. However, his armour of fat kept him out of most games. 'Because I was fat, my masters did not think I was good at games, but I longed to play in all the matches,' he told journalist and friend Bunny Reuben.

The entire paraphernalia, all the pomp and show that went with the games, dazzled him. Certainly it must have appealed to the dormant showman in him. 'The hockey and football uniforms striped shirts with white shorts and boots, excited my fancy and I yearned to wear them.' But above all it was the rainbow at the end of it all: 'The players got lemonade and sandwiches after the match. I pleaded with the games master to take me as a linesman!'[3.]

It was the same with acting: the craving for food was the hidden motive behind his desire to act in school plays. Of course, the long cassock-like robes the school children wore for the Passion Plays his school in Bombay staged during Easter dazzled him. But what he was really after were the coupons they were given for free coffee, sandwiches and chips after each performance. 'Acting is in my blood,' he told the concerned teacher in order to persuade him to give him a part in the plays. Unimpressed, the teacher made the ambitious schoolboy an extra. Undaunted, the fledgling star, adept at embellishing the truth, told his parents that he was a lead player. And on the big night, carried away by his histrionics, caught his foot in the long robe he was wearing and fell—he wasn't even supposed to be onstage for the concluding act. The audience laughed. The drama master was not amused. Furious, he threw him out of the play, and with this came the premature end to the coupons as well.

His acting skills helped in his pursuit of food offstage as well, as did his blue eyes and fair skin. His brother Shammi Kapoor relates an amusing incident. 'With his blue eyes and his *gori chamari* Raj Kapoor looked like an *angrez da puttar*. He was always up to his pranks. Whenever he was reprimanded by Dwarka [their family servant who escorted the two brothers to town], the goras took Dwarka to task. They thought Raj was one of them. "*Kyon pareshan karte ho gora ko*," they would tell Dwarka, when they saw him scolding Raj on the streets. The Englishmen would then take my brother to a restaurant for cakes and sandwiches. He would gulp it all down. And I would sit outside, hungry and waiting.' Obviously little brother was not amused at the time.

Raj didn't let honesty come between him and food as a child even in Samundari. Occasionally his grandfather used to give him money to eat chaat in a nearby village. But since he wanted his money to go a long way, he tried to get the chaatwala to give it to him for half the price. When that didn't happen, Raj bought the chaat and then stopped eating it when he was halfway through and tried to get half his money back by insisting that the chaat had gone bad. The chaatwala, shocked by the crooked ways of the great-grandson of tehsildar Dewan Keshavmal, complained to the family. That evening Raj got quite a beating from his grandfather.

Adulthood didn't change this inspired quest for food. The grown-up Raj Kapoor, dressed in his simple but impeccable white clothes and hat, was a regular visitor to the racecourses in Pune and Mahalaxmi Racecourse in Bombay. Many presumed he was a great gambler, as addicted to the game as he was to showmanship. How wrong they were. There were other instincts much stronger than gambling at work here, according to close friend and Chembur neighbour, industrialist Vinny Ahuja. 'At the races, Raj Kapoor would sit and I would go to place bets. We had a budget of five hundred rupees and would go fifty-fifty. He used to make a five sign, which was for fifty rupees. People thought we were betting five lakhs. We had intense discussions between the races. We used to go there because of the nice *mahol*.'

It wasn't the horses and the thrill of winning which drew him to the races but the ambiance, the parade of society women and men dressed in their faux Ascot best, and the pomp of it all. An equally if not more powerful draw were the chicken sandwiches and pakodas served there. 'When the races were over, we would go to all the stalls and eat. There was always a group of people, including VIPs, who would come up to say hello to Rajji. So, we would order round after round of sandwiches,' says Ahuja. Raj usually picked up the tab at the racecourse. But the feasting didn't stop here: from Mahalaxmi they usually went to a south Indian eatery in Matunga to devour endless rounds of idli and sambar. Ahuja paid for this round. 'No matter how much you ate, the bill never came to more than twenty-five rupees,' he adds.

Raj Kapoor may have looked much older than his years but gambling brought out the child in him. Specially on Sundays when, as his wife says, he used to ring up bookies with Dr Ghanti, their family physician and friend. 'When Rajji said "dus" into the phone, you would think that he was betting a thousand rupees, but it was really just dus—ten rupees, five his and five the doctor's! And when they won fifteen or twenty rupees they would go mad with excitement—the telephone would ring and Rajji would jump to answer it, the syringe hanging from the arm, Dr Ghanti running after him, holding on to it...They were like little boys together.'[4]

The samadhis of Prithviraj and Ramsarni Kapoor lie next to one another in Raj Bagh, Raj's 100-acre farm in Loni, a little outside Pune. Raj wanted it thus. Ever one for the melodramatic gesture, he even wrote a little postscript for himself. He told his family to put his samadhi between his parents'. Not quite between them but lower down, closer to their feet, in due deference to them. Raj Kapoor's family finally sold the farm at the turn of the century. But the three samadhis remain, with Raj Kapoor finally resting between his parents—the way he often did as a child and late into adolescence in his parents' bed.

It looks peaceful, this trinity of the departed. However, Raj and his father had a complex and often troubled relationship. Just eighteen years separated the two; a mere sixteen separated his mother and him. In a sense father and son were both growing up together. The teenager father was defiantly struggling to find an identity and a vocation different from what he was born into; the son was merely growing up. Raj was the tag-along, the portable child, in the early wandering days of his father's film career in Bombay and Calcutta.

He also bore the first-born's burden. Not only was he witness to the hard times and the uncertainty, he had to contend with an immensely successful, charismatic and impossibly handsome father. Prithviraj was tall, impressively built and had a manly voice that resonated. Raj was short and chubby in his adolescence. His voice was never his calling card, and later, in early manhood, his muscles were not his major asset. Rather, his intense blue eyes were. But more than anything else, the baggage of the first child he carried also made him the repository of his father's hopes.

The senior Kapoor had made it on his own, and he wanted his eldest son to do so as well. There were no safety nets under the slippery ladder of show business which the younger Kapoor had decided to climb. Perhaps, the father expected too much from him. Perhaps, he didn't quite read him well. Those who knew the father when Raj was barely out of his teens affirm the close relationship between the two. However, they also talk about a strange tussle between them. Not only was Prithviraj exceedingly tough on Raj Kapoor, he was unable to perceive his son's intensity and dormant creativity. His great fear, according to close friends and colleagues, was that Raj would turn out to be a good for nothing.

Ali Raza minces few words when he describes the relationship between the two. 'Every man has great hopes for his son to become something. But Prithviraj thought Raj Kapoor was *nalayak* (useless). Raj's *gham* (sadness) was within him, and his talents were hidden. The tragedy is that Prithviraj did not realize this about his first son. The talent was dormant within Raj Kapoor. In fact, the father must have thought that his son was a little dumb.'

Those who knew them well admit that Prithviraj was quite worried about his son and what he was going to do with his life. Ironically, he wanted his son to have a proper education, followed by a proper job, even though he himself had rejected the conventional career route in his life. Nor did he know what to make of his son. He shared his fears and doubts with V. Shankar who was for many years revenue commissioner in Bombay, and had also been the home secretary and right-hand man of Sardar Patel. His daughter Rashmi Shankar recalls her father telling her about his conversation with Prithviraj Kapoor. 'He was very concerned about Raj Uncle. He wanted him to make something of himself. He asked my father: "What do you see in my son?" My father told him: "There is no middle ground here. He is so creative. Either he struggles and makes it to the top, or he goes to the bottom. Just allow him the space he needs...to express himself."'

V. Shankar was one of the few who recognized the young Raj Kapoor's latent creativity and the seething intensity that appeared to be consuming him from within. Equally urgent was his need to find an outlet for it. The bureaucrat became a surrogate father and a close friend. It was an odd friendship. The formidable ICS bureaucrat who helped in the reorganization of the states into the Indian Union was only three years younger than Prithviraj Kapoor. Yet, it was the younger Kapoor with whom he bonded emotionally.

Why did Raj Kapoor need a surrogate father? Was he reaching out, beyond the boundaries of the family, for kindred souls? Intense love for his parents did not translate into conversations, but declamations. His conflicts as a young man centred round his father, whose long shadow fell over him no matter how far he ran. 'My father and he had a father–son relationship,' explains Rashmi. V. Shankar first met Raj Kapoor during the Presidency when he was on a panel and Raj had to testify about the export of films. 'Raj Uncle had to give some evidence. There had been some objection about something concerning what he had done. Standing in the witness box he said that he was full of the rebellion of youth. My father heard him out and then leaned across and said: "My dear young man, one swallow does not make a summer." And then he explained to him what the problems were.'

In his book, Professor Dyal describes an evening that he spent with the Kapoors in Bombay. Raj was particularly lively that night since he'd just given the finishing touches to *Barsaat*. 'Krishnaji sits quiet with a smile playing on her chubby face and enjoyed [RK's] jokes...What made him leave the stage and go to the screen? Was it money? I do not think so...Raj felt that on the stage his father would overshadow him. He did not want to shine in reflected glory nor that the people pointing to him should say: "There goes Raj Kapoor—the son of Prithvi." In the exuberance of youth he would prefer people to exclaim: "There goes Prithvi—the father of Raj Kapoor."'

It was a strange love between father and son. Raj Kapoor has never publicly expressed any resentment. Yet in the subtext of some of his remarks you can catch a trace of disappointment over his father's disappointment in his abilities. 'When I was working with my father in Prithvi Theatres, where I did all kinds of work, right from the lighting of the sets to art direction, he asked me to play a small role on stage as Ramu, the servant, in *Deewar*. I was young and I could not refuse my father. "Right, sir, I will!" On the opening day of that play, I was discovered as an actor after ten years of acting in the film industry.'[5]

When talking about Prithviraj Kapoor's relationship with his children to a friend, Krishna Kapoor compared her father-in-law to an elm tree who dwarfed his three sons. Ironically, so was Raj Kapoor with his three sons. In order to find his own place in the sun, from under the shadow of his father, Raj Kapoor had to move away and do something different. Explains Prayag Raaj: 'Rajji decided that since everyone knew him because of Prithviraj Kapoor, he had to be different from Papaji. So, he broke away from the theatre style of acting. He started doing skits. He did more comedies, musicals, and romantic roles.'

The younger Kapoor adopted a more natural, soft-spoken manner of speaking, quite unlike the declamatory and, in later years, hammy style of his father. Because of his patrician bearing, Prithviraj usually incarnated icons and figures of authority in most of his stage and screen performances—kings, patriarchs and gods dominate his repertoire of characters. He represented the status quo: Akbar in *Mughal-e-Azam*, Raghunath the judge in *Awara* and Sikandar in *Sikandar*. Raj on the other hand liked to play the small man—the one who was always against the establishment—like the vagabond in *Awara*, the country bumpkin with funny pants and all his possessions in a little bundle at the end of a stick who goes to the big city with great expectations in *Shree 420*, Raju the common man who goes into a building complex for a glass of water in *Jaagte Raho*, the country bumpkin in *Jis Desh Mein Ganga Behti Hai* and the little man–sad clown in his magnum opus *Mera Naam Joker*. Raj Kapoor was always the quintessential smaller-than-life figure.

The anger bottled inside Raj Kapoor seems to have found an outlet in his first film *Aag*. There is an amazing rawness about the film. It reveals a rebellious Raj Kapoor in whom an inarticulate fire smoulders. He was only twenty-two when he began work on this film. Raj started making the film as early as 1947, even though it was released in 1948. *Aag* focuses on the fire in the belly of the youth in the afterglow of India's hard-won, bittersweet independence. These were the early Nehruvian days of optimism when people actually worried about the small man, and socialism was in its heyday. They believed in the pot at the end of the socialist rainbow. The clarion call was to dismantle some of the old hierarchies of privilege and wealth. Raj Kapoor has often described his film 'as the story of youth consumed by the desire for a brighter and more intense life'.

His directorial debut is more significant because he lays bare his soul in this film. Here you see his fledgling romantic yearnings, his first love, and his anger at the ways of the world. A poignantly revealing line in the film is: '*Kahin, sau saal pahle jab mein das saal ka tha*...' (A hundred years ago, when I was ten years old...) The line is a refrain, and the first time he uses it is when he is just twenty—a young man with a lifetime's hurt already burdening his young shoulders.

In *Aag*, Raj Kapoor was not speaking for the lost generation, but for a generation that was in a hurry. He plays a figure pitted against authority and icons. The debate in *Aag* centres on authoritarianism versus individuality and creativity. The simple storyline is about a young man, Kewal (played by Raj), who runs away from home to join the theatre. The film is fairly autobiographical: Prithviraj had done just that. And yet he, in turn, expected Raj Kapoor to study law.

Raj often argued with Prithviraj about the merits of learning from the school of life as opposed to going to university. There are several slanging matches in this film in which the young protagonist and his screen father angrily debate the worth of a college education. One scene takes place after Kewal, who has fared poorly in an exam, refuses to take it again. In the film he angrily mocks the importance given to facts like whether King Henry VIII had six or eight wives. Kewal's arguments against university education and stuffy history teachers and their obsession with dates and irrelevant facts closely echo Raj's own contretemps with his father when he failed his school exams. (In fact, when Raj Kapoor told his parents that he was giving up school—he had failed his prelims for the matriculation exam—to make films, even his mother was angry.)

Interestingly, a few of Raj's early films resonate with the subterranean tensions between Raj and Prithviraj. They explore the disruptive nature of the relationship between father and son. The two were literally pitted against one another in *Awara*. The film has an Oedipal twist to the Ramayana-like tale with the son taking on his father (not knowing he is his biological father). The fact that Prithviraj Kapoor plays the recalcitrant father and Raj Kapoor the abandoned son who hates him gives the film an added frisson. In *Kal Aaj Aur Kal* (1971), Randhir Kapoor's directorial and acting debut film, the Kapoors represent the divide down three generations, with Prithviraj Kapoor playing the patriarchal and unbending grandfather, Raj Kapoor the caught-in-between-generation father and Randhir the son fighting for his independence. Babita plays his 'modern' on-screen love, much to the consternation of the paterfamilias. Art imitating life gives a poignant edge to the film: at the time, Randhir Kapoor was dating Babita much against the wishes of his family.

There was a degree of competitiveness between Prithviraj and his eldest son, and Raj knew that he had to be better than his father. Prithviraj was a proud man and didn't want to play second fiddle to anyone. It is said that he was initially reluctant to play the hero's father in *Awara*: he agreed only after he was told that he was also a hero, and that the character played by his son was the hero's son.

The age difference between Prithviraj and his first-born was so little that Raj was never quite overawed by his father. Yet, the need for his father and the intensity of their relationship never quite diminished. Raj Kapoor moved away from his parental home in Matunga after his first child Randhir Kapoor was born in 1947. But it was not a rare sight for neighbours to hear a troubled Raj calling out to his father from the street. Recalls Shashi Kapoor: 'There was a very strong relationship between Papaji and Raj Kapoor. Papaji used to say that his elder son was a *darpok* (coward). He needs *aar* (support). Sometimes, Rajji would get very high and come to Matunga and yell from below for Papaji and then go up and sit with him. The whole gali knew he had been there.'

The Kapoors have traditionally not been—Prithviraj Kapoor apart—academic achievers. Most found it difficult to even finish school: Shammi Kapoor was the only one of his generation to go to college. None of Raj Kapoor's sons went to college. Raj Kapoor himself didn't even finish school. When he failed to matriculate because he had failed his Latin prelims, he was mortified by the thought of having to repeat the class. Depressed, he made his way home, all sorts of negative thoughts flitting through his mind. How was he going to break the news to his parents? But then he came across a dead man who had been run over by a train. The lifeless body set him thinking. Remembering this turning point moment in his life he has said: 'I realized that it was wonderful to live, and that one could live a full life. I put aside all morbid thoughts of death which were filling me because I had failed.'[6]

His early academic disasters explain Raj's detour from books—and his aversion to conventional norms. His nemesis at studies was, according to his brother Shammi, 'the compulsory second language, Latin'. On his web page, Shammi writes: 'He [Raj] achieved the unprecedented distinction of winning the All India Elocution Competition for three successive years but failed in Latin and that was the end of his academic career. When Papaji asked him why he wished to leave school and not try again, he replied, "Sir, if I graduate what happens? If you want to become a lawyer you go to a law college; if you want to be a doctor you go to a medical school; and if you want to be a film-maker, where do you go? So, instead of wasting the next five years studying something I don't want to learn, I'd like to join a studio right away." Papaji had no answer. It was ordained.'

But a deep sense of the inadequacy of the schoolboy who could not cope with rules, structure, and Latin and mathematics lay beneath the surface arrogance. He turned his inability to master the simplest concepts or anything analytical into a badge of honour. No wonder he bragged about reading only comics, even though he undoubtedly—and secretly—read books, given his profound understanding of Indian philosophy and the epics. Perhaps he was a closet reader.

A series of academic failures was responsible for his entry

into films. He failed school. He failed to get into the cadet corps. He failed to get into the navy. Making a film seemed to be the next stop after all these rejections. And here, too, it didn't come about easily. In fact, when he told his father that he wanted to make films, his mother made a disdainful remark: '*Thukh mein thori pakode bante hai.*' (You can't fry pakodas in spit.)[7] A colourful colloquial expression, it was meant to convey that you can't make something out of nothing. It needs a lot of money and resources before you can even begin to make a film. Raj's mother was making a case for her husband to help her son. There may, however, have been a hint of sarcasm in the remark.

Prithviraj Kapoor, however, was a tough taskmaster. Mrs Seth tells an interesting story of Raj waiting outside his father's house, who was about to set off for work. 'Pritheeji asked him why he had not already left for the studio and then got into his car and drove away. Raj had to take the bus.' Their destination was the same but the senior Kapoor wanted to toughen his son. The lesson was not lost on Raj. One of the stories he loved to keep repeating whenever the Kapoor family sat down for a meal—which was not very often—was about his father's response when he told him he wanted to become an actor. 'Do you know what my father told me? He said that he would give me a job for one rupee a month. And for this I would have to sweep the studio.'[8] Apparently, he used to become very melodramatic at the dining table. 'Do you know how I created R.K. Films?' was a frequent refrain in the Kapoor home in Chembur.

Prithviraj possessed only one car for most of his life—his beloved little Opel. Raj Kapoor's first car was a Ford—it had a Rewa licence plate, and was used as his office while he was making *Aag*. After *Barsaat* became a big hit, he bought his convertible Oldsmobile. Mrs Seth remembers another telling incident about the difference between the father and son. 'My mother had financed *Barsaat*, and that had done well. Raj asked Papaji to go down to see his new car. Papaji went to the balcony and looked down below. There was a convertible Oldsmobile, the car Raj had just bought. But Papaji said, "I can't see it. Is it yours?", adding, "*Ma de pese de dithe hain*? (Have you returned mataji's money?) Only then can it be your car." Raj promptly gave Vishwa money and told him to return the money to my mother.' Raj later wrote a beautiful two-page letter apologizing to his aunt and explaining his lapse.[9] (The son was always the big spender. Flush with success and money, he once presented a blank cheque to his father to buy a new car. Prithviraj pocketed it, and filled the space for amount by drawing hearts on it.)

In his childhood pictures Raj Kapoor always looks much older than his age, a flicker of sadness on his face frozen in silver nitrate. The camera seldom captured the prankster in him. His joker persona seems absent in these photographs. Perhaps it was an artificial construct, as was Charlie Chaplin's screen alter ego which he later assimilated into his screen genealogy. Even at age one, there is something uncannily lived-in about the infant Raj's face. Underneath the embroidered cap—perched at a slant on an apparently oversized head—his alert eyes look as if they have already seen a lot of life. There is nothing baby-like about this knowing gaze: it appears to be taking in and, perhaps, even questioning the photographer.

Photographs of him as a child also betray a maturity quite beyond his years. A telling picture of him is a family portrait with his parents and sister Urmi. Raj Kapoor is barely eight. His parents look positively happy; they gaze confidently into the camera. Chaiji, beautiful with perfect features, appears almost coy, playful with the camera. Prithviraj takes in the camera head-on, with the smile of a successful American matinee idol. Young Raj, however, has a diffident, almost disgruntled look about him, his eyebrows captured mid-wriggle. Posing with his brother Shammi in another photograph—he must have been in his early teens—Raj looks much older than the seven years that separate him from his sibling. The Pathan turban sits, like the baby cap, at a slant on his head. His eyes don't sparkle; the air of self-confidence is missing. There is an air of the loner and a maturity in the photographs of Raj Kapoor as an adolescent and as a young man as well. In Kidar Sharma's *Neel Kamal*, his acting debut as an adult, he looks youthful. However, in *Awara*, a few years later, still in youthful prime, the traces of youth are barely visible. His fine features no longer stand out.

It almost seems as if something was eating him up from inside. Had experience nibbled into his innocence, shrinking his childhood? It could well be. Certainly, responsibility came too early, and tragically at that. Shashi Kapoor believes that the deaths of Raj Kapoor's two younger brothers—Devi and Bindi—within a fortnight or so of each other must have affected him deeply. Raj couldn't have been more than six years old, if that, when four-year-old Bindi ate some rat poison and became violently sick.

At the time the Kapoors lived in Khar, a suburb of Bombay. It seems that Bindi had gone to play in a neighbour's garden. When his mother called out to him to return home and bathe, he went to her, and choked in her arms. Prithviraj was away shooting for a film at Imperial Studios. Raj's mother, home alone with her three sons, hastily dispatched Raj to the doctor. And as soon as he returned, his mother sent him in a taxi with a servant to the studios to bring his father home.

In his book, Bunny Reuben quotes Raj Kapoor's account of this incident. 'All the way back my father kept asking me what was wrong with Bindi, but I maintained a stoic silence, for mother had asked me to say only that Bindi was not well, and nothing more. For hours, mother and father sat by Bindi's bedside—watching him sinking. Mother was weeping. Father sat silent and dry-eyed. I was sick, not knowing what was happening. Why was Bindi lying there like that? Why didn't he get up and play with me? Till then I did not know what death was.'

This was Raj's first—and brutal—encounter with death. Death also left its calling card on its first visit: about a fortnight later Devi succumbed to high fever—it could have been pneumonia.

In fifteen days Raj must have aged that many years. His role as messenger, and later as an uncomprehending witness to the enormity of this double tragedy, must have indelibly scarred him. His parents, caught up in their own grief over the loss, could hardly have dealt with their surviving son's trauma. After this, Raj clung even more to his mother. And she, in turn, became even more protective about him. He was the only son for whom she would rush into the kitchen and cook the food he liked. The others followed the communal eating habits of the ever-enlarging Kapoor clan and its fellow travellers. There was no high table: the family ate the same food as the strangers. But whenever Raj came home, his mother cooked pulao for him. He was the only one to get any special treatment, remembers Surinder Kapoor.

Since Raj led a lonely childhood—not only was his father perpetually on the road, there was a seven-year gap between him and Shammi—fantasy had the space to move in and make itself comfortable: whether it was the elaborate funeral for the bird he killed, falling in love with every second girl he saw or, finally, and most importantly, his magnificent obsession with cinema. The need to escape into an inner world was all the more pressing because while Raj was growing up, the Kapoors lived the life of the commune. Prithviraj's patriarchal embrace took in, literally, far more than the traditional joint family. Somebody was always dropping in. Or more likely, just staying on—interminably. Public and private spaces spilled into each other; nobody even knew the meaning of privacy.

Crowded out at home, Raj created a persona, one perhaps that had very little to do with the real him. This might have been at a juncture in his life when the line between what he created and what he was as a person began to blur. Lies and fabulations became the truth; reality and fantasy became entwined. Many writers or cineastes use their lives as a blueprint for their creative work, at times making sure they live the life that is tailor-made for being realized on screen or in print.

Boosting truth became a habit with Raj Kapoor early on. At times he made himself fall in love just so that he could transport the experience to the screen. He might even create scenes in life, only to later transfer them to screen. As Rashmi Shankar says, at times he 'transferred gestures to the screen'. 'Raj Uncle would cup his face when lost in thought, his head leaning towards one side. You know the "I-am-caught-don't-know-what-to-do" kind of look. And he would take the self into the scene.'

Sometimes, he even relished the pain of an experience or heartbreak, knowing that he could use it in his cinema later. Says Simi Garewal: 'He enjoyed the mourning period; he loved it—

even the mourning period after Nargis. Rajji loved going deep into every experience and feeling it and letting it have its effect. He got the maximum emotion out of it and used this emotion in his films.'

The cineaste in him never took a break. The director's eye never shut, editing as his life unspooled before him. Even as he suffered, he was spinning the emotions and images onto the projector in his mind. 'It seemed as though my own shadow was watching me, seeing everything in terms of shots, with all the wipes, dissolves, fade-ins, cuts—everything telescoped into a mass of unedited celluloid scripts, caught by the camera's unblinking eye, in the tireless gaze of life's arc lamps.'[10] And when it came to work, the private Raj Kapoor disappeared.

It seems he always knew he would make films. Like a magpie, the teenage Raj swooped down on bits and pieces of information and visual images, anything that attracted him. And, like a squirrel, he would hide these treasures for future use. Sneaking around in Raj's room one day, a curious Shammi Kapoor could not stop himself from 'hacking' the two locked cupboards in the room. Raj was a little over sixteen and already an assistant by then. 'I found scraps...cuttings from newspapers, foreign magazines, fashion magazines for ladies and pictures of hairstyles and different dresses and designs, and storybooks and scenarios and scripts.'[11]

Raj Kapoor was already making films in his head. Nothing was lost on him: everything went into this data bank. And he kept tapping into it for his films. 'My father had amazing grasping power,' says Rishi Kapoor. 'He was observant and stored things in his mind. He had a sharp memory, like an elephant. Papa could remember any face. He had a bank of knowledge that he depicted in his films.'

Raj may not have been a good student. But he enrolled early on in the school of the street. As a teenager, he used to observe the middle and lower middle classes in Matunga: he was a habitué of the *jhopar patti*s there. Prayag Raaj says: 'He used to sit with the sabziwali outside his home in Matunga, or the one near his school in Byculla. There was a woman who was quite similar to the banana seller character in *Shree 420* which was played by Lalita Pawar. In Loni he would be bindaas, sitting for hours in the dhabas, speaking to the locals in Marathi.' Having learnt Marathi in school, Raj was later to use his fluency with the language to communicate with Maharashtrians both in the film industry as well as with the farmers and workers on his farm in Loni. The farmers became his friends; they spent a lot of time cooking and eating together.

Raj was quite at home in the world of those who worked for him—as dependent if not as close to them as he was with many in his family. His driver, Gopal, was more than just somebody who drove him around. He was more like his caretaker, always watching over him, often after a late night out drinking. 'Sometimes he would sit with the driver and put his head in his lap,' says B.J. Panchal, Raj Kapoor's photographer. Gopal's job was to make sure no harm came to his boss. Raj had a unique way of saying thank you: he uses the name Gopal in many of his films. In *Sangam*, Rajendra Kumar (Raj's best friend in the movie) is called Gopal. He was equally dependent on John (the cook) in his cottage and on Revati (his personal assistant) at home.

Similarly, Raj was quite close to the people who worked in the dhabas and restaurants like Gita Bhavan and Ranjit Café near R.K. Films. No wonder he had the pulse of the common man. Perhaps the father and son had a volatile relationship because they were very similar: Prithviraj used to sit with fishermen in their kholis in Juhu during the last decade of his life, talking to them for long hours. Prithviraj's other sons did not mingle with the man on the street in the same way. Both father and his first-born were a curious mixture of the traditional—caught up in the customs and rituals of the Kapoor khandaan—and the bohemian. Essentially, they were wanderers whose circle of friends extended to those outside the furthest ripples of their social orbits.

Ironically enough, Bollywood's greatest showman—there hasn't been another worthy of this mantle yet—had very simple needs. He never slept on a bed, but on the floor. Wherever he went, he pulled the mattress on to the floor—even in his suite at the George V hotel in Paris. Sometimes this got him into trouble. His wife recounts an interesting incident. 'Rajji was a simple man. He always slept on the floor. In London, at the Hilton, he was ticked off for pulling the mattress down and when he did it the second time, he was fined. He paid the fine every day till he left the hotel.'[12] To paraphrase what they said about the Mahatma—it took a lot to keep Raj Kapoor in simplicity.

The showman in him insisted that his table have everything possible. There had to be several kinds of chicken and mutton, and, of course, yakhni in all its avatars. But the man himself ate quite selectively, and simply. Raj Kapoor could whip up a perfect biryani and chicken curry but preferred to eat the common man's food. His favourite staple was idlis and street food. In her account of her husband's eating habits in Ritu's book, Krishna Kapoor says: 'The great cook was a poor eater! He could not bear to see a poorly laid table, it had to overflow, but he himself merely nibbled at the food and then settled for his usual pao and eggs and a little daal. For years he ate no lunch, only dinner. At parties he merely pretended to eat. When he got home—sometimes in the early hours of the morning—he promptly had his fried eggs.'

Raj Kapoor was very happy with the Ambassador car he bought much later in his life: the fancy cars of his youth no longer thrilled him. The Mercedes was for his wife. 'He tasted life at a basic level,' says Bina Ramani. Raj stayed with Bina and her former husband Andy Ramani in New York for nearly two months when his father was being treated at Sloane-Kettering in the early seventies. This was a particularly painful time for him because *Mera Naam Joker* had been a box-office disaster and both his parents were terminally ill. 'He was down and depressed and hurting from the loss. We had a very small apartment. He used to pull the mattress to the floor. Rajji used to take the bus to the hospital, changing two buses to get there. Black Label became Red Label in New York: it was all we could afford. He wanted to fit into our life,' recalls Bina. Interestingly, Shammi Kapoor stayed in the suburbs and cabbed it to the hospital in Manhattan.

Comics had a lot to do with the sentimental education of Raj Kapoor. They gave him ready-made, easily digested bits of illustrated wisdom about human relationships and adolescent love. He only read Archies, Sad Sack, Little Lulu and Richie Rich and a few other American comics—they formed the library of his mind. Not just while growing up, but all through life. Simi Garewal added to his stock of Little Lulus and Richie Richs. Did he read Little Lulu, the fat girl, because he empathized with her adolescent predicament? Dimple Kapadia's wardrobe (the knotted blouses and short skirts) in *Bobby* was largely inspired by the clothes of Betty and Veronica in Archie comics. Even while producing *Biwi O Biwi* (directed by Rahul Rawail and starring Randhir Kapoor), he told make-up man Sarosh Mody to design a Mr Lodge look for Sanjeev Kumar and an Archie look for his son.

Raj Kapoor's considerable knowledge of life and human nature also came from his having done much of his growing up on cinema sets and backstage. His higher education, you could say, was in an academy without walls. Life's emotions were his alphabets. His vocabulary was enriched by his father's long years in the films, beginning with silent films and the numerous mythologicals and historicals. Later, the texts of the plays staged during his years of apprenticeship with Prithvi Theatres expanded his mental library of insights into human behaviour and instincts.

Raj was five when he first acted. It was in the play *Mrichakatikka*. 'It was then that the whole thing just entered me, and I could not think of anything except belonging to the world of show business.'[13] Since he grew up in the arc lights, he wasn't really familiar with anything else. Raj Kapoor was just eleven when he acted in his first film, *Inquilab*, made for New Theatres in Calcutta in 1935 with Prithviraj Kapoor and Durga Khote. As a child he also acted in *Gauri*, a film his father was starring in. While still in school, he also appeared in *After the Earthquake*, a film directed by the renowned film-maker Debaki Bose. Apparently, he was also 'borrowed' by actor–director Gul Hamid to work in another film while still a child.

Aware of the tragic fate of most child actors, Prithviraj

Kapoor was against his son becoming a child star. When Reuben asked him why he did not want to make a child-star out of Raj, he replied: 'I am a great admirer of Hollywood child-star Jackie Coogan, and I never wanted any of my sons to go through what Coogan experienced—early glory followed by problems, obstacles and difficulties in later life.'

Barely out of school, Raj Kapoor began to work for his father, and as 'sixth or seventh assistant, trolley-puller, clapper boy, somewhere in the laboratory picking up odd shots and in the editing department...'[14] This is because Kapoor senior didn't believe in lending his shoulders for his sons to climb to success. No papa's boys for him. 'One nice thing about our father was that he never pushed anyone,' says Shashi Kapoor. 'He only pushed once with Rajji: he first got him to work with Kidar Sharma. My father told him that he was worried about his son: "He plays the tabla, sings, and talks a lot about what he will be." Kidar Sharma reassured my father and asked him to send Rajji to him.'

Raj Kapoor started his career in the film world in the lower depths, as third assistant to Kidar Sharma, who was then working with Ranjit Studios in Bombay. Hardworking and driven, he swept the floors and did everything those starting out at the bottom do. His days as an apprentice film-maker were varied. After his stint with Sharma he became an assistant to Amiya Chakraborty, then at Bombay Talkies. He soon left Bombay Talkies and began to work as an assistant director with Sushil Majumdar who was at the time directing a film for S. Mukherjee at Filmistan. Raj was particularly happy to work on this project because Majumdar allowed him a lot of freedom: since he was away from the sets for large chunks of time, Raj got the opportunity to make many of the major decisions about the film. *Begum*, as the film was called, starred Ashok Kumar and Naseem (Saira Banu's mother) and was shot in Kashmir.

Hungry for work experience, Raj Kapoor juggled several jobs, oscillating between Bombay Talkies and Prithvi Theatres. Married and a father of one by this time, Raj Kapoor needed to work double shifts to support his family. His father paid him Rs 201 a month for his work as an assistant in Prithvi Theatres. It was a rupee more than what Bombay Talkies was paying him at the time.

His break as lead actor came accidentally when he was an assistant clapper-boy. Kidar Sharma hardly noticed him until the day Raj got carried away and goofed during the making of *Vish Kanya*. Recalling the incident, Sharma says: 'I wanted to film a scene during sunset, but Raj Kapoor was late. He would first go to the mirror and comb his hair, look at himself in the mirror and only then do the clap. Once he caught the beard of an actor in the clapperboard, and it came off. I lost my temper and slapped him. Raj never said a word. The next morning I felt bad and I gave him a contract promising him the role of a hero in my next film, *Neel Kamal*.'

Raj Kapoor started crying when offered the lead role: this was in 1944, three years after he had been Sharma's junior-most assistant. When Sharma asked him why he was crying now and hadn't when he had been slapped the night before, he replied it was because the director had given him some work. And then he added: 'Violence has no emotion, goodness has emotion.' Relating this, Shashi Kapoor adds, 'God knows where this was coming from at that age. He cried because *dil bhar aya tha*.'

It is hard to imagine Raj Kapoor in costume dramas (*Chittor Vijay* among others), so indelibly marked in our minds is the screen image of his urban down-and-out persona. However, he did act in a few mythologicals. In fact, he worked with his father in a few which were filmed in Kolhapur by Bhalaji Pendharkar. In *Valmiki* (1946), Prithviraj played the title role while Raj played Narad, a comic role. The young Raj Kapoor had quite a flair for comedy.

Life as a hero really began in Kidar Sharma's film *Neel Kamal* in 1947. It proved to be a bonanza year for the budding actor. Three other films were also released that year: *Chittor Vijay*, *Dil Ki Rani* and *Jail Yatra*. Madhubala was his co-star in three of the four films. Kamini Kaushal was his heroine in the last. Interestingly, both the heroines were rumoured to be Dilip Kumar's amours.

Prithvi Theatres was the crucible where the director in Raj Kapoor was forged. Plunged straight into the world of theatre whilst not quite out of his teens, he learned all aspects of stagecraft: from lighting and acting to direction. His assorted jobs there allowed him to explore his many-faceted talents as actor, designer, backstage hand, general dogsbody and composer. Prithviraj soon made him the art director of the group, a responsibility that allowed him to discover his considerable aesthetic sensibility.

Zohra Segal describes Raj Kapoor as a perfectionist with an eye for detail. 'For the play *Pathan* he went all the way to Peshawar to get authentic old silver jewellery. He disbanded the sets often—the chowki in the mountains and the haveli front—because he felt they were not just right. In the opening scene of the play, there was an azaan, the morning prayer before sunrise. On the stage you had a small diya and smoke—*dhuan*. And as the sun rose, the light became stronger, while the diya's light became dimmer. It evoked a brilliant response each time.'

His apprenticeship in Prithvi Theatres taught him the value of stage lighting—how to place it, how to play to it, how to make it more dramatic. Consequently, the lighting in the debut film of the ingénue film-maker often appears stagey. In some of the scenes in *Aag* you can see where the light is coming from: intense and focussed, it gives the effect of a spotlight rather than diffused lighting. So while the rest of the scene is dark, the person who is speaking is bathed in light. Often, characters are grouped as they are in plays. For example, in a scene between the young Raj Kapoor and his parents, one of them is seated on the sofa and two behind it, just as it is done in theatre. Moreover, the contrast between black and white is sharp. The music in the film is quite theatrical. Veteran composer Ram Ganguly had worked with Prithvi Theatres for many years, and the music he composed for *Aag* was heavily melodramatic and static. The lyricism and contemporary feel came with *Barsaat*, when his new team of Shankar–Jaikishen was in place. And, of course, with the advent of Lata Mangeshkar.

Scene-stealer that Raj Kapoor was, he managed to place himself in the limelight, never mind if his role was marginal—just as he had done in school. In Prithvi Theatres' first production, *Shakuntala*, he was only meant to be in the background. But he drew attention to himself by mime and comic antics. However, his acting abilities really surfaced in 1945 in the play *Deewar*, in which he excelled in his role as Ramu the servant. Studio owner Chandulal Shah was so impressed by the young Kapoor's histrionics on stage that he asked Prithviraj Kapoor for his son. In *Pathan*, Raj's interpretation of the role of Bahadur Khan was also remarked upon.

Raj Kapoor spent less than four years with Prithvi Theatres. He left in 1948 when he formed R.K. Films to make *Aag*. But the theatre didn't quite leave him: it was the nursery from where his films got their initial sustenance. When he left Prithvi Theatres for R.K. Films he took along quite a handsome dowry in fact: writers like K.A. Abbas and Inder Raj Anand, actors, musicians and lyricists like Shankar, V.P. Sathe, Premnath, Prayag Raaj and B.M. Vyas among others who had cut their teeth in Prithvi Theatres, and to a lesser extent director Ramanand Sagar who gave direction and thrust to his early films. This was Raj's charmed circle—'a unique assemblage of reformers, romantics and dream-weavers'—as Rajni Bakshi so succinctly puts it in her essay on Raj Kapoor's films.[15] His first film is studded with actors from his father's repertory company.

It wasn't just the people: much of the ideas, ideology and spirit of Prithvi Theatres also piggybacked into R.K. Films when the writers moved there. They were the springboards for the golden age of the banner. Raj Kapoor's early films reflected the spirit of a nascent nation. Burnished with the Nehruvian brand of socialism, these films achieved the delicate balance between entertainment and idealism. A desire for social justice and a degree of optimism not yet gone weary underwrote many of these films. Just as they had in the plays staged by Prithvi Theatres.

IPTA was both an influence and a catalyst for many of the writers and actors of the time. Balraj Sahni, Sombhu Mitra, Chetan Anand and briefly Dev Anand were also part of IPTA. Many flirted seriously with communism, as did a large number of intellectuals of the time. Closely associated with the Communist Party of India (CPI), the association had on board writers K.A. Abbas and Inder Raj Anand. Both brought some of its ideology to the plays they wrote for Prithvi Theatres, and later to the films for Raj Kapoor.[16]

Marosa, the restaurant where Raj used to clandestinely meet his Sikh girlfriend in the mid-forties, was also the nursery for his ideological grooming and political education. He hung around, eating the famous chicken patties and listening to IPTA members talk about the impending partition, an equitable society and a new India. Raj must have soaked it all in passively. But on occasion he did step out of this chatty world of 'adda' and on to the streets. Two years after independence communal tension still simmered. IPTA, Prithvi Theatres and several writers and film-makers took out a procession from Azad Maidan to Shivaji Park for communal harmony on Mahatma Gandhi's birth anniversary. Abbas and Raj Kapoor were among those who led the spirited peace procession.

The two men could not have been more different. Raj was religious, superstitious and apolitical, even though he was a romantic nationalist—mildly socialist and secular by instinct. Describing his brother, Shashi Kapoor says: 'Raj Kapoor was very conservative and very Hindu.' Abbas on the other hand was an agnostic and a committed Marxist. Shaken by the Bengal Famine in 1942, the writer–journalist had made the film *Dharti Ke Lal* in 1946, highlighting the tragedy. A founding member of IPTA, for whom he'd made this film, Abbas's columns in the *Bombay Chronicle* and later in *Blitz* continued to espouse his socialist concerns until the day he breathed his last.

Abbas was a major player in the shaping of Raj Kapoor's mind. The writer enlarged the world of the young director, coaxing him to step out of his life and get under the skin of others. Raj acknowledges his debt to him but also considers Nargis another major influence on his way of understanding people: 'Both of them in their own way have taught me to speak with the voice of all rather than with my own voice.' The director's 'little man' did not come out of a vacuum. Nor was its creation entirely inspired by Charles Chaplin's tramp. Abbas, with the help of V.P. Sathe, helped build the persona of the 'little man' with all the cards stacked against him in films such as *Awara*, *Shree 420*, *Jis Desh Mein Ganga Behti Hai* and *Jaagte Raho*. It was an ideal working relationship. As Rajni Bakshi puts it: 'Abbas was the ideological guide and Raj the faithful choreographer of dreams.'[17]

But revolution was not part of Raj Kapoor's vocabulary. Karl Marx was not his Bible, as it was for many of his adda members. He did not want to turn society topsy-turvy. He was, as Ali Raza puts it, 'a humanist with *zameen ki philosophy*. He had no ideology. A great romanticist, he believed nobody should be hungry, everybody should have a roof on his head. This was *jazbati* (emotional) Marxism, not ideological Marxism.'

Kapoor had a one-point programme: cinema. He began *Aag* six months before partition when communal bloodbaths had already begun. Although he completed the film after the brutal division of the country, he did not reflect upon it in the film. His only nod to the cataclysmic event was the inclusion of a victim of partition, a character played by Nargis. Moreover, Raj just hints at her predicament, and leaves it there. She has no name: Raj calls her Nimmi after his childhood love. The Nargis character is initially dishevelled and looks as if she has emerged from some horror chamber. Her eyes vacant, her demeanour lets you know that something quite unspeakable has happened to her. When asked about her family she replies that she has lost them all.

At one level the film is about creativity, the desire to be creative. 'I want to take theatre to transcendental heights,' is a refrain mouthed by the protagonist played by Raj. The film is also about love, explains Shashi Kapoor. 'Rajji was happiest and his best in the company of beautiful women. In *Aag* he says, "If I was not so handsome, the girl would not have liked me and then I would not do this natak." *Aag* has his *halki* (light) romances—the girls in school, the cycle of infatuation, love. Then it broke and he burned his face.' By getting personal, and moving away from the obviously political, Raj Kapoor was able to speak to the youth of the day, according to the late film commentator Iqbal Masud. 'For many not in the north, politics did not dominate their lives. 1947 was not a cataclysmic year. Young people were going about their lives, falling in love, being disappointed, being heartbroken.'[18]

Raj Kapoor's relationship with cinema was very complex. In his films he moved between the personal and catering to the masses. *Aag* and *Mera Naam Joker*, for example, were deeply personal films: he laid himself bare in them, at times wearing his soul on his sleeve. And then there were films like *Satyam Shivam Sundaram*, *Bobby* and *Ram Teri Ganga Maili*, made for the frontbenchers as well as the balconywallas. However, strangely enough, there was another lesser-known side to the film-maker: he also hankered after the 'other cinema', or what is commonly labelled art cinema. There was a secret wannabe intellectual lurking within this Kapoor. One might say that he had a Satyajit Ray complex.

In fact, Raj Kapoor and Nargis called on Ray after they had seen *Pather Panchali*: they were impressed and showered the Bengali film director with praise. Kapoor even offered the film-maker a blank cheque to make a film for him. Ray, who had seen *Jaagte Raho* and admired it, refused: he said that his Hindi was very weak. Apparently, Ray did visit Raj Kapoor in Bombay to discuss a film. Shashi Kapoor recalls a meeting between the Bengali maestro and the Kapoors in his apartment. 'Both of them edited their own films. *Pather Panchali* lay incomplete until the Bengal government stepped in. Dr Hemant Ganguly, a distributor from a good Bengali family who later distributed *Junoon*, was fond of Ray. Since *Pather Panchali* had gone over budget, he contacted Raj Kapoor for money. The two men met and discussed the film. But Raj Kapoor could not pitch in—he was broke at the time. Later, after *Sangam* and its success, Raj Kapoor approached Ray. Ray came to Bombay. He came home for dinner. But I think Ray realized that the two were strong film-makers. It would have been the clash of two giants.'

So when Nargis in her off-screen avatar as Rajya Sabha member criticized *Pather Panchali* for displaying India's poverty to the rest of the world, it was like a bolt out of the blue for Ray. 'Ray told me that he was shocked,' says director Kumar Shahani. 'He did not expect this since she seemed to have liked his film. Raj Kapoor and she had seen the film in Madras when they were both acting in *Chori Chori* (a spirited remake of Frank Capra's *It Happened One Night*) for A.V.M., and had at the time admired the film.'

Kapoor's sneaking admiration of Ray continued, unabated. The fact that *Pather Panchali* had been given an award in Cannes was not lost on cineastes in Bombay at the time. Several directors began to believe that it was essential to make a Bengali film to get international recognition. *Jaagte Raho* was also made in Bengali. 'Raj Kapoor got Sombhu Mitra to direct both versions, and the Bengali version was titled *Ek Din Ratre*,' says P.K. Nair. Fluent in Bengali, Raj Kapoor acted in both versions. And Chhabi Biswas played Motilal's role in the Bengali version. Sombhu Mitra may have directed the film but, according to Nair, Kapoor could not help making changes in it after the Bengali director returned to Calcutta. Kapoor added the scene at the end when Nargis pours water for the thirsty protagonist (Kapoor) who has spent the entire film looking for water to drink.

Years later he enticed Ray's cinematographer, the eccentric but brilliant Subrata Mitra, to become a regular in his *baithak*s in his cottage. The *addabazi* used to continue late into the night, with Kapoor plying Mitra with whiskey and prodding him to talk about his techniques of lighting and composition. Mitra could barely stay awake beyond 2 a.m. However, Kapoor, the perfect host, refused to let him go—and kept him talking.

Hungry for knowledge about cinema, he grabbed it wherever and from whomever he could. Kapoor didn't turn to books to learn about his trade; he just listened attentively to practitioners of the art. Raj Kapoor was the true apprentice. While still a stagehand at Prithvi Theatres he used to work there during the day and spend the evenings learning editing from Babubhai Takar, who was then with Murari Pictures. Takar used to work at night, and his young apprentice often stayed there until two in the morning watching him. Raj would snip off the buttons on his shirt and pants so that he wouldn't be tempted to leave. Panchal, with Murari Pictures at the time, recalls Raj Kapoor 'sleeping on the floor of the editing room, after sweeping it. Sometimes Takar would tie a string on him to wake him up as he slept on the floor.'

Bombay Talkies was another training ground. Jairaj, a fellow assistant there, was familiar with Hollywood cinema. Lekh Tandon remembers the long discussions on cinema. 'Jairaj taught Raj a lot about Hollywood. He used to tell him that while making a film one hand should not know what the other does. Jairaj would talk about who was the best in Hollywood, how a film should be made, how Nargis copied Joan Fontaine. Raj would see those films and tease her about it.'

Raj Kapoor's interest in parallel cinema continued alongside. He even discussed a film project with Kumar Shahani, among the more abstract pundits of the 'other' cinema, as different from Kapoor as chalk from cheese. The two film directors happened to be in Tashkent for a film festival. *Satyam Shivam Sundaram* was being shown there that year. 'We were waiting in the wings to go onstage. Kapoor sahib asked me what I was doing. He said that he was thinking of making the Mahabharata. When I told him that I had a Bhabha fellowship to study the epic form, he said, "*Kya baat*. Will you do this film for me?" He told me that he was planning a film called *The Hindu*. Evidently everybody who heard this conversation was shocked: what could be more surreal than the showman and the arty film-maker making a film together?'

Of course nothing happened. It was just serious daydreaming. Raj Kapoor also planned to make a film called *Ajanta*. He had spent hours discussing the project with Nargis. His talented art director M.R. Achrekar had even made sketches for this ambitious project. After Nargis left R.K. Films, Kapoor talked about the film with Vyjanthimala. 'There would have been many classical dances in the film, authentic Bharatnatyam,' explains the actress. The epics had long fascinated Kapoor, as had Hollywood's spectacular epics like *Ben-Hur* and *The Ten Commandments*. His ambitions were no less than those of Cecil B. de Mille.

India's classical lore and philosophy had enthralled him for a long time. It was something he soaked in—imbibed—rather than read about. After all, he had seen his father act in innumerable mythologicals and historicals—and been a bit player in a few himself. However, the younger Kapoor developed cold feet. He was not confident about making a period film, especially one with larger-than-life figures. And so it was back to the common man, the man of the street and the man of the moment, the man he knew, the man on-screen whose identity he subsumed into his own. Interestingly, while Raj Kapoor always gave himself names that were derivatives of or similar to his (Raj, Raju, Rajan), the names of his leading ladies had nothing in common with their own. Meanwhile, the wonderful paintings in the old Ajanta-derivative Sharda Ukil style gathered dust.

Kapoor was a perfectionist: he had to be completely confident about a project before embarking on it. Moreover, he wanted Indian cinema to be as great as what was coming out of Hollywood. While the Charlie Chaplin[19] fixation is well documented and much commented upon—the tramp of *Shree 420*, the desi country bumpkin avatar in *Jis Desh Mein Ganga Behti Hai*, and, of course, later in life the sad clown of *Mera Naam Joker*, so obvious an inspired homage to Chaplin's *Limelight*—what is not so well known is his close study of the works of Western cineastes. According to Randhir Kapoor, he was aware of what was happening in Europe and Hollywood.

The international film festival held in Bombay in 1952 left a deep impression on Indian film-makers, including Satyajit Ray, Bimal Roy and Raj Kapoor. Vittorio de Sica's *Miracle in Milan*, *Bicycle Thief* and *Shoeshine*, and Roberto Rossellini's *Open City* were eye-openers for them. Kapoor was particularly taken by Frank Capra and three Italian cineastes: Roberto Rossellini, Vittorio de Sica and Cesare Zavattini. 'Certain film-makers nearly changed my art, like Frank Capra. In all my films it is the common man, the underdog who ultimately manages to get the best deal from life. I have always shared the optimism of Capra's *It Happened One Night*.'[20]

From the Italians, Kapoor learned about 'slice of life' realism. 'De Sica and Zavattini brought to the screen what they saw and felt. Something real. Slices of life. In an American film you could never see a little boy piddling. In *Bicycle Thief*, the boy piddles and the father waits on the other side of the road with his bicycle...However, the most effective part of the whole movement was the allegory that was part of the film.'[21] In his 'long chats' with the directors he also realized the importance of taking the camera out of the studio.

Before the Italians, Orson Welles had a profound influence on the way Raj shot his films. In his little lectures on cinema to Simi Garewal, Raj Kapoor often used to talk about the director–actor. 'He was fascinated by Orson Welles and used to talk about his use of light and shade. He was also quite taken by expressionist film-makers. He went to see *Citizen Kane* with his cameraman,' says Simi.

Raj Kapoor often acknowledged his debt to the techniques of Orson Welles. 'I was influenced by Orson Welles's camerawork during *Barsaat. Aag* had very low-key lighting. The contrast between black and white was very vivid. I wanted my cameraman to give me black and grey pictures. But at that time nobody liked my low-key lighting. Those days bright pictures were in vogue.'[22] Raj Kapoor wanted to use lighting to create mood; above all to do it subtly as he had for the opening scene of *Pathan*. Shashi Kapoor sees some touches of Welles, especially his use of the wide-angle lens, as early as *Aag*. Apparently, his *Aag* cinematographer, aghast by the idea of pillars and columns getting shortened, refused to do so for Raj Kapoor's next film. Kapoor replaced him with Jal Mistry for *Barsaat*.

It's been nearly twenty years since I first went to R.K. to interview Raj Kapoor for an article on sensuality and sexuality in Indian cinema. I was immediately directed towards the cottage.

In the early days when Raj Kapoor lived and worked in Chembur there were long green stretches, and an air of country about the place. You could even hear the roosters crowing at dawn and chickens clucking in his garden. The Kapoor home is almost at the end of a tree-lined undulating road with large bungalows on either side behind the Tata Institute of Social Sciences. Today, as you make your way to R.K. Films from Sion circle it is through an endless stretch of shops, crowded tenements and small industries. The air is heavy and oppressive with the myriad enterprises.

It is quite easy to miss R.K. Films, about 4 kilometres from the Kapoor home. It looks sleepy, and has an air of a ghost town about it. The gate is rusty, as is the guard who opens it. The iconic R.K. logo—Nargis arched backwards in Raj Kapoor's arms, forever enacting the passionate love scene in *Barsaat*—is on the gate. The logo also sits on the two-storeyed building which houses the offices where his three sons come to work each day, around lunchtime. Their father used to come to work at two in the afternoon.

The iconic R.K. logo

Dating from the early fifties, the office building recalls cantonment architecture, with its high-ceilinged large rooms that open out from a long, covered corridor. The caucus, the inner group that made all the films, has long since gone: Shankar, Jaikishen, Radhu Karmakar, Allaudin, K.A. Abbas, V.P. Sathe, Inder Raj Anand, Shailendra and Mukesh. Many of the old retainers and fellow travellers of the R.K. family have also died or left; only a few employees shuffle about. The only one who remains from the early days is Vishwa Mehra—Mamaji—the last of the Mohicans and the keeper of most of Raj Kapoor's secrets, who moves almost imperceptibly, ghost-like, through R.K. Films.

Raj's famous cottage is behind the office building, a little to the side. Built before even the studio was, it had a room at the back which was Nargis's room. After she walked out of R.K. and Raj Kapoor's life to make *Mother India*, it was kept just the way she had left it. Apparently, Raj Kapoor wanted to keep her room like a shrine, with a few of her clothes and crockery in place.

Raj Kapoor often used to refer to the cottage as his sanctum sanctorum. Cinema was his life. The world outside mattered. But, increasingly, it mattered only if he could transfer his experiences—or those of others—to the screen. Life was fodder for his creative imagination. The door of the cottage was the line of control between Raj the film-maker and Raj the husband, brother, father, grandfather and social animal. His family never crossed the line: the division between his home and work was complete. Says Rishi Kapoor: 'If not interacting with the outside world, my father lived in his cottage only. He was not interested in politics.

He was interested in his own films, not in those of others. He lived in his own world.'

The real Raj Kapoor dwelled here. It was a temple to his inner life. Modest and cosy, the cottage housed what was dearest to him. Besides the ladies in white, the walls had a garlanded photograph of his father. Deities of all religions hung on the walls. Besides the Hindu deities, he had a cross, and something from the Koran. He even had a Jewish scroll (his hairdresser Bertha was Jewish).

The cottage was also his adda, a gathering of kindred spirits, especially over long drinking sessions. Tape recorders spooled silently, recording many of the brainstorming sessions of Raj Kapoor's creative team. Ideas, baked and half-baked, stories, intimate revelations, stray bits of music and melody which teased his mind, impressions and plain gup-shup went on to those tapes. Apart from the core group, there were those who came and went, temporary habitués, like Rajesh Khanna who used to go to the cottage to drink when Raj Kapoor was wooing him for *Satyam Shivam Sundaram* for the role Shashi finally played. Raj had wanted to cast the reigning superstar—before Amitabh Bachchan's coup de grace in *Anand*—with his new wife Dimple Kapadia after their sensational, headline-grabbing marriage. The actress had become the sweetheart of the nation after Kapoor's *Bobby* and the canny director wanted to cash in on this. Zeenat Aman eventually managed to prise the role from him.

Describing the all-night sessions in the cottage, Bunny Reuben says: 'We used to sit and talk late into the night with him. He used us to get reactions. We would begin at midnight. Once shooting was over, he would bathe and say his prayers to all the deities in the cottage. He never drank until he had done this. All this would finish by three in the morning. Not even one sip of whiskey until then. We would drink until four or five in the morning. He would get to work at 2 p.m.—his working day began then.'

Somewhere behind the façade of the showman–ringmaster was a lonely man who wanted people to listen to him. Raj Kapoor was all right as long as he was making a film, though financial difficulties dogged him most of the time. But his dependency on the adda was acute: he often said that he wanted all his cast and crew with him while he was shooting, even if they were not part of the scene being filmed. There was another reason for his friendships with people from all walks of life—his obsessional curiosity about everything, even *matka*. Panchal remembers him quizzing a certain Rattan Katri for a long time on details of this very special Indian form of gambling. He was even interested in the workings of boilers, and would spend hours picking his friend Vinny Ahuja's brain about them. Curious about his friend's livelihood, Raj Kapoor wanted to know everything about his business. 'Once at a fair he ran after President Zail Singh who had just walked past my stall. Rajji asked him to come to our stall. He wanted to know everything about boilers. In fact, he even expressed interest in being on the board of my company BAMCO,' recalls Ahuja.

The cottage is still there, sort of. What was Raj Kapoor's creative crucible is being used as a storeroom. Peering through dusty windows all one can see are logs of wood and bits of broken furniture. Some of the cottage has been rebuilt, some of it destroyed. There is nothing for relic hunters of the fifties here—the trail has gone cold; there isn't even a whiff of nostalgia.

Fortunately, you can find it elsewhere, in what used to be Nargis's dressing room on the first floor of the studio, located behind the administrative building. The custodians of the R.K. legacy moved the memento mori here. Post Nargis, it was used as a make-up room by subsequent leading ladies. And opposite was Raj Kapoor's make-up room. An embryo of a museum of Raj Kapoor's films waits in this dark forgotten corner of R.K. Films, gathering the dust of indifference. For many years, R.K. used to rent out the *Jaagte Raho* staircase, but eventually that had to go: there were no godowns to store things.

Mamaji, the keeper of the memories of the place and its sole archivist, directs me to the 'museum'. A chowkidar leads the way, switching on one light after the other, interminably it would seem as we walk down a long, dark corridor. And as he does so, faces from the past swim into view from the old posters of R.K. films on the walls—a luminous Nargis in *Barsaat* and *Awara*; Raj Kapoor, both intensely young and ageing, in *Aag* and *Mera*

Naam Joker; Rishi Kapoor and Dimple Kapadia, caught in transit between childhood and adulthood, in *Bobby*.

A door opens and memories stir. The ghosts haven't quite fled. Bits and pieces from Raj Kapoor's life and work lie scattered, like a dust-covered jigsaw puzzle. A stack of Archie comics lies in one corner. Incongruously, next to them, in a glass cabinet, are two dog-eared books: *The Miracle of Fasting* and *Live in Agelessness*. A huge black umbrella that partially protected the love-struck couple from studio rain in the unforgettable anthem for lovers 'Pyar hua, ikrar hua' in *Shree 420* is propped up, without a context. Nargis's elegant long black dress from *Awara* drapes a mannequin. Even the knife with which Raju kills Jaggu the daku in the same film is on display.

Glass-fronted cupboards line the wall, spilling over with clothes and accessories from his films: Vyjanthimala's saris from *Sangam*, Mandakini's cholis and lehangas from *Ram Teri Ganga Maili*, Dimple Kapadia's funky frocks from *Bobby*, Padmini's saris from *Jis Desh Mein Ganga Behti Hai*. There's even a separate cabinet for the many *topi*s (hats) Raj Kapoor wore in his films. Tucked away is the torn frock Baby Naaz wore in *Boot Polish*: her performance in the film won her the best child actor's award at Cannes. (Interestingly, she later married Raj Kapoor's cousin Subhiraj Kapoor.)

But suspend disbelief for an instant, switch off the mind's censors and open an inner ear. The saucy magic of 'Mur mur ke na dekh' wafts by as you gaze at the shimmering evening dress Nadira wore with such élan in her maiden vamp role in *Shree 420*. Never mind that the cigarette holder she held so enticingly between her lips has long been dispatched to Israel, to the then prime minister who was infatuated with the actress after seeing the film. Let your eyes rest awhile on the torn coat and oversize canvas shoes and you can almost see Raj Kapoor's indigenous tramp figure walk by jauntily singing 'Mera joota hai Japani'. Even the stick he slung over his shoulder with the pathetic little bundle at the end is intact. Flutes, a mandolin, an accordion, a set of drums and many of the instruments that made the memorable music of his films also have a place here. Dimple's infamously pesky bikini from *Bobby* is also there somewhere, hidden from view.

But the most heart-tuggingly poignant prop is the self-referential life-size clown figure of the joker from *Mera Naam Joker*—the film's failure at the box office almost led to Kapoor selling R.K. Films. The painted clown has become an even more pathetic figure with the passage of time. He has lost his wig, and is slumped on a chair, though his red suspenders and the patch on his blue pants have survived in their original state.

We leave this repository of Raj Kapoor's dreams. And as we walk back up the corridor into the present, the guard switches off the lights one by one, plunging them once again into darkness.

Raj Kapoor had the strangest relationship with god, rather with his gods. To begin with there was his wide-armed embrace of deities and messiahs from all religions evident on the walls of his cottage. The showman in him revelled in festivals of all kinds. Just as Pandit Nehru donned the hat or dress of any community or tribe he visited, Kapoor celebrated all occasions. Ahuja recounts: 'During Durga Puja, he would get fish from Shivaji Park. I had to bring langar for him from the gurudwara on Guru Nanak's birthday. He went to Shirdi. He made a big thing about Lohri. The Tata Institute of Social Studies was next door, and during Christmas the children would sing carols. His birthday became a big occasion, and he wanted to have a three-day-long party for the New Year.' And his Holi parties were legendary.

Raj Kapoor was also on first-name terms with Christ. He often talked out loud to a picture of Jesus Christ. Lekh Tandon saw him talking to it. 'When he was drunk he would say, "You are Jesus Christ and I am Raj Kapoor."' When he was staying with Bina Ramani in New York, she heard him 'talking loudly to a picture of Jesus Christ. He would talk to him in English. And he would be cursing: "Why did you put me into all this? All this has come together at the same time, and now you have to get me out of this."' When a surprised Ramani asked him how he could talk to Christ in such a manner, he replied: 'He is a human, just like us. Not like those gods on rocks. He can curse me and I can curse him.'

The intimacy with Christ was obviously a childhood habit. Recounting the incident when he tripped on his robe and fell onstage during a school play, Raj Kapoor said: 'Everyone laughed, even Christ laughed and I was happy that I made Christ laugh.'[23] In *Mera Naam Joker*, the young, pubescent Raj (Rishi Kapoor), mired in misery and loneliness, talks to the figure of Christ.

Not only was he on intimate terms with Jesus, Raj Kapoor was keenly interested in the tenets of Christianity. He often said that he poured his philosophy of life and love into *Mera Naam Joker*, a film in which he deftly achieved an unforced blending of comedy and sadness, especially in the first part. The joker learns and teaches through the process of love and sorrow, until the film's 'memorable climax', which Raj Kapoor felt attains 'supreme Christian proportions'.

Raj Kapoor had a personal equation with the Grim Reaper as well: his conversations with Yamraj (the Hindu god of death) appear to be something straight out of a mythological film. Ahuja recalls a strange dream Raj Kapoor told him about. 'He was convinced that someone in his larger family wanted him to die. He dreamed that Yamraj had been called to take him away. But to do this he had to have eyeball-to-eyeball contact. Rajji turned on his side and closed his eyes. Yamraj got angry. Since Rajji was not ready to go with him, he went away. The next time they tied him to his bed and Yamraj was invited once again. Rajji looked at him eyeball-to-eyeball and said, "My departure is organized, Yamraj. You can't kill me. *Maarne wale mere apne hai.*" (My own will kill me.)'

Raj Kapoor's unconventional life and lifestyle belied his deep-rooted conservatism and an unstated craving for the spiritual. He searched for answers elsewhere, and once even went to the Rajneesh Ashram in Pune during a particularly unhappy passage in his life. A practising Hindu, he did not, however, wear his religion on his sleeve. Shiva being the deity of the Kapoor khandaan, on a holiday in Kashmir, he insisted on going on a pilgrimage to Amarnath, the cave-temple in the mountains. Every R.K. film begins with Prithviraj Kapoor performing a pooja to the deity. Of course Raj Kapoor became even more observant of the tenets of his faith just before the release of a film. Not only did he become vegetarian during those crucial days, he donned the avatar of a pilgrim: Vaishno Devi, Nizamuddin Aulia, Haji Ali, Ajmer Sharif, Shirdi... The conservative streak surfaced at home as well. Rites and rituals and the Kapoor brand of conservatism were followed to the last detail. The Kapoor daughters were not encouraged to act, and the actress daughters-in-law said goodbye to the arc lights and doing the rounds of studios after taking the *pheras*, although all of them left willingly.

Inevitably, actors become narcissists. And Raj Kapoor was no exception. But he was subtler about it than many of his contemporaries. He didn't go down the Peter Pan path like Dev Anand, frozen in an indeterminate age zone. Nor did he spend time on the couches of psychoanalysts for help in coping with being a legend, as did his on-and-off friend Dilip Kumar, who boasted about having shared an analyst with Sir Laurence Olivier. It was just those implacably blue eyes of his. Raj Kapoor was very proud of them. Unfortunately, their magic did not come through in his black and white films, though they caused a flutter in the hearts of many of his leading ladies.

When small cysts began to form around his eyes, he did the round of doctors. However, he didn't have the courage to go under the knife. Then, one evening at a party a few days before he was going to Tashkent with his film *Satyam Shivam Sundaram*, he told Dr Narendra Pandya, a renowned cosmetic surgeon and friend, that he had decided to undergo surgery as soon as he returned from Tashkent. Dr Pandya was quite surprised when he actually did turn up. Raj Kapoor had been talking about it for years. 'He came as promised. And after the stitches were removed he was happy. I asked him why he had suddenly decided to have it done. He told me, "I was in a *nasha* and I saw your eyes without your glasses that evening at the party. I saw that they were like mine, the same colour. My eyes are the most precious things for me. I realized that you would not play around with them since we had the same kind of eyes,"' says Dr Pandya.

His famed humility was inverted narcissism. At a party when

he walked into a room, the whole room would rise. But he, slightly bent forward, with folded hands, would go up to people and say, '*Mujhe Raj Kapoor kehte hain.*' (I am Raj Kapoor.) There wasn't a person in the room who did not know who he was. Yet there was this in-your-face faux humility and the body language to go with it.

At the same time, he knew that he was good-looking, with his fair skin, light hair, and of course the 'ole blue eyes. He often referred to the advantages of his fair looks: women—relatives, teachers and actresses—showered him with a lot of affection because of it. The dandy in him didn't stop with his looks: a waft of Je Reviens used to envelop him. It was his signature olfactory aura, despite the fact that this French perfume from Worth was for women.

But underneath it all, many leagues deep, Raj Kapoor had the complex of a short man. Like most Pathans, his father and two brothers loomed large over him. Not only did he get his blue eyes and light hair from his mother's side of the family, he also inherited the Mehra height: his mother was barely five feet tall. Raj Kapoor seldom let his sensitivity about his height surface, apart from his stray remarks about his brothers being taller and better looking than him. But obviously he never got over his height. One day when Nargis came to meet him, he was devastated: she was wearing heels. 'I knew then that it was over,' he told Simi Garewal. Raj Kapoor had a 'seventh sense', according to her. 'He told Nargis that he knew she had a tall man in her life. *Mujhse milne aayee thi aur heel mein*! I looked at her heels for twenty minutes. And then she left.'

Sunil Dutt was a tall man.

Alcoholism is the hamartia of the Kapoor men. An alcoholic haze hangs low over them, like stubborn dust-laden clouds that refuse to lift. Shammi Kapoor calls it 'the curse of the Kapoors'. The curse certainly did not start with Prithviraj Kapoor: he only began drinking when he was fifty. According to B.M. Vyas, a doctor had told Prithviraj to drink whiskey after he turned fifty.

'The doctor told Papaji that it was good for his voice. He used to pour some local whiskey into a *katora* and sit under the tree in his jhompra. And even then he drank with restraint.'

His three sons, however, have had to struggle with this demon of the spirits. As do Raj Kapoor's three sons. Raj Kapoor didn't really drink until he was in his mid-thirties: it was more like *Devdas* with a twist. Mamaji says that he turned to the bottle after a fight with Nargis in 1955. 'Rajji started very late. It was while we were shooting *Chori Chori* in Madras. He drank half a bottle of whiskey when he saw a letter written to Nargis by some man. She lied and said that it was not hers. He put this scene in *Sangam*, the scene in which Raj finds a letter which Vyjanthimala has torn up and thrown away.'

The letter, explains Mehra, was a proposal of marriage from a producer. Was this really the catalyst tripping Raj Kapoor into dependence on alcohol? The 'letter' was certainly important to him. It still rankled over three decades later when he showed it to journalist Suresh Kohli during the course of an interview in 1986. Kapoor had glued together the torn bits of the letter. He had even had the reconstituted letter framed. Raj Kapoor went on a marathon binge when Nargis walked out of R.K. Films and his life to work with Mehboob Khan in *Mother India*. Apparently, she left a note on his tape recorder in the cottage.

There was a pattern to the drinking bouts. Anger often preceded the binges. 'When Rajji used to get angry, he drank. He would keep it [his anger] in all day and take it out at night,' says Mehra. 'During the day he was normal.' Family members talk about the 'midnight hour' when, after a few drinks, Dr Jekyll became Mr Hyde. It was the time for them to slip away, before the darker side and irrepressible demons of the showman surfaced. Sometimes, however, it was just an act: Raj Kapoor played the part of a drunkard, but for a purpose. 'Alcohol was not just for pleasure. Raj Kapoor used alcohol to say what he wanted to, things he would not be able say otherwise,' says Madhu Malik. 'He would drink and become semi-abusive and start rambling. He started *sunaoing* people (telling people off). He pretended to be drunker than he actually was. If he was angry with his distributors and wanted to say something to them, he'd do so under the guise of being drunk. This way he said what he had to, yet kept the relationship intact.'

Actor Raza Murad was a victim of this 'act' when *Prem Rog* was being made. Raj Kapoor did not like the way the actor had interpreted a particular scene during the rehearsals. Stone sober he started behaving like a drunkard and ticked off the actor. Recounting this incident, Tanuja says: 'Rajji told Revati to bring him a drink. And then, actor par excellence that he was, he wheeled downstairs to the sets as if he was drunk. He took a sip, sat down, leaned forward, and started on Raza. "Who do you think you are, Raza?" All he had to do was a simple scene—to look up and hold his look when he sees Padmini Kolhapure. Rajji asked him if was ready. Raza said, "Yes, sir." And then made all kinds of faces and noises—Raza was trying out some method acting. He muttered something like "Mood ata hai". That really got Rajji, and he took off. Raza told him not to bring his father and mother into it. At which point Rajji started to imitate Raza. This is not acting, he told him. "It is a simple thing that you have to feel inside and not make a noise." And that man had eyes at the back of his head: he told me he could see what I was doing with my hands—I was trying to signal to Raza to stop.'

Work was sacred for Raj Kapoor. Alcohol was banned from the sets. He never drank while he worked—not even when the unit had packed up for the day. He would wait until he had removed the last traces of his make-up before he wet his lips with his beloved Black Label. Drinking on the set was for him tantamount to disrespect for his profession. Naturally, he was averse to anybody drinking on the sets. So, one day when he spotted a drunk Dharmendra sleeping on a bench in a corner of the studio on the sets of *Mera Naam Joker* he lost his temper. He began to shake the sleeping actor. 'Papaji, Papaji,' babbled a contrite Dharmendra, before falling at his feet and apologizing. Dharmendra never drank on the sets again.[24]

Raj Kapoor's relationship with alcohol was quite unique. If he loved women, he loved good Scotch even more. This was his true passion, one that he was never fickle about. Raj Kapoor was not comfortable in five-star hotels. Yet the whiskey he drank had to be Black Label. 'He was the only commoner who liked Johnny

Walker Black Label,' says Randhir Kapoor. And that too, only the Black Label bought in London. Says Rishi Kapoor: 'He would open his cupboard. It was full of bottles, even gallon bottles. He was possessive about his Black Label. When he went to parties, he carried his own booze. He would tell us that others got their Scotch from the market, but his was *asli*. He did not trust anybody.'

In fact, Raj Kapoor had a neat caste system for his whiskey. He would get the top-of-the-line Black Label from London for himself. Like a deity he shared it with the chosen few of the moment, dispensing it like prasad or a blessing. Only a few friends and the favourites of the moment were given this ambrosia from London. The next in the hierarchy got Black Label as well, but only from bottles that had been brought from Dubai. Mamaji was dismissed with Red Label—because Raj Kapoor didn't think he deserved any better than this whiskey that 'tasted like piss'.

Raj Kapoor banished his sons to the lower end of the whiskey hierarchy. Much to their chagrin their father shared his elixir of life with his friends in front of them but gave them an inferior whiskey. Tanuja was one of the privileged few to get the genuine stuff. 'We had a strange connection. We were friends, pals. He would always pour me whiskey from his bottle of Black Label. Daboo [Randhir Kapoor] would plaintively ask me, "Why do you get it and I don't?" He used to notice his father serving it to me.' Raj Kapoor's close friend, neighbour and drinking companion, Vinny Ahuja, was the other privileged recipient.

Alcohol was at times like a wall between him and his family. However, there were occasions when it also brought down that wall. Raj Kapoor did not spend much time with his family, totally immersed as he was in his films. But once in while, the whiskey made him play at being father as well. Recalls Rishi Kapoor: 'My father used to become emotional when he drank whiskey. He'd keep talking about how we were his real sons. And he would tell us, "You drink junk."'

Whiskey coursing in his veins also made him more voluble and melodramatic, more over the top. Especially when he was happy with the way the film he was making at the time was going. Tinnu Anand recalls an incident when Kapoor landed up, quite inebriated, at their doorstep in the middle of the night. 'It was 1.30 a.m. We had just returned from a party in Chembur to our flat on Warden Road. I heard the bell. There, in front of me, was an exuberant Raj Kapoor, standing, pressing the bell continuously. I touched his feet. He said, "Tinnu bete, you have to see *Sangam*. My car is downstairs. Drive to R.K. and tell the projectionist. I want you to see your father's work." He was drunk. I woke up my father and when I returned to the living room there he was, full length, on the floor. He kept calling my father chacha. And then started talking about the film. "Have you seen *Sangam*?" It was like a stuck record. He went on until 5.30 in the morning, repeating the dialogue and the climax of the film. Later, he called for ice. He put some in his whiskey. I have never seen love flow out of a person as I did that night. He embraced you every two minutes.'

Drinking with those he cared for was a secular act of communion for him. Dr Pandya recalls a dinner party in the Kapoor home. 'It was after 2 a.m. As my wife and I were leaving the party, he asked me why we were going home so early. We sat on the swing in the backyard of the house. He'd hold our hands and give us cognac: he would bring a glass and we would all sip from the same glass.'

Drinking in solitude was not his style. In fact sipping from the same glass seems to have been a trait he shared with his father—like passing the peace pipe. Manmohan Malhotra remembers an evening he spent with both of them in Delhi. 'Papaji did not drink much. But one day we were all sitting together. Raj went out to their car and brought a whiskey bottle. We poured it in one of those long glasses and we kept passing it round. We all drank from the same glass.' Perhaps, these were atavistic Pathan traits of eating from the same plate. Here, of course, communal eating had been replaced by communal drinking.

It was a movable bar all right. Raj Kapoor's court continued wherever he went, even in Breach Candy Hospital. And even there he tried to play host. One evening when Dr Pandya dropped in to see him, he insisted that the doctor have a drink with him. 'Rajji was drinking and he told me, "*Aaiye* Doctor sahib", and asked Krishnaji to give me some whiskey. When I hesitated, he insisted. I told him that as a doctor I could not, what if the other doctors and nurses saw me. Then he became soft. "*Mujhe maaf karna*. You are a doctor and in an important position." There were tears in his eyes.' The actor in him was seldom at rest.

'During the shooting of *Tarang* we were at the creek in Chembur. Smita [Patil] dances a few steps on the highway bridge, as the sun rises slowly. We had just forty-five minutes to catch this, and we had to take crane shots. We needed the police to help us. They had been there on the first day. But where were they today? Not a single cop had turned up on the second day. Where was everybody in Chembur? I was livid; there wasn't a soul. I sent somebody to find out. Apparently, they were all drunk, including the police. The night before had been Rajji's birthday—it was like a raja's birthday. All the people had been invited. It was almost mythological,' recalls Kumar Shahani.

It wouldn't do for a showman extraordinaire like Raj Kapoor to throw a mere birthday party marking the addition of a year to his life, as most people do. No, his birthday had to be celebrated as workers' day, just like a nation commemorates the birth anniversary of a political leader. And for the Kapoor 'event' not only did the world and his friend land up, a film was usually launched on that day as well with a mahurat. His father would perform the puja.

Today the word showman is synonymous with Raj Kapoor. His parties were laid out like a Cecil B. de Mille production. Excess was a good word in his vocabulary. He still does not have a successor, though Subhash Ghai may have tried to borrow the mantle. Even his enemies granted him that: nobody threw a party quite like he did. Holi, Diwali, weddings, post-premiere celebrations—these parties were not just, well, parties. They were like manna falling from some gourmet heaven.

Devnar Cottage, the Kapoor home, with its vast lawn became a Disneyland of world cuisines during these gargantuan feasts. The tables were laden with an infinite variety of preparations of mutton, chicken and fish. He would be devastated if anybody asked for a liqueur he did not have. 'He'd move heaven and earth to get it. You could get whatever you wanted on earth,' gushes Shahani. Meanwhile, Raj Kapoor played—and the word is not used lightly—at being the perfect host. He would attend to every guest. His wife did the same, often asking each guest what he wanted and personally dishing it on to their plates.

The front door of Devnar Cottage opens into a huge hall. Often Raj Kapoor sat on a gaddi placed on the floor and surveyed people coming in—like an emperor. Evidently, he wanted to see everybody as they entered. Sometimes he got up to receive the guests. Occasionally, he'd play sentinel, especially at weddings. Recalls Dr Pandya: 'During Rishi's wedding he stood at the main entrance and checked all the guests. He used to say that there are too many badmashes, and he would actually tell gatecrashers that he had not called them, and ask them to leave. I think he did not want gatecrashers because there was too much jewellery around.'

His daughter Ritu's wedding was a major production. According to Panchal, the Nandas played a joke on the occasion. Panchal recalls burqa-clad persons walking on the tarmac towards Raj Kapoor, waiting for the Nandas at the airport. 'Rajji was asked to identify Rajan, and he did.'

Long before that, when Ritu was a child, the Kapoors celebrated her doll's wedding. 'I remember a grand wedding for my guddi. I must have been six. Shammi Uncle took an 8mm movie of the event. The barat came in an old Studebaker. My tailor's daughter had the gudda and I was shocked when she came and took my guddi away,' says Ritu Nanda.

Raj Kapoor's showmanship went much further than hosting the best parties. He was also a great performer on life's stage. Larger than life, his gestures spoke much louder than his soft-spoken utterances. Particularly pleased about a script Abbas had written, Raj Kapoor—filmi style—went to his home and handed him the keys to a new white Ambassador which was parked outside his flat.

His flamboyance leaps from Panchal's photographs. As Panchal rummages through them it is Raj Kapoor the performer who emerges. Posing with Soviet sailors, a beaming Kapoor holds the huge fish they have brought for him. He invited them to have dinner with him to eat the fish. Reminisces Panchal: 'Rajji was a *tirath* (pilgrimage) for the Russians. Whenever they visited Bombay they would come, especially the navy guys. They knew he liked fish and the crew stepping off steamers brought special fish for him.'

In another photograph you see him, his hair wild, locks falling over his forehead, playing the drums. At a party for Premnath's wedding in Green Hotel, Kapoor sent the drummers away and began to play. Playing the bagpipes, the sitar, the guitar, or singing and dancing, the performer in him seldom took rest.

Not even when was ill. Lying on his mattress on the floor he played host by remote control, instructing the family. Recalls Kamana Chandra, on whose story *Prem Rog* is based: 'We were invited to a party after the trial show of *Ram Teri Ganga Maili*. Rajji remained in his bungalow. He was not well, but he said that the show must go on. He told Rishi, "*Dekh, yeh teri film ki writer hai*. Look after her." He kept telling the family what to do.'

Relationships were very important to Raj Kapoor. He built up the R.K. team very carefully, and cultivated it assiduously like a precious private garden. He had that ability to reach out to people from all walks of life. He surfed different worlds, making them his own, even if they did not quite intersect. Raj Kapoor had mastered the old Nehruvian pan-Indian trick: he'd speak a few words in Marathi to a Maharashtrian, of Bangla to a Bengali, or toss around the little Tamil he knew in Gita Bhawan, the south Indian restaurant where he often went for his afternoon tiffin of dosas and idlis.

Raj Kapoor had a romanticized notion of the common man, and boasted to friends of his ability to empathize with him. 'He used to say how proud he was of not being an intellectual, pointing to his brain as he said so,' says Rashmi Shankar. 'He felt he was able to identify with the common man because of this.

Thank God, I am not one of those, he used to say.' To drive home the point he always used his white Ambassador while his wife Krishna travelled in their white Mercedes.

There was restlessness in his genes, and a need to reach out to strangers. 'Inside in him he was unhappy. Deep inside there was some deep kind of wanting, a *talaash* (a search),' says Ali Raza. His family and friends were not enough for the affection he sought or wanted to give. His coterie—his creative team, close friends and passing fancies—were not able to satisfy his need for emotional intimacy. Nor his insatiable hunger for affection and adoration. Curiously, many of his really close friends were seldom the same age as him: they were either much younger or much older than him.

Raj Kapoor reached out to strangers, drawing them closer to him than his family, at least for certain phases in his life. V. Shankar was almost as old his father. Vinny Ahuja was fourteen years younger than him. Actor Rajendra Kumar and singer Mukesh (whom he once famously described as his 'soul') were, according to Randhir Kapoor, his closest friends. His choice of friends was nothing if not eclectic: businessmen, bureaucrats, even his doctors and dentists were regulars at his court, both in Bombay and at his farm in Loni. There were, of course, his workmates who formed a sort of inner circle—the intimacy of collective creation, when long hours of work dissolved into personal revelations. The outer ripples included an assortment of women of diverse ages, most of whom were his confidantes, or he theirs. Simi Garewal, Bina Ramani, Madhu Malik, Devyani Chaubal and many such other friends were decades younger than him.

One of his more intense friendships was with Dilip Kumar. The families knew each other and the two often spoke in Peshawari Punjabi. Both were in Bombay Talkies. And both shared a love of food. Though while Kumar would eat, as Ali Raza puts it colourfully, 'charbi, champe, all the roadside rubbish, Raj only wanted good food'. Their other shared love was cricket and football: they often played charity matches and Raj Kapoor even contemplated buying the Western India Football Association.[25] They were like blood brothers when it came down to the crunch.

When Krishna Kapoor moved out of the Chembur home after the *Sangam* premiere, Kumar offered to go to Natraj Hotel and bring her back to the Kapoor home. Recalling this, Ali Raza says: 'Raj told him, "Who are you to come between me and my wife?" The two men had a love-hate relationship. He was family—in their fights, loves, struggles, everything, he was there.' Nevertheless, Kumar continued with his patch-up efforts, even visiting Krishna Kapoor after she had left her husband. After *Andaz*, the two actors never shared the screen, but at Kapoor's funeral the normally restrained Kumar wept inconsolably.

In photographs with both in the frame you can detect the easy, equal camaraderie. Yet if you look closer each appears to have a watchful eye on the other. The two realized that they weighed in as equals in the arena of showbiz: two kings of the celluloid jungle. Dilip Kumar once compared his fellow Pathan to an 'automatic rifle'. 'I am a muzzle load. An old gun in which you first load the gunpowder and then the *goli* and then you fire.' Apparently, Kapoor never rehearsed his scenes in *Andaz*. He was shooting *Barsaat* at night and acting in Mehboob Khan's film during the day, and needed to catch up on his sleep. Recounting this little duel between the two actors, Shashi says: 'While Rajji slept, Dilip Sahib rehearsed. Rajji used to tell people to wake him up when the shot was ready. And then he would just steal the scene away from the other.'

The strong streak of competitiveness in Raj Kapoor was responsible for the rather volatile nature of their relationship. The fact that the two had a lot in common made it more of an intimate rivalry. After all, both Nargis and Vyjanthimala had been Kumar's heroines before Kapoor prised them away from him.

Impulsive about the people he chose to draw into his charmed circle, he also became very possessive about them, at times even childishly so. Recounts Simi Garewal: 'Raj Kapoor was very possessive. When Satyajit Ray chose me for his film (*Aranyer Din Ratri*), Rajji would not allow me to leave: he would say that there was something or the other that had to be done. Once when I was shooting in a forest in a remote location, another world really, his distributors turned up. They told me that Rajji was ing me to Delhi. Manik da [Satyajit Ray] observed that this happened every time I shot with him. So, I said, "What do I do?" He just said that he would take the shots in the next schedule. I rushed to Delhi with my make-up on. I had to be very dark for this role, and my scalp was all black. And that's the way I rushed to Delhi.'

Raj Kapoor was also moody, especially when his dark moods descended. During those spells he wanted to be left alone, more so as he grew older. He wanted solitude, preferring the company of his hens and dogs in Ram Bagh, or a few friends. Recalls Vinny Ahuja: 'Sometimes he would tire of people. One day when he was sick—he had reacted to some medicine and had convulsions—I drove him to Breach Candy. He kept his hand on my shoulder all the way. It was difficult to drive. In the hospital he removed his clothes and asked me to tell visitors that nobody could come in. "Tell them, *nanga baitha hoon* (I am naked)."'

Raj Kapoor's relationship with animals was rather special. His two dogs Bonzo and Toddy (a Doberman and a Labrador) used to sleep beside him on his mattress. He also had a Cocker Spaniel who, according to Ahuja, was his guardian angel. 'The dog used to know when the time had come for him to leave. He'd sit down silently when Rajji was drunk. When he felt it was time for Rajji to stop drinking he'd pull his lungi. Rajji would hit the dog, but the dog would shake its tail and escort him back home from our house.'

Raj Bagh had a small house for his hens and kennels for his dogs. Raj Kapoor loved his hens as much as he did his dogs: he fed the feathered creatures every morning when he was at his farm. The hens obviously reciprocated the love. After Raj Kapoor died, one of the hens made her way to his room and laid eggs on his bed. The bond with his animals was very special. His favourite hen sat outside his bedroom door for days after he died. Adds Ahuja: 'She waited until the door was opened for cleaning and then flew inside and sat on his pillow. The *murgi* died soon after Rajji died.'

The reigning trinity of the golden age of Hindi cinema, the fifties, comprised Dev Anand, Dilip Kumar and Raj Kapoor. Dev Anand, with his flouncy puff and mannerisms, was the early chocolate boy romantic hero. Rajesh Khanna and a thousand other head-shaking heroes went down that breezy path. Dilip Kumar with his brooding looks was the great thespian—the tragic hero. Sanjeev Kumar and Amitabh Bachchan belong to the same school of acting. Romance was light and frothy for the Anand inheritors, and usually star-crossed for the Kumar aficionados. Kumar's *Devdas* became a template for these loser–lovers. Sublime in both love and sacrifice, they seldom got the girl.

While Dev Anand and Dilip Kumar brought romance to the screen, neither could do so with passion. Certainly not in its least refined form—lust. Raj Kapoor filled that gap. He was, in a sense, sui generis. Puppy love was not what early Raj Kapoor's screen personas were about. Here was raw passion on screen at last. It was about 'possession' as well, according to film director Subhash Ghai. 'This poverty-bitten roadside character could say this is my woman because I love her.'

Meanwhile, Nargis sent the suppressed woman into temporary hiding: she did not hide her love. Coyness gave way to passion and sprightly aggression. That slap across Nargis's face in *Awara* still resounds in cinematic memory. The intensity of the passion between Raj Kapoor and Nargis sears through the screen in *Barsaat*, even when one watches the film today. In *Jis Desh Mein Ganga Behti Hai* and *Sangam*, the camera knowingly caresses a woman's body, not that of a child-woman or an overgrown filly.

Raj Kapoor was the master of the sensual, teetering in his post-Nargis films into voyeurism, witnessed in almost full flower in *Satyam Shivam Sundaram* and *Ram Teri Ganga Maili*. The departure of his muse—*spruhti* as he called it—coincided with the time his erotically charged romantic stories acquired their prurient tint, when sex overtook sensuality. Somewhere along the line, the poetic choreographer of romance became a Peeping Tom of sorts. *Jis Desh Mein Ganga Behti Hai* and *Sangam* mark the beginning of the change.

Vyjanthimala had never danced the way she did for the 'Kya

karoon Ram mujhe budha mil gaya' cabaret spoof sequence in a Paris hotel suite in *Sangam*. Fantasy in this film is very nitty-gritty, not mere daydreaming. It's almost the celluloid equivalent of John Donne's immortal line, 'For God's sake, hold your tongue and let me love'. Raj Kapoor loosens his tie after the song, and without speaking a word, throws her across his shoulder, caveman like, and carries her into the bedroom. The door shuts and the camera rests on a bewildered-looking ceramic gnome. The sexual chemistry between the two screen lovers is palpable. Raj is no longer the mama's boy, like most Indian film heroes; family barely intrudes in this 'adult' film.

There's a sexual charge to *Sangam*, Kapoor's first foray in colour. Underneath the humour of the Paris number he is talking about sexual chemistry going cold between husband and wife. Vyjanthimala uses the wiles of a courtesan to arouse him. Earlier in the film she swims in the river in her bright-red swimsuit, flashing broad expanses of flesh, while 'Raj' plays the bagpipes and sings the famous 'Sangam hoga ke nahin' song. This Sangam does not refer to the coming together of two rivers but of a man and a woman.

While discussing the sexual connotations in this film, historian Rashmi Doraiswami writes: 'The bagpipe is the shifting signifier par excellence: Kapoor has earlier referred to it as the only other beautiful thing in the world apart from a woman's body. His hand gestures when he refers to it in the scene make it indistinguishable whether it is a woman's body he is referring to or the bagpipe. In the bedroom scene, Vyjanthimala's blowing on the bagpipe, given the sexual references of this section of the sequence, can be seen as having phallic connotations.'[26]

Raj Kapoor once told Dev Anand that since all that the audience wanted was sex that's what they were going to get. Much before the Indian Miss Universes began to surface in swimsuits, Raj Kapoor was putting his actresses in them—as early as the fifties with Nargis in *Awara*, with Vyjanthimala in *Sangam* (1964) and later with Dimple Kapadia in a bikini in *Bobby* in 1973. (Sharmila Tagore of course scooped them all in her pert two-piece in Shakti Samanta's *An Evening in Paris* [1967]; Shammi Kapoor is her leading man in the film.)

However, the real disillusionment set in after the inordinately expensive *Mera Naam Joker* flopped at the box office in 1970. There was a sea-change in both the man and the film-maker after this film. This was Raj Kapoor's most personal film. A thinly disguised autobiography, he poured his soul and his philosophical musings about life and love into the film. Hence, the failure of what he considered his magnum opus affected him profoundly. He felt the rejection at all levels. In an interview with *India Today* about *Satyam Shivam Sundaram* he is quoted as having said: 'In the end they will go and see it for her tits.' The photograph that he sent the magazine to be used on the cover for a story on him was Zeenat Aman with her breasts showing.

Passion can turn dark too in Raj Kapoor's films. In *Awara* he drags Nargis in a swimsuit—a first of sorts in post-independence cinema—and then slaps her. 'That was the real Raj Kapoor in his twenties—the man and not just the director. I had never seen anything like this before in Indian cinema. You never show a hero beating the heroine,' says P.K. Nair. Raj Kapoor in *Awara* recalls Clark Gable's Rhett Butler in *Gone with the Wind*. The two men are charming. Yet there is a dark lining to the charm—a sense of menace lurking beneath it, laced as it is with potent sexuality. The atavistic caveman instincts surface. Prayag Raaj reads the slap as 'an outburst of frustration'. According to him it is wounded pride. 'It is a class complex in *Awara*. When Nargis calls him a junglee, *ubal ke chaante par athe hain*. It is like when you call a *tawaif* a *tawaif* and she is only doing it because of circumstances, she will slap you.'

Women obsessed Raj Kapoor. It was an early malady. Kapoor has famously stated that his preoccupation with women started when he was a child. The world of show business was his nursery. Innocence took some early knocks, both backstage and in the film studios. In Ritu's book, Raj Kapoor talks of feeling excited when actresses used to cuddle him whenever he visited the stage. Precocious as he was, he learnt to conceal his emotions.

Raj Kapoor may not have read Freud. But he certainly applied some of the Viennese psychoanalyst's theories to himself. He even discussed his childhood Oedipal stirrings with a frankness that was indeed rare then, and is in fact even today. Describing himself as a 'worshipper of nudity' Raj Kapoor said that his initial sexual stirrings could be traced to his mother. She had been beautiful as a young lady, with the sharp features of a Pathan woman. Mother and son often bathed together. Kapoor traces his enduring obsession with women and female nudity to those early bathing sessions, responsible perhaps for his wet see-through saris decades later. According to Raj Kapoor, the Urdu phrase *muqaddas uriyan* (sacred nudity) describes this perfectly. He was always upfront about his own sexuality, unlike others in the industry whose public postures of prudery were at complete variance from what they did behind closed doors.

Nothing was lost on this sexually precocious child. Another childhood experience that marked him took place in a village near Lyallpur. Village women used to roast chanas on the fire. One afternoon, when Raj went to buy some, all he had on was a shirt. Amused by the sight of the little boy naked beneath his shirt, the woman behind the earthen oven told him that he need not pay her for the chanas if he raised his shirt and made a 'bowl' to receive the roasted gram. The innocent Raj did so, and she laughed her head off looking at him. The incident, however, left a lasting impression on his mind. 'Years later when the memory came back to me and I understood the trick she must have been up to, it disturbed me a great deal. For some time in my life, chana itself became almost a sexual object.'[27]

Women, increasingly, became sexual objects in his films. *Jaagte Raho* was the turning point. It was Nargis's last film with him. And it marked the end of an era of the idealist phase of the director's engagement with the emerging new India. The Pandora's box of Raj Kapoor's fantasies was now wide open. Erotic images and sensations surfaced, freeing themselves from the censoring anchors holding them down. Most ended up in his films. The memory of the alabaster skin of his petite mother, with her perfectly chiselled features and her bow-shaped mouth, was among his early erotic fantasies. Equally powerful were his mid-adolescent and adolescent fantasies.

Raj Kapoor was always in love. Crushes were as common as a cold for him. Raj's first real love was a young, rich and pretty Sardarni. They were both sixteen when they met. Diddo, as she was called, was a friend of his uncle Prannath Khanna's sister. The two used to meet at Marosa. He used to take the bus from Matunga to Churchgate and then make his way to Marosa, near Flora Fountain.

Metro cinema was another haunt of theirs, as it was for many romantic couples. According to Vishwa Mehra, 'They would always miss the beginning and end of the movie because they'd deliberately go into the cinema hall after the lights had been switched off when it was dark so that nobody could see them. And they would leave early, before the film ended and the lights came on.' Lands End on Malabar Hill was another favourite spot for the two: there were rocks to sit on, the sea lashing them gently. And most important of all, it gave them privacy. One day, however, this privacy was rudely interrupted, according to Mamaji: a corpse washed up beside them.

The first love had a sad ending: when her parents found out, Diddo was promptly married off to a suitably rich contractor in Bombay. But it wasn't forgotten. Raj Kapoor immortalized their romance in his film *Aag*. He gave it a happy ending of sorts in the film though, with actress Nigar Sultana playing his first and only real love. Raj remained good friends with his pretty Sardarni until he died. Decades later he invited her for a private screening of *Bobby*.

Diddo went to R.K. Films with friends and family. Kusum Chohan was amongst the privileged audience that day. 'There was just Raj Kapoor and another person from his studio. He was very warm, and kept swinging on his chair and getting nostalgic, with tears falling down his cheeks. We started watching the film, but then he stopped it before it ended. Should he have the young star-crossed lovers die, he asked us. After all, this was yet another take on *Romeo and Juliet*, and the point of the film according to him was to show the parents how wrong they had been. It was to teach them a lesson, he explained. I told him, with tears streaming down my cheeks, that it would make sense to have the two die but then I wouldn't be able to see the film. His distributors told him the same. It had to be a happy ending. The two lived.'

The next coup de foudre was Hemavati. 'Raj was in love with

a dancer, Hemavati, who eventually married Sapru,' says Zohra Segal. Papa Kapoor was not amused. Hemavati was part of a dance group from Hyderabad, which was assimilated into Prithvi Theatres after it came to Bombay. Raj, the general dogsbody at Prithvi Theatres, was put in charge of teaching the pretty young danseuse acting. She acted in *Deewar* with Raj, as well as in other plays. Interestingly, she left a year later when Raj got married, and switched to the world of cinema.

The woman in white is an enduring figure in the mythology that has wrapped itself around the persona of Raj Kapoor. There has been a lot of speculation about who the original woman in white was. All those women who came under his spell switched to white—it was a uniform of love and allegiance to the blue-eyed piper. The roll call is long: Nargis, who wore bright and filmy clothes before he came into her life; Lata Mangeshkar, his muse and fellow traveller on musical journeys; Simi Garewal, his *cheli* and friend; Devyani, the late gossip columnist and film journalist who didn't hide her infatuation with him. And above all his elegant wife Krishna, ever draped in her crisp white organzas. There must be many unknowns on the list, in whose private fantasies the great showman dwelled.

But the original lady whom Raj Kapoor has referred to in many conversations was a woman who came with her husband to visit his parents when he was a schoolboy in Calcutta. 'I remember to this day how the colour white came to be imprinted in my memory,' he once told Bunny Reuben. He overheard his mother telling the cook to buy chicken: there were people coming for lunch that day. Chicken was a magic word, and Raj decided to play hookey from school. Glib at lying, he told his father that his school was only half-day. 'Among the guests was a young woman. She was dressed in white. I looked at her, and then I could not look away from her. She seemed to me to be the most beautiful woman in the world...Of course I fell in love with her. Then it was time for them to go...I went into the garden in front of the house. I plucked some creamy white tuberoses and was still plucking them when the woman in white came down the steps. Stammering, my cheeks burning, I gave her the fragrant gift. She took the flowers from me, murmuring her pleasure. She walked through the garden and entered the road. "Turn around," I pleaded within my heart. "Just once, please look back."'

She didn't. However, that memory was indelibly imprinted and his famous love for white was born—including, equally famously, his love for white mogras and tuberoses. You wonder whether Raj Kapoor didn't invent this memory too. He certainly must have embellished it. Rashmi Shankar believes that the lady in white was Damayanti Sahni. Damoji, as she was called, was Balraj Sahni's first wife—she was an actress and was Prithviraj Kapoor's first choice to play Shakuntala, the title character of his first production for Prithvi Theatres. 'Raj Uncle was bowled over when Balraj Sahni walked in with his wife to visit his parents. Damoji was in all white. That left quite an impression on him. Later he told me that when he first saw Krishna Aunty she was playing a sitar and was dressed in white. That's what he remembers.'

Raj Kapoor's films are so thoroughly autobiographical that what he showed was what he was. His storyboard was often his own life. Which is why at times one wonders whether he went through certain experiences and motions of love—his mind ticking away, storing all his feelings and emotions—just so that he could transfer them to the screen. He often admitted that some incidents came back to his cinema at a subconscious level. Just like those chanas which finally found a place in *Bobby*. 'There's a scene in *Bobby* when the boy flashes a mirror into Bobby's face while she is sitting in the library. The girl comes out, first in rage, and then in playfulness. The boy says, "Let's have tea." Bobby says, "No, let's have chana." This was a private joke with himself.'[28]

Raj Kapoor let go of nothing. Films were his life, and he introduced all of his problems into them. Raj Kapoor's romantic obsessions appear, successively, in his nearly four-hour-long saga *Mera Naam Joker*. The chubby, gawky pre-pubescent schoolboy fell in love with his teacher at New Era Boys' School. And, there she is, on film, as the long-legged, lissome Simi Garewal. Stepping out of the sea like a dusky Botticellian Venus Primavera, pearly drops of water glistening on her body, she is an early version of the Raj Kapoor wet dream.

The teacher is, as he says, no fantasy of the scriptwriter. Raj Kapoor went into a big sulk when his father decided to move the family to Calcutta. He was so attached to this teacher that he told his parents he would rather stay in the school hostel than pack up and leave. During his last few days at the school, he would bring her flowers every day. The parting was tearful. His son Rishi Kapoor plays the infatuated young Raj—perhaps a first on the Indian screen of unequivocal pubertal longing. The strong autobiographical elements of the scene, especially its intrinsic honesty and endearing charm, recall some of the great cinematic moments of sexual awakening in young boys—one such is Federico Fellini's depiction of his childhood sexual stirrings in his film *Amarcord*.

Rishi Kapoor became Raj Kapoor's alter ego on screen, a surrogate Raj Kapoor. Crushed and disheartened after the dismal failure of *Mera Naam Joker* at the box office, Raj hung up his leading man boots in his own productions. He bestowed the R.K. banner's mantle of hero to his middle son. Rishi Kapoor says he was too young at the time to know anything about the women in his father's life but could tell then that he knew romance. 'In *Bobby* it was him. I was the body in which he put all kinds of colours.' If Raj Kapoor incarnated bits of himself in his films from *Aag*, through *Aah*, *Barsaat*, *Sangam* and *Mera Naam Joker*, his son (after his cameo in the last) would do so for him in *Bobby*. Since he died before he could make *Henna*, his eldest son Randhir made it for him, following his script and instructions.

Women and romantic love formed the core of Raj Kapoor's films. The notion of love at first sight was very strong in the Raj Kapoor school of romance. Talking about his philosophy of love, Raj Kapoor told me that his generation, and the ones before it, who had been fed on the Heer–Ranjha tradition of love at first sight and for ever, put love on a sacred pedestal. True love justified all acts in its pursuit. Suicide was thought of as a poetic expression of love, an accessory to romance.

Raj Kapoor rambled on in the interview. But when he came to the subject of the echoes of his life and romances in his films he became animated. Pointing at the photograph of Nargis on the wall, he began to tell me the oft-repeated story of how the iconic scene in *Bobby* in which Rishi Kapoor first sets eyes on Dimple Kapadia was exactly what had happened when he met Nargis. Nargis was a big star, and Raj Kapoor who was but a mere assistant to Kidar Sharma had yet to make his first film. He wanted to cast her in it. On an impulse he went to Chateau Marine where Nargis lived with her mother Jaddanbai. 'She had been frying pakodas when I rang the bell. And when she opened the door she accidentally brushed her hand, which had besan on it, over her hair.' The sight of the actress, slightly embarrassed and with the yellow streak of besan batter on one side of her forehead completely floored Raj Kapoor.

An unwritten canon in the Raj Kapoor credo was that only those films in which he was involved with his leading ladies would succeed at the box office. The failure of *Mera Naam Joker* not only broke his spirit, it convinced him of this, according to Madhu Malik. 'He really suffered when this film flopped. He believed it was a sterile movie because he was not involved with any of the actresses in it. The audience had rejected the film because the electricity, the chemistry was missing. Padmini was an old love. And there were Simi and the Russian ballerina, but he did not have a romantic entanglement with any of the actresses in the film.'

There was another lesson he learned from this failure. The circus fascinated him—it always had, as it did his father. But he realized that you could not make a film about it. In a way *Mera Naam Joker* closed the circle: it was the culmination of his clown persona which started with *Shree 420*. In fact, he sliced bits of *Shree 420* into *Mera Naam Joker*. The lesson was well learnt, almost too well. After a long interlude of introspection and self-pity at its dismal failure at the box office, the showman bounced back with *Bobby*. Raj Kapoor as a visibly ageing lover was out; young actors with obvious screen chemistry between them were in.

There are hidden love messages scattered in many of Raj Kapoor's films. The picturisation of the 'Pyar hua, ikrar hua' song in *Shree 420* is one of Indian cinema's most iconic love-affirming moments—Raj Kapoor and Nargis, one black umbrella and Bombay city lit up at night as the rain falls on the couple.

The two, perfectly in tune with one another, are oblivious to everything but themselves. The song is no less a love anthem than Gene Kelly's 'Singin' in the Rain' number. But there is much more going on here, subliminally. During this song sequence, three of Raj Kapoor's children (Randhir, Ritu and Rishi) walk across the rain-drenched road, in raincoats. Raj Kapoor had arranged for them to miss school for their run-on parts. He told a close friend that the three little Kapoors were meant to symbolize the children that he and Nargis could have had. Was this superimposition of fantasy on film wish-fulfilment? A compensation for all that could have been?

Strangely enough, Ritu's first memory of her father is taking part in this sequence. It is also one of the more important early memories of Raj Kapoor for Randhir. 'We got a holiday from Campion School. We came in raincoats. Raj Kapoor was very affectionate, and so was Nargis. And then he took us to Nanking for a Chinese lunch.' Ironically, while this was a happy moment for the children (they got to keep the raincoats and hats and miss school), for the screen couple this scene was an affirmation of their love, a shared moment of intimacy in a public space. Nargis told Simi Garewal that she wanted her own and not just screen children. 'I am tired of living in cardboard houses, pretending somebody else's child is my own child. I want my own home. I want to hold my own child in my arms.'

There are more coded exchanges between the couple in their films. Usually, it is Raj Kapoor sending her a message after she had left him. In many of his films he played *Amurskiebog*, a Russian tune which was first rendered as the 'Anniversary Song' by Al Jolson in 1946 ('Oh, how we danced the night we wed...'). Says a confidante: 'Raj Kapoor was reminding Nargis about their "marriage". They played this song the day they got married in a temple.[29] Strains of the song can be heard in "Jeena yahaan, marna yahaan", and in between the segments in *Mera Naam Joker*. It is there in *Bobby* and in *Kal Aaj Aur Kal* in the background. His movies are full of his clues—they are his life.'

Sometimes the coded messages in the films before Nargis's sudden departure are more like shared whisperings between the two. The more obvious ones are in *Aah*, one of his least known films. For example, while explaining the design of the ideal home he envisions for Neelu (Nargis) and him after they marry, Raju (Raj Kapoor) describes their future garden with lots of flowers. He lists champa, chameli, gulab, etc. And the last flower he mentions is nargis, at which point he makes a sweet gesture with his hand. In yet another instance, towards the end of this film, Neelu's arranged wedding is taking place in Rewa and Raju is shown rushing, almost dying, in the middle of the night to Rewa in a tonga. There is more than a touch of the tragic Devdas here. Raj Kapoor and Krishna got married in Rewa. Was he alluding to his own arranged marriage?

> '*He was like a lion in front of a prey. The way he looked at a woman, the way he looked into her eyes—no woman could turn away*. Jhuka nahin sakthi thi ankhen.'
>
> —B.J. Panchal

B.J. Panchal was Raj Kapoor's photographer for thirty-five years. Like the thespian's shadow, the man and his camera followed him everywhere, on the sets and off them. After hours, too. Panchal is old and ailing, but his memory is sharp as if it all happened just yesterday as he sifts through hundreds of photographs he has taken. There's Nargis, incandescent in Moscow, as she gazes into Kapoor's eyes at the time of the *Awara* blitzkrieg, oblivious to the world around her; Vyjanthimala mesmerized as her eyes lock into his during the *Sangam* days, like a snake in the snare of a snake charmer; Padmini, voluptuous; Lata Mangeshkar, all coy and coquettish in his cottage. There were others besides his famous women in white, the anonymous many who formed part of his eclectic court in his cottage. They came in all ages, sizes, backgrounds and dispositions. A few even started donning white, as if they were adherents of a cult of the guru of romantic love.

Those blue eyes got them all—for a while at least. The great showman was also the ultimate seducer. Raj Kapoor had outsize passions, and was not afraid to live them. His affairs were not in camera, unlike those of his contemporaries. He would often tell his close friends that he wanted his epitaph to read: 'Here lies a man who only wished to love.' And like many of the world's great seducers he worked his way through the defences of even the most reluctant with large measures of charm, genius and guile. He wooed his heroines with hyperbole and flowers. The women didn't stand a chance, according to screenwriter Ali Raza: '*Pagal kar deta tha*. (He would drive them mad.) He had the ability to make a woman feel that there was nobody like her.' Tanuja, who spent many of her growing up years near the Kapoor home in Chembur and was one of the privileged few with whom he shared not only his Black Label but also confidences, says, 'Women were crazy about him. He was a romantic. He brought romance into their lives, and women want romance. He was more about romance than about sex.'

Romantic love lies at the core of his films. The iconic R.K. logo says it all. A man, his hair a bit wild, his body taut, holds a violin in one hand, his arm stretched downwards in line with his body. In his other arm he holds a woman arched backwards in a pose of sublime submission. The logo recreates this epiphany of passion of the scene in *Barsaat* when Nargis, overwhelmed by the plaintively lovesick strains of Raj Kapoor's frenzied violin, rushes to him and falls into his arms. Over the years the original, more fleshed-out figures metamorphosed into these stick figures. Countless films copied that scene but failed to recreate its magic. The legendary chemistry between Raj Kapoor and Nargis made this the epitome of screen passion in Indian cinema history.

However, the truth of it may have been more complex. An element of mystery surrounds the R.K. logo. Was there a third, invisible presence there, between the lines, so to speak, of the logo? Raj Kapoor used to say that a white sari draped both Nargis and Lata Mangeshkar in his logo. Nargis was the physical manifestation of his object of love; Lata was its aural avatar. Nothing is very simple with this Kapoor: the truth is layered and open to interpretation. Some in the industry maintain that R.K. did not stand for Raj Kapoor alone. Perhaps it was a secret code between the two when both were at the height of their partnership—both romantic and professional.

R.K. Films was really a Nargis–Raj Kapoor banner. She was a partner, alongside him at the helm of R.K. Films for much of their golden years together. They were to make sixteen films together, beginning with *Aag* in 1948 and ending with *Jaagte Raho* in 1956. Six of these were made under the R.K. banner. Others in Raj Kapoor's coterie may even have resented her influence on him and on the management of the studio. Mamaji says that she was 'quite bossy', often ordering him about. P.K. Nair recounts an incident when he visited the studio during the filming of *Jaagte Raho*. 'When I was on the sets she was virtually directing a scene. There was a multi-storeyed building with a spiral staircase. Nargis was involved with the preparation of this scene. Raj Kapoor was running in one of the corridors, while she was giving instructions to the light people. She became important in the running of the studio.'

It is easy to forget that when Nargis and Raj Kapoor met, she was a star, a veteran of eight films by 1948. She was twenty and one of the stars from the camp of movie moghul Mehboob Khan. Raj was twenty-two, new to the world of celluloid, yet to direct his first film. When she agreed to act in his debut film, her mother Jaddanbai insisted Nargis be given top billing over Kamini Kaushal and Nigar Sultana. In deference to Prithviraj Kapoor, her mother agreed to a fee of just ten thousand rupees for her daughter. However, Nargis's brother Akhtar Hussein insisted it be raised to forty thousand. And it was.

Aag was the tentative beginning of a partnership and on-screen pairing that recalls the chemistry of Katherine Hepburn and Spencer Tracy, the resonance provided in the case of both by their long and intense affairs. Both actors were married and unwilling to leave their respective wives. But by the time *Barsaat* was being made, Nargis was totally committed to Raj Kapoor. Midway through, she pegged her future to his. She began to put her heart and soul—and money—into their films. Nargis even sold her gold bangles when the studio was short of funds. She acted in films of other producers (*Adalat*, *Ghar Sansar*, *Lajwanti*) to fill the depleting coffers of R.K. Films. One could say that she was the fledgling Mother India of R.K. Films.

Raj Kapoor has famously—and rather callously—said that his

wife was the mother of his children and Nargis the mother of his films. Ironically, she was also his 'wife' in the world of cinema, within the cordon sanitaire of the studio. Dara Singh tells an amusing story about his visit to R.K. Films. 'I went there with a pahalwan friend. It was summer. Nargis and Raj were sitting there. She was cutting mangoes. Rajji told her that there was no need to cut the mangoes, he is a pahalwan and will swallow it whole. *Chus lega*.' Nargis was also his Girl Friday (apparently, Nargis clipping Raj Kapoor's nails was not a rare sight). When his children came to the sets, she would spoil them with presents.

According to Shashi Kapoor, Nargis was the 'life of R.K. He made films after her. But there was a strange electricity in the air when she was there. She would visit the sets even when there was no scene and give him *aam ras*.' She veered between playing Mother Hubbard and Madame Boss in the studios and on location. When they were filming *Aah* on a lake near Nasik, Raj Kapoor invited his cousin Colonel Khanna to join them. Reminiscing about those days, the Colonel says: 'I went down to see him. We went hunting each evening. Nargis used to sit behind us in the jeep and keep giving us sandwiches and drinks. We would return at 3 or 4 at night, after which she would go round in that tented colony and ask people why the generators were still on. She was very conscious of wastage. She would tick them off in the jungle.'

The obvious chemistry between the two was more than skin deep. It was a meeting of minds as well. Nargis was Raj Kapoor's friend, muse, partner-at-work, actress, lover, love. She was involved in all aspects of Raj Kapoor's films, from the conception of an idea to its final execution. Well-read and familiar with international cinema, her inputs during the countless brainstorming sessions in the cottage were significant. Scores of ideas were tossed around, many of them hers. T.J.S. George quotes an interview she gave to *Filmfare* in 1954 in his book. 'Before I started working with Raj, my ideas were bottled up. There was no one with whom I could discuss them freely. With Raj it was different. We seem to have practically the same views and ideas, the same outlook on all subjects.' Interestingly, unlike the prevalent Bollywood etiquette, she doesn't refer to him as Rajji. Raj Kapoor had, in another context, said, 'She understands me and I understand her.'[30]

The two were a study in contrast. To begin with he was a married man—one of the tragic ironies of his life was that he met Nargis a mere four months after his marriage. Religion separated them: although Nargis's father Dr Mohan Babu was a Hindu, she was brought up a Muslim. She grew up a Bombay girl in their ground-floor flat in Chateau Marine on Marine Drive in Bombay; his life was more nomadic growing up. She was better educated—a voracious reader (John Galbraith, Kazantzakis, Maulana Azad), she graduated from Queen Mary's Convent, and had wanted to be a doctor like her father. Raj Kapoor never finished school and only read comics—or, as Bunny Reuben puts it, pornographic books from Olympia Press. He came from a close-knit, respected bourgeois family with tehsildars on the family tree—and an illustrious father who was a friend of Jawaharlal Nehru and who became a Rajya Sabha MP. Her mother was a singer, and her parents were not married. She was the caring sort, always keen to help the less fortunate. His world was his films. Her language would often be punctuated with colourful expletives. He was more circumspect, more indirect when he wanted to snub someone. Eric Segal couldn't have scripted this love story better; this was a post-independence Bombay love story.

Their first meeting is now a part of film lore immortalized in his film *Bobby*. He was looking for a studio for his debut film and because he heard that Nargis's mother was making *Romeo and Juliet* in Famous Studios he wanted to know how good the facilities there were. Nargis opened the door, and the rest is history. He introduced himself as the son of Prithviraj Kapoor—he had yet to make a film. Nargis, however, had seen him in *Deewar*. He left, flustered on finding her alone in the apartment, but as he said later, 'I did not leave her behind; her memory stayed with me.'[31] From Chateau Marine he rushed to Inder Raj Anand's house on Warden Road to ask him to write Nargis into the screenplay: she was an accidental addition.

Less known is Nargis's reaction to their first meeting, which George describes in his book on Nargis. 'Narrating the incident to her intimate friend Neelam—her real name was Lettitia—she put it in characteristic terms. "A fat blue-eyed pinkie had visited the house," she said. During the shooting of *Aag*, she tells Neelam, "Pinkie has started getting fresh with me." They were obviously terms of endearment indicating the recognition of someone out of the ordinary.'

Soon Nargis's family sensed the growing attraction between the two. Since *Aag* was shot on location in Khandala, a suspicious Jaddanbai went with them. She put her foot down when Raj Kapoor wanted to film *Barsaat* in Kashmir. There were many scenes between the weary mother and her wilful daughter. On her insistence it had to be closer to Bombay. Eventually Mahabaleshwar became Kashmir. The Kapoor household was also in turmoil, with Prithviraj Kapoor attempting to restrain his son. He soon gave up. However, by the time *Awara* was on the floor, Nargis's mother had died and there was no holding her back. She had lost her father two years earlier.

They soon became inseparable. Talking about their relationship, Neelam said: 'There was nothing that could stop them, nothing that could separate them. There was not a line between them, there were no dots. She was everything that life meant to him. The loves, the quarrels, the tears, the fights, the reconciliations, the oneness—they were like one soul.'[32]

The two became a working pair, travelling to festivals everywhere, including Moscow twice. Recalls Dev Anand: 'I got to know him rather well when we were in the USSR for six weeks. It was in 1954, the first delegation. We went to parties together, ate and drank together. He and Nargis were in the same room. Whenever we went anywhere, they would play "Awara hoon" on the piano. Sometimes he would drink too much and had to be pulled out of bed. We would all be waiting for him, and then Nargis would rush off and try to bring him down.'

The partnership went much further than their fabled screen chemistry. What was important was the way the two balanced each other on screen. They brought out the best in each other, one a catalyst for the other. Raj Kapoor's searing, at times maudlin, intensity was offset by Nargis's spontaneity; his clowning by her innate dignity. Nargis was her own person. A New Woman of her times, hers was the sensuality of the spirit. A misfit in the mytho-historical mould, Nargis refused to do the coy eyelash-fluttering, sari-pallav-twisting, twittering heroine number. Going against the grain, she wore her hair short, got into pants and swimsuits and refused to wear wigs.

Barsaat launched the greatest romantic pair of Indian cinema, pushing screen love in a new direction. Sacrifice was sidelined when Raj Kapoor stormed in with this ode to love. When I interviewed Manmohan Desai in the nineties, he said, 'Raj Kapoor revolutionized romance in Bollywood by bringing in possession and the physical.' The tragic lover became passé. The blue-eyed passionate lover even slaps the girl he loves in *Awara*. Guilt about passion and love was exiled, and love became the prerogative of the young. Kapoor and Nargis introduced an element of earthiness in their on-screen relationship.

The director–actor relationship was equally special. Nargis was never as luminous as when caressed by Raj Kapoor's camera. In *Aag* she does look awkward, as if she's just stepped out of a post-partition Manto play like *Khol Do* or *Kali Salwar* with her hair wild and unfocussed gaze. But from *Barsaat* onwards there is a subtle transmogrification of the screen Nargis: her face often looks as if it has been lit by the rays of the moon. The camera lingers on her profile, gingerly exploring the landscape of her face, incandescent with an inner glow. The inner beauty more than made up for her unconventional looks: until then Nargis was not considered a cinematic beauty in the league of Devika Rani or Madhubala. Kapoor's use of close-ups wrapped his star in an aura of mystery and glamour, akin in a way to the German-born director Steiglitz's framing shots and close-ups of Marlene Dietrich. His use of softly spoken dialogue lent a degree of intimacy seldom seen in Hindi movies. It was almost as if the audience was eavesdropping.

Eventually, however, the spell he cast on Nargis began to weaken. The magic began to gradually seep out of their relationship. Initially, when her brother Akhtar Hussein used to tell her that Raj Kapoor was sidelining her in his 'hero-oriented' films, she would snap at him. She refused to believe that Raj Kapoor was using her to become famous at her expense. Her brothers tried to convince her that he gave her the bit roles while he hogged the limelight. But when she went to Moscow, she began to believe that they may be right. Nobody really asked for her there. In fact, many thought that she was Mrs Raj Kapoor. It was bad enough with *Awara*, but when she went the next time for *Shree 420*, it was more of the same. Her ego was hurt. It was the beginning of the end. Here she was, the star whose name on the marquee brought in the crowds, being relegated to second fiddle. Unable to stomach the adulation—canonization almost—of Raj Kapoor, Nargis abruptly left Moscow.

Nargis was also beginning to get restless. She longed to become a wife and a mother—Mrs Raj Kapoor. So important was the sanctity of marriage for Nargis that she apparently even cornered Morarji Desai, then Home Minister in Bombay and asked him for his advice on how she could legally marry the actor. Kapoor was a Hindu and already married. Neelam later told Bunny Reuben that Raj Kapoor used to keep telling Nargis that he would marry her. Her patience ran out when she realized that Raj Kapoor would never leave his wife. Nor was she happy with her roles for the R.K. banner. Nargis wanted to play more spirited characters, more in tune with her confident personality. In fact, she was quite unhappy with her docile and 'unglamorous' role in *Shree 420*. Says Ali Raza: 'Nargis finally left because she had reached that *manzil* in life when emotions have to be left behind and instincts take over. The biological clock was ticking. She was desperate to settle down. The *Mother India* fire happened. But it would have finished anyway. Both had reached a stage of exhaustion in their relationship.'

The exit was quiet—and final. There were no retakes. Nargis did not even let on what she was going to do. Normally she used to ask Raj Kapoor before she accepted any film outside the R.K. banner. When she decided to work in *Mother India*, everybody knew it was over. The writing was on the wall. Just a few months earlier Nargis had refused to act as an old woman in a film Raj Kapoor was planning to make. Kapoor told journalist Suresh Kohli in an interview in 1986: 'She betrayed me again by refusing to play an old woman in the script I had bought from Rajinder Singh Bedi...She said it would spoil her image and the next day went and without telling me signed *Mother India*. What would you say to that, Sir?' She did not hesitate to 'age' all those decades for Mehboob Khan. Nor did she dither over her decision to marry Sunil Dutt in March 1958—after he famously rescued her from a fire while the film was being made. Their marriage was a secret until *Mother India* was released: since she played his mother in the film it would not have gone down well with the audience had it become known she was his wife in real life.

Raj Kapoor was devastated. Caught up in his work, he had no inkling that Nargis was going to leave him. He broke down and cried in front of his friends and colleagues when he found out that she had married Sunil Dutt. Raj Kapoor took it very badly: he would reportedly burn himself with cigarette butts to check if he was not dreaming, wondering how she could have done this to him. In his book, George writes: 'After Nargis left, the showman brooded, mourned his loss, and wept. Never the Devdas lover on-screen—he always got the girl there—he became one off it, for a while. The long drinking binge began. He began to weep like a child, using almost any shoulder to weep upon, repeating his sad tale like the ancient mariner. There was a deluge of tears in the cottage.'

Nor was the Kapoor home in Chembur spared the tears. Talking about this dark period in her husband's life, Krishna Kapoor told Reuben: 'Night after night he'd come home drunk...He'd come and collapse almost unconscious in the bathtub weeping bitterly. Night after night. Do you think I thought he was weeping for me? No. Of course not. I knew he was weeping for her.'[33] The weeping continued next door in the home of Vinny Ahuja. 'He used to come and sit here and cry inconsolably,' recalls Ahuja.

Says a friend whose shoulders got wet with all those tears: 'Nargis was his only true love. He never spoke against her publicly. He blamed her brothers for driving a wedge between them.' In private, he often babbled on about what he termed 'a great betrayal'. It wasn't an amicable goodbye. Raj Kapoor talked at length to Suresh Kohli about the 'betrayal'. It was in 1974, almost twenty years after Nargis's exit. Yet, the showman talked about her as if it had just happened the week before. Kohli, then chief editor with Sterling Publishers—they had just brought out a novelized version of *Bobby*—wanted Kapoor to write his autobiography. During the course of the conversation, Kohli mentioned that columnist Devyani Chaubal wanted to write his biography.

His remark was the trigger, and all the bitter memories began to pour out. 'Raj Kapoor said, "What does she know? She will write about whom I went to bed with. *Kya bataun*—what should I tell?" Then he took out a framed letter from a drawer. It was pieces of paper glued together, with two or four of the pieces missing. He had glued it together. Rajji said: "The world tells me I let Nargis down. It was she who betrayed me. *Sahib, isne woh kiya tha*. We were going out to a party. It was getting late. I went to her and she had a paper in her hand. I asked her what it was. She said *kuch nahin, kuch nahin*. And tore the letter and walked out. When we reached the car I said *rumaal bhool gaya hoon* and went back. The maid had already swept it away and put it into the waste paper basket. I picked up the waste paper basket and put it in my cupboard. The next day I joined the torn pieces together and saw that it was a proposal from a producer. She did not tell me about it. This was her first act of betrayal. I put this sequence just the way it happened in *Sangam*.' The proposal was from producer–director Shahid Latif, who was then married to the writer Ismat Chughtai, according to Kohli.

Raj Kapoor then went on to talk about subsequent 'betrayals' to Kohli: 'Raj Kapoor had acquired the rights to *Phagun*, written by Rajinder Singh Bedi. Nargis kept delaying the shooting. She kept telling him that she was not ready for the role. And then she went off quietly to Kolhapur where they were filming *Mother India*. Rajji told me: "When I confronted her, she said that she did not know what the story was. *Wah, picture ka naam* Mother India *hai*, and she did not know...Nargis's driver came from Kolhapur and said Baby has asked for her heel ke sandals. I said *le jaiye*. The driver came again, this time for the *baaja* (harmonica). I then realized that it was all over. Heels, baaja, and Sunil Dutt was six feet tall."'

If the two met accidentally, the encounters were largely silent. Nargis was neither sentimental nor bitter. Interestingly, she even confided in Kohli: 'She told me that when she went to a party she was shocked to see him and thought: *Maine is Ganapati se ishq kiya tha*? (How had I fallen in love with this portly man?)'

Their last film together—particularly the last shot of *Jaagte Raho*—turned out to be symbolic. Nargis plays a *jogan* (a role she was not keen to do) who finally quenches the Raj Kapoor character's thirst. Ironically, the memorable and haunting song 'Jago Mohan pyare' plays while she pours water into his mouth. Nargis had been his inspiration, a pillar of R.K. Films, his partner, but now here she was in the robes of a jogan, and not his leading lady. The film flopped at the box office: the audience missed the electricity between the screen pair.

That last scene was a real fade-out. Years later at her funeral, Raj Kapoor preferred to be the outsider, part of the general public. Rashmi Shankar recalls going to Nargis's funeral with Raj Kapoor. 'There was such a crowd. Everybody kept telling Rajji to move up front. But he stayed behind and told me to just sit down where we were. "*Yahin se toh guzrenge*," he said, and then added, "All my friends are going." He had his dark glasses on and remained one of the crowd.' It was almost like a melodramatic end when the lover returns just as his beloved is going around the nuptial fires.

The Nargis chapter closed like a heavy door, slamming shut the most intense and creative phase of his life. Nargis had been the centre that held his working life for a decade. Raj Kapoor now needed another heroine. Padmini, one of the famous Travancore sisters (the other two were Ragini and Lalitha), was a natural successor. When Raj Kapoor fell ill after Nargis's sudden departure from Moscow, Padmini happened to be there. The south Indian actress nursed him through his cold and high fever. Raj Kapoor even told a few close friends that he made *Jis Desh Mein Ganga Behti Hai* as a thank you gesture to Padmini. Or was it on the rebound from Nargis?

The voluptuous dancer–actress had hovered in his field of vision. When shooting for *Chori Chori* in Madras, Padmini had been on another set in the same studio. Nargis, it seems, did not miss a flicker of interest in the southern belle. Her biographer George quotes a 'piquant' remark Nargis made in 1957 to a writer–director about Raj Kapoor's fascination for the exotic. 'Madhu [Meena Kumari's screen name as a child actress was

Madhuri] could offer three lakhs for Amrohi's love. Raj does not need money. He wants variety and the south is providing that.' Observes Simi Garewal: 'He had a thing about south Indian women. We used to joke about it. Everybody knew about his weakness.'

Padmini and Raj Kapoor got to know each other well during the Youth Festival in Moscow, where she had gone with her sister Ragini. Padmini was acting in Abbas's *Pardesi*, a co-production with the Soviet Union. The two sisters were bowled over by the Russian adulation of the director and star of *Awara*. Kapoor was mobbed like a pop star: his clothes were torn, girls fainted at the sight of him and the Russians sang 'Awara hoon' and 'Ichak dana, bichak dana' whenever they saw him.

Padmini didn't stand a chance. She was a leading star in the south when Kapoor worked his charm and lured her to Bombay. The Madras film industry was up in arms when she headed north. She had been a popular star of Tamil, Malayalam and Telugu cinema, including several devotional films. Apparently, this screen goddess of the south received many threatening letters when she became a Raj Kapoor heroine. So did Kapoor, from producers and directors who feared that she would no longer be available for their films and worse that she was going to become the 'second Nargis'. Padmini's mother, Saraswathi amma, was equally apprehensive about the effect of Raj Kapoor's seductive charms on her daughter, just as Jaddanbai had been about Nargis. Hawk-like, she watched over her daughter, scolding her more than once for any perceived intimacy with Kapoor. She almost dragged Padmini from Jabalpur where the famous waterfall song sequence 'O basanti pawan pagal' (*Jis Desh Mein Ganga Behti Hai*) was being filmed. The clever showman was indefatigable: he turned on the charm for both mother and daughter. The R.K. machinery was set in motion, wooing the two ladies with whatever they wanted.

Padmini's induction as an R.K. heroine in *Jis Desh Mein...* in 1960 marks a significant departure in the films of Raj Kapoor. Until *Jaagte Raho* his films were not overtly sexual. In the post-Nargis era they are: the journey from sensuality to sexuality was a short sprint. Raj Kapoor's camera lingers longingly on Padmini's curves and cleavage, the way it used to explore Nargis's face. He may have put Nargis in a swimsuit, slapped her and pulled her unruly locks of hair, but she was never a sexual object in his films. In *Jis Desh Mein...* the camera has turned voyeuristic: it seldom strays from Padmini's ample body, especially her large breasts which the cut of her choli and the embroidery on it accentuated.

She is also the prototype Raj Kapoor draped-in-a-wet-sari heroine: the zenith (or nadir depending on the readers' point of view) was Mandakini in *Ram Teri Ganga Maili*. Padmini oozes sexuality in the song sequence when, suddenly aware of the fact that she is in love with the character played by Raj Kapoor, she jumps into a pond and swims, exposing large expanses of luminous flesh as she keeps getting in and out of the water like a drunken mermaid. Her face is a study in sensual arousal, her eyes full of dreamy longing. She wears a black sari wound tightly round her body. There is no blouse. And, of course, there's a waterfall. Padmini looks like a woman who has stepped out of a Raja Ravi Varma painting. The Travancore painter invented the wet-sari look in his canvases, which Kapoor later immortalized on celluloid.

Raj Kapoor makes her a sexual object in *Mera Naam Joker* as well. The screen sizzles in the song 'Ang laga ja balma' when she sheds her male disguise and puts on a sari for the first time in her life. A flesh-coloured sari is draped tightly over Padmini, once again without a blouse. When she goes looking for her hero–joker in the middle of the night she is drenched in torrential rain. Even today, with less scissor-happy censors and more body flaunting, most directors can't approximate the eroticism of Raj Kapoor's song sequences.

Obviously the on-screen chemistry between Raj Kapoor and Padmini worked. *Jis Desh Mein...* did very well at the box office. Its success restored Kapoor's self-confidence. After Nargis's sudden departure he had begun to believe that he was finished as a film-maker: *Jaagte Raho* had been a miserable flop. He was so unsure of himself that he put down Radhu Karmakar's name as the director of *Jis Desh Mein....* Kapoor may have had a sense of indebtedness to Padmini—this was the second time she had bailed him out. In fact, she also acted with him in *Aashiq*, a film produced by Bunny Reuben and V.K. Dubey. However, the film was never completed. Midway, Padmini got married to a doctor and moved to the United States.

Padmini was just an interlude: the actress came at the right time into Raj Kapoor's life but she did not fill the void of professional and emotional intimacy that Nargis had left behind. Theirs was a nice, somewhat placid relationship, without any emotional tempests. The two remained friends even after she married and went away.

It was time to look for another heroine. Buoyed by the success of *Jis Desh Mein...*, Raj Kapoor wanted to make *Sangam*. Once again he turned to the southern comfort zone, this time to Vyjanthimala. Raj Kapoor's wooing of the actress, who was rumoured to be tenuously connected to the Mysore royal family, is even more diabolically interesting that any courting he did on-screen. One of the obstacles was Dilip Kumar: Vyjanthimala had been romantically paired with him in many films—*Naya Daur*, *Madhumati*, *Paigham*, *Ganga Jamna* to name a few. The two Pathan actors might have been close as thieves, but they were ardent rivals as well. It had happened before. Nargis and Dilip Kumar had been a star pair in several films. Later, Kapoor had even prevented Nargis from acting with Dilip Kumar. And now it was happening with 'Paapa', Vyjanthimala's pet name.

Her grandmother–guardian Yedugiri had already snubbed Raj Kapoor when he had wanted the voluptuous, saucer-eyed south Indian belle to act in *Jis Desh Mein Ganga Behti Hai*. Vyjanthimala was no less indifferent when the two were acting together in *Nazrana*. Raj Kapoor, however, was wilful and seductive enough to know how to move the world in the direction he wanted. B.R. Chopra tells a wonderful story. 'Once Raj, I and Vyjanthi were on a plane from Delhi to Madras. I was doing *Naya Daur* at the time. I was sitting next to Vyjanthi. Raj came up to me and said: "Chopra, you come and sit in my seat and I will sit in yours." Vyjanthi was upset with me and said: "Why are you leaving me?" I told Raj: "You want to sit next to her? What about your wife?" He replied: "This is for the artist, not the woman." He sat next to her and before you knew it, he was reading her hand. "Let me see your future. There is some relationship and love here." He went on saying things like that. I asked him: "*Kya dekh raha hai*?" He answered: "Chopra, for once don't ask me." Later, when I went to Vyjanthi to fix some dates for another film I wanted her to act in, she said that she was making a film with Raj.' Raj Kapoor's way of showing gratitude to him was quite unique. According to Chopra: 'In *Sangam*, they used my portrait.'

Vyjanthimala tells the story differently. 'Nobody got me away from anyone. I had done *Nazrana* with him. He was planning to make *Sangam*. He saw me as Radha and asked me if I would be his Radha. I told him to talk to my grandmother. Then the telegram "*Bol Radha bol, Sangam hoga ke nahin*" arrived. I sent one back: "*Hoga, hoga, zaroor hoga.*"'

Once the tall and cherubic-faced actress with the trademark big mole on her cheek and the fluttering eyelashes stepped into the R.K. arena, things were never the same again. They did only two films together: *Nazrana* and *Sangam*. Yet, their relationship caused more havoc in the Kapoor household than did Raj Kapoor's decade-long partnership with Nargis. Krishna Kapoor actually left Raj Kapoor and checked into Natraj Hotel on Marine Drive, at the other end of town, with her children. A few weeks later she moved into an apartment in Chitrakoot on Carmichael Road. It was the closest the Kapoors ever came to a split.

This particular Sangam may not have been of the minds, as was probably the case with Nargis. But Vyjanthimala's initial disdainful response to the invader from the north soon melted to incredible warmth. Whether Raj Kapoor actually fell in love with his heroines or convinced himself that he was is open to question. Those who know him well believe that his films were his real obsession and love—like a man possessed he sacrificed anyone and anything that came in the way, including, perhaps, personal happiness. During the Vyjanthimala phase, Kapoor made himself fall in love with her, according to Simi Garewal, who made a documentary on his life for Channel Four and became a close friend of Raj's when he was shooting *Mera Naam Joker*. 'He wanted to create an aura of love. Over the phone he would suddenly become dramatic while talking to her. He loved south India, and he used Tamil words now and then. You could just see him getting into that state. He was in love with love. Even if he did not fall in love with his heroine, Raj Kapoor wanted to make himself believe he was: he felt it was important for the film.' Always the Svengali, Raj Kapoor was very particular about the looks of his heroines, at times putting the finishing touches of the make-up himself. In the case of Vyjanthimala, he ensured that she put less oil in her hair and look more like a north Indian actress.

The grand seduction continued through the long months of filming in Europe. Kapoor, the great romantic, pioneered the trend for location shooting abroad.[34] It was more than a Roman holiday: the honeymooning screen couple traipsed through Rome, Paris, Venice, Interlaken and Hamburg for over two months. Of course, she had come with baggage from Madras: there was her stern guardian grandmother, an aunt and her make-up man Sarosh Mody. But the bodyguards could not dissuade Kapoor. Just as he had disarmed Padmini's mother, he charmed the formidable Yedugiri, showering both her and his second southern belle with expensive presents and flowers. The unit worked during the day and went nightclubbing most evenings.

It wasn't too difficult for Cupid on this grand European tour, where India and its social and familial restraints seemed galaxies away. Vyjanthimala obviously managed to get under Raj Kapoor's skin, and he hers—as Panchal's photographs reveal. If he had mesmerized her, she had him in a trance as well. 'Vyjanthimala had a strong, sensual sense about her. She cast a magic spell around him,' says Bina Ramani. 'They did not snap out of their mutual enchantment when they returned to India.'

The famous 'Budha mil gaya' song sequence in a Paris hotel suite was actually filmed at R.K. Films after their return. It is obvious that she is performing her dance of seduction for Raj Kapoor and not for the camera or posterity. The come-hither posturings come with emotion. Raj Kapoor could get his heroines to do anything for his films. Today, Vyjanthimala can't quite understand how it all happened, why it happened. She says: 'Even when I see it today I can't believe how modern it is. How fusion came in a number like that—in the sixties. I had never danced like that. It was not a dance, there was no choreography. It came spontaneously. It was the first time I wore sleeveless. It was quite a daring number. All the movements were mine. He just told me to do a sort of Can-Can. I have to show that I can do the Can-Can better than the dancers in the nightclub where he is going, and I have to stop him. It was done in one take. I could never have done it a second time. I had to dance on such a small table. I had to wear heels; if I slipped I would have broken my ankle or teeth.'

The carefree mood of the idyllic European sojourn continued in Bombay. Film journalists began to write about the romance between the director and his actress. Grandma Yedugiri had been packed off to Madras, and Raj Kapoor and Vyjanthimala became less than discreet. This time Kapoor tested his wife's patience. In his biography, Bunny Reuben writes: 'I remember one picnic day four of us spent at Powai Lake—Raj and Vyjanthi, me and Devyani Chaubal. The two of us were included as eye-wash...when we returned to R.K. Films late in the evening we were sitting in the cottage...the door suddenly burst open and in walked Bhabhiji [Krishna Kapoor] with the children...They came and sat on the divan (Vyjanthi, Devyani and I were on the floor as usual, as also Raj himself) staring at us, saying nothing. The atmosphere was electric with tension. Hurriedly the three of us said our goodnights and came away from the cottage. There was a fierce quarrel that night.'

It didn't stop here. Raj Kapoor was so captivated by Vyjanthimala that he could not hide his involvement with her, even in the presence of his wife. The last straw was the Bangalore premiere of *Sangam*, where he took both Krishna Kapoor and Vyjanthimala. Describing what happened there, Panchal says: 'Vyjanthi is there, and so is Krishnaji. And they were playing a very romantic song on the piano, with Vyjanthi standing near him. Krishnaji says, "Panchal sahib *bus*, don't take any photographs." She was crying.' Mrs Kapoor returned to Bombay with Mukesh, and shortly afterwards moved to Natraj Hotel.

But no matter how besotted Raj Kapoor was, he was not about to break up his marriage. The Kapoors don't divorce: he didn't do it for Nargis, and it was unlikely that he was going to do so for Vyjanthimala. In fact, he made it clear to her that his home and his work belonged to two mutually exclusive worlds, just as his wife and his actresses did. 'He would often describe a scene of Chaplin's wife, Oona, and his mistress walking down these long stairs. He would say: "There is Oona on one side walking down the steps gracefully. His actress and mistress is walking down on the other side." And then he used to add: "The two never meet,"' recalls Vyjanthimala.

Vyjanthimala, like Nargis, wanted marriage. And remarks like these must have irked her. Just as his previous comments about his wife being the mother of his children and his actress the mother of his films hurt Nargis. Once again Raj Kapoor was oblivious to the romance blooming right under his nose, this time during the making of *Sangam*. Dr C.L. Bali, Raj Kapoor's personal doctor, accompanied the unit to Europe. In fact, Kapoor even asked the doctor to look after Vyjanthimala in Bombay when he went to London for three months of post-production work on the film.

When she quietly left and married the doctor, Kapoor was stunned. Years later, he told a friend that Vyjanthimala used to 'disappear into the bathroom for long spells and write letters to Dr Bali while she was very much with him in London'. This particular Sangam did not last long, though it took its emotional toll. Vyjanthimala turned her back on both Raj Kapoor and cinema. She returned to dance, started playing golf and eventually became a Rajya Sabha MP when Rajiv Gandhi was prime minister. Interestingly, both she and Nargis became members of the Rajya Sabha. Raj Kapoor never did, although his father was a distinguished Rajya Sabha member.

Raj Kapoor's trinity of women—Nargis, Padmini and Vyjanthimala—is widely known. Less so is his very special relationship with Lata Mangeshkar. He was entranced by her voice, and she by his *chikna* face and blue eyes as well as his formidable talent and powers of persuasion. She looks girlish and coy in photographs taken during the early days of their collaboration. There is an air of intimacy, of unspoken complicity in a photograph in which Raj Kapoor is grooming Lata. He is standing behind her as she sits. A cigarette dangling from his lips, he is dressing her hair, while she looks like a blushing teenager. Lata Mangeshkar became yet another woman in white: she only wore white saris, but with coloured borders. While Nargis was his screen beloved, Lata Mangeshkar was her voice and the aural incarnation of the poetic soul of Raj Kapoor in his early days.

Lata, like Nargis, was also his collaborator in creation—in this case his partner in creating some of his most memorable songs. Raj Kapoor pushed her to the limit, extracting her best, and she willingly gave it. The intensely heady experience of composing and recording the three songs for the nine-minute dream sequence of *Awara*—an R.K. epiphany—had meant so much to both. She sang through the night, beginning at nine at night, and continued until day broke, after which she, Raj Kapoor, Shankar and Jaikishen went to the Irani restaurant opposite Famous Studios in Tardeo. Years earlier, it had been the same sort of exhilaration after they finished recording the music for *Barsaat*, when they went out and sat on the pavement outside the studio, wondering if the film would make it. In his biography of Lata Mangeshkar, Raju Bharatan writes: 'Lata in white was for Raj a replica of Nargis in white; somewhere the voice and the vision merged.'

The singer with her tanpura spent many evenings in the cottage—sometimes singing through the night. Raj Kapoor was besotted with her voice. In the fifties, after *Barsaat* and *Awara*, he even planned to make a film with her as a heroine. He was going to call it *Soorat aur Seerat* (Face and Soul). It was a film Raj Kapoor and Lata Mangeshkar had developed together around the theme of the body versus the soul, beauty versus ugliness. Kapoor had first touched upon the theme of internal and external beauty in his film *Aag*. In that film the disfigured persona is a man, the hero, who is shunned by women after a fire destroys his face. There is a poignant line in the film in which the hero says that had he not been so handsome, with his golden hair and blue eyes, the subsequent rejection would not have hurt. Here was Lata with a magical voice and face slightly disfigured by the smallpox she suffered when she was five.

Raj Kapoor shelved the idea, returning to it years later when he made *Satyam Shivam Sundaram*, with Zeenat Aman playing the Lata role. In an interview years later he spoke about making a film about an ugly girl with a beautiful voice—like beauty and the beast. According to Bharatan, Lata Mangeshkar felt insulted by Raj Kapoor's choice of Zeenat Aman. The singer thought these were pointed references to her because 'her vocals had been the inspiration for the *Satyam Shivam Sundaram* theme, which was first written as *Gharonda* by Inder Raj Anand'. Unfortunately, while talking about casting Roopa (form), the role Zeenat plays, Raj Kapoor is supposed to have bragged: 'Give me a girl with big boobs and I will make her an actress.' Initially he had planned to cast Hema Malini in the lead role: he had acted with her in her debut film *Sapnon Ka Saudagar*. Lata was not averse to the Dream Girl playing Roopa. 'What she did not like was the body beautiful theme,' writes Bharatan. 'She expected the fusion of emotion and vision, and got fusion of vision and passion.' She was apparently aghast by the 'Zeenatising of *Satyam Shivam Sundaram*'.

People forget that Lata Mangeshkar was a sensual being, and not just a disembodied, ethereal voice. She had acted in plays and in movies long before she became a playback singer. In photographs, the young Lata may look tiny, shy and fragile. Yet, hope and ambition stare out of those limpid, sad eyes. She toughened up fast when the mantle of supporting her entire family fell on her with the demise of her father, the actor–singer Dinanath Mangeshkar.

Lata Mangeshkar may have had a weakness for Raj Kapoor. But she was the only woman to make him dance to her tunes. The two fell out over Lata's levy: two-and-a-half per cent royalty for her songs from the music companies in addition to the fee Kapoor paid her for each film. Film producers used to get ten per cent from the music companies. Raj Kapoor used to give half of what he got from HMV to his music director. He believed in a one-time payment to the singer. The problem with Lata arose when *Mera Naam Joker* was being made: the singer realized that she had not yet been paid for *Sangam*.

It was a draw; neither of them budged. Raj Kapoor's nightingale became a prima donna: she kept going abroad for tours. She returned to Raj Kapoor four years later when *Bobby* was being made. Both *Mera Naam Joker* and *Kal Aaj Aur Kal* were commercial flops. Raj Kapoor must have realized that Lata was his talisman: he needed her more than she needed him. Obviously, Raj Kapoor's infatuation with Vyjanthimala rankled—ironically enough, like Krishna Kapoor, Lata was wearier about Vyjanthimala than Nargis or Padmini. She also resented the danseuse–actress getting all the credit for the 'Man dole, mera tan dole' song sequence in the film *Nagin*.

Lata Mangeshkar did turn up for the recording session of the final song of *Satyam Shivam Sundaram*. Unit members recall seeing her sitting in her white Ambassador in the courtyard of Famous Studios—and Raj Kapoor waiting with folded hands by the door. She looked at him and drove off. 'The look on Lata's visage as she thus took off was one of score-settling triumph,' writes Bharatan. Was she still simmering over what she perceived as an insult: the choice of Zeenat Aman with a half-scarred face to play the character that is supposedly based upon her? Whatever, there was no final song in *Satyam Shivam Sundaram*.

Raj Kapoor and Lata had more in common than music. Both their fathers had been part of travelling theatre groups. Dinanath Mangeshkar's Marathi play *Raj* was staged at the Royal Opera House in Bombay. Prithvi Theatres staged their plays there when they were in the city. As children, and later as adolescents, both grew up in the world of greasepaint. She used to sneak off to see movies as a child, as did he. Her first acting role was when she was seven. Raj Kapoor wasn't much older. Both shared a passion for cricket. Theirs could have been a meeting of the minds as well.

They also had Dilip Kumar in common. The thespian was her rakhi brother, and in a sense a blood brother of Raj Kapoor. What is puzzling is the fact that Raj Kapoor did not make Lata Mangeshkar tie a rakhi on him, as he did with other actresses. Nadira and Nimmi were two of his sisters; in fact he asked Nimmi to become his '*muhn boli behan*' as soon he cast her in *Barsaat*. Were his feelings less than brotherly towards the singer whose voice enthralled him and gave him a high?

Raj Kapoor was the high priest of romantic love on the Indian screen. The R.K. logo certainly heralds the fact. Scores of directors—from Subhash Ghai to Karan Johar and Sooraj Barjatya—have been 'inspired' by him. But the big question that looms over his romantic interludes and intense love affairs is: Was he just taking notes? Was he in love with his actresses or was it just for the sake of his art? Perhaps Nargis was the only heroine he really loved; his colleagues and friends believe that his only real love was his films, and if there was anyone else he did love, it was Nargis.

Although Raj Kapoor was convinced that he had to be romantically involved with his heroine for a film to work, to do well at the box office, did he really fall in love with his leading ladies? Or did he make himself do so for the sake of verisimilitude, to make the screen sizzle with sexual chemistry? Cynics say that not only did the star pairing off-screen bring the vibes on to the screen, it also brought great publicity—that all-important buzz which is crucial for a film to be commercially successful.

One only has to look at the romantic scenes in the earlier films of this alchemist of screen love. Nargis, Padmini, Vyjanthimala—Raj Kapoor was able to make them glow with an inner light. His heroines don't look as if they are acting when they gaze into his eyes—something they did not quite achieve in their films with other directors. Whether it is *Barsaat*, *Jis Desh Mein...* or *Sangam*, the leading ladies don't appear to be performing for the camera but for the director. Their respective gazes directed at him are being returned, to which they respond: the astute Raj Kapoor is provoking them. For them, the audience at that particular moment does not exist.

But for the audience it was the shock of the real. Take *Barsaat*, Kapoor's first hit. It appealed to the youth because such raw passion had not really been seen on screen before. Referring to the film's treatment of passion, George writes: 'His fingers tenderly probing around her mouth, her head tilting in a gesture of total submission, his hands fondly rustling her hair, her eyes catching fire as she looked at him—this was intuitive romancing, honest and unpremeditated, and audiences accustomed to lovers running around trees were enthralled.'

Raj Kapoor's need for women went beyond romantic love or sex. He was a grabber, a collector of other people's experiences and emotions. 'He needed women to replenish his creative juices, to stoke his creative fires,' says Madhu Malik. She remembers him telling her that he was 'a professional emotionalist. He sought friendship with people who had what he called emotional depth. The only reason he got up in the morning was to look for things that he could put in his films.'

Kapoor fell in love with celluloid in his first film. From then on not only did he prise open other people's hearts and minds in search of fodder for his films, he was always 'on', collecting 'material' for his films—images, sensations, feelings, emotions, even unpleasant experiences. It isn't surprising that there was a thin line between the reality of his life and his films. Says Simi Garewal: 'He loved the emotion of going through a heartbreak, of acting out a scenario from a film.' It was all grist for his cinematic mill.

Raj Kapoor sought intimacy outside the pale of the family, whether it was with women or men—even casual acquaintances. His obsessive quest for creativity is perhaps one of the reasons he sought intimate friendships with women. The self-confessed 'professional emotionalist' reached out to women of all ages and backgrounds. Apparently, he felt the need to do so more intensely after his father died. On his way back from Haridwar after he had immersed his father's ashes in the Ganga, he stopped in Delhi. Madhu Malik met him at the time and recalls his being 'obsessed by the very idea of mortality. He seemed very bitter about man's inability to reproduce. He said that no matter what a man could do, no matter how many films he made or how creative he was, he could not do this.' Obviously, he envied women their ability to bear children, the ultimate act of creativity.

Raj Kapoor was also apprehensive about women, often playing a cat-and-mouse game with them. The director used to tell his friends that a man should never let a woman get power over him. Says Simi Garewal: 'In this baby style of talk he would say, "Never tell a woman too much, never show her you love her." He did not trust women too much. He always used to say that the women he cared for would always walk out of his life.'

Much mythology has been spun around Raj Kapoor's women in white. The man liked everything white—from gajras, mogras and tuberoses to white furniture and clothes. There is some irony in the colour: brides wear white in the Christian tradition, but according to Hindu custom it is the colour of mourning. Raj Kapoor may have loved more than one woman but in the end he reserved his fidelity for his films. His women inevitably ended up R.K. banner widows.

In spite of all his relationships, Raj Kapoor could not do without his wife. He may have strayed, but never irredeemably far. She was like, with due apology to the metaphysical poet John Donne, the fixed foot of the compass leg which stays in place while the other leans away from it, venturing outwards.

As he lay dying in 1987 in the ICU of the All India Institute of Medical Sciences, he apparently asked for the venti box, a device through which those who are unable to speak can express themselves. Tragically, he wasn't able to do so. Most people believe he wanted to say his last goodbye to his wife—perhaps to tell her finally what he had left unsaid all these years. Simi Garewal recounts a touching conversation she had with Mrs Kapoor. 'Krishnaji was an amazing wife and woman. Rajji was emotional with unspoken gratitude to her. When I asked him whether he had told her that he loved her, you know what he said: "I don't want to do that. She will get power over me. *Ek baat hai, jaane se pehle* I will tell her." He did ask for the venti box when he was dying. But they didn't give it to him. He wanted to tell her how much he loved her. Deep down in his core he was in love with Krishnaji.'

It had been an arranged marriage. The Kapoors believed in early marriages. A note of dejection is unmistakable in a remark Raj Kapoor once made about his marriage. 'Mine was the only arranged marriage among us brothers. Actually Krishna is my bua, my father's second cousin. One fine day my father said, "You are getting married", and I said, "Yes, Father." That was in 1946 when I was twenty-two years old.'[35] Were they too young to marry? Krishna Malhotra was only sixteen.

Raj Kapoor's first meeting with his wife was no less romantic than his first meeting with Nargis. He had gone to her home in Rewa (now in Madhya Pradesh) with his cousin, the actor Premnath, who was Krishna Kapoor's brother. Their father, Raisaheb Kartar Nath Malhotra, the inspector general of police of Rewa, was opposed to his son becoming a film actor. Raj Kapoor wanted to cast him in *Aag*. On entering the large bungalow he heard the distant strains of a sitar. He followed the sound to a room and saw Krishna playing the sitar. Next to her on the floor was a tabla. He quietly sat down next to her and began to play the tabla. They obviously struck the right note together.

Raj and Krishna Kapoor belong to the same clan. But the Kapoors and the Malhotras were worlds apart. Prithviraj Kapoor and his travelling theatre represented the heady Bohemia of an emergent India. The Malhotras were the establishment. Raj Kapoor was a wanderer at heart; Krishna Kapoor always hankered after a beautiful home and beautiful clothes. An elegant woman, she also had expensive tastes. The transition from the leisurely, ordered life of the burra sahibs to the uncertainties of show business must have been difficult for her. For years they led a very simple life. Her friends say that she would often weep and compare her home to those of the people they knew.

Krishna Kapoor became the perfect Kapoor bahu. Supportive to a fault, she even sold her jewellery to raise money to enable her husband to make *Barsaat*. Few people know how difficult the early days of this young couple were. Prithviraj Kapoor believed that once a man became a father, he should move out of his parental home. Randhir Kapoor was born in 1947, within a year of their marriage. The young family moved to Chembur when Raj Kapoor was still a struggling assistant with Kidar Sharma.

Life was hand to mouth in the early days of the young couple, according to Tanuja, who lived with her mother Shobhana Samarth and sister Nutan in the same neighbourhood. 'At one point they were dirt poor. They lived in a rented house after they moved out of the family home in Matunga to Chembur. Krishnaji did beautiful embroidery on saris. There was a group of women who supported each other. She must have used this to support the family. The recognition only came with *Barsaat*.' In fact, as Vinny Ahuja says, Raj Kapoor bought the R.K. house after the success of *Bobby*. 'He owned no property before that. It had no meaning for him unless it involved work.'

Meanwhile, Krishna Kapoor was the keeper of the house. Raj Kapoor has often said that she was his pillar of strength. He once told Tanuja that he didn't know what he would do without her. 'Krishnaji's house ran on oiled wheels,' says Tanuja. 'The train would go off the *patri* without her. She was the foundation on which he built everything.' She kept the home front going, despite Raj Kapoor's emotional and financial fluctuations. When any film flopped—and some did—he took it very badly. There was a lot of turmoil and upheaval in the early years of their marriage as well.

For Rishi Kapoor, his second son, his mother is the 'anchor for the family'. She had to be both mother and father for them. 'I was close to my mother. Krishna Kapoor was the woman behind my father. She took all his nonsense. She is shy and bore it all because of the children. We were her priority: she did not want us to be teased in school. She did not want us to get a complex. She kept us away from the arc lights. We were not spoiled. Raj Kapoor's children were not academically the best. But our mother sent us to the best schools. We went all the way from Chembur to town for our education.'

She was also the show woman behind the great showman. Raj Kapoor's legendary hospitality would not have been possible without her. Rishi Kapoor regrets the fact that his mother didn't get enough credit for what she did. 'My mother did all his parties. Actually, she was the show woman. She had no great education, but despite this she managed beautifully. Raj Kapoor had guests from overseas, many of them celebrities. Krishna Kapoor is the real woman in white: she epitomized the woman, the psychological force. My mother had to be strong to take his life.'

Behind the façade of the rambling Devnar Cottage, Krishna Kapoor led a fairly lonely life, shedding quiet tears. The romantic that he was, Raj Kapoor believed in love at first sight. Or at least convinced himself that he did—whether it was the first time he set eyes on his wife or the first look exchanged between his screen lovers. In most of his films the camera turns away after the nuptials—at any rate it never lingers on after the honeymoon. On-screen obsession never loses its intensity because time stops still, with passion frozen at high pitch. In real life, however, a marriage keeps rolling, and 'love' becomes a secondary obsession. So, Raj Kapoor sought it elsewhere—in his heroines, but above all in his cinema.

At times he could be quite callous. When asked at a party in Delhi how he managed to gather so many beautiful women around him, he is supposed to have said within earshot of his wife that he had a wonderful wife and beautiful children, but that is not what he needed. The amazing thing was that he appeared to be addressing her while he was talking to the others.

Explains a close friend of both Raj Kapoor and his wife: 'Krishna had the slot of the mother of his children. There was no room for romance—Nargis filled that. She started life like that. She would lie on her bed, put on the radio, and the song "Aa ja re mera dil pukare" would come. And then she'd say: "I am the one the song should be for. I lie in bed and wonder if he will come home tonight." He would come once in a while.' Raj Kapoor's bedroom was on the ground floor; his wife's on the first.

Most people in the industry believe that Krishna Kapoor eventually resigned herself to her husband's relationship with Nargis: the couple had acquired an iconic status as a pair. They were almost like ambassadors of India. Raj Kapoor and Nargis travelled extensively overseas with film delegations. Photographs show them in the company of prime ministers and international dignitaries, and with Hollywood royalty. Moreover, Nargis was sensitive to Krishna Kapoor's feelings. In his biography, George quotes Neelam, Nargis's close friend: 'Nargis never spoke ill of Krishnaji, nor did she attempt to deprive her of her place unlike those who came later into his life. During a pooja at the studio she would go to the back and stand with the workers. Krishnaji wished her, talked to her, kept a brave front.'

Perhaps, the two women understood each other. Both kept their poise and distance. And finally, they made their peace with one another. During a party, Nargis went up to Krishna Kapoor and apologized for whatever pain she may have caused her. In his book, Bunny Reuben gives Krishnaji's account of the incident to him. 'She came out with it all, saying how much she regretted all that happened and how sorry she now felt for all the pain and humiliation I had been subjected to because of her. I interrupted her and said, "Please do not speak of it any more. It is all over and you don't have to feel sorry because if it hadn't been you, it would have been someone else."'

When Nargis married Sunil Dutt, Krishna Kapoor hoped that she would finally have her husband to herself. But it was not too long before Raj Kapoor began his southern excursions. Says a friend of Krishna Kapoor: 'Before she could take a breath, he was doing *Sangam*, and Vyjanthimala had started wearing white. Shammi Kapoor alerted her—watch out, she is wearing white. She counted on Shammi, he was like a brother to her.'

The Vyjanthimala chapter was perhaps the most painful for her, according to Raj Kapoor's friends and people in the film industry. Reuben mentions that reports about the budding romance between the director and his actress in Europe reached Krishna Kapoor in Bombay. And Mrs Kapoor was not amused. So, when Raj Kapoor returned to London for post-production work, he took his wife with him. But that didn't help. Asked by a close friend in London how she could bear it, Krishna Kapoor replied: 'I carry a heavy rock and hold it to my heart—that is the only way I can survive.'

But at times even her famed patience ran out. While Krishna Kapoor's moving to Carmichael Road (after the Bangalore premiere of *Sangam*) is well known, few people know that she left her Chembur home several times. Once, she left Raj Kapoor and went to her family in Jabalpur. At other times she moved into a friend's house. She, too, like her husband would cry on the shoulders of friends. But she never allowed any cracks to surface in her façade of cool composure. She remained, as she still remains, elegant in her white organdy saris, her carefully coiffed hair and pearl strings.

Why did she always come back? Perhaps she knew her husband's complete dependence on her. It was almost childlike.

Says a friend of many years: 'He would search for her fragrance among her things when she went away to Jabalpur. He was a coward. I have seen the letters from him.' Simi Garewal also saw some of these epistles of love from Raj Kapoor to his wife. 'When I was making the documentary I saw a box of letters—it was quite a revelation. He was in the USSR with Nargis when he wrote them. Love poured out in these letters.'

Obviously, Raj Kapoor was a complex man. And in the end, like the shorter compass leg, he always came back to the fixed centre in his life. Tanuja recounts an incident when she was shooting the film *Bhoot Bangla* in R.K. Films. 'It was the 7 p.m. to 2 a.m. shift. At about 12.30 he was pissed—well not drunk, he was never drunk. And suddenly he said: "See, see Tanu, she has come back." She was wearing a beautiful powder pink salwar kameez. He had Satyanarayan pooja done the next day and declared a holiday for R.K.'

Ironically, it was the taxman who reunited them. There was a tax raid after *Sangam*. Raj Kapoor had no idea where his papers were. But his wife did. Recalls Ritu: 'Papa was absent a lot. My mother had moved out. Funnily enough, the income tax guys brought them back together. They wanted to raid my father, and he knew nothing about his accounts. So, my mother was brought in. That's how they got back together. Some of the women would pinch my mother and say how lucky she was to be married to Raj Kapoor. Little did they know what she was suffering.'

Krishna Kapoor returned to help him out, and stayed—pretty much a safety net for her husband for the rest of his life. Meanwhile, she carved out her own life: playing cards with a group of close friends who live in Bandra. Nor did she always accompany her husband on his long sojourns to his 100-acre farm, preferring to stay on with her band of friends and her family. She was and remains a matriarch for her immediate family, and a bulwark of support for the family at large. Meanwhile, the film industry divided itself into two camps: those aligned with Raj Kapoor and those with her. The sympathy was, overwhelmingly, for her. Not only was her public relations impeccable, she always maintained her dignity.

It seems that behind the public face of the imperturbable, rather serious-looking Mrs Kapoor, there is a less serious, humorous individual: it's easy to forget that she is also the sister of comedian Rajendranath. Her grandson Ranbir, Rishi Kapoor's son, says that she has a 'great sense of humour. My grandmother says these really funny things with a poker straight face. She will be standing in line at some serious function seeing off guests and she'll say these funny things from the corner of her mouth. She loves to have fun too. She was reluctant to go to Disneyland. But once we got there she went on the maximum number of rides. She is really cool.'

Today, Krishna Kapoor has survived Raj Kapoor, and cancer. And, it seems, is finally turning a page on the R.K. saga. She even tried to sell Devnar Cottage and move to Bandra—a world away from R.K. Films and her life with Raj Kapoor. The matriarch of the Kapoor clan—she keeps an eye on the extended family—took up the Raj Kapoor mantle and presided over Karisma Kapoor's wedding to Sanjay Kapur in 2003.

Whiskey was a passion, one that Raj Kapoor used to inflict extremes on himself, veering between the two poles of creation and destruction. He so wanted to play god, to make the world—certainly his world of cinema—move in the direction he wanted. And when it didn't, when a film flopped, the dark moods took over and a haze of alcohol descended.

The family often bore the brunt of those moods and the ensuing hours of unquiet desperation. There was, as well, an ineffable air of sadness about him, almost as if loneliness were eating into the core of his being and creating a vacuum. The long Nargis interlude isolated him further. The Kapoor clan stood by Krishna Kapoor, as did their children. She had their sympathy. The film industry was also, down to a man, with her. She was the epitome of the long-suffering wife.

According to Vinny Ahuja, Raj Kapoor sought to fill the vacuum by gathering people around him—ready listeners, companions in drink and a consistent court. If the Ahujas spent

Wednesday evenings in the Kapoor home, Raj Kapoor spent his Saturdays with them, that is, when he was not working. 'Rajji wanted people to listen to him. His young boys were busy and Chimpu was too young. He was fine as long as he had work to do. He always had financial problems running the studio, and felt the pinch.'

Family was certainly not enough to fill the void. He often made remarks like: 'To be honest with you, I don't think I have been a very good family man.' While he credits his wife for standing by him and describes her as the perfect wife, mother and daughter-in-law, the bluntness of his remarks to her could be devastating. He has admitted that even though they may not have got along very well, they have always been together.

Curiously, Raj Kapoor's children's memories of him while they were growing up are rather vague and hazy. Images of him from his films appear more alive in their recollections of him than do actual events and real conversations. Ritu Nanda has famously said that she got to know her father only after his death. Putting together a book on him was an act of reclamation of her father: 'I really got to know him when I started writing my book [*Raj Kapoor Speaks*] on him.'

As children they never really saw him. Recounts Ritu: 'We were asleep when he came back, and he was asleep when we went to school. He used to start work late.' Her first memory of him is her fleeting appearance in *Shree 420*, in the iconic umbrella sequence. She barely recalls any conversations. The communication was usually through notes. 'I used to write him little letters. I used to leave them on Papa's pillow, with some mogra that I plucked. He used to love fragrances. So, I would put some harsinghar on a leaf with the note and place them on his pillow.'

Raj Kapoor seldom replied, but whatever she asked for was granted. He was like the good tooth fairy for his children. Once Ritu asked for a piano, and voila, it came. As Ritu puts it expressively: 'Papa was always there for us. We would call him the ambulance. There when needed, in both happy times and sad times.' Their mother, however, looms much larger in their respective memories, and much more in focus.

Like many actors and inhabitants of the world of cinema, Raj Kapoor was more emotional about his children when he was away from them. Nor was he always demonstrative with his children. For example, when Ritu got married, he remained dry-eyed until the end, waiting for the moment he was alone to shed his solitary tears. Krishna Kapoor reveals this intimate moment in Ritu's book: 'When Ritu got married and she was departing for Delhi with her husband, everyone broke down. Only Rajji controlled himself. He waited for her to leave and then got into his car and drove to the studio. After an hour, when one of his personal attendants walked into his cottage, his master was still in tears...That was Raj Kapoor, the father. But he did not like others watching him.'

Often an absentee father, he appeared to be a little distant to his sons. There was a certain formality in his relationship with them, just as there had been in his relationship with his father. Moreover, Raj Kapoor was tough with his sons. Close friends believe that he was disappointed with them because his expectations of them were far greater than what they had of themselves. Rashmi Shankar was a frequent guest at the Kapoor table and remembers the lectures he used to give his sons: 'They were fascinating stories, morals really. He would talk about the way he had struggled.' Clearly, he wanted them to go through the grindmill, as both he and his father before him had done. *Kasar rahi, Kasar rahi* (still not perfect) was a constant refrain in his 'lectures' to his sons.

Rishi Kapoor was mortally afraid of him, rarely uttering a word in his presence and never contradicting him. He even fainted on the sets during *Prem Rog*: his father had been particularly demanding that day. It seems that he was angry with somebody else in the cast and took it out on his son. So much so that Krishna Kapoor had to be called to the studio to handle her husband.

When his children were young, he was hardly there. And when they were older, they did not have much time for him. Their interests were different. However, some of that 'distance' might just have been another role. Raj Kapoor was, according to his wife, deeply attached to his children but left the parenting to her—especially the disciplining bit. He would stay awake till his sons came back late from parties, never revealing this to them. Nor did he ever scold them, leaving Krishna to take on the unpleasant task.

If Raj Kapoor was demanding with his sons, he was indulgent with his two daughters. The younger, Rima, was more like him, in fact the only one who talked back to him. But he had a soft spot for Ritu, according to Lekh Tandon. 'If he parted with Nargis it was because of her. One day he got up late. I was staying with them that night—we had been discussing the storyline of a film. Rajji slept on the ground floor. He went upstairs. Ritu was in her mother's bedroom. She saw him all dressed up and said: "Hi handsome, where are you going?" When he told her that he was going to the races in Poona, she asked him, "What's wrong with my mother? Is she ugly, uneducated, uncouth? Why don't you take her?" He quietly went down, changed his clothes and went to sleep.'

Perhaps he was more comfortable in his role as grandfather. If he parted with his Black Label for his close friends, he parted with his precious desi eggs—from the chickens that used to roam freely on his Pune farm and at home in Chembur—for his favourite grandchildren. Ranbir Kapoor remembers his grandfather doling out chocolates and cooking omelettes made from his special desi eggs.

Raj Kapoor could not have scripted a better end for himself. It was a showman's death; the last encore. 2 May 1988 was to have been the apogee of his career. Years earlier, in 1972, he had gone to Delhi to receive the Dadasaheb Phalke Award posthumously given to his father. This day, it was his turn, and he sat in the front row of the Siri Fort Auditorium, in his favourite white suit, waiting to be called by President R. Venkataraman. His wife Krishna was by his side.

It had been a struggle for him to get there. Just hours earlier the country's premier showman had been reluctant to move out of his suite at the Maurya Sheraton for what would be his last performance. The time of the award ceremony was drawing near. His wife tried to hurry him up, telling him that they should get there before the president. She brought out three suits for him to choose from. Irritable, Raj Kapoor said: '*Mein logon ko pahnata hoon, banata hoon. Mein sundariyon ko banata hoon*, and she is telling me.' He then chose the white suit, the one most people admired.

Something was bothering him that fateful evening. The night before they left Bombay for Delhi he had a strange and surprisingly intimate conversation with his younger brother Shammi Kapoor. Recalling his last moments with his brother, Shammi says: 'We became close towards the end. I was shooting that side and dropped in at Chembur. Rajji was alone at home. Krishnaji had gone shopping. I wanted to go home after a bit but he said no, stay. I had a bath, a drink and rang up Neela and told her I would be late. I stayed on until ten that night. We talked about Papaji, about how he had got the same award posthumously. Rajji had gone to Delhi to pick it up then, and now he was going for his. We were comparing this moment in the history of our family, and how happy we were for our family to be up there. Then we talked about what had happened between us, why we were not close. Rajji talked about how his two brothers had gone. Bindi and Devi had been like his two hands, one his left, the other his right. He talked about being lonely, about losing his two friends. I told him that they were my brothers too, and would have been my friends as well. My brother had never realized that I also felt the loss, that I, too, was lonely. This conversation removed the chasm between us. We became pals. I was the only one he talked to before he left for Delhi and went into a coma.' Shammi Kapoor was never to see his brother again, alive—out of coma that is.

Raj Kapoor had to be given oxygen during the short ride from the Maurya Sheraton to Siri Fort. It was a particularly hot summer day, and he could barely walk from the entrance to his seat in front of the auditorium. Each step was a major effort, and, according to Vinny Ahuja, by the time he got there he was breathing very hard. 'Sitting next to him was his son-in-law Rajan Nanda. I kept saying that Rajji was not well at all, but I was told that I was overreacting. The ceremony began and they started calling people to the stage. I saw Rajji get up—he looked uncomfortable, and he called out my name. I took him outside. He said that he could not bear it inside the auditorium. The car was parked far away, and the oxygen was in it. The security men did not allow me to take the oxygen cylinder in; they thought it was a bomb. One sardar recognized me. The president's military secretary was there, and finally Rajji was given oxygen. I rushed to Anil Nanda. They put on the airconditioning and I took off his shoes and his tie so that he could breathe more easily. We removed his coat. Finally, H.P. Nanda came out and the organizers took us back inside for the award. Rajji went back in reluctantly.'

When it was time for him to go up to the stage, Raj Kapoor could not get up: he suddenly suffered an asthmatic attack. He turned to his wife and said: '*Krishnaji jao, aap jao*.' Seeing Raj Kapoor sway, lurch forward and almost collapse in his seat, President R. Venkataraman stepped down from the stage and started walking towards him. Watching his friend's discomfort, Ahuja rushed to him. 'I virtually lifted Rajji. He was like a deadweight. The president came down and Rajji collapsed in his chair.'

The nation watched the drama unfold on their television screens. This was reality television, before its time. Raj Kapoor, pale and gasping for breath, being propped up by his friends and wife; watching them, a perplexed president and a hushed audience. The ceremony suddenly came to a halt. Raj Kapoor was taken to the All India Institute of Medical Sciences in the president's ambulance. Krishnaji sat by him and began to pray. Vinny Ahuja remembers it being quite hot and suffocating inside the ambulance. 'There were no doctors and no oxygen in it. It was hot, and Rajji felt claustrophobic. He kept saying, "*Vinny, le ja bahar*." The VIP syndrome took over. It had become a jamboree. Rajji was quite upset. "*Bade log, yeh mujhe maar denge*," he said.'

Raj Kapoor went into a coma. A month later, at 9.30 p.m. on 2 June, he breathed his last.

Did Raj Kapoor have a premonition about his death? Certainly he could not have scripted anything as melodramatic as what transpired during the hours leading up to his departure to Delhi.

According to people close to him, he had become quite restless a few months earlier. He was reluctant to leave his home—despite the fact that Devnar Cottage was being renovated and all that paint would not have helped his asthma. Vinny Ahuja remembers him being quite apprehensive about going to Delhi to receive the award. 'He insisted I accompany him to Delhi. "*Mere bhai*, please come with me," he persisted when I told him that bhabhiji [Krishna Kapoor] could take care of him. We went to the airport together. There was no seat for me. He called for the duty officer and told him that he wanted to take his brother.

'He really did not want to go. We were the last people left after the rest of the passengers had boarded the plane. It was difficult for him to climb the aircraft—it was an Airbus 300. The duty officer brought a wheelchair but Rajji said, "*Chodo*" (Leave it) and almost ran up the stairs: when he gets angry he becomes a rebel. Unfortunately, he became quite breathless. I rushed to get an oxygen cylinder. Finally, after the airconditioning become more effective, he settled down. But as we were landing we could see a dust storm, and he exclaimed, "Oh meri Maa." It was poison for him since he was asthmatic. I insisted on a wheelchair, and we went to the hotel.

'There were four of us, including the servant, that evening for dinner. We wanted to eat at the Bukhara, but the general manager sent all the chefs up to the suite. Rajji ordered so much. That was strange: he never wasted any food. There was a lot of vegetarian food from Dum Pukht and Bukhara. He was turning vegetarian towards the end. He liked kichadi. When anybody asked him why he was eating ghas-phus, he'd say, "*Gandi machli satyanas kar degi whole pond ko.*" I had never seen him eating so much—there was nothing left, even for the servant. It was as if he was eating his last meal. I was scared.'

It was almost as if he wanted to script his death, making his last exit with his show boots on. Just as he would have had his film *Mera Naam Joker* end the way he had originally planned it to. His ageing and tragic clown persona was supposed to have died during his grand finale performance to which he had invited those he had loved in his past—many of whom had left him and gone on, making the clown persona even sadder and lonelier. The curtain came down on the dying clown in Chaplin's *Limelight* with the audience oblivious about what was happening onstage. The curtain in Kapoor's film comes down on his tragic-comic persona falling ill in the circus ring and being carried away. But then comes a legend, not quite in tune with the rest of the film, promising his return.

In life, there was no return. If Raj Kapoor's death was surreal, his funeral was even more so. Randhir remembers his father talking about his death: 'Whenever I die, take me to my studio—for it is possible that amidst the glitter of all the lights I may get up again and shout "Action, action!"' And that's how it happened. The Government of India, courtesy Prime Minister Rajiv Gandhi, flew his body to Bombay in a chartered plane. Raj Kapoor made his last journey from his home, down the winding road to R.K. and then to the Chembur crematorium. Some amongst the milling crowds may have heard him say 'Cut' in that soft-spoken voice of his. But this time, the sad ending remained: there would be no rewrites.

3

The Junglee and the Gent: Shammi Kapoor

The 'Yahoo!' man who first unleashed adolescent sexuality on the Indian screen and hurled that still-resounding lustful cry was a long time in the making. Born prematurely and worryingly thin on 21 October 1931 in Ajinkya Hospital on Charni Road in Bombay, Shamsher Raj Kapoor (Shammi is his pet name) didn't exactly get an auspicious start in life: his mother was pregnant with him when his two brothers Bindi and Devi died within a fortnight of each other.

Did this tragic double death in the family affect his mother's pregnancy? Was there some guilt on his mother's part? Losing two of her children in quick succession must have weighed on her conscience. The tragedy was no doubt like a shroud over the Kapoor household, a family secret both Raj and Shammi Kapoor had to bear like an albatross. Their mother was twenty-three at the time, and insisted they not tell anybody. 'My mother said we don't share our happiness with anyone, so why should we share our sorrow,' says Shammi Kapoor. 'She actually told me, "When we are in the bedroom we don't share our happiness with others. You have to bear this."' Perhaps the burden was too heavy for his frail young shoulders. Shammi Kapoor may have been asked to erase the family secret from his mind but he could not block out the sense of foreboding that overwhelmed him. 'I was in my mother's womb when the two children died, so death has always weighed heavy on my mind. I have always had a fear of death and thoughts of rebirth kept coming to my mind. There has been so much death in my family,' says Shammi.

Ironically, the hunkiest Kapoor who emulated Elvis Presley's swivel-hipped dance movements on screen was so scrawny as a baby that his family feared he would not survive. 'He looked like a little *chooha* (mouse), we thought he might not live,' recalls Mrs Jagat Singh Ahuja, Rama Kapoor's friend. Born with a patch on his lungs, Shammi Kapoor was a sickly child for most of his childhood. Prayag Raaj remembers him as an exceptionally thin child. 'We all made fun of him. We used to play *jal tarang* on his ribs,' he recalls. The dancing star's early teens must have been trying: a frail Pathan is something of an oxymoron.

Shammi Kapoor says that he was inhibited until he was about fourteen. 'I was four foot something and very thin. But then in 1946 I went to stay with bhabhiji [Krishna Kapoor]. She took me to her *maike* (maternal home) in Rewa. There I learned to swim. I shot up four or five inches. I was in the right place at the right time. I didn't stop after that. I grew to over six feet. Shashi stopped at 5'11", Raj Kapoor was a little over 5'7", and Prithviraj Kapoor was 5'10$^1/_2$".'

The one who turned out to be the tallest of them all did not like being short—or the weakling—when growing up. He was like a shrinking violet at home until he suddenly grew up, like Popeye after swallowing his can of spinach. While the chubby-cheeked Raj was ebullient, ever the prankster hogging all the attention, Shammi remained withdrawn and quiet at home. 'I was an introvert growing up. I was very shy at home,' says he.

Slinking into the shadows in their home bursting at its seams with people, outside the home he found an outlet in sports for his irrepressible energy. 'I was an outgoing person on the sports field,' recalls Shammi. Table-tennis, cricket, football and hockey—there was a hardly a sport this spindly Kapoor didn't take up, and with a vengeance. In fact, when he was about eleven, he broke a few bones in his hands while roller-skating: he had actually tried to jump over a manhole. The accident, however, did not prevent him from taking part in a table-tennis tournament a few days later: he just put his arm in a sling and played. Breaking bones became a habit with him through much of his acting career, dancing wildly as he did in most of his films.

The neighbourhood of Matunga was perfect for the sporting life. There was enough space for this Kapoor to work off his excess energy. Matunga had two playgrounds—one belonged to Khalsa College, the other to the V.J.T. Institute. Shammi Kapoor also prowled the Five Gardens behind the Custom's Quarters and the playgrounds of his school, Don Bosco.

The Kapoors were probably the first 'filmi' family to move to this middle-class area situated a few kilometres from the tree-lined Parsi Colony in Dadar. Civil engineers, customs officials, doctors and bank employees had made Hollywood Lane (as College Back Road where the Kapoors lived came to be called) their home; many of the families had moved here from West Punjab after partition. It was, according to Shammi Kapoor's childhood friends, a life most ordinary. 'Shammi's childhood was amazingly normal for a family in the movies,' says Parminder Sandilya whose family lived on Hollywood Lane from 1938 to 1952.

Mr Sandilya still marvels at the fact that there were no incipient traits of a movie star in Shammi Kapoor. He never talked about films to them: the focus was on sports and on pranks. The gang of friends may have gone to different schools but they played together each afternoon. They had a coded, bird-like whistle; it served as the signal to gulp down a glass of milk and come down to play. When they were not playing, they used to sit on the railing of Five Gardens or on the Khalsa College wall and chat.

Talk at home amongst the elders centred on the freedom struggle: there was always somebody from the IPTA, and Prithviraj Kapoor alluded in his plays to the politically volatile times the country was going through in the early forties. However, for Shammi and his Hollywood Lane friends the struggle for independence and partition seemed to have been nothing more than a backdrop, not impinging on their conscience in any significant way. 'We never talked about homework or serious things,' remembers Parminder Sandilya. Afsal Sharif, whose family moved to Pakistan eventually, stood tall at 5'3", and talked about wanting to become a heavyweight boxing champ like Joe Louis. Shammi was more reticent. However, his actions spoke louder. Glimmers of the prankster persona of his later films were already there: he was not averse to flicking somebody's car when he felt like going for a spin. His pranks were never less than imaginative, and certainly indicated early entrepreneurial skills.

For pre-teen schoolboys the boundary between borrowing and stealing can be quite blurred. Shammi Kapoor often hitched rides. Once, a doctor generously offered to drop him somewhere. He quietly flicked a syringe out of his bag and later sold it. But these little 'borrowings' were not always only for his benefit. While touring with Prithvi Theatres in Hyderabad, he entered a shop and slipped a small shoe into his pocket. The shoe was for his nephew Randhir Kapoor. But the exercise was in vain: he had forgotten to steal a pair.

There was something of the daredevil about him from the beginning. Perhaps, it had to do with his fascination with Errol Flynn movies. The actor was an early idol of his, and Parminder Sandilya remembers his friend speaking fondly about the film *Captain Blood*. But he was not obsessed about films, as his elder brother was. Shammi Kapoor enjoyed seeing them, but he liked emulating screen heroics on the streets of his neighbourhood even more.

Unlike Raj Kapoor who was forever falling in love as an adolescent, Shammi was more diffident. The actor who was later to incarnate the Playboy of the Eastern World was quite shy in school. 'I had to sing in a play when I was thirteen. I had to kiss a girl. I remember I came home and washed and washed my face,' Shammi reminisces. Hollywood Lane bristled with pretty young girls but they would come to his house generally during rakhi and he had to give them presents.

Like his elder brother, Shammi, too, changed schools quite often. He attended St Joseph's Convent, a co-educational school, in Wadala until the fifth standard, before moving to Don Bosco School, behind Khalsa College, in Matunga. However, the bohemian lifestyle of the Kapoors resulted in his being made to leave the school after a year. Shammi used to act as Bharat in *Shakuntala* on Fridays, Saturdays and Sundays at the Royal Opera House, for which he had to leave school early on these days. One day, the principal of Don Bosco finally put his foot down. Prithviraj Kapoor asked his eldest son to handle the matter. Raj Kapoor went to Shammi's school, picked up his books, took his brother by the hand and walked out of the school. This is how Shammi Kapoor started attending the more elite New Era School on Hughes Road, where Zulfikar Ali Bhutto was also a student at the time. 'This was the school of the rich and the elite. I was the only poor guy there,' recalls Shammi.

This Kapoor was in a hurry to grow up, and to grow up manly. To be macho was a Pathan thing. Akharas were ubiquitous then, as gyms are today. Young men from middle-class backgrounds were into muscle building, as his father had been. So when nature let him down, Shammi Kapoor turned to artifice. His fair complexion and large hazel-green eyes made him look almost pretty, all the more since his upper lip remained unadorned by hair until his early teens. But he soon found a remedy. Before going to a party Shammi used to light a match, let it cool and then draw a thin moustache on his face with the black deposit on the tip of the matchstick. Lekh Tandon observed him doing this quite often. The moustache was his ticket to an adult world he was keen to gatecrash into.

Cigarettes and alcohol were the other entry tickets. He began to smoke in his early teens. Somebody had told him that smoking would add depth and timbre to his thin voice. The long affair with alcohol began early as well. Lekh Tandon remembers the night a fourteen-year-old Shammi stole a bottle of champagne, helped by accomplices: cousin Rajendranath and friend Bhappi Soni. 'Kamal Kapoor and some of Shammi's other cousins were sleeping in the dining room. The champagne was in a cupboard behind them. They tried to open the door by standing on top of one another. The three then went to Wadala Station. It was late at night, and they had forgotten to take any glasses. They took a few from a tea stall, bought a bucket and put some ice in it to cool the champagne. All of them got drunk.'

Obviously, the adolescent Shammi Kapoor was the difficult son. A bit of a buccaneer he often turned tradition on its head, rarely playing by the rules of the Kapoor clan. Actor–singer B.M. Vyas who worked with Prithvi Theatres from its inception tells an interesting anecdote. The group often rehearsed for their plays in the Royal Opera House. There was an upper storey. Prithviraj Kapoor often stood there and observed his players down below on the stage. 'Papaji used to watch Shammi from above when we were rehearsing in Opera House. He used to shake his head in despair when he saw him drinking beer. He never said much to his son though.'

Raj Kapoor on the other hand kept up appearances. He never smoked in front of his father. In fact, he literally burned his fingers one time when his father suddenly walked into the room while he was smoking. Raj Kapoor quickly put his hands behind his back, with the burning cigarette between his fingers. He kept holding on to his cigarette even as it burned down to the very end. Shammi was open about everything he did.

Raj and Shammi didn't have the most comfortable of sibling relationships while growing up. The seven years between them stretched like infinity, an unbridgeable gap for a long time. The relationship was one of silences and brooding, of unexpressed resentment. Later, to be at the receiving end of his brother's hand-me-down roles in Prithvi Theatres must not have been easy. But they made their peace on the eve of Raj Kapoor's fatal trip to Delhi to receive the Dadasaheb Phalke Award. While the relationship with his elder brother was not easy, nor was being the middle son: Raj Kapoor was the precocious darling of his father and Shashi was his mother's pet.

The only one of the Kapoors of his generation to go to college, Shammi Kapoor did not initially want to become an actor. Aeronautical engineering fascinated him. Ever curious about how things worked as a child, he used to spend hours with Meccano sets. He also liked to take radios apart and put them back together again. A perpetual tinkerer, he took up science in Ruia College, in south Bombay.

However, he didn't do anything as prosaic as attending just one college. Since he didn't find Ruia College 'stimulating enough', he juggled three colleges at one time. He used to go to Ruia College most mornings, where he would leave his books. Some days he didn't even do that and got his friends to give proxy for him. Later in the day, he sat in on the classes at the more elite St Xavier's College, where he also played table-tennis. Several afternoons found him attending practical classes at the Royal Institution at Elphinstone. And nobody was the wiser.

The honeymoon with college lasted just a year: Shammi Kapoor got 'bored'. He decided that science was not for him, and asked his father if he could join Prithvi Theatres, just as his elder brother had done before him. His father offered him a job at fifty rupees a month.

Shammi Kapoor joined Prithvi theatres in 1948 as an extra after his brief fling with college. When he left four years later to act in films, his take-home pay had grown six-fold to three hundred rupees. By then he had acted in *Deewar*, *Pathan*, *Gaddaar* and *Ahooti*.

The Kapoor brothers were left to their own devices in Prithvi Theatres. Shammi recalls: 'I learned the ropes by watching. It was like being thrown into a pool at the deep end. I got to remember all the roles since I was an understudy. For a senior role I donned a beard and make-up. In *Pathan* I played Bahadur Khan. In *Ahooti* I was the understudy to Sajjan. The second day he had a toothache. I had merely watched him rehearsing, and on the third day I just went on and did the main role. I didn't need a prompter. I was told if you forget the dialogue, just make it up.'

But the person whom Shammi Kapoor watched the most closely was his elder brother. 'In the theatre you saw and performed. I mostly saw Raj Kapoor,' he says. He was given most of the roles his brother had grown out of. And he did exactly what Raj had done in those roles—nothing more and perhaps nothing less. It was only with the play *Kalakar* in 1951 that Shammi Kapoor came into his own. His role in the play is the blueprint for the Yahoo persona that was to emerge years later.

Kalakar was a new play. Prithviraj Kapoor had asked his friend Ramanand Sagar to write the play. *Kalakar* was a rather romantic play about a painter who falls in love with a beautiful mountain belle and takes her back to the 'corrupt' city. Contrasting the pristine innocence of the *pahadi*s (hill dwellers) with the cynical and predatory people of the plains became a favourite theme with Raj Kapoor as well. Incidentally, Ramanand Sagar also wrote *Barsaat*, Raj Kapoor's first commercial success which, too, had at its core the contrast between the purity of hill dwellers and the cynicism of urbanites.

What is important about *Kalakar* is the fact that Shammi Kapoor's character was written into the play by his father. In fact, the third act of *Kalakar* was completely rewritten by Prithviraj Kapoor. Says Shashi Kapoor: 'It was inspired by characters in the plays of Shakespeare—Bassanio in *The Merchant of Venice* and Mercutio in *Romeo and Juliet*. My father wanted this character to be the complete opposite of the painter—urbanized, flamboyant, but not a baddie.' Prithviraj had played both Shakespearean roles while working with the Grant Theatre Company.

Shammi Kapoor's character, Ramesh, is a playboy who seduces the painter's naïve wife. Not only did Prithviraj Kapoor recast the third act, he also showed his son how to enact the role. Adds Prayag Raaj: 'That whole persona of the rebel, of rebellion, was actually conceived by Papaji. I saw him showing Shammiji what the character was all about. Shammi was surprised. He wondered where his father had got that walk and gestures. It was from Shakespeare. Papaji had also played a negative character in Ishara's film *Sharabi*. In this film he acted as a drunkard, with a similar kind of walk, and the same expression in the eyes. It was a sideways walk, and he would shake his head as well.' That shake of the head is probably the blueprint for many of the muscle-defying head movements Shammi Kapoor later did in many of his films.

For Shammi, *Kalakar* was the first turning point in his career, although the more significant one was to come later on the screen. 'Finally, I was able to add my own colour to a role. In the play I was a playboy. I did things with the flourish of a city character. The changing aspects of city life gave me the occasion to play a villainous role,' recalls Shammi.

Prithvi Theatres for Shammi was merely a stepping stone, as it had been for Raj Kapoor. Raj Kapoor left Prithvi Theatres when he very young. Shammi Kapoor on the other hand stayed on much longer, well into his mid-twenties. But when he left to join the movies, he left alone, unlike his brother who absorbed many people from Prithvi Theatres into R.K. Films.

The elder brother started an institution, the younger one became one. The moment he found his profession, he was on his own, the lone star who unlike his father or brothers was not part of or head of a repertoire.

Even though he never completed college, Shammi Kapoor continued his education, informally. He was a voracious reader, quite the opposite of his elder brother. He consumed books with the same frenzied passion as he did food, whiskey and women. Books probably had more to do with the shaping of his mind than anything else. How else can one explain how different he is from his father and brothers, and the larger Kapoor clan. There is obviously an introspective and enigmatic personality behind the hedonist façade.

Prithviraj Kapoor and Raj Kapoor had been influenced by Nehruvian socialism: leftist ideology bolstered the work of both, and the collective prevailed over the individual. Shammi Kapoor did not have any such burden. The philosophy of the high priestess of capitalism, Ayn Rand, may have had more of an abiding influence on him. Vehemently anti-communist, the American novelist–philosopher of Russian origin had influenced generations of young people with her advocacy of the 'virtue of selfishness'—the pursuit of happiness and the American dream. Her novels were a paean to capitalism. From her came the ideas of personal freedom as well as free markets, and most important, the idea of the heroic personality.

Her two most well-known protagonists—Howard Roark in *Fountainhead* (1943) and John Galt in *Atlas Shrugged* (1957)—certainly left an indelible mark on Shammi Kapoor. The Rand men were nothing like the heroes he saw around him. Shammi Kapoor admired the intransigent, unbreakable, rebellious spirit—and the go-for-it philosophy. 'I liked *Fountainhead* very much—the character had an influence on me. To design the self on the man who would not accept second best. Just imagine naming his yacht "I do". I liked this "nothing holds me" philosophy. You can live in a book at an impressionable age,' says Shammi.

To say that Shammi Kapoor was obsessive in his reading is an understatement. Producer Surinder Kapoor remembers him tearing out each page after he had finished it—there was a pile of pages on the floor after he had finished. 'I think he used to tear out each page after he read it because this way he would not end up reading the same pages again. I have never seen anybody read like this.' For Shammi Kapoor reading was often like a marathon race: he did not even stop to take a leak. Or at least that is the way he describes reading *Atlas Shrugged* on his web site. 'Before starting *Dil Deke Dekho* I did a reading stint. Ayn Rand, the author of *Fountainhead*, had written a new book called *Atlas Shrugged*. It was a massive novel comprising some 1000-odd pages and I was bent upon doing a start-to-finish job. It took me thirty-six hours of non-stop reading but left me with a kidney ailment. I do not know how the two are connected but the pain was excruciating.'

Nor was it just a solitary activity. He used to discuss books with his sister, Urmi. He has often said to friends that books were not something he could discuss with his brothers. Shammi Kapoor loved to talk about books with the women he dated: perhaps he thought it would be considered wimpish to discuss books and ideas with his drinking pals and colleagues in the film world. He used to read to his first wife, Geeta Bali. She was illiterate, but loved to listen to him. 'I used to read out loud to my wife—every night a chapter. She would cry, especially when I read Dumas's *Camille*.'

Shammi Kapoor found his heroes not only in the fiction of Ayn Rand but also in the macho men of the screen in the Hollywood movies of the fifties. Errol Flynn was a significant influence on his impressionable young mind: 'It was a different world and time. I saw Errol Flynn in *Robin Hood* and read his autobiography *My Wicked, Wicked Ways*. I was impressed and I modelled myself after him...his kind of persona.' The young Shammi Kapoor also admired and tried to emulate the 'romantic tough guys' like John Wayne, Kirk Douglas and John Barrymore.

'They were men. Wayne with his hip flask...watching them you got the feeling that if you were like them you could knock on any door,' says Shammi. The character of Nick Ramon really appealed to him. 'At twenty-two you live fast, die young and make a good-looking corpse. This was a Bible for us.' He often talks about his fascination as a young man with being 'male'—hunting, riding off like a cowboy into the wild country with a hip flask and a girl on his arm, and driving cars at breakneck speed. He was the original Alpha male of Malabar Hill.

Which is why the young Shammi had to have a Buick convertible, which he would drive at 90 miles an hour. The Kapoors loved their cars in different ways. Prithviraj Kapoor loved his Opel and was faithful to it till the end. Raj Kapoor bought a car, a convertible Oldsmobile, soon after his first film as director. Later, however, he was quite happy with his white Ambassador. Shashi Kapoor loved driving his white Mercedes. But it was Shammi Kapoor for whom a car was much more than getting from one place to another in comfort.

It was more like a relationship between a cowboy and his horse. Shammi Kapoor just loved cars, even if he had to 'borrow' them. On his web site he evocatively writes about his love affair with them. It started in Hollywood Lane with a small Austin that belonged to a certain Mr Mani. Shammi and his friends used to push the car to get it started. 'Then one day, unknown to him, we started to push it around with one of us at the steering to keep in practice, and ultimately when I jumped into the driver's seat, I fixed some ignition wires and got it started. The rest jumped in and we took a short drive. We got away with this routine a couple of times till we were apprehended one day by Mani and got the firing of our lives.'

Shammi also coveted his elder brother's car. One day before going to school he started Raj Kapoor's car, and before Dwarka, their servant, could get in and close the door, the car took off. The result was disastrous. The open door crashed against the lamp post and got wrenched off. The noise brought Raj and his parents to the balcony. Before he could be hauled up, Shammi ran from the car to the nearest bus stop.

Before the ink could dry on the contract for his first film,

Jeevan Jyoti (1950), he began to scout for a car. He fell in love with a second-hand sky-blue Buick convertible that belonged to actress Nigar Sultana. Shammi Kapoor spied it at the Car Mart on Hughes Road, and borrowed five thousand rupees from Aspi Irani, a producer friend, for the down payment. Two years later on 12 June 1952 he finally took possession of his beloved Buick. He was twenty-two.

Subsequently, the flamboyant film star owned many cars. A former friend remarks: 'He changed cars as often as he did his women.' His garage witnessed a passing parade: a Desoto followed by a Chevy Belair, a Chevy Impala, a Chevy Intercontinental convertible, a Ford Thunderbird, a Sunbeam Alpine, a Triumph, a Malibu, some foreign and Indian Fiats and a number of jeeps for shikar. But as Shammi Kapoor notes on his web site: 'To this day the one and only beauty which has always remained dear to me in both my memory and my heart is the Buick BMY 3009.'

Shikar was his other passion. His home looks like a hunterwalla's abode. There are trophies on the walls, on the floor, in photographs, in the images on his sleek iMac, testimony to Shammi Kapoor's past as a shikari. Tiger skins, heads and once-glorious horns of various fleet-footed deer and stags populate his living room. Actually, you don't even need to enter the apartment on the ground floor of Blue Haven on Malabar Hill to realize it is one of his major passions. Right at the door, just above the traditional garland of dry Ashoka leaves and green chillies to keep out evil spirits, stag horns greet you, eerily.

Hunting was more than a mere sport for the actor. It served as an important tool in the moulding of himself in the image of the macho man, the desi equivalent of the Marlboro man. He could not become a cowboy on the prairie, like the romantic image etched in his mind after watching Westerns—taciturn men ever ready to fell an enemy or win the heart of a beautiful woman. Becoming a shikari took him some distance towards this coveted image. It wasn't just about killing animals and being a real man, in the way Hemingway talked about blood sport and bull fights. Or the thrill of the tango of death between hunter and the hunted. It had to do with a mood, the evocation of a romantic life in the wilds of nature. 'More than the killing, it was being out there under the stars in the jungles, seeing the wild *dhuan* (smoke) of the village, of the camp fires, of driving in the jeep. I would do anything to go back and enjoy those moments,' he says wistfully.

Nature was as big a draw, and Shammi Kapoor spent many a Christmas and New Year in the forests of the Terai. On his web site he writes: 'There is no electricity in most of the dak bungalows in the forests and the sky is full of the stars you never get to see in the city. The winters are very cold, so the camp fire is something you don't want to get away from. The local tribal scene blends beautifully with the local sounds or radio or tape music and potluck...Sometimes you just drive around in the forest for hours, looking at the different hues of colour and shade among the trees and foliage along the streams running amok. There are days when you don't even use the gun to shoot with (except of course to bring something for the kitchen) and instead look through a camera.' Is there a touch of the incurable romantic in him?

Reading Jim Corbett and Kenneth Anderson fed his young imagination. Their tales drew him to the jungle. But the catalyst in his becoming a shikari was his meeting with the maharani of Jodhpur in 1946. Prithvi Theatres was staging a play in the city at the time, and the fifteen-year-old Shammi Kapoor was mesmerized by the maharani and the trappings of royalty. Her two sons took him blackbuck hunting and on duck shoots. The memory of 'travelling with them in their convertible and Rolls Royce, custom-made for shikar, chasing the herds of blackbucks' still lingers. He shot his first partridge here with a 20 bore double-barrel.

The maharani presented him with his first weapon, a BSA air gun, as a farewell present. Recounting his royal encounter, Shammi Kapoor dramatically finishes his story, trailing off with 'I never forgot that maharani...she was the most beautiful woman I had ever seen.'

Having tasted blood, Shammi Kapoor did not wait too long before he bought his own guns. As soon as he turned twenty-one, he bought a .32 bore Webley Scott revolver and a 12 bore double-barrel gun by Wright & Sons. Later, he added a .375

Holland & Holland rifle, a 450-400 Purdy DBBL, a .370 Strech & Co rifle along with a hornet, a .22 for small game, and a PPK Walther to his arsenal. He also bought jeeps for his jungle excursions, naming the first one Dinky and the second, aptly enough, Yahoo—his famous call in *Junglee* which later became his battle cry.

Shammi Kapoor's favourite shikar companion was comedian and friend Johnny Walker, with whom he shot his second tiger (he notched three all together) when they went hunting in the Terai. He shot his first tiger near Bhopal in the Barasia forest in 1958. On his web site, Shammi recounts: 'In big game hunting it is customary to select who gets to shoot first as the trophy belongs to him who draws first blood. So Johnny and I took turns on alternate days and fortunately for me, the night we spotted the tiger, it was my turn. It was a huge male measuring 10'3" and there is a photo of how I looked the next morning with this beauty.'

There were some close shaves in the Terai. The tigers didn't get him, but a bear almost did. 'It was dangerous…at that time and that age to do stupid things. I was attacked by a huge mother bear. I was in the middle of a nallah, and felt something behind me. I heard someone say, "Sahib ghumo." She snarled at me. I would have been a goner had it not been for my instinct.'

Geeta Bali and he often went off on shikar on the spur of the moment. 'We would just get into the car and drive off,' recalls Shammi. She loved the outdoors as well, and they took turns driving from Bombay to Dehradun. They had a Dunlop mattress at the back of their car: this way one of them could sleep while the other drove. The memory of the food from the dhabas they stopped at along the way still teases his palate.

Hunting also led him to his other great love: cooking. Instead of heating beans over camp fires, as they do in the movies, Shammi Kapoor developed his famed culinary skills in the jungle. 'You know how it is. You are in a jungle, with that atmosphere. You are killing something and you open it up, put some salt on it, some brandy. I used to build a fire of wood and then pour brandy on the shikar…That's how I started to cook.' As he talks, his voice slows to the kind of drawl you hear in American

Westerns, and a image of the iconic cowboy in a checked shirt squatting over a camp fire, his gun secure in his holsters, comes to mind.

While Shammi Kapoor tried to construct a persona for himself in the image of the macho men he read about or saw in films, there was another crucial element in the crucible forming him: music. It was critical in his development as a person and as an actor. His Elvis-like gyrations on screen belie his profound understanding of the rhythm and intricacies of all kinds of music. He started young.

Shammi is an accidental musician, courtesy his mother when he was a child and later, surprisingly, Nargis. His mother had kept a tutor, Jagannath Prasad, to teach her how to sing classical Indian music. However, she lost interest and made Raj Kapoor learn in her place. But when her eldest son became too busy and started bunking his music lessons, she sat Shammi down for the lessons. 'Chaiji said, "*Isko bithao*", and I struggled. I got over five years of classical training,' remembers Shammi. Jagannath Prasad had taught K.L. Saigal and Mukesh and he found an attentive student in the young Shammi. Later, when he joined Prithvi Theatres, Shammi Kapoor continued his music apprenticeship. The plays had original compositions, and among his early friends were the young duo of Shankar and Jaikishen who worked with Prithvi Theatres before they moved to R.K. Films. His feet tapped to another beat as well: Shammi Kapoor was very fond of Western music, particularly Latin American music.

That Nargis was Raj Kapoor's muse is well known. Less known is the fact that she inadvertently played muse to the musician in Shammi Kapoor. As a teenager, Shammi Kapoor used to spend a lot of time at R.K. trying to learn the ropes of film-making. But the real motivating force behind his regular attendance on the film sets was the free lunch. One day, on the sets of *Barsaat* he happened to pass by Nargis's make-up room and saw her crying. Apparently, her family had forbidden her from acting in any more films with Raj Kapoor. She was particularly keen on acting in *Awara*. Shammi Kapoor promised to pray for her, and Nargis promised to give him a big kiss if her wish came true. *Barsaat* became a hit. Meanwhile, Shammi Kapoor graduated from school and joined college. He had grown into a young man when he went for his customary free lunch and to collect on her promise, this time on the sets of *Awara*.

Taken aback, Nargis told him: 'I know, I promised, but now you are a big boy. Ask for anything else.' Shammi Kapoor was waiting for this: he actually wanted a gramophone and asked her to get one for him. 'She did not blink. She led me by the hand to her Riley car and drove out of the studio to an HMV shop,' he recalls. He chose a red gramophone, after which she drove to Rhythm House and asked him to select twenty records. The first one he chose was *The Gypsy Love Song*. Others included Arty Shaw's *Jungle Drums*, Glen Miller's *In the Mood* and several rumbas and sambas.

At that time he thought his day had been made. But the red gramophone actually made his life. Recalls Shammi: 'It was going to be my life that was taking off. And thus the music grew within me. The beat and swing engulfed me completely. I spent every moment of my sober and not too sober life in the ensuing period involved with different types of music. I was totally spaced out...blending with the music to such an extent that there were times I danced to it in the middle of the night, lone and lost. At last I had found it: my way of expressing. Every form of music reached a state where I did not need to hear the music itself. It had embedded itself so deep within me that I even lost track of it. It lay dormant for a long time. And the day I had need for it, I found myself dancing and singing to every type of music. I had created a style. And it all started from a red gramophone I received instead of a kiss.'

That red gramophone and the faraway rhythms it brought to Shammi Kapoor's eager ear helped him find his own path to success. The 'style' he concocted is what made him, enabling him to carve an original niche for himself in Hindi cinema. Until then the golden trio—Raj Kapoor, Dilip Kumar and Dev Anand—mostly stood while their heroines pouted and moved around a bit. The dancing, fairly acrobatic actor who moved to inner rhythms which Shammi incarnated was new.

He had swivelled himself to this while still a teenager by learning to dance to different kinds of music. There were no dancing classes for budding films stars then as there are today: you did your own training. At seventeen he enrolled in dancing classes in a certain Pritam Hotel in Dadar. 'My dancing beat came from all this. Pritam Kohli had these classes. I paid twenty rupees an hour. I learned the tango. All this was lying dormant. It took the film *Tumsa Nahin Dekha* to bring it all out. It evolved and grew,' says Shammi.

Raj Kapoor was equally nimble footed—dancing as well to an inner beat in his films (just watch his feet), but Shammi Kapoor took the art of dancing much further. 'Raj Kapoor did the samba in *Dastan*. But for me it was dancing to a mood, not just a movement. I never had a dance master in films. My heart told me to do this. In *Junglee* I did not dance, I moved. I jumped from one place to another. I slid down the stairs. I slid down the snow. It was really an expression of a mood,' says Shammi. At home, alone, he often went into 'a frenzy' listening to his 'haunting rumbas and gypsy love songs' that he 'performed in the mind'.

Ragas and rumbas led a harmonious existence in his canon. This Kapoor was also very fond of European classical music. 'I particularly like Brahms, Mozart, Chopin and Pavarotti,' he says. His eclectic taste embraces jazz, the blues and Indian classical music. And he occasionally exercises his vocal chords, mainly for his own benefit. The actor even sang a few lines in his maiden film *Jeevan Jyoti*, along with S.D. Burman and Asha Bhonsle.

'I was a male starlet.'

—Shammi Kapoor

In the history of Hindi cinema, the sixties belong to Shammi Kapoor. But he had to work his way out from under the long shadows cast by not one but three elm trees before he could find his own place in the sun. 'It took me five years to wipe out the basic image in which I was clubbed as Prithviraj Kapoor's son, Raj Kapoor's brother and Geeta Bali's husband,' says Shammi. His first wife Geeta Bali was almost two years his senior and already a well-established star in 1955 when he married her, while he was getting nowhere.

So, to get somewhere, Shammi Kapoor reinvented himself: he took on a new identity. He went as far away as possible from the trademark fair and lovely Kapoor look. He traded the image of the thin, gangly youth with slicked-down hair and a pencil-thin Errol Flynn-ish moustache for that of the macho man. He cut his hair short and adopted a cowboy swagger. His green bedroom eyes now shone with lust. He yelled Yahoo!

The Indian audience had never seen anybody or anything quite like this. The wimp-lover was buried, and the Yahoo lover was on his way to becoming a cult. Shammi Kapoor appealed to the rebel in men. Here was a man's man: he did on screen what they wanted to but dared not do. He introduced the feel-good factor: men and women came out of the cinema halls laughing. When video cassettes first came to India, those of his songs flew off the shelves the fastest. And today, songs from his films inundate radio and television.

Shammi Kapoor was barely twenty-one when he acted in his first film. Director Mahesh Kaul spotted him in *Kalakar* and *Pathan* and cast him as his lead hero in *Jeevan Jyoti*. Chand Usmani was his leading lady in this historical. Alas, this film sank without even a ripple. The tall, fair and skinny actor with a far from resonant voice, a pencil-thin moustache and a lock falling over his broad forehead didn't impress the audience. Nor could his green bedroom eyes make an impact: it was the black and white era.

Shammi Kapoor in his early days

The actor may have tossed out the provocative remark about having been 'a male starlet' casually, but he was serious. Shammi Kapoor made eighteen successive flops in the five years that followed his debut film, despite being paired with actresses like Nutan, Meena Kumari, Madhubala and Suraiyya. Most of these films were mythologicals or historicals. In costume dramas like *Laila Majnu* and *Shama Parwana* and several B-grade films, the actor was not much more than the foil for his leading ladies—an attractive prop whose magnetism and sex appeal had been strapped in, much like a chastity belt.

Failure appeared to be the only constant in Shammi Kapoor's career. No wonder he was despondent. There was also that matter of being dwarfed even further by his family. Prithvi Theatres had become a national asset. As his father alternated between the screen and the theatre, his fame spread throughout the country—a sort of national hero. Raj Kapoor had proved himself an ingénue with his first film *Aag*, made before he had turned twenty-three. Moreover, his second film *Barsaat* had been a big hit, and R.K. Films was up and running, subsequently turning out celebrated films like *Awara* and *Shree 420*.

Shammi had chosen to debut at the wrong time. It was the golden age of Indian cinema, and sitting pretty at the top was the reigning trinity of Dilip Kumar, Raj Kapoor and Dev Anand. Dilip Kumar's terrain was the tragic hero, and he invested his screen characters with the kind of intensity seldom seen since on the Indian screen. Raj Kapoor invented himself as the little man of the screen, also donning the persona of Charlie Chaplin's tramp. Dev Anand played the debonair romantic hero, and his good looks and mannerisms had the women swooning.

There was no room for Shammi Kapoor. Not the way he was then at any rate. He was even refused the role of Salim in *Anarkali*, losing it to Pradeep Kumar. The actor had to find his own identity. It turned out to be a fairly long journey till 1957 when he was cast in *Tumsa Nahin Dekha* directed by Nasir Husain. Apparently, Nasir Husain's screenplay for *Munimji* (one of Dev Anand's most loved films) was so successful that producer S. Mukherjee of Filmistan asked him to direct a film for him. Husain found his manly, brash hero in Shammi Kapoor, and the actor found a film which would finally break the curse of failure. 'With that film I took on a new identity. I was going no place, nowhere until then. *Tumsa...* was a musical comedy romance. It was a complete break. I changed my style, off went the moustache, I gave myself a crew cut, wore jeans, tight clothes and went out and did Yahoo,' recalls Shammi.

The film was an instant hit; its songs are still perennial favourites. A breezy romantic comedy with the usual Nasir Husain staple fare (mistaken identities, misplaced letters, lost and found parents and children, a villain who wants to marry the rich heroine, and great feet-tapping music), it became a great hit despite the fact that the heroine was debuting actress Ameeta and the hero the little-known Shammi Kapoor.

In this film one gets to see the first glimmers of the flamboyance and swagger which were to become Shammi Kapoor's trademark. The hero no longer looks virginal: love and longing now acquire shades of lust. With this film—you could call it an embryonic Curry Eastern—the desi cowboy has also arrived. Shammi Kapoor wears rough-hewn checked shirts, boots, various kinds of caps, and is forever getting on and off horses, and letting out strange kinds of yells. Villain Pran does some nifty bit of horse riding as well. There is even a ranch-style house.

But what makes the film are the numerous song and dance numbers, especially Shammi Kapoor's boisterous movements on a rapidly moving tonga. O.P. Nayyar's music and Mohammad Rafi's voice combine to produce unforgettable songs. Rafi obviously stretched his vocal chords to their limits, putting enough force into his voice to match the actor's exuberance. The actor's signature head movements and uninhibited gyrations captivated the audience. As did his patented pout.

In *Tumsa Nahin Dekha*, Shammi Kapoor also found his comic voice: he was that rare combination of a romantic hero and a comedian. In this film he gets a chance to display his talent for mimicry, not to speak of making funny faces—more Jerry Lewis than Charlie Chaplin. He dons many disguises, including that of a Pathan—a leftover perhaps from his Prithvi days—and something that he would continue to do in films that followed. He even plays the harmonica, an act he repeats in his next film

Dil Deke Dekho. Apparently, the actor was left to his own devices since the film was supposed to be the launch pad for Ameeta. The proprietor of Filmistan, Tolaram Jalan, was personally interested in promoting her career. So, Shammi just let himself go.

From *Tumsa Nahin Dekha* Shammi Kapoor was on a roll. *Dil Deke Dekho* in 1958 with Asha Parekh was an even bigger hit, and the actor became a cult figure.

Shammi Kapoor was the architect of his new look, and he did his own packaging. An avid fan of American films, particularly Westerns with John Wayne, he simply emulated their wardrobe in his films. He wore lumberjack or leather jackets, casual, open collars, tee shirts, jeans and checked shirts. The actor could also be debonair in bow ties and white dress jackets.

His screen metamorphosis involved more than just his wardrobe. With his moustache gone, Shammi Kapoor's eyes became more prominent. He also drastically altered his hairstyle, sacrificing the sleeked-back look for his infamous puff and ducktail. 'I used to watch the Bandra Christians. I often went to Bandra to eat *maska pao*. I imitated the way they did their hair. I would put some oil, curl it, puff it and just push it up,' says Shammi.

Shammi Kapoor also changed his body language. It became free and uninhibited. He walked with *jhatka*s, a sideways swagger, emulating his *Kalakar* persona. But the most fundamental change he brought to the Indian screen was the expression of raw sexuality. The dancing hero brought a current of sexuality, as opposed to sensuality. 'He was the first actor to portray adolescent sexuality on the Indian screen,' explains Mumbai psychoanalyst Udayan Patel. His song 'Jawania yeh mast mast bin piye, jalati chal rahi hai raah me diye' in *Tumsa Nahin Dekha* expresses the unstoppable urges of youth.

Shammi Kapoor's famous Yahoo cry was heard for the first time in *Tumsa Nahin Dekha*. It was not just a cry from the heart: it seemed to embody the hormones and uncontrollable urges of the characters he played. He is part caveman, part romantic lover. He manages to convey the fact that he is turned on. In *Junglee*, when Saira Banu and he are stranded in a hut after a snowstorm the cry expresses his awakening sexuality—until then he is immune to women in the film. The burning fires symbolize passion; the sight of Saira's hair spread on the pillow, the red shawl highlighting her fair skin, her eyes closed in the abandonment of sleep arouse his latent desire.

Where did this iconic cry spring from? Of all places, he picked it up from Hollywood movies. Shammi Kapoor was trying to imitate the cowboy's shout while rounding up his cattle or horses. Strangely enough, in *Junglee* it is not his voice but that of Prayag Raaj which one hears as Shammi lets out that life-affirming yell on-screen. As the actor puts it: 'The Yahoo sound was something one heard in the movies with cowboys and horsemen. I thought it was apt for the occasion. Yahoo was not a word. I used it as an expression for the mood of the actor at that moment. In *Dil Deke Dekho* the boy is teasing a girl. He is loud and exuberant, and this boy shrieks and jumps in the fray. I thought about it. I enjoyed doing expressions. It culminated in *Junglee* as an expression of complete freedom, an expression of love. I was able to portray what I felt at the moment...I could identify with the junglee...to put her [the heroine] on my shoulder and ride into the sunset yelling hurrah.'

It is difficult to imagine the impact Shammi Kapoor must have made in his aggressive, uninhibited screen lover avatar from the late fifties and through the sixties. This was also the era of Muslim socials, reticent lovers, and the good and noble men in Bimal Roy's films. You also had heroes like Rajendra Kumar whose eyes were seldom dry: he incarnated the noble Indian male. And then along came this lover who did not take no for an answer. Observed director Manmohan Desai on Shammi Kapoor's contribution to the depiction of romance in Indian films: 'With him Paro will be teased and molested on the way to her father's house.'

Asha Parekh, Sadhana, Nanda and Sharmila Tagore—heroines with that peculiarly desi combination of pallav-twisting coyness and sensuality—kept up with him. They danced and pranced, their eyelashes batting. Asha Parekh must not have been more than sixteen in *Dil Deke Dekho*. In the scenes where her make-up is not so thickly laid on, she looks like a schoolgirl playing hooky. Yet, she spunkily tries to match Shammi Kapoor step for boisterous step. As for Sharmila Tagore, it was a quantum leap from Satyajit Ray's *Devi* to the coquettish *Kashmir Ki Kali*, and later the sexy heroine in *An Evening in Paris*.

No one quite danced the way Shammi Kapoor did in his reinvented screen persona. His head would jerk one way, his feet point in another direction and his arms would move as if according to their own volition. He could not have been more uninhibited and less conscious of the camera. Yet, underlying the jerky movements and sudden jumps was an inner rhythm. He knew what he was doing. His directors and leading ladies, however, did not know what he was going to do in those song and dance sequences. Cameramen did not know where to place the camera and were caught wrong footed when he began to dance: the actor would suddenly move in an unexpected direction, continuing to sing. In *Dil Deke Dekho* he jumps up and lands, cross-legged, on the floor; in *Junglee* he does that famous tumble down the snow-covered hill, a physical act to match his resounding cry.

So directors like Shakti Samanta decided to leave the choreography to the star himself. He directed him in several films, amongst them some of the actor's biggest hits: *An Evening in Paris*, *Kashmir Ki Kali* and *China Town*. 'When you gave him a song, he would create his own movements, better ones,' says Samanta. 'There were no dance directors in my films. Shammi was different. There was no point giving him soft scenes. Whatever you gave him, he would be aggressive and dynamic with the girls. *Gaana ka or mara-mari ka same movement tha* (His singing and fighting had the same movements).'

Shammi also knew his music. In *An Evening in Paris* he hangs from a helicopter and sings 'Aasman se aya farishta'. During this song sequence, shot in Beirut, the helicopter made so much noise that the actor could not hear the music he was supposed to move his lips to. Samanta found a solution: 'I began to give him lip movements, and he followed that. He was very musical, he knew everything.'

Extremist is an adjective Shammi Kapoor often uses for himself. Nowhere is this more evident than in the way he abused his body. He probably broke more bones than he can remember. Knee pads didn't exist during his days and as a dancing hero he was forever falling on the floor. 'When I used to dance, I used to fall on the floor, and the floor was hard. The cartilage is gone. I fell four times on my knees. My knees are gone,' he tells me.

His 'knee trouble' began when he was on location in Ooty in 1964 for K. Shankar's film *Rajkumar*. On his web site, Shammi Kapoor goes into great detail about his bone-breaking days.

'I was singing a song seated on an elephant and to steady myself on its bare back I entwined my feet in the rope tied round its neck. At some time during the shot the elephant started twisting its neck and I could not extract my right leg from its neck. That I think was the beginning. I must have torn some tissue or ligament but I did not take any notice at that moment. The next day we went to Bangalore where I was to shoot for *Kashmir Ki Kali*. I started feeling a shooting pain in my right knee and in spite of this I went for the climax fight at Khemmangundi (some iron ore depot where they had a rope trolley) and while hanging from it I was supposed to jump on the villain's back. In so doing I landed on my right foot and the pain I felt in my knee was something I cannot define. I thought I had broken my leg. They carried me to a car and sent me back to the hotel where a doctor examined it and said I had strained my knee cartilage.'

Soon after, he resumed filming for *Kashmir Ki Kali* in Bombay. Recalls Samanta: 'His knee had not quite healed after his accident in Ooty. We were shooting the climax of *Kashmir Ki Kali*. Shammi was supposed to jump from a jeep. I told him not to do it. In this scene there was a factory where he had cut wood, planks. He has come here to save the heroine. So, he backs out of the gate, jumps and breaks his knee.' From then on, it was a series of mishaps.

During the filming of a song sequence for *Laat Saheb* in Mahabaleshwar he jumped from a height into a pond only to land on a square piece of rock which was hidden under the water and cracked both his knees. During the making of *Tumse Achcha Kaun Hai* he had to jump over a fence, a ditch and a small stream before landing on the cemented road. He slipped and fell on his knees.

He hurt his back when shooting an action sequence for *Tumsa Nahin Dekha*: the horse he was riding tripped on top of a hillock and when he fell, the other horses in the chase scene went over him. There were to be many more such mishaps. Perhaps they should have insured his legs, as they did with Marlene Dietrich in Hollywood.

Shammi Kapoor realized the importance of music in films, particularly the role it played in making a film a box-office hit. At Prithvi Theatres he had learned a great deal about various aspects of music. And like his brother Raj Kapoor he, too, made it a point to be involved in the music sittings of his films, unlike most actors at the time. He also played the drums or the harmonica in his films. But the younger brother went one step further: he made sure that he had as many songs as his heroines, if not more. In *Dil Deke Dekho*, his leading lady is almost an accessory in the song and dance numbers.

Frustrated at his long wait in the antechamber of the hall of fame, Shammi Kapoor was determined to remain in the spotlight for as long as possible. Lekh Tandon who made two films with him (*Professor* and *Prince*) maintains that the actor did this at the expense of others: 'Shammi wanted to be taken seriously. But the tragedy was that he wanted to take away the success of the others to do so. Nobody wanted to work with him. Kalpana (*Professor*) was a good dancer. Bela Bose was a better dancer than him, but he would stop in the middle of a scene and ask her whom she was sleeping with. He did this only to upset her and spoil her performance. Sadhana refused to act with him after a while. Asha Parekh, however, was able to stand up to him.'

Regardless, Shammi Kapoor's career graph went up steadily, pushed part of the way by music directors—O.P. Nayyar's breezy music in *Tumsa Nahin Dekha* and *Kashmir Ki Kali*, Usha Khanna's magic in *Dil Deke Dekho*, Shankar–Jaikishen in *An Evening in Paris* and *Junglee*. And then there was Mohammad Rafi. The singer was to Shammi what Mukesh was to Raj Kapoor: an aural avatar. For, even though he sang for the actor's contemporaries, the image Rafi's voice evoked was that of Shammi Kapoor. Rafi didn't yodel like Kishore Kumar but he stretched himself to match the actor's boisterous antics on screen, interjecting the sounds cowboys in Westerns made while spurring on their horses. Who can forget 'Yun to humne laakh haseen dekhe hai, tumsa nahin dekha' from *Tumsa Nahin Dekha* and 'Ai ai ya karoon mein kya, suku suku' from *Junglee*. Equally unforgettable are 'Aasman as aaya farishta' from *An Evening in Paris* and 'Deewana mujhsa nahin' from *Teesri Manzil*.

Shammi Kapoor's songs spelled energetic defiance and defined the mood of the young in the sixties. Rigid hierarchies in the home were loosening and people were moving into the cities. The cities themselves were beginning to swing. Love had less to do with kismet than with going out and getting what you wanted. Young men wanted to be like this romantic hedonist with his scene-stealing bravado. Songs like 'Badan pe sitare lapete huye' (*Prince*), 'O haseena zulphonwali' (*Teesri Manzil*) and 'Aaj kal tere mere pyar ke charche' (*Brahmachari*) provided young men many of their courting lines, or just plain lines.

As for the women, there are many closet fans of the politically incorrect actor. Confesses a rather prim blue stocking friend who usually turns her nose up at anything less than nouvelle vague and earnestly gritty third-world cinema: 'I just love him, the way he lets himself go. He doesn't care about anything. He is not doing it for the audience, nor posterity, but for himself. The way he dances, it's so, uh, uninhibited.'

Another major reason for his popularity was the fact that he was also a consummate comedian, and a trained actor. It is easy to forget that he belongs to a family of performers; performing was their family business. Even as a schoolboy, Shammi Kapoor occasionally entertained the audience before a film show. Recalls Shashi: 'We went to see *Kismet* in 1945 or 1946. It was a Congress show. Shammi and Urmi sang "Delhi se dulhan laye rahe" before the film started. The choreography was by Mumtaz Ali, Mehmood's father. Shammiji must have been about fourteen.'

Of Prithviraj's three sons, Shammi Kapoor had the best flair for comedy. He was a natural, with his sense of timing and gift for mimicry. A master of the disguise, he had the audience in stitches whether he was a Pathan (*Tumsa Nahin Dekha*), an astrologer (*Dil Deke Dekho*), a doddering old professor (*Professor*), a Frenchman (*An Evening in Paris*) or a sadhu

(*Junglee*). These slapstick skits or comic interludes were often used as narrative devices to push the plot further.

Shammi Kapoor is one of the first comic heroes of Indian cinema. He was able to move between joker and lovesick protagonist, from slapstick to emoting without a glitch. Until his arrival, heroes remained aloof from comedy, leaving the job of tickling the audience's funny bone to comedians. Johnny Walker, Mehmood and Rajendranath played his sidekicks, his comic foils. However, he also had his own comic track. A classic vignette is the train episode in *Teesri Manzil* where he makes a fat passenger go into paroxysms of laughter. Catch Dilip Kumar or Dev Anand, or for that matter Raj Kapoor, doing that. And again unlike the Trimurti, he was an action hero.

Shammi Kapoor knew a great deal about film-making as well. Shakti Samanta says, 'When we were outdoors, he knew how to face the camera, even when we had to use reflectors. He would turn his face in such a way that the light would fall on it. Even in the emotional scenes he would do well—I found him a perfect actor.'

The sixties were Shammi Kapoor's halcyon days. In most of the films he played a rich young man, often from a feudal background. If his father was not an autocrat, his mother was. And almost always, his family did not approve of the woman he wanted to marry. Shammi Kapoor continued with his successful run of romantic comedies for much of the decade. However, Geeta Bali's tragic death in 1965 brought about a change in his lifestyle that would eventually affect his acting career. Recalls Samanta: 'I was making *Jaane Anjane* with Shammi and Leena Chandavarkar when Geeta Bali died. Shammi was very perturbed. He loved his wife very much. He cancelled the shooting, started drinking and began to put on weight. The film was delayed; there was a problem with continuity.'

Jaane Anjane flopped, and Samanta moved on to a younger, slimmer, more bankable hero. Rajesh Khanna, who made such an impact after *Aradhana* with Shammi Kapoor's former heroine Sharmila Tagore, proved to be his nemesis—the way Amitabh Bachchan was to be later for Khanna after *Anand*. Meanwhile, Shammi Kapoor soldiered on, acting with the next generation of heroines like Babita (*Tumse Achcha Kaun Hai*) and Leena Chandavarkar (*Preetam*).

His second round of films with Asha Parekh did not repeat the magic of *Dil Deke Dekho*. *Pagla Kahin Ka* in 1970 and *Jawan Mohabbat* the following year were forgettable. Age, and his expanding girth, had become more visible. That shock of hair, his Elvis puff, had also lost its bounce. The Rajesh Khanna wave pushed other actors to the margins of mainstream cinema. Shammi Kapoor's mature and measured interpretation of the role of a widower in love with a widow (Hema Malini) in Ramesh Sippy's *Andaz* in 1971 didn't create any ripples. Unfortunately for Kapoor, Khanna's cameo appearance in the film garnered all the praise. Khanna also got the best song—'Zindagi ek safar hai suhana'.

Shammi Kapoor saw the writing on the wall, and switched to character roles. In fact, he had realized the need to stop playing the romantic hero after his film *Prince* in 1969.[1] 'I couldn't do the footwork any more. I had broken my legs so many times. I closed shop,' says Shammi.

Once the kilos came on, and finally the beard, it was time to play uncle or patriarch—to become, in fact, his father. While he acted in several successful films in the eighties (*Hero*, *Betaab* and *Desh Premi*), he was less than discriminating in his choice of films in the next two decades: *Tahalka*, *Aur Pyar Ho Gaya*, *Jaanam Samjha Karo* and *Wah Tera Kya Kehna* among the more forgettable. However, some of the supporting roles did enable him to tap his considerable talent as an actor. Shammi Kapoor's performance as the patriarch in Raj Kapoor's *Prem Rog* is among his more memorable, and he won the Filmfare Award for Best Supporting Actor in *Vidhata* in 1982.[2]

Raj Kapoor's huge fan following in the Middle East and the erstwhile Soviet Union is common knowledge. Shammi Kapoor also had his share of admirers in the Middle East and countries like Morocco in the seventies. He almost made it to a Hollywood film: George Cukor had cast him as Ava Gardner's Hindu boyfriend in his screen adaptation of John Masters's novel *Bhowani Junction*. However, the Indian government refused Cukor permission to shoot in India. (Eventually, the film was made in Pakistan.) The closest brush Shammi Kapoor had with Hollywood was in 1978 when he acted in Krishna Shah's film *Shalimar*, a comedy crime caper which starred Rex Harrison, Sylvia Miles and John Saxon, along with Dharmendra and Zeenat Aman.

Shammi Kapoor also tried his hand at direction. But his avatar as a film director was short lived, even though he had been an assistant to Raj Kapoor during the making of *Awara*. He was keen to see what happened behind the camera, and did a stint in editing song picturisations.

Shammi Kapoor directed two films—*Manoranjan* in 1974, produced by F.C. Mehra, and *Bandalbaaz* in 1976 produced by the Nadiadwalas. In *Manoranjan*, Sanjeev Kumar plays a naïve policeman in love with a streetwalker (Zeenat Aman). Despite R.D. Burman's catchy music, the film did not do well at the box office. Perhaps the film was too bold for its time. It was not just the theme of this boisterously entertaining film. In it you see prostitutes waiting under streetlights, below the hotel where they take their customers after a deal is struck. Interestingly, the girls don't look that unhappy. And then there's Zeenat Aman in a short skirt, her black panties often showing. Kapoor even has her in bed with Sanjeev Kumar many mornings-after. However, Shammi Kapoor's camera does not linger lasciviously—and unnecessarily—over the actress's body as Raj Kapoor's did in *Satyam Shivam Sundaram*. The film could easily have been vulgar and voyeuristic. Instead it is naughty-but-nice. Zeenat Aman wears her sex appeal with a certain amount of grace. It's almost as if her innocent face does not know what her naughty body is doing. Almost three decades later, Raj Kapoor's granddaughter, Kareena Kapoor, played a streetwalker in *Chameli* and was critically acclaimed for it.

Shammi recalls his days behind the camera. 'I had seen the play *Irma La Douce* in 1961 in London, and I liked it. Billy Wilder made it into a film, and it was banned in Bombay because it was the story of a prostitute. We had a private trial in Bombay in 1964 for me to do the Jack Lemmon role. My wife thought it was too risqué a proposition. F.C. Mehra wanted me to direct a film and gave me the script of *Irma*. I had grown a beard by then and knew my aptitude, what I could and couldn't do. So, I played a bartender, and Sanjeev Kumar the policeman. I enjoyed making the film. But it was too sophisticated a comedy—you have a prostitute who actually enjoys her work. Here you would have to have a girl doing it because her father is dying of cancer, or she has been kidnapped. Then I made *Bandalbaaz* for the Nadiadwalas. It was a comedy and a ghost story. I offered the main role to Amitabh Bachchan, but he was doing *Adalat* at the time. I asked Rajesh Khanna. I had a miserable time making it. Rajesh Khanna was on his way out. The film was meant for kids. And even they did not enjoy it.'

Ironically, Shashi Kapoor's only directorial venture, *Ajooba*, in 1991 was also a costume drama in the Arabian Nights vein. But this time round Amitabh Bachchan was in the film as its main protagonist. Shammi Kapoor acted in his brother's film, which like his own version of Oriental tales didn't do well at the box office.

Shammi Kapoor never picked up the director's baton again. The critics had not been kind. Stung twice, he retreated and went back to doing supporting roles in films.

'It was known that Shammi Kapoor had to have a new girl for each new film. Compulsive, he did not spare anyone. So when he invited me for lunch during a film shoot, I said no. I told him I didn't go to make-up rooms. Then the producer came to me, the director came to me. And for the fifteenth time I said no. We were all eating lunch outside. Shammi came up to me said, "Now maharani sahiba, please sit here." But I smiled, pretending not to hear. He sat down next to me and asked if I wanted to eat butter chicken. "What will you eat? Breast? Leg? Me?" And I replied, sweetly, "The neck." I wanted to be sarcastic. Then he said, "If you are not satisfied with the chicken neck will you eat mine?"' Thus recalled Madhumati, the dancer–actress who was known as the poor man's Helen and now runs an acting school, in her interview with me.

This vivacious, still coquettish Parsi actress (Hitakxi Doctor is the name she was born with) says she was terrified of Shammi Kapoor until that day on the set. For, when the actor found out that she was married (and that too to a musician working with Raj Kapoor), he dropped the playboy patter like a hot brick: 'He pulled back his chair, and his whole attitude changed. He invited my husband and me home.'

The enfant terrible of the film industry certainly terrorized many actresses and starlets in the sixties. Women may have feared Shammi Kapoor, but they were also inexorably drawn to him. There was something about the young Shammi Kapoor, beyond the fair good looks and petulant swagger, something that the camera did not quite capture. Could it have been 'electricity'? Strangely, it is the word two actresses as diverse as Madhumati and Tanuja use to describe him. Says Madhumati: 'My god! What charisma he had. He'd just appear on the set, and it was electrifying.' And Tanuja concurs: 'Even at seventeen, he had a presence. Wow! He had electricity. He was electric.'

His reputation of being a playboy of the film world preceded him wherever he went. Shammi Kapoor doesn't deny his Casanova image nor his recklessness: it was all about being the 'tough romantic guy'. 'I was the only guy with guns, the only one to shoot tigers and leopards, and that whole thing about women came along as the baggage of being a famous man,' he says.

He also takes pride in the fact that there was a string of debuting actresses cast opposite him during his matinee idol days, indicating that he could carry a film on his own broad shoulders, without the star appeal of his leading lady. 'I created my own world. I picked my own subjects. I took a new girl every time—Saira Banu, Ameeta, Sharmila Tagore, Kalpana, Ragini. I was not dependent on a star cast,' he says.

There was something of the swashbuckling braggart about Shammi Kapoor. It may partially have been due to his Errol Flynn fixation, influenced greatly as he was by Flynn's autobiography *My Wicked, Wicked Ways*. His friends and families maintain that Shammi wanted to emulate the sexually adventurous Hollywood actor and his exploits, both on-screen and off it. A director who made a couple of films with Shammi Kapoor describes him as being 'very indiscreet during his wild days.

Geeta was aware of her husband's affairs but overlooked them. Shammi was like a spoiled brat. He was bold, and would make it a point to let others knew what was happening. Once after a party he was making love to a woman on the lawn while his wife was sleeping inside the house. He was double-edged: he could be charming but also obnoxious, a male chauvinist, specially the way he treated women. If a girl did give in, liked him, she would have certainly wanted it to be discreet. But Shammi's attitude was, so what. And, he would catch her in public, put her over his shoulder and walk off with her, like a caveman. He was the total rebel.'

He may have been the kiss-and-tell playboy of the film world of the sixties, but nobody can accuse Shammi Kapoor of being a hypocrite. While other actors also seduced their leading ladies, they did so behind a shroud of secrecy. In those days, magazines did not follow stars into their bedrooms and bathrooms as they do today. The film industry kept its secrets to itself, as did film journalists who were perfectly au courant about all their peccadilloes and affairs. As for most actors and actresses, they made sure their public images were in keeping with the 'goodie-goodie' characters they portrayed on-screen.

Shammi Kapoor has generally been disarmingly frank about his love life—even with his family—and quite early on in his life. In an intriguing photograph posted on his web site, a beautiful Egyptian girl possessively holds on to a lean, moustached Shammi Kapoor, her arm entwined in his, while his grandparents stand alongside. The young couple appears to have stepped out of a fifties black-and-white Hollywood movie: he is elegant in a tuxedo and bow tie and she equally elegant with her gloved hands and gown. The picture was taken outside Liberty cinema in Bombay in 1953 during the silver jubilee function of a Raj Kapoor film. His caption for the photograph reads: 'With me are my grandmother, grandfather and my girlfriend, Nadia Gamal, a belly dancer who I met in Ceylon. As we were in love we were to get married. Somehow things did not work out and she went back to Cairo and I resumed my work in films, but with a sad heart. At that age, she was seventeen and I was twenty-two, it gets broken very early and quite often.'

Was Shammi Kapoor really a macho, Alpha male? According to the actor himself it was just an 'image thing'. 'I gave the impression of being macho, but I was actually an introvert and protective of these girls. Asha Parekh was a young girl when I saw her in Mehboob Studios. She was reading the novel *Carpetbaggers*, and I told her it was for adults. I had read it ten years earlier. Since it was a sensual novel I did not want her to read it. She called me chachu. I am shy, and not very outgoing. Earlier, the environment was different. The days were different when I worked. For a girl to come to my make-up room and garland me and say, "You are a dream husband" in the fifties, this kind of adulation was unheard of. I would go home and tell my wife. I would brag about it,' he adds with a long sigh.

Actors often fall in love with their leading ladies, and Shammi Kapoor was no exception. An early infatuation was legendary beauty Madhubala, with whom he acted in a few films (*Rail Ka Dibba*, *Bluff Master* and *Boyfriend*) at the outset of his film career. Kidar Sharma, who discovered the actress, says that Shammi Kapoor proposed to her. 'Mumtaz [Madhubala's pet name] was in love with him. He proposed to her. She had become popular. She did not marry him.' It seems Shammi Kapoor even took her home to meet his parents. She was dressed in a white sari. Obviously, the parents did not approve. Later, his relationship with another Mumtaz, also a co-star, became serious. Apparently, he proposed to her also while they were both acting in G.P. Sippy's *Brahmachari*.

What was it about the Kapoor brothers that made them so irresistible to the women they acted with? It wasn't just their fair, good looks that won the women over. With one look, Raj Kapoor's blue eyes had the ability to make any woman he spoke to believe she was very special for him. Shammi Kapoor's green bedroom eyes and cocky persona were equally seductive. Shashi Kapoor was immoderately handsome and quite the prince charming of Hindi cinema with his crooked canine teeth and disarming style.

Shammi Kapoor's aggressive manner and overt sexuality was tempered with romanticism. He may have played out his patented screen rebel image in life, but he could also be an ardent suitor, wooing with poetry and music, and above all pesky persistence. There was an air of the incurable romantic about him.

After Geeta Bali died in 1965, Shammi moved for a brief spell to Chembur, next to Raj Kapoor's home. The self-confessed hedonist didn't waste any time getting on with his infamous binges—both with alcohol and women. On a wild spree, he would often bring his lovers home. His name at the time was linked to Sonia Sahni, Mumtaz and Sharmila Tagore. Worried about his 'wicked, wicked' ways, the Kapoor khandaan began the search for a second Mrs Shammi Kapoor.

Krishna Kapoor, ever his guardian angel, took on the role of Cupid a year after his wife died. Shammi Kapoor was lonely and had two small children—Aditya Raj and Kanchan—who needed looking after. She wanted her young brother-in-law to meet Bina Ramani, whose parents were friends of Raj and Krishna Kapoor and lived in London. Krishna introduced them at a Christmas party Raj Kapoor had given. Bina recalls walking into Bombellis, a favourite watering spot for the young on Warden Road in Bombay: 'I was with my girlfriends and as soon as we entered the live band began to play my favourite song, "The Breeze and I".' Flowers from the actor would surface. Sometimes, Shammi would mysteriously materialize, or call her there. He obviously had an understanding with the restaurant's manager.

Not only did he put his wallet where his mouth was, he was the master of the melodramatic gesture, behaving the way people do in, well, movies. When he won a fairly huge amount at the races at the Mahalaxmi Derby he flamboyantly placed the entire amount at the feet of Bina Ramani. For her birthday he bought her a yellow Sunbeam, the spitting image of the car she drove in London. He once drove his car to Bhendi Bazaar in central Bombay, hopped on its bonnet and started singing out loud—a song with words to the effect of never getting involved with a Sindhi girl. But it was a short romance. Perhaps the age gap between the two was too much: he was in his mid-thirties and she in her early twenties.

The indefatigable Krishna Kapoor got Cupid to shoot another arrow, and in 1969 Shammi Kapoor married Neela Devi from Bhavnagar. It was an arranged marriage, unlike his first. The interlude between his two wives was about four years. But the wedding nuptials were most unusual in both cases.

> *'I am an extremist...I married my two wives in the middle of the night.'*
>
> —Shammi Kapoor

A man of the moment, rushing wherever whimsy led him, Shammi Kapoor married Geeta Bali on the night of 23 August 1955 on the spur of the moment. 'We were together in my room at the Juhu Hotel, where I was staying because my parents were out on tour with Prithvi Theatres, and she said, "Okay, it's now or never. Can we get married now?" I asked her did she mean like right this moment and she said yes, tonight,' writes Shammi on his web site.

Talking to me almost half a century later, he says: 'I told her I couldn't wait. I said let's get married tonight. I was twenty-three. We went to my friend Johnny Walker's house. He had married a week earlier, eloped. We asked him if we could get married the same way. He said, "Stupid fool I am a Muslim...You go to a mandir." The idea struck us and we arrived at the mandir later that night. It was after ten and raining. The gods were sleeping—the temple was closed. I knocked on the door for the pujari. I told him that I would come back at four in the morning. We then went to Matunga. Geeta was a vegetarian. She ate some aloo sabzi, and we waited. At about three I started my Buick convertible with the hood down. She put on some lipstick in the car. We got married.'

The sole witness to the wedding was his friend Hari Walia, producer and director of *Coffee House*, a film in which both Geeta and Shammi were working at the time. Walia, in fact, had guided the couple to the cluster of Banganga Temples near Napean Sea Road. They were married in the Hindu tradition. After the ceremony, Geeta took out a tube of lipstick from her purse, which Shammi applied on her *maang* instead of sindoor.

The nuptials over, Shammi took his bride to his grandfather, asking for his blessings. Bashesharnath Kapoor congratulated the couple. Shammi also took his new wife to Lachcha masi's house for her blessings. She called Prithviraj on the phone and told him about the fait accompli. A surprised Prithviraj asked Shammi to take his wife to their house. They spent the night in Matunga.

For Shammi Kapoor marriage was a passage to adulthood. Somehow, he thought he would feel more grown-up after getting married. In fact, only after he married Geeta Bali did he smoke in front of his father. When Prithviraj Kapoor used to egg him on to take out his cigarettes in front of him, Shammi told his father that he would do so only once he was a married man—only then would he be a grown-up, a man in full in other words. Shammi recalls: 'On Raj Kapoor's birthday, my father and I used to drive in Papaji's Opel to Chembur. My brother would vanish every five or ten minutes to smoke. In the car my father told me that he knew my brother smoked and wondered why he didn't in front of him. And then he said: "What about you? I am missing those moments by your hiding..." I was twenty-two at the time and told him that when I got married I would smoke and drink with him. I kept that promise.'

As he keeps reiterating, for him marriage was the proof of maturity, independence. 'Dilip Kumar was a bachelor for a long time. I on the other hand married when I was twenty-three, when I could stand on my own feet and owned my convertible. I was self-made and a father at twenty-four,' says Shammi.

Shammi Kapoor was the first in his family to marry for love. Raj Kapoor had quietly capitulated and agreed to an arranged marriage, even though it was love at first sight when he saw sixteen-year-old Krishna Malhotra playing a sitar in her home in Rewa. Shammi, on the other hand, was always a bit of a rebel, straining at the leash of convention and the rules of the house. Apparently, his family was not keen he marry an actress, which perhaps explains the dramatic elopement in the middle of the night.

Shammi was apprehensive about the reaction of his family. After all Geeta Bali had been Raj Kapoor's leading lady in Kidar Sharma's *Bawre Nain*. The delightfully spontaneous actress had also worked with his father in *Anandmath*. Moreover, she was two years older than him, and the two could not have come from more different social strata. Prithviraj Kapoor was a member of parliament, a friend of Jawaharlal Nehru; his grandfather had been a tehsildar. The Kapoors were Hindu Pathans, proud of their fair good looks. Geeta Bali, a dusky and vivacious sardarni, came from an impoverished background. Although her father was a teacher, she herself was illiterate. Her family was too poor to send her to school. Nor did she have an easy life as an adolescent: her mother pushed her into acting when she was a teenager. She had to support her family.

'Her mother was domineering, like Madhubala's father...Geeta's father, Kartar Singh, was blind, and she had a fear of becoming blind,' the late Kidar Sharma told me during an interview two years before he died. He played Professor Higgins to her Eliza Dolittle, and she became his protégé. Reminiscing about his first meeting with her, he said: 'Mazhar Khan, a producer and director, told me about a poor girl in Delhi who wanted to act. He said that she would sign free. He asked me to find a place for her to stay. Her guru, dance teacher Pandit Gyan Shankar, brought her to Bombay. My office was near Ranjit Studios, and he came to me and said, "*Taras kar meri beti par.*" (Have pity on my daughter.) He told me that she was too afraid to come to the office and that I was to accompany him to the railway bungalow. There was a big room inside, but no chair. They were poor. There was a bathtub in the middle of this room, over which they had put a wooden slab. Geeta's mother asked me to sit on the slab, and I sat down. But there was water in the tub, and I fell into it. I asked for a towel. Geeta, who was standing in a corner, burst out laughing and said you can't go home like that...'

And that was it: her impish, irrepressible personality had won Kidar Sharma over. The poet–director cast her in *Suhaag Raat*, her debut film. From there, she danced and sang her way to stardom, infecting those along the way with her exuberance. *Albela*, a film in which she co-starred with dancer–actor Bhagwan, was a big hit, and is a perennial favourite even today. She was one part Lucille Ball, two parts Judy Garland: no one could match her liveliness on screen (perhaps Tanuja and more recently her daughter Kajol come close). Interestingly, for Shammi Kapoor the one actress who most approximates his first wife is Urmila Matondkar: 'When I saw her, I said I have seen that look before, the impish look. She has little nuances. Geeta had a versatile canvas. *Bawre Nain* had all shades in it.'

No wonder that after Shammi Kapoor swept her off her feet and away from his Svengali hold, Kidar Sharma was quite distraught. He never forgave the actor for taking his actress and protégé away from him. We were both seated when I was interviewing Kidar Sharma. But when the conversation turned to Shammi Kapoor, he suddenly stood up, his face all flushed with anger, and described the actor as a 'sadist'.

Shammi Kapoor met Geeta Bali while they were both acting in *Coffee House*. It wasn't quite love at first sight, but at second or third, and culminated in Ranikhet during the filming of Kidar Sharma's *Rangeen Raatein*. Sharma did not have a female role in the film for her to play. But that did not deter the effervescent actress who wanted to go along—she suggested to Kidar Sharma that she could play the role of a man in the film, and she did. Describing how they fell in love on location, Shammi Kapoor says: 'She had a cameo role in the film, and I saw a wonderful side of her there, the way she behaved with everybody else in the unit. We vibed. We sang together. She was a very outgoing person, gutsy and down to earth. I was honest, and she fell for that. She had a sense of humour... We had very similar tastes. We both loved the outdoors, jungles and the snow and ice in the hills.'

The Kumaon hills were obviously alive with the sound of romance: they fell in love with the climate, scenery, the people and their music, and each other. When they returned to Bombay they couldn't live without each other. Initially, Geeta Bali was unsure, but 'four months of agony, tears, cajoling, pleading, non-togetherness, desperation', as Shammi puts it, finally made her give in.

The marriage also proved to be a turning point in Shammi's career. Geeta Bali urged him to let some of his irreverent self seep into the characters he portrayed in his films. She convinced him of the need for a screen metamorphosis. 'Geeta bhabhi encouraged him to get over the "family hangover" and to be an individual,' explains Shashi Kapoor.

Talking about Geeta Bali's influence on his film career, Shammi Kapoor says: 'She came from a poor family, yet she was very strong. She gave me strength; she was my backbone. She kept telling me you can do it when I was making films like *Laila Majnu* and *Shama Parwana* and going nowhere. While I was working in *Tumsa Nahin Dekha*, she used to come to the studio. She often brought my dinner and kept telling me that I could make it. You see, when we met, she was a star. I was just Prithviraj Kapoor's son and Raj Kapoor's brother.'

The Kapoors were displaced Pathans. While they brought along a few traditions from the North West Frontier Province, they also evolved a few new conventions and rites of passage for their khandaan. Prithviraj Kapoor's sons continued to stay with him in his Matunga flat after they married. But each one had to move out after the birth of his first child.

Shammi Kapoor and Geeta Bali got a bedroom to themselves in Matunga after their wedding (only married couples were eligible for individual bedrooms). In fact, he was the first to get an air-conditioner in the Kapoor home: he bought one with his own money for fifteen hundred rupees. However, when their son Aditya Raj was born, they moved to a bungalow in Chembur.

Unlike his elder brother, Shammi Kapoor was not enamoured with suburban life. Nor was his wife. The two moved to their apartment in Blue Haven on Malabar Hill in south Bombay in 1960. 'Geeta and I wanted to be in Bombay, in an elite locality. I bought my own flat,' says Shammi. Life acquired a sophisticated patina, not normally the case in many film families. They used to go to Calcutta—to Blue Fox, Joshua Bar, Princess in Grand Hotel—for Christmas and New Year's.

Shammi Kapoor often talks about his fondness for the good things in life, especially his cars. His wife also wanted to acquire the accoutrements of success, particularly jewellery. Geeta Bali used to wear gold anklets. When Mrs Jagat Singh Ahuja remarked that gold anklets were the prerogative of maharanis, she countered, 'If I don't put them on my feet how will people know that I have so much gold?' 'You see,' explains Mrs Ahuja, 'she had five hundred *tola*s of gold.'

Geeta Bali was quite content to concentrate on her home and children, leaving her husband to bask in the arc lights, and cheering him on from behind the scenes. She encouraged him to continue in the *Tumsa Nahin Dekha* vein. The few films Geeta Bali acted in after she married were to complete her commitments. Husband and wife even acted in one film together, *Jabse Tumhe Dekha Hai*. In fact, she was acting in Rajinder Singh Bedi's film *Ek Chadar Maili Si*, based on his play of the same name, when she fell fatally ill. The unit was filming in Moga (Punjab) and Dharmendra was her co-star. The film was never completed. Geeta Bali died of smallpox on 21 January 1965.

The Kapoor men can't do without their wives, despite their wandering eyes. Shashi Kapoor puts it succinctly: 'The Kapoors need strong women, to keep the home together and to keep them from straying. They need wives whose mission it is to take care of them.' It was the same with Shammi Kapoor: he became a widower when his son Aditya was just nine and his daughter Kanchan only four. A second marriage was arranged to Neela Devi; she is from Kathiawad, and the present maharaja of Bhavnagar is a cousin of hers.

Shammi Kapoor's two wives are a study in contrast. While Geeta Bali came from an ordinary Punjabi family and had never been educated, Neela Devi, a colonel's daughter, belongs to Gujarati aristocracy. Draped in the feudal uniform of chiffon saris, she always keeps her head covered in public. Soft-spoken, Neela Devi speaks crisp English, and is nothing if not elegant and correct. Tea in their home comes in a well-dressed trolley, a well-behaved white poodle in cheerful pursuit.

Shammi had seen Neela earlier, in Bhavnagar, when she was much younger. Many years later, in 1969, Krishna Kapoor and his sister asked him to 'see' her again. 'I used to pull her chotis,' says Shammi. 'I knew the family. We met. And then one night I rang her up. It was 26 January 1969. I talked to her for four hours and told her what I wanted. I talked about how I used to drink in the past. I told her that I was a widower with two children. That I had had two strong affairs: one wanted a career, the other I was not keen to marry. I told her that if it has to happen it has to be tomorrow. She said okay. I spoke to my mother and bhabhiji. Both came at 11 the next morning. They came and put the proposal to Neela's father. I insisted that I wanted to get married just then, and not the day after, right then. It was not a love marriage. She brought up my kids. She rules. I gave her all the keys.'

The junglee was finally tamed. Life proceeded at a more measured pace. It was also a transitional stage in Shammi Kapoor's professional life. His matinee idol image was losing some of its shine: he had begun to put on weight and his films were no longer doing as well. His last role as lead hero was in Ramesh Sippy's *Andaz*. The film was made in 1969 but released only two years later.

Was life imitating art? In the film, Shammi Kapoor plays a widower who remarries. The irony is double peg here: not only did his brother act in a film of the same name (Mehboob Khan's *Andaz* with Nargis and Dilip Kumar), Sippy's film anticipated the subject of widow remarriage, the subject of Raj Kapoor's comeback vehicle, *Prem Rog*, after his box-office debacle, *Satyam Shivam Sundaram*. Recalls Ramesh Sippy: 'Shammi was going through a phase. He had already seen stardom and was kind of peaking. He was also stuck in the rebel image. When I told him about *Andaz*, he asked me if I was sure. There were no songs. The story was about a widow and widower. The whole world thought I was mad. There is a man who has lost his wife and a woman who has lost her husband. Why can't they be together? The film was about widow remarriage, but I did not put it into a social context, as Raj Kapoor later did with *Prem Rog*. He identified it as a social problem and gave it a traditional setting. Shammi saw my film and became my fan. He used to call me Jonas, after the character in *Carpetbaggers*.'

Neela Devi not only *sambhaloed* (steadied) her husband, as Shashi so cogently puts it, she brought up the children as if they were her own. Apparently, she chose not to have any of her own in order to look after her husband's children better. And Shammi began another phase in his life. Lachcha masi believes that the second marriage began the Gujaratification of Shammi Kapoor:

'Shammi has become a Gujarati. His wife and his daughter-in-law are both Gujarati. His son married Neela's niece.'

On his web site, Shammi Kapoor includes his wife's version of how they got married. The prankster and fabulist in him won her heart. Interestingly, she never takes his name. 'I first saw him when I was nine and he was nineteen. He had come to Bhavnagar with his father's troupe to perform on the stage. My family was in the auditorium watching Prithvi Theatres' *Pathan*, and along with my cousins I was allowed to watch from the wings. He came and pulled my pigtails, something which I have never forgotten. And that is how I became a fan of a person who one day was to become my husband. The year was 1955, he had just married Geeta Bali, somebody I had always loved and respected both as a film person and a human being. I had once met her and taken her autograph, which is still one of my proud possessions. He often came home to visit us as he was a good friend of my brother, but I knew better—it was mostly to share a bottle of whiskey with my father who was a retired colonel, and being the prohibition period, it was often my father who ended up producing the whiskey. He would regale us with his stories of shikar and film shooting and various other escapades, which kept the whole family enthralled while he walloped off the bottle.'

Flash forward to the portly patriarch in his den. Photographs of his children and grandchildren surround him. The grandfather has become the chronicler of the Kapoor family, intermittently scanning photographs of his family into his iMac. During one of our meetings in his study I ask him to show me his electronic family album. He flips through the photographs of the larger Kapoor clan. When he calls up the images of Geeta Bali (there is a special file for her), his voice drifts away, muffled it would seem by nostalgia.

On the screen appear photographs of a moustached and lean Shammi Kapoor with his wife at a premiere, feeding her at breakfast, the two of them outdoors and laughing, cutting a cake during the birthday of one of their children. All the while his back remains turned to me. But when he turns around, after he has finished with calling up the Geeta Bali file, he appears to have retreated into the past as well, as if the world of memory is more real than the present. When I tell him that it is strange how technology helps us hold on to and relive the past, he replies, 'This you can't take away from me. They have taken everything else.'

It's quite a mise en scène, Shammi Kapoor's office, or the room where he works and receives people. The delicious title of Arthur Koestler's book, *The Yogi and the Robot*, flashes through my mind as soon as I enter the glass-encased room in which he sits, lost on the highways of the Internet. A digital camera sits next to the computer, both obviously much in use. The room is full of gizmos and electronic objects, like a futuristic cabin in a nineties' movie. But the man himself is a study in contrast, at the other end of the spectrum from the high-tech world that surrounds him.

Massive and imposing, he looks like a cross between a maharaja and a guru: long hair in a ponytail, luxuriant beard, wearing a luminous turquoise silk kurta over an equally colourful lungi. His string of brown stones as big as ostrich's eggs has a pendant with a photograph of his guru Dera Khan Baba. The guru's photographs embellish both the actor and the walls of the study. The piercing eyes in the photographs seize you, looking out as they do from a young face framed by wild hair. Shammi Kapoor does a long, maharaja-ish namaste. For a moment all you see are his rings and earrings—emeralds, diamonds and rubies that could be a king's ransom. Bedazzling.

It is difficult to reconcile this image with the original jumping jack and 'roadside Romeo' of the Indian screen, though those (in)famous green eyes still flash insolence and *masti*, albeit tempered with a soupçon of vulnerability. Shammi Kapoor has obviously reinvented himself once again, this time after hitting midlife crisis. It happened in the seventies, when his career as matinee idol slowed down.

While he was busy hunting on one side of the Terai, unknown to him on the other side was the man who was to change his life. Neela Devi had tried to introduce her husband twice, without luck, to Dera Khan Baba, as Shammi today refers to him, when he came to Bombay. This guru lived in Dera Khan village in Kumaon, near Bhim Tal. Shammi Kapoor was a reluctant disciple, yet the minute he begins to talk about his encounter with his guru, his demeanour changes, his voice becomes more wistful.

'There is a temple in that village with that name, and he is the reincarnation of the original Dera Khan Baba who built that temple,' says Shammi. 'He keeps coming back. My contact came through my family. Neela's family went for kirtans. My father-in-law, Colonel Godha, had read *The Autobiography of a Yogi*, where he came across a description of Mahavatar Baba. Neela asked me to come for darshan. She took my children to him when he came in 1970. But I did not get Baba's darshan for years, arguing as I did over the stupid conception of god on earth and a human being two hundred years old. When he came again in 1974, my wife asked me to come along. I was shooting in Ville Parle for Manmohan Desai. This was big: Babaji was coming to our house. When she insisted, I asked Manmohan Desai if I could leave early. The film was *Parvarish* with Amitabh Bachchan and Amjad Khan on the set. He said no, and I told him that it was my duty to ask. So, we continued shooting. But some things are ordained in life. After lunch, about 2.30 p.m., Manmohan Desai was called to the phone. He returned and hit me on my back. "*Aise kaun sa guru aya hai*?" he asked me. "My wife's mother has been in hospital for the last six months and she has just kicked the bucket. Is your darshan so important that you got it [the shooting] cancelled?" I went home. I had a camera and I took his photographs. But he looked at me as if he was taking an X-ray. It was as if he was taking my photograph with his eyes. The way he looked at me, I was totally lost. I went to his ashram in 1976. I was curious to begin with. What was it all about? Hocus-pocus? Four hundred years old and feet curled up like a child, so beautiful. Could it be a melting of years? It was something far beyond my comprehension. I wanted to know, and after that my surrender was total. He accepted me. My Babaji never spoke in those days.'

But his guru transformed him. Shammi Kapoor was forty-three years old, and both his parents had died, within a fortnight of each other, in 1972. Describing the pre-Baba days and the post-Baba days he says: '[Growing up] we lived in the aura of bhajans. My mother said the Gayatri mantra, and there was no meat cooked in our home on Tuesdays. But I was not aware about rituals, rites and fasts. In 1972, I went to Badrinath for the first time with the ashes of my mother. Shashi and I took her ashes to Haridwar. He was supposed to go back, he was shooting a film. I persuaded him to go with me to Badrinath. I took an icebox with beer, and we drank. We went to Srinagar and Rudraprayag. The circuit house was empty. We got Ganga water and whiskey. We got non-vegetarian khana from a dhaba, ate and slept. I was a strict non-vegetarian, a shikari. I also went to Joshimath, where I stayed in Hotel Ashram, a one-star hotel. I opened my whiskey bottle, drank and slept. The panda gave us a 3.00 a.m. darshan. We ate vegetarian food, had a darshan of Bhagwan Vishnu. We gave some money, got into our car and drank beer.'

When Shammi Kapoor travelled with Babaji to several pilgrimage places, including Gangotri, Yamunotri and Badrinath, things were certainly different, as he tells it. 'I went with Baba to Devprayag. We stayed outside an old school. The bathrooms were in the open air. At 3.30 a.m. we would bathe in the stream, put on chandan. We reached Joshimath at night, ate aloo, dal, puris and slept. We bathed in the stream. I was not well, so I slept all day. I saw the same aarti very differently. A transition had taken place: this was a yatra; that was a picnic.

'The first time I went to Tirupati, it was 1962 or 1963. I was shooting in Madras. I took a car, but was late. [At the temple] they said "Bhagwan so gaye" (God has gone to sleep). I was alone, god was not with me. I opened a bottle of whiskey and drank all the way from Madras. I saw Tirupati and went back: it was only *naam ke vaaste*. Then I went again in 1977 [after he had met Baba]. I recall it was during the making of *Shalimar*. We were in Neela Bungalow in Bangalore. We reached the temple complex, but I had gastroenteritis. I went straight to the circuit house, bathed, and had Electral. We got tickets for Rs 3, went in there and joined our hands. After darshan, it was raining very hard, and we had only one wiper, and the driver wore very thick glasses. It was the Andhra Pradesh cyclone. We drove all night, one wiper, and reached Bangalore...*Yeh yatra hua.*'

The biggest change after meeting Baba was when he began to wean himself from alcohol. Recalls Shammi: 'I was ill once when I was in his [Baba's] ashram. He took care of me. I had fever. He sent me brandy, but I never touched it. The first time I had gone there I took whiskey and tinned sardines and tuna. But this time there was no need. I cherished the vegetarian meals, delicious *kaddu*. Babaji gave me the meals. I shared a plate with him. When I used to go and smoke outside, he would tell me, "*Rail gaadi chala ke aye ho.*"'

The guru and his ardent actor disciple had a very special relationship for a decade, till Baba's demise in 1984. 'On 14 February 1984, I was in Bangalore, shooting *Ek Se Bhale Do*. I got a call at 5 a.m. I had woken up with a start. I was dreaming that there was an anchor to which we were tied which had broken. It was like being cut off from a mooring, like ships on a sea, or floats tied to a buoy that had broken and drifted off into the sea. Babaji has gone, said the voice on the phone. I was surprised. I had just met him. I used to spend Makar Sankranti (14 January) with him every year. We had left Dera Khan on 16 January after a havan at 5 a.m. He asked me then to tell everyone in Bombay that he would leave Dera Khan on the 14th. I thought he meant that he would come to Bombay. We drove all night to get to him. I even took a ride on a military truck. I made his samadhi. I carried him,' says a sombre Shammi.

'The Internet set me rolling again. It introduced me back to life.'

—Shammi Kapoor

Crisis and critical turning points have regularly punctuated Shammi Kapoor's life. At a crucial juncture in his midlife his guru had buoyed him for a decade, until 1984, guiding him not only down the path of spirituality, but also through the quotidian milestones of life. Baba Dera Khan even organized the marriage of his son

Aditya. The guru had become a father figure for his ardent, formerly reckless disciple.

Computers took on the role of his new life support system in 1988, shortly after Raj Kapoor died. The black clouds of depression hung over Shammi Kapoor. His work life had hit a new low. Although he had started doing character parts in the seventies, his career as a director had not taken off. Shammi Kapoor had to cope, as do all movie stars, with the fact of no longer being a star. He had already put on a lot of weight. How close Raj Kapoor and he may have been is anybody's guess, but his elder brother's death suddenly left a vacuum in the Kapoor family. He now found himself wearing the mantle of the 'head of the family'.

It was in such a state of mind that he first spotted a computer. As the new patriarch of the family, Shammi Kapoor used to visit Devnar Cottage every day. His niece, Ritu Nanda, had brought her computer from Delhi to Bombay, where she had moved for a short while to be with her mother after the death of her father.

'It was quite small and she would sit every afternoon, typing, and look at Rajji's business affairs,' remembers Shammi. 'I would sit with her. Computers were only available in government or corporate worlds. For the next few days I did graphics, besides using the word processor. Here, I thought, was a technology which was so vibrant, and of which I had no knowledge. After a week I went to Moscow with my wife to act in Shashi's *Ajooba*. We stopped in London on the way. I went to Harrods, and just opposite the store I saw a small shop that was selling Apple computers. I went there every day during our three days in the city. I picked the software. But I had no hardware. Back in Bombay I contacted Macintosh and got a computer with a fourteen-inch monitor. That's how I got into the world of computers. I read manuals, learned to load it myself. The next time I went to London I bought a scanner. It got me away from the depression of death—my parents, my wife, my brother.

'The day a mouse came in my house, the cigarettes flew away. I used to smoke hundred cigarettes a day at one time. Eventually I stopped after forty-five years. My drinking went down. I had no definitive job, so I wandered up and down different software. I thought technology was something to get involved with, to grow with. People play golf when they retire. I played golf thirty years ago. I smoked, I drank, I womanized, and I cooked. I have done it all. You have to move on, evolve. It is not a question of shedding one's skin—that means you are removing one self and waiting for the other to grow. There has to be growth, movement. You know, time hangs heavy. What happens when you are no longer the star? All those people around you will disappear, and then time will be waiting for you. You take a drink. You think it will make time go a little bit, that time will move faster. But it does not. That entire crowd around you disappears. I found technology instead. The Internet opened up. The globe shrank.'

Shammi's life is now organized around the computer. His day, which has found structure, begins late. He surfaces in the afternoon, available for phone calls only after two. From then on he is at his computer until dinnertime, that is, on days he isn't shooting for a film or a commercial, or attending an Internet club meeting. He no longer does fourteen-hour days on his computer though, as he did when he first began to use it to cope with his sense of grief and emptiness.

Shammi Kapoor joined the Mac users club, and made many friends through it. He also became a member of the Apple web site, after which he became part of the Internet users club started by VSNL to create awareness about the Internet. When the group was first formed it met once a month at VSNL. Shammi Kapoor has been its chairman for the last decade and is even today actively involved in creating awareness about broadband—its cost and availability.

After he surfs the net to find out what is happening in the world at large, he settles down to his own world. Shammi Kapoor's scanner has become his time machine, transporting him to, perhaps, a happier past. He scans photographs of old films, of himself, and of his family, immediate and extended. Occasionally, he puts them on his web page, but more often than not he places them in his personal memory book, an electronic photo album—a refuge from the present.

He often pulls up photographs of Geeta Bali, of the two of

them together, of the two of them with their children, of his parents, of his grandchildren, of Raj Kapoor, of the whole Kapoor clan. He has got them all in there, and keeps topping up his bank of family pictures. He even did some detective work and found out more about his family by consulting the pundits in Anantnag, Haridwar and Badrinath.

The computer has helped him retrieve friends from the past. One day he received a letter from Afsal Sharif, his childhood friend from his days at Hollywood Lane. Afsal, whose family moved to Pakistan after partition, had seen Shammi's web site and wrote a letter asking him if he was the same Shammi Kapoor who had lived in Matunga. The two now communicate regularly through e-mail.

January 2004. It has been almost six months since I last saw Shammi Kapoor. He has reinvented himself, yet again. For this meeting, he is in a blue striped T-shirt and dark-blue loose-fitting trousers. The gorgeous jewellery has gone, as have his beard and ponytail—and twenty-five kilos. His hair has been cut close to the head. An air of fragility envelops him; his eyes now look even larger, more limpidly vulnerable.

His daughter Kanchan is responsible for the 180-degree sartorial turn. In July 2003, Shammi Kapoor had a very close brush with death: he was coughing blood and his lungs had practically collapsed. He spent almost two months in Breach Candy Hospital, much of it in intensive care and most of the time in a critical condition. Just before he was to come home from the hospital, Kanchan went shopping for pants, shirts, T-shirts and shoes. She laid them out on her father's bed and asked him to try them out. The new wardrobe was more suited to the new life that his illness had scripted for him. 'It was conducive to a new way of thinking, a new life,' Shammi tells me. 'It is also a different world I have come back to. I have a hospital bed at home, a day and night nurse, a physiotherapist. My lungs collapsed, so did my kidney, and I have weekly dialysis. It feels different—I have been so close to it [death], and came back because of the blessings of my guru, friends, family and fans.'

His circle of friends has also shrunk. 'I have inhibitions,' he says. 'I would rather walk in my garden. I still feel shy of people because I suppose I don't have much to share, either work wise or view wise. I don't go out much, not even to the movies. I talk about books in my circle of friends—the computer-minded. I am comfortable with them.'

It is a quiet existence in his little oasis on Malabar Hill, calm, all passion spent. In his current real-life role, Shammi Kapoor is the patriarch of the larger Kapoor clan, overseeing weddings and funerals, and other ceremonies of the family. For Karisma Kapoor's wedding, he was the understudy who got to play his late brother Raj Kapoor's role as paterfamilias. No doubt he will don the robes again for the wedding of Raj Kapoor's other granddaughter, Riddhima Kapoor, in 2006. In this life of quiet contentment, he is happy being grandfather to his own small family.

You don't see the junglee, beloved of successive generations, any more. Yet you can't escape the feeling that when the rest of the household sleeps, the Yahoo Shammi Kapoor emerges, travelling into the past on his time machine, his computer.

4

The Perfect Gentleman: Shashi Kapoor

It was just a curl, a loving little swirl his mother made each morning. She felt kiss curls would make his unusually large forehead appear smaller. No doubt his schoolmates at Don Bosco or childhood friends on Hollywood Lane made fun of him. But for the school-going boy the curl was sacrosanct. For Shashi Kapoor, arguably the most handsome actor of the Indian screen (actress and friend Tanuja describes Shashi as simply 'Shashlik'—good enough to eat), that large brow seemed to trip narcissism early on in his life. Recalls Prayag Raaj: 'Shashi was very touchy about it. If anyone disturbed it, he would say, "I will beat you." At times he even said, "I'll kill you." He used to stand in front of the mirror and make sure the curl remained intact.'

As a child his large head sat atop a small body, and his unbelievably long eyelashes triggered sniggers from his friends and family. His looks may have been inadvertently responsible for his being an angry young child—one who, ironically, did not grow into an angry young man on the screen like his famous co-star, Amitabh Bachchan. In fact, the joke in the Indian film industry in the late seventies and eighties was that this Kapoor, with his perfect and fair Pathan looks and easy charm and crooked canines, was Bachchan's favourite heroine. Of course there was nothing feminine about Prithviraj Kapoor's youngest son. It was just that he always came across, and was, The Perfect Gentleman of Indian cinema—the nice guy, ever chivalrous and gallant with a sly sense of humour. Contemporaries like Dharmendra and Amitabh Bachchan cultivated a more macho image, while he was more nuanced, less melodramatic and obviously uncomfortable running around trees and singing about the birds and bees. However, he was not always the nice man—a label slapped on him by many of his fans in India and abroad.

Under the urbane, good-natured surface there was complexity and unarticulated anger—a spark could set it off. It was more evident in the films he made for European and American directors. Shashi Kapoor was our first real international star, and till today the most significant overseas. It took more discerning film directors like James Ivory (*Bombay Talkie*, *Heat and Dust*), Stephen Frears (*Sammy and Rosie Get Laid*) and Nicholas Meyer (*The Deceivers*) among others to explore his complex or dark side. In Indian cinema, Shyam Benegal brought out this side of the actor in both *Junoon* and *Kalyug*.

Growing up, the youngest Kapoor son had a lot of anger bottled up inside him. Perhaps he did not like being called Napoleon by those around him. 'Being a little fellow, uncles and aunts would call me Napoleon,' says Shashi Kapoor. 'I had a big head, big forehead and a small neck and body...I used to fall down as a baby because of my big, heavy head.' Perhaps being the baby of the family he was spoiled. As he puts it: 'I was an angry child. I was the youngest, and could almost get away with murder. When I was about eight or ten, I challenged a friend. I had an air gun and I shot him in the leg—I put a lead bullet in his leg. We used to call him Gulu...Everybody thought Shammiji was the angry young man, but I was the angry young boy. Papaji used to put oil on my head to take care of my *gussa* (anger). He used to say, "*Sar garam hai*" (He is hot headed), although he never slapped me.'

Who would have thought that the angelic-looking Shashi Kapoor had a bad temper? That head used to get garam quite often. Once during a family dinner, Shashi, who was not quite thirteen at the time, tore Shammi Kapoor's kurta. 'Shammiji was teasing me. I got angry and said something to him. He then dipped his finger into the *salan* (curry) and flicked it on me. I got up and tore his kurta that he had got for Diwali. It was expensive, made from silk which Chinese men used to bring on their bikes. Shammiji got angry. I began to cry. My father called me and asked for an apology. He cut the amount for the kurta from my pocket money,' recalls Shashi.

Any incipient or remaining narcissism took another knock when the skinny Shashi began to put on weight. You can already see the chubby Kapoor gene at work in *Awara*. In the film he acts as the child (not quite twelve at the time) who will grow into Raju, the young man Raj Kapoor plays. His face is podgy, and he fills his shirt quite well. The film apparently was a long time in the making, during the course of which the fledgling actor put on some weight. Recalls Shashi: 'Raj Kapoor started with the child's portion, and he added some scenes later, by which time I was plumper and taller.' Says Prayag Raaj, who used to play with Shashi and his friends in Matunga most evenings: 'When he was eleven his thighs would rub against each other when he walked. He was such a fat kid, coming, rather waddling, back from school. People teased him, and he cried. But he was the *ladla*, everybody's favourite.'

The child Shashi also had a surprisingly foul tongue. 'I followed the example of others around me and spoke the *gali wali* (street) language. Once I even gave a *gaali* to my mother. Rajji overheard and slapped me. I cried a lot and ran up to the terrace on the third floor of our Matunga home. Rajji followed me and patiently lectured me about the use of language—what bad language really meant, what should or should not be said. Later he took me out for a Chinese meal to Kamlin. He had a beautiful Oldsmobile. I was about eight.'

Another slap followed when Raj Kapoor was making *Barsaat* in 1948. He used to work nights on his own film, and days on the sets of Mehboob Khan's *Andaz*, completing the triangle with Dilip Kumar and Nargis. The schizophrenic life was getting to him, juggling as he had to the shooting schedules of Nargis and his own. It was also Diwali. Shashi, ten at the time, could not have enough of firecrackers. 'We were bursting firecrackers and I did it in the staircase. Naturally it resonated—it was really loud. Rajji woke up, disturbed,' recalls Shashi and slapped him, following it up with yet another Chinese meal. This was to happen again.

But happily for Shashi a slap was usually followed by a slap-up meal.

His mother was forever slapping him as well. But Prithviraj Kapoor never raised his hand on Shashi, preferring to leave the disciplining to his first-born. Fourteen years separated the two brothers. 'Raj Kapoor treated me like a son. He used to say, "Shashi is my first son, and Daboo my second,"' says Shashi.

Shashi Kapoor was first named Balbir Raj, a name chosen for him by his step-grandmother because the pundits had decreed his name should begin with B. However, his mother 'hated' the name and called him Shashi since he was always looking at the moon. The youngest Kapoor was born on 18 March 1938 in Calcutta, where his father was working as an actor with New Theatres. It was not an easy birth. Not only was there a problem with his oversized head, he was born at home: a *dai* (midwife) brought him into the world in the Kapoor house on Hazra Street. Prithviraj Kapoor could not afford a hospital for his wife. Although he earned a fair amount at New Theatres at the time, he was also supporting his expanded family: his father, stepmother and their children. 'My father was the sole earner. His sister was pregnant at the same time as my mother was with me. He paid for his sister's hospitalization. Earlier, when my mother was pregnant with my sister Urmi, Khasho buaji (his father's stepsister) was expecting. My sister was born at home and Subhiraj was born in a hospital. My father was a *shravan puttar* (devoted son),' recounts Shashi.

Prithviraj Kapoor returned to Bombay in 1939. And Shashi, barely one at the time, spent the next twenty years of his life in Hollywood Lane. Memories of childhood surface, buoyed along by images and aromas of what he ate. The highlight of each evening was the adda of friends that surrounded the *golewala* (seller of ices) with pink and orange flavoured ice balls. 'I remember I always had tonsillitis, yet we ate ice fruit, ragara patties and all those horrible things. I went there a few years ago and that man, now in his seventies, was still there. Shammiji used to go there too,' remembers Shashi. Shashi's initiation to hard-boiled eggs took place in Peshawar, where they were usually served on top of biryanis and pulaos. A vivid childhood memory is of his father holding aloft fried eggs, sunny side up, in his palms: the logic of the exercise was to determine which ones had the perfect yolks. Of course, there would be a scramble for those.

His father started Prithvi Theatres in 1944, and was seldom home after that: the group was constantly on the road. Shashi was six and too young to go on the road. He spent much of his early childhood in Bombay with his mother while the rest of the family was away. His father was a remote figure: the devoted son was not indulgent with his own sons. Prithviraj Kapoor didn't want his sons to become spoiled brats. The gentle giant was quite a formidable patriarch: children were supposed to be seen, not heard; spoken to, rather than speak. Shashi was perpetually in awe of him. 'Everybody used to fall silent when he came home. I was scared of him when I was little and growing up, in fact till my school days,' says Shashi. Later, when he joined his father's group, Shashi Kapoor continued to be 'tongue-tied with him. I didn't talk. I listened...When I was in the theatre he did not treat me as a son but as a theatre person—as a member of Prithvi Theatres.' Yet, surprisingly, this Kapoor seemed to have relished the shade of the proverbial family elm tree—unlike his siblings who struggled to get out from under it to find a distinct identity in the world of cinema. Nor was there a sense of rivalry with his brothers.

Notions of hierarchy were more fluid when it came to his relationship with his mother: he could get away with a lot with her. 'We were friends with my mother. We would bully her all the time. She was so gullible and very simple,' recalls Shashi.

Growing up with relatives and strangers in every nook and cranny of the Kapoor home, life was seldom less than eventful. The tragedy of the deaths of Bindi and Devi evidently affected the elder brothers—they have often said as much. Shashi, on the other hand, claims that his parents did not allow the tragic deaths to impinge on their lives: 'My parents never talked about the two brothers who died. My father was strong and my mother was so fond of him that he was able to make her forget this tragedy.' Yet, when he talks about his childhood and his mother, an unmistakable note of melancholy creeps into his voice. Napoleon may have been a family joke but Shashi is convinced that 'his big head' was in some way responsible for his mother's uterine cancer. Apparently, his mother used to tell him that his birth caused her a great deal of pain. 'I gave my mother a lot of trouble when I was born,' he says a little sadly.

The 'baby' of the family spent more time within the enveloping fold of their home than his brothers did, much of the time in a household dominated by women because the men were at play. Shashi's mother and the women of the extended Kapoor clan, including her best friend, Lachcha masi, spent hours each day playing cards. They played rummy and chatted about clothes and jewellery. During family holidays in Peshawar and Murree, Shashi often found himself sequestered with the women. 'We used to sit outside on the bed in summer. During the winters we were indoors, where it was always dark, and there were very few windows. We remained under *razai*s (quilts). There were narrow steps going up. Women sat on bricks on the terrace, chatting, gossiping. Sometimes I felt embarrassed being with women,' recalls Shashi. His mother used to go see a film in a purdahwalla tonga. He used to go along and sit in the women's section with her.

While Raj Kapoor spent many of his impressionable years in the North West Frontier, for Shashi Kapoor it was just a place his father had left behind when he went to Bombay to become an actor. It was somewhere he went for a holiday as a child, or to attend a family wedding. Being a Pathan was more central to the identity of the eldest brother. Pathaniyat for Shammi Kapoor did not go much beyond a Pathan servant of the family. For Shashi it was not the place, Peshawar, but the journey there that is more vividly imprinted on his imagination.

Recalling the time he went there as an eight year old in the summer of 1946 to attend a family wedding, he says: 'As children we hated to go to Peshawar. It was very hot in the summer and very cold in the winter. The elders loved it. But for us the journey of two days and nights on the Frontier Mail was more fun. We ate different things at different stations. We also drank different kinds of tea along the way. Between Lahore and Peshawar we used to get delicious deep-fried *bater*s (partridges). Even the toys sold at each station were different. In Agra they sold fruit sellers made of clay in cardboard boxes lined with cotton wool. In some places you found koli (fisherwomen) in clay or south Indian Brahmin ladies.'

Memories of Peshawar are more intangible. The smells rather than the sights of the city lingered on, and surfaced when the actor visited the city in 1997. Shashi Kapoor was in Pakistan for three months to act in the controversial international film *Jinnah*, in which he plays the angel Gabreel (Gabriel). 'There was a funny smell in Peshawar in different areas, like the Sadar area. I got the same whiff last time, not in Lahore or Karachi but in Peshawar. It was not a *khushboo* (good smell) or *badhboo* (bad smell)—just a *boo* (smell). Lahoriyan di Gali [where his mother grew up] had open drains, and still does. When I went there as the governor's guest, women on the first floor threw flowers and yelled. I went to Sadar Bazaar, the cantonment area where Edwards College was located. It was a very emotional experience.' The city remembered the Kapoors: flower sellers gave him flowers and called him Sishi Kapoor, pronouncing his name the Pathan way.

For Shashi the stage became his world early in life, much more so than it had been for his brothers. 'At six I started going to Royal Opera House. I was taken to Tamil plays—plays by R. Manickam and others. I remember I used to look around and go to sleep. After six I never wanted to do anything but theatre,' says Shashi. Everything else was just a matter of waiting in the wings, even school.

Shashi Kapoor went to Don Bosco in the suburbs when he was six, where he initially shared a bench with Faroukh Engineer, later to become one of India's best-known cricketers. The two used to bunk their last two classes—Shashi to go to the movies, Faroukh to play cricket. Shashi's first and last hero had to be his father. The first film he saw or remembers is *Sikandar*: his father played the title role. And the first play he saw was *Shakuntala*: his father was the hero in this as well. Shashi packed in a lot of films during those stolen hours. A little ingenuity went a long way: the truant schoolboys used to see films in Palace Heights and Broadway, cinema halls in which matinees were cheaper. 'You had two classes—A class and B class. Matinees were cheaper. We used to buy a five-anna ticket for the front benches and sit in the ten-anna seats. Or, pay one rupee for the stalls and go to the balcony,' Shashi says.

The fledgling movie buff was eclectic in his tastes: he liked Hedy Lamaar and Robert Walker, was keen on Westerns, and even devoured films full of *jadu* (magic) made by Mohan Picture Company. B-grade and kitschy films occupied the same hallowed space as did the more classical cinema. *Jalpari*s (fairies) and *jadugar*s (magicians) populated the world of his imagination. Unlike his two brothers, Shashi was not a sportsman. His playing fields were the darkened movie halls.

Meanwhile, there was school. Just as Professor J. Dyal and Norah Richards played a seminal role in forming the character of Prithviraj Kapoor, Charles Farrow, his mentor–teacher, had a lasting influence on Shashi Kapoor. Farrow, who later became headmaster of Don Bosco, taught him for four years—until he was eleven. Recalls Shashi: 'He used to tell me that I'd do well. He made me paint. I even won a contest. I loved history and English. We used to call him Sir Charles, or Sir. He was always optimistic and never allowed me to be pessimistic. He taught me to never use the word "can't". I was weak in Sanskrit. Whenever I said I can't do something, he said, "You can and you will." I learned to have faith in myself.'

However, the hard work was short lived. Shashi Kapoor started getting bored when he was fourteen. School ceased to interest him after studying was reduced to *kitabi* knowledge, learning by rote. 'There were fixed questions, and *mujhe ratna nahin tha*. I refused to remember what I didn't like. So, I decided it had to be theatre,' Shashi informs me. Interestingly enough, his aversion to blindly remembering lines without absorbing their meaning carried over to films. 'I used to fight with Salim–Javed over commas and pauses. You couldn't change a word. Amitabh Bachchan had a photographic memory, not me. Until I accept something and internalize it, nothing registers.' No wonder bombastic and hyper-melodramatic dialogue did not sound right coming out of his mouth. The actor did not look convincing, unless he was convinced. On the other hand, plausibility of plot or dialogue did not hinder Shashi Kapoor's rivals like Rajesh Khanna and Dharmendra, or even friend Amitabh Bachchan, who came across on-screen as believable.

Unlike his father and Raj Kapoor, Shashi did not act in school plays. 'At Don Bosco they preferred Christians for all extra-curricular activities,' says Shashi. His initiation into the world of theatre took place in Prithvi Theatres. When he was six, he acted as Bharat in their debut production *Shakuntala*. As a child he was always hanging around the theatre after school or during school vacations. The Royal Opera House in central Bombay, where Prithvi Theatres usually staged their productions when they were not travelling, became Alibaba's cave of wonders for the awestruck young boy. Backstage became his real school.

It was also the school of life, and first crushes. It seems he was infatuated with the leading ladies (and sometimes loves) of his father and brothers. His first crush was on his father's leading lady Vanmala. The blue-eyed Brahmin actress with 'pinkish skin' co-starred with Prithviraj Kapoor in numerous films, and often dropped in at Prithvi Theatres. Recalls a wistful Shashi who was a chubby child at the time: 'I told my father I wanted to marry her. He took me to her and said, "*Boloon, kya*?"(Shall I tell her?) Nargis and Geeta Bali were early infatuations. I used to call her Babyji, and Geeta bhabhi was so sprightly and *chalu* in *Albela*—we could identify with her.'

It is easy to forget that Shashi Kapoor was a child star on the screen as well. Long before all his milk teeth were in place, he was put on the shuttle between theatre and film, moving between the respective realms of his father and his elder brother. His performance as the young Raj Kapoor in *Awara* was widely appreciated. It is generally believed that this was his debut film. However, his first screen appearance was nearly five years earlier, in *Aag*. Shashi was almost nine when his brother began the film. Shashi plays Raj Kapoor's younger self: a young schoolboy passionate about theatre and his schoolmate named Nimmi. The younger Kapoor gives a remarkable and assured performance. It rings true because he was, like the protagonist, under the spell of theatre. At eleven he also worked outside the R.K. ambit in a Bombay Talkies film, *Sangram*.

The adult Shashi Kapoor is not known for his starry, prima donna ways on the sets. Yet, as a child actor he was not beyond getting his way by means fair and foul. Recalls Prayag Raaj who plays a friend of the young Raj Kapoor in *Aag*: 'We used to go to the film set every day. It was our film. Rajji used to give us money to see films. There were many night shoots. Rajji used to wake us up at twelve. When it came to Shashi's shot, he'd say, "I won't give the shot, I am sleepy." Rajji would then ask him if he wanted an omelette and send a car for it. Only then, his stomach appeased, would the young star deign to act.'

Somewhere along the way food got inextricably linked with film in the young Shashi Kapoor's mind. Even today, over five decades later, he still remembers what he ate, when, and what it cost. 'I was attracted to the food served at film studios, whether it was R.K. Films, Jagriti or Asha. The canteen at R.K. served both desi and *vilayati* (western) food. The sahib actors ate fried chicken or fish and chips. The others had the desi dishes: rice plates. You could get *daal-chawal* for five annas or fish and rice for ten annas.' Both Prayag and he used to saunter into R.K. at lunchtime, pretending they had casually dropped in. Raj Kapoor would inevitably ask them to eat with the cast and crew at a long table placed outside his famed cottage. It wasn't just their tummies they filled. R.K. was Shashi Kapoor's film school, and Raj Kapoor his first teacher. The young, chubby boy took it all in, watching his brother on the sets. 'My guru was my father to begin with, both in acting and in life. Raj Kapoor was my guru as far as film-making goes,' says Shashi.

Following in the Kapoor tradition Shashi Kapoor and academics soon parted company. Perhaps his early trysts with cinema, playing Raj Kapoor's fledgling alter ego, sparked his abiding love for show business. He was hooked on grease paint, backstage cacophony and a whiff of desi bohemia. When he was twelve he flew (his first flight) to Calcutta with Raj Kapoor and his wife for the *Awara* premiere. No doubt the world of glamour had seduced him. School would have been incredibly dull after this.

One of Shashi Kapoor's favourite lines to journalists is: 'I am a Matric fail', uttered with a broad grin as if it is a badge of honour. 'I was not good in studies, and I did not pass. I was in awe of my father's reaction. When I failed, nobody scolded me. Shammiji took me to Matheran, a hill station near Bombay. When my roll number did not come in the papers, he did not react at all. Later, my father asked me to appear again. I told him that I did not want to waste his money sitting in college canteens. I asked him whether he would rather I did four years of canteen,' recounts Shashi.

This was clever dialogue. What he, in effect, was telling his father was that going to college was all about skipping classes and marking attendance in the college canteen for four years, downing endless cups of tea over endless chit chat, when not bunking college and going to the movies. Prithviraj Kapoor was impressed by the wisdom of his son's words. Khalsa College was situated opposite the Kapoor home, and he was aware of what the students were up to. Shashi told his father that he wanted to do theatre, and the best 'school' for it was his father's company. So, in 1953, at the age of fifteen, Shashi Kapoor became an employee of Prithvi Theatres for a kingly salary of seventy-five rupees.

The moving caravan of players became Shashi's college. He was involved with all aspects of theatre, from acting, lighting, arranging props to management. The roles Shashi Kapoor usually performed were hand-me-downs from his brothers. The Kapoor family also stood in as extras: Shashi played an *ashramvasi* (ashram inmate) in *Shakuntala*. Sometimes, however, the fair and lovely looks of the Kapoor clan went against them: for the play *Kisan*, Shashi and Tiger (his cousin) were far too *hatta-katta* (robust) to play starving farmers.

His beard had just begun to sprout. The baby fat had melted

and the chubby torso of the *Awara* days stretched into quasi-thinness. 'Napoleon' was no longer top-heavy. For the by-now-almost-handsome Shashi Kapoor, travelling with Prithvi Theatres was like going away to a movable feast—a cross between a boarding school and a circus. Recalls Shashi Kapoor: 'For my first professional tour (Nasik in Maharashtra) I had a *nai nai* (new) beard. I did not need it. Krishnaji gave me shaving *saman* (kit). I had already toured with the group during school holidays and I knew the excitement and adventure of touring. Chaiji gave me a steel trunk and a holdall. I didn't have a quilt, so I pinched one from Tiger.'

The angel-faced Shashi Kapoor may have looked as if butter would not melt in his mouth but he knew how to get what he wanted. He cajoled his sister-in-law Geeta Bali into buying him a record player by continuously talking about the famous red gramophone Nargis had bought for Shammi Kapoor when he was a teenager. Geeta Bali bought him a small foldable one in 1955: it went along with him when he travelled with Prithvi Theatres. Shashi Kapoor did not have as eclectic a taste in music (nor the talent for it) as his brothers. However, he too was fascinated by Western music. Doris Day, the early Sinatra, Bing Crosby and Pat Boone were to keep him company during his travelling days. He was not overly fond of Elvis Presley, preferring instead Danny Kaye, Nat King Cole, Rosemary Clooney, the Andrew sisters and a group called Rum and Cola. 'There were jukeboxes, but they were a luxury at the time. It cost four annas for a song in Irani restaurants. We used to eat *maska pao* or *puri bhaji*, drink tea and listen to the music,' recalls Shashi.

Eventually, he graduated to assistant stage manager of Prithvi Theatres—a job that often required him to sit on top of the truck, guarding trunks full of stage props and costumes as they moved from city to city. During his long apprenticeship at Prithvi Theatres—1953 to 1960—Shashi was given increasingly significant roles and took on more responsibility backstage, including how to play boss.

When his father was a Rajya Sabha member, Prime Minister Jawaharlal Nehru asked him to stage a play for the inauguration of the All India Fine Arts and Crafts Society (AIFACS) in New

Delhi. Prithviraj Kapoor dispatched his son to organize things. 'I went to meet Tapas Sen who was the wizard of theatre. At the time I knew exactly what I wanted. I was cool, and in charge. Tapas said, "Don't touch my lights." I told him all right but re-angle them, don't shift all the lights. My ego was hurt. I had learned about lighting from Dhanji Shah Mistry.' The bruised egos soon healed. The two became friends. Later, when Shashi Kapoor opened the current Prithvi Theatre in 1978 in Juhu with his wife Jennifer Kendal, he asked Tapas Sen to be an advisor.

Double shifts began early in his life. Like a trapeze artist, he swung between Prithvi Theatres and R.K. 'I educated myself in film work. I used to go to R.K. I loved the magic of theatre, but I was also interested in the technical side of cinema. Raj Kapoor had three good cameramen: Radhu Karmakar, Tarun Dutt and Jayant Pathare. Hrishikesh Mukherjee used to be there as well. Rajji sent me to the top to see how they do the lighting. He told me: "*Garmi mahsus karo*" (experience the heat).' No doubt he was building up his CV.

As a teenager, Shashi Kapoor also oscillated between Prithvi Theatres and Shakespeareana, the touring theatre company run by Geoffrey Kendal, his future father-in-law. It was quite a double act: the actor went back and forth from Shakespeare to contemporary Indian plays like *Deewar* and *Gaddaar*. Shashi met Jennifer Kendal when he was eighteen. She 'arranged' for him to join her father's company. Moving between two such different worlds was not easy. Shashi Kapoor had to struggle to offload the Indianisms and accent and speak like a pucca angrez.

In her splendid book, *White Cargo*, Felicity Kendal (well-known British stage actress and Jennifer's younger sister) writes: '*Arms and the Man* and *The Merchant of Venice* were to be staged in Bangalore, but a few actors had gone back to England. Shashi came by train, clutching copies of Shaw and Shakespeare, and for the following five days Jennifer tutored him, until he was ready to take over as Gratiano and Sergius. He had never acted in English in his life and was shaking with nerves, but he carried it off with great success and was reluctantly welcomed into the fold by my father, who was never keen on any boyfriend Jennifer had.'

But it was the old Bard who was to leave a lasting impression on the young man stepping over the threshold into the world of English-language theatre. Shashi Kapoor played Cassio in *Othello*, obviously with great enthusiasm. Carried away with the fencing, he broke a piano during rehearsals. Another role he remembers fondly is Laertes in *Hamlet* (his father had also acted as Laertes during his days with J. Grant). An early ambition of Shashi Kapoor was to play Othello but he never dared. However, he did do a warm-up exercise as the Prince of Morocco in *The Merchant of Venice* in which he plays a black man in one scene and has to say 'dislike me not for my complexion'.

Shashi Kapoor was with Shakespeareana in an informal capacity from 1956 until 1963, and with Prithvi Theatres from 1953 until the curtain finally came down on it in 1960. In between, he acted in films. Shashi believes that his 'acting skills' were honed during his days in Shakespeareana, watching both Geoffrey Kendal and Laura Liddell (his mother-in-law) act.

The first thing his father-in-law told him was to stand erect. He also corrected his pronunciation—though not always in the happiest of circumstances. 'I joined the Penang tour of the group in the winter of 1957. They were not doing well: the organizers had cheated us. Everybody was growling and in a bad mood. We were staying in a cheap Chinese hotel, with a cheapie bar. Geoffrey Kendal was sitting there and drinking the cheapest beer he could have, Tiger beer. We had very little money. I would sit and wonder what to do. He would fight about Jennifer, and he was often rude. I ordered a bowl of rice, but I said "bowel of rice". The beer spluttered out from his mouth and he laughed loudly. Everybody wondered what had happened: here was a man who never laughed. Now what, I wondered. He came to me and said: "Bowl, not bowel you silly bugger." I was not offended, but happy he had come up to me,' recounts Shashi.

The English lessons continued. Shashi Kapoor acquired the trappings of the Perfect Gentleman. The unKapooring of the Pathan had begun.

Theatre couldn't pay the bills. This Kapoor had a wife by the time he was twenty, and a son—Kunal—a year later. He also realized that Prithvi Theatres would soon pull down its shutters. Shashi Kapoor reluctantly turned to cinema to feed his young family. It wasn't easy: how could there be room for yet another Kapoor? He did the rounds of the studios, and was turned away from Filmistan: film pedigree alone did not open doors in those days. Nor did Prithviraj Kapoor give him a leg up in the movies, although he had spoken to Kidar Sharma about giving Raj Kapoor a break in films. So, Shashi Kapoor did what many young men who flocked to Bombay to become actors did: he sat on a bench outside Filmistan and waited to be spotted. For a while he shared the bench with Dharmendra and Manoj Kumar—all three vying for a role in the film *Picnic*. Recalls Shashi: 'Dharmendra used to tell me I don't mind if you get the role, but not him.' Eventually, Kumar got the role and Dharmendra walked away despondently. Shashi Kapoor knocked at Kidar Sharma's door in his Sri Sound Studio office. The director, who had given Raj Kapoor his first break in films, offered him tea, sympathy and chana—but no role. Movie moghul Sohrab Modi was terser: even the tea was missing.

Meanwhile, like many aspiring, down-at-heel actors, Shashi Kapoor hung around Gaylords, a restaurant near Marine Drive, which was the closest Bombay had to Hollywood's legendary drugstore where Lana Turner was discovered, probably languorously sipping a milkshake. Started by two refugees from Lahore, Gaylords with its icing-cake décor, famed pineapple pastries, cold coffee and chicken sandwiches was an adda for several directors and producers. Shashi Kapoor and other aspiring actors like Feroz Khan, Joy Mukherjee, Shashi Puri and Sudesh Kumar frequented Gaylords, hoping to be spotted.

Shashi Kapoor loitered with intent around Gaylords twice a week for six months in 1959. Jaikishen, one half of music composers Shankar–Jaikishen, had given a standing order that all newcomers be given tea and snacks. Another restaurant nearby, Bombellis, was also a place for actor-spotting. One day, on his way to Gaylords, Yash Chopra saw Shashi Kapoor waiting outside the restaurant. The director invited him to his table, and advised him to go to Kardar Studio after Shashi told him whose son he was.

Talking about his early struggle, Shashi Kapoor says: 'My initial attitude towards films was to earn enough money to look after my family. I had a family when I joined films. I had a *biwi* (wife) and I had Kunal. Jennifer was earning two hundred rupees a month and I was earning two hundred. Prithvi Theatres closed down in 1960. It was panic stations for us. I was living with my parents, and touring with Shakespeareana. *Char Diwari* was my first release... It did not do well. There was *Ek Anar Sau Bimar*—they were looking for a new *chehra* (face). I was a disappointment. My second film was *Dharmaputra* (1961), made by Yash Chopra for B.R. Chopra. Yashji's *Dhool Ka Phool* had been a great hit. But then came *Dharmaputra*, based on the novel *Gunahon ka Devta*. I played the title role and the film bombed. It was the first disaster for B.R. Chopra, and he couldn't take it. My third film was *Prem Patra* for Bimal Roy. All failed. Panic stations again. I became a jinx in the industry. Producers cancelled my roles. "Shashi Kapoor *nahin chalega*," they said and took back the signing amount. I had signed a film with Sadhana but two days later the producers asked for their money back. I was replaced by Ashok Kumar. I went to Rajji, and he said it's all right, this will happen again. And it did, again and again.'

Family history seems to have repeated itself. Just like Shammi Kapoor made flop after flop for five years until *Tumsa Nahin Dekha* in 1957, it took five years of flops before Shashi Kapoor made it with *Jab Jab Phool Khile* in 1965. What made it worse for Shashi Kapoor was the fact that even the films he made with major directors like B.R. Chopra, his younger brother Yash Chopra and even Bimal Roy flopped. Insecurity took a long time to leave the lives of Shashi and Jennifer. 'I got five thousand rupees in 1966 for signing a film. Jennifer said let us not touch it, and put it in a corner. We feared the producer might ask for it back. After six months we decided to spend it.' What saw Shashi through the trying times was his father's advice: '*Nahin chala to dukhi raho, chala to dukhi raho* (If you fail, you will be unhappy; if you succeed you will be unhappy). Keep both aspects neutral. See your face in the mirror, are you capable of success and failure.' Says Shashi: 'I think what he told me saved me, that and the ability to laugh. Thank God I had Jennifer. I was not too involved with my profession.'

Until *Jab Jab Phool Khile*, directors, producers, and even heroines turned their backs on Shashi Kapoor. Actors whose films flop are avoided like the plague in the world of cinema: superstition determines many decisions, and consequently fates. A godfather or a reigning actress is essential for an actor. Actress Nanda, Master Vinayak's daughter, was supportive and proved to be his lucky mascot. However, quietly and in the background, Raj Kapoor also played godfather. Big brother actually called Nanda to watch over Shashi when she was about to play leading lady in his debut film, *Char Diwari*. Remembers Nanda: 'Rajji told me that he had heard that I had signed a film with Shashi. He told me, "You are senior, so please take care of him. He is not my brother. He is my son. It is a very new experience for him."'

Nanda acted in seven films with Shashi Kapoor, including *Mehendi Lagi Mere Haath*, *Char Diwari* and *Jab Jab Phool Khile*. She has fond memories of working with him: 'It was great. He was spontaneous, and did not need rehearsals. A family man, he was a little angrez and always punctual because of Jennifer's influence. During location shoots Jennifer was often with us. We used to feel we were all family. All were young, and we played cricket. Once, when a scene was over, it became overcast and Shashi was very protective. In Kashmir, Jennifer and he would follow my car. He knew I was shy. He wasn't shy but I was an introvert. I had a difficult role in *Jab Jab Phool Khile*. Until then I'd been a sister or a wife, and here I had to be modern and gregarious. The climax of the film was also very challenging. The scene was shot at Bombay Central from two to four in the morning. I had to run with the train, all tense and in a sari. The train was speeding too much. Shashi was on it and had to time it well because he was supposed to pick me up at the right moment. While I ran I had to say dialogues and I couldn't see where the platform ended. It was dangerous. If he missed pulling me up onto the train I would have been under the train. Shashi concentrated hard and did it.'

The film was a 'superhit', and Shashi was on his way up. Not only was *Jab Jab Phool Khile* commercially successful in India, the film was screened in Algeria's cinema halls every two days for a couple of years: there was, in fact, public demand for it. Shashi Kapoor was one of the most successful Indian actors in North Africa in countries like Algeria, Morocco and Libya. In the souks of Marrakesh, even today some of the older shopkeepers will give you a discount if you are from the land of Amitabh Bachchan and Shashi Kapoor. And women—both Arab and Indian—of a certain age get all woozy when they talk about Shashi Kapoor.

Psychoanalyst Udayan Patel believes that the actor came across as an ideal, believable lover. 'In *Jab Jab Phool Khile* all of us fell in love with the way Shashi Kapoor loved Nanda. And the way she loved him. It was our fantasy to find a girl like Nanda, and to be like them both. The fantasy about him as a lover was great. You believed him, you believed his romantic feeling.'

Shashi Kapoor's lucky streak continued through the latter half of the sixties with romantic comedies like *Pyar Ka Mausam*, *Pyar Kiye Jaa*, *Neend Hamari Khwab Tumhare* and *Haseena Maan Jayegi*. This streak continued through much of the seventies with films like *Aa Gale Lag Ja*, *Chor Machaye Shor* and *Fakira*.

Prakash Mehra brought out the hidden mimic in Shashi Kapoor in *Haseena Maan Jayegi*, his debut film as a director. The actor is marvellously witty in the long cross-dressing song sequence in which he spoofs stereotypes of Bollywood heroines: Sharmila Tagore in *Kashmir Ki Kali*, celluloid tawaifs, pallav-twisting demure maidens and liberated 'modern girls' in flared skirts and flipped-out hair of the sixties. In the film, Shashi Kapoor plays a double role that allows him to stray from his goodie-goodie image. As the bad one he gets to be menacing and pure evil. The actor also lets himself go when he dances: boisterous, he does all kinds of acrobatics on the dance floor, often falling flat on the floor like his brother Shammi Kapoor. He even shakes his head like his brother, plays the saxophone and has the same Brylcreamed Elvis puff.

Had he not been so picture-perfect, Shashi Kapoor may have been a successful villain. At times he is more convincing as the worse half in his double roles, often overplaying the dark side.

The actor is aware of the fact that as the bad guy he tends to overshadow the good guy. He cites the example of *Paap Aur Punya*: 'I came on too strong as the bad one. Consequently, the hero appeared weak. The same thing happened in *Aan*. Premnath was too strong, and Dilip Kumar appeared *pheekha* (insipid).'

Shashi also acted in a spate of indifferent films in the sixties. However, he bounced back with *Sharmilee* in 1971, his second coming. Rakhee, in a double role, sparkled in the film, responsible in large measure for its tremendous success. And Shashi Kapoor as a young Indian army officer is convincing. He is more nuanced, even in his romancing. And once again his dark side appears, however briefly, adding complexity to his character.

From here on he was on a roll. Producers loved him: he was always punctual, easy to work with, professional, occasionally deferring or forgoing money owed him. Shashi Kapoor made so many films that even he has lost count. Some time in the seventies he accelerated into double and triple-shift mode, going in and out of film sets as if he were perpetually walking through a revolving door. Journalist Sunil Sethi remembers Jennifer Kendal telling him: 'He was working almost round the clock. Both of us just sank into a kind of non-thinking state.'

Consequently, there were some bloomers in his hyperactive seventies. Films like *Jaanwar Aur Insaan* in 1972 with Aruna Irani were embarrassingly bad and did not do well at the box office. Shashi Kapoor even fell—as did his father—through a trapdoor to B-grade films. There came a stage when he was willing to fight a tiger with a stitched-up mouth. He even acted in films titled *Jai Bajrang Bali*.

Shashi Kapoor was on an eighteen-hour cycle, with four or five films on at the same time. His Sundays were no longer sacrosanct—reserved for the family. 'We had no driver and no servants. I used to help Jennifer at home,' recalls Shashi. Not exactly the best time for Raj Kapoor to ask him to act in *Satyam Shivam Sundaram*—it became the last straw that almost broke the camel's back.

Raj Kapoor famously called his younger brother a 'taxi actor' on the sets of *Satyam Shivam Sundaram*. The epithet describes an actor who goes with any producer who hails him, like a taxi: you could get in and ask him to go, and he would go anywhere once the meter was put down. Obviously, his brother's sarcastic remark still rankles almost three decades later: 'Rajji was a great showman, and very sentimental. But as a director he could be...I had to pass through a very difficult time. When Rajji was going to start the project [*Satyam Shivam Sundaram*] I was working with directors like Yash Chopra and Manmohan Desai. He asked me how much money I would take. I cried and touched his feet, and he said, "*Bade log ho gaye. Aap ke date mushkil se milte hain.*" (You've become a big star. Your dates are difficult to get.) I told him that my secretary would place my diary in front of him, and he could choose whatever he wanted. I gave him my first dates, and in the process annoyed all my producers. Yet, one day on the set he said, "*Shashi Kapoor sahib aap taxi ban gaye* (Shashi Kapoor, you have become a taxi)."'

Raj Kapoor was quite testy during the making of *Satyam Shivam Sundaram*. Things were not going as he wanted. His muse Lata Mangeshkar was in a sulk and was making the showman dance to her tune. It seems Raj Kapoor soon realized that he had miscast Zeenat Aman in the lead role of the village belle with a beautiful body and a disfigured face. Shashi suspects that his brother took his anger out on him. 'There were five thousand people, and he had a mike when he made that remark. *Kisi ka gussa kisi pe* (Anger on someone else taken out on me). He told me to walk properly, when he actually wanted to tell off somebody else.' Life must have become unbearable for Shashi Kapoor because he asked his sister-in-law Krishna Kapoor to come to Loni to calm her husband down.

Meanwhile, Shashi Kapoor went into robotic mode—'like a zombie', as he puts it—shuttling between Pune and Lonavala where he was acting in G.P. Sippy's film *Trishna*. The Lonavala shift was from seven in the morning to 1 p.m., when Shashi Kapoor would rush down to Pune, only to return early the next morning.

Was Shashi Kapoor too good-looking to be taken seriously as an actor? According to Shyam Benegal, who directed him in *Junoon* and *Kalyug* (Kapoor produced the two films), he was 'an exceptional actor' who did not get the kind of films that would have given him the stature of an actor and a star that Amitabh Bachchan was to get subsequently. Nor was he given the opportunities to suit his personality. 'He was only seen as a romantic star. People took him for his looks—nobody in Indian cinema was quite as good-looking as he. In *Heat and Dust* and *Kalyug* you see the nuanced actor,' says Benegal.

Evidently, Shashi Kapoor tiptoed around narcissism: the grown-up 'Napoleon' did not stare at his image in the mirror. 'I never thought of myself as good-looking, the way Prithviraj Kapoor and Raj Kapoor were,' says Shashi. 'Shammiji was very attractive and magnetic. Since I never thought of myself as handsome, I never thought of looks as a handicap. In Indian films it was the face that mattered. It was so in the thirties, forties, and even in the sixties. Dilip Kumar was the first to come out of it. He was never a craze like Raj Kapoor or Dev Anand. But he created an aura, *ban gaya* (he became) attractive. He worked on it. I first came to films to earn for my family. We never used to talk about the films at home...I was never into the narcissism of an actor—my wife would never let me think of it.'

Why didn't Shashi Kapoor become a superhero or a cult figure? He was more than handsome, a versatile actor, a great mimic, was part of the blue-chip Kapoor film dynasty and had a sense of humour that came through on-screen. He danced well—going his own way—and had good comic timing according to James Ivory. The American director also believes that with the right directors he could have been an Indian Cary Grant. Kumar Shahani believes that Indian directors did not properly exploit the actor, and somewhere the actor lacked the killer instinct: 'Shashi never had the courage; he could have been a better actor than Raj Kapoor.'

As he grew older and his sideburns acquired a touch of white, the good looks distracted less from his acting, and the romantic lover boy image morphed into a mature character with a more lived-in face. The dramatic actor overshadowed the romantic lover. The graph of his acting prowess in Indian films jumps considerably with *Kalyug* and *Vijeta* (directed by Govind Nihalani) through Ramesh Sharma's *New Delhi Times* to Ismail Merchant's *Muhafiz*—adapted from Anita Desai's novel *In Custody*. His understated yet convincing performance in *New Delhi Times* (he plays an investigative journalist exposing political corruption) won him the National Award for Best Actor in 1986.[1]

In Kapoor's own productions such as *Junoon* and *Kalyug*, the actor taps into the complexities of human nature and the nature of obsession. In *Kalyug*, a modern-day Mahabharata said to be based on the Walchand Hirachand industrial family, Shashi Kapoor's interpretation of a contemporary Karan is impressive. Cunning as a fox and a master of manipulation, he manages to show his character's vulnerability as well as impotent rage and pain.

One of Shashi Kapoor's major regrets—and an unrealized dream—is that he did not work with Satyajit Ray, even though the two men did discuss the possibility. 'Manikda had promised to take me in *Shatranj Ke Khiladi*,' he told me during the course of our interviews. 'He came home and explained why he did not take me in his film, asking me, "Do you think your wife will not be satisfied with you and go to other people to appease her sexual appetite?" I was stunned by what he was saying. And when I shook my head, he said, "Precisely. This character is deep down in lethargy, alcoholism and nawabpan, and does not touch his wife. Does Shashi Kapoor look like this? No."'

Meanwhile, in mainstream Hindi cinema, stars like Dharmendra, Rajesh Khanna and Amitabh Bachchan overshadowed him and hogged the limelight. Dharmendra was Mr Macho, Rajesh Khanna Mr Boy Next Door and Bachchan was Mr Angry. Explains Udayan Patel: 'Shashi Kapoor's showmanship did not create the impression that he was a power who could create anything. Would he have been "Hero" even if the screen didn't exist?' In other words, the actor did not come across as an action hero who could take on a dozen armed baddies bare fisted off screen as well: the illusion of superman did not continue after the lights in the cinema halls came on.

Perhaps the inner angrez gentleman in Shashi Kapoor, nurtured by his British wife, restrained him, kept him from becoming the typical hero of Hindi films. Clearly, in his early films this Kapoor is not looking for a cinematic signature. There are no mannerisms—like Dev Anand with his tilted head and voice with the hint of a tremor, Raj Kapoor's clowning or Rajesh Khanna's blinking eyes. However, Shashi Kapoor blurred into Shammi Kapoor in a few early films. Unlike Shammi, Shashi never talks about struggling for a screen identity different from his siblings and father. He began to act in Hindi films to support his family, and eventually to finance the revival of Prithvi Theatres: theatre as he keeps reiterating has always been his real passion. A professional actor, he switched off once he left the sets.

Or, perhaps, he was too intelligent an actor, and his penchant for nuanced performances in a Bollywood of over-the-top performances and stereotypical characters came in the way of ascendancy to superstardom and icon status. Explains director Ramesh Sippy: 'Take *Deewar*. If Shashi had to play that role and be sincere to it, he had to underplay it. He did it right, and was sincere in his performance. However, if he had tried to stand out as a performer and give the kind of performance that gives you stardom, he would not have done justice to the role.' Shashi Kapoor had the best line in the film, indeed one of the most iconic lines in popular Indian cinema: '*Mere paas maa hai*' (I have mother). Yet, it was screen bad brother Amitabh Bachchan who dies a marvellous cinematic death and walks away with the film and the mantle of Angry Young Man—and gets a comfortable niche in scholarly studies of Indian cinema.

Shashi Kapoor's career in mainstream cinema zigzagged. Fortunately, he had a parallel track outside the boundaries of Hindi cinema—a savings account of sorts. Arguably, he is Indian cinema's first crossover actor, not counting Sabu of Mowgli fame. It all started with his encounter with Ismail Merchant and James Ivory in 1961, the beginning of a beautiful relationship—and six films, so far.[2] The actor's first film (*Char Diwari*) was yet to be released, and the duo's first feature film was still a glint in their eyes. Ismail Merchant and James Ivory were planning to make *The Householder*, based on a novel by Ruth Prawer Jhabvala. Merchant recalls his first meeting with the actor: 'Betty del Garno, an Australian friend who worked for an advertising firm had told us about a wonderful actor, Shashi Kapoor, whose first film was about to be released. I went to his apartment in Olympus in Bombay and barged into a party for journalists. There was a brawl; all were getting drunk. We gatecrashed, and were offered *nimboo pani*. I said, "I am Ismail Merchant. I am making a film. How would you like to be in it? We will send you the script." Jennifer Kendal read the script, which she liked very much. We worked on it, and immediately a friendship was born.'

However, *The Householder* (1962) was not the first film for which they considered him. James Ivory had actually gone to Bombay to make a film about an American anthropologist in Devgarh, with Shashi Kapoor, Leela Naidu and Durga Khote. Ivory met Shashi and Jennifer Kendal in Delhi at an outdoor party with sofas on the lawn. 'He looked like a movie star, and I was struck by the couple. The other film had collapsed. Ismail wanted to make *The Householder*, and I jumped in and said sure,

Shashi Kapoor and Leela Naidu in The Householder, *the first English-language film he acted in (Photo courtesy Merchant–Ivory Films)*

we have a ready-made cast. Shashi came from theatre. He was expressive in English, expressive when he spoke, and unusually good-looking. This was his first English-language film. He did not have much experience then. I cast actors partly because of their personality—how they are as people themselves, what they convey about themselves. Shashi had that—his own personality. Those who have that, build a part out of it: a way of speaking, of carrying themselves.'

Jhabvala, on the other hand, became nervous when she saw Shashi when the cast went to her home in Civil Lines in Delhi. She wondered how such a handsome man could be transformed into her character of Prem, a schoolteacher. 'He was a dashing, movie star type, a far cry from her idea of Prem. Her worries made me worry about Ismail's casting,' reminisces Ivory.

Distributed by Columbia, the film opened at the Guild Theatre in New York in October 1963, and did not exactly set the Hudson on fire. Bosley Crowther—god of the film world and the much-feared film critic of the *New York Times*—gave it a thumbs down. Recalls Shashi: 'He killed *Householder*. We were sad and depressed. Crowther had praised Leela's beauty, but had hated Jim. He reviewed it later and liked it. Jim and I went to the Plaza. He used his father's credit card and we plastered ourselves. He introduced me to Pernod.[3] We got tight and sentimental and felt sorry for ourselves.'

Meanwhile, the never-say-die Ismail Merchant was running around, his mind already on the next project. Recalling their first snub, Merchant says: 'I said never mind, we will do other films, and we drank at the Plaza. Then we started thinking about the *Shakespeare Wallah* screenplay, partially based on the Kendal family.' Jhabvala based part of her story on the diaries of the Kendals.

They made the film just three years later, in 1965. This time all of them participated in the film: Shashi, Jennifer, her sister Felicity Kendal, their parents Geoffrey Kendal and Laura Liddell. Merchant played a cameo role, and Madhur Jaffrey came on board the Merchant–Ivory bandwagon. Satyajit Ray loved the film, and did the music for it. The maestro, revered by the duo, even loaned them his cameraman, the late Subrata Mitra. The film was shot in Delhi, Lucknow, Kasauli, Shimla, Alwar and Bombay. The Kendals, however, were not amused: they did not like the idea of the theatre company going downhill in the film.

Merchant–Ivory had better luck the second time round. *Shakespeare Wallah* made it to the international film festival circuit: Berlin, London and New York. And Jaffrey got the best actress award in Berlin. Compensation came in a different, unusual form for Shashi Kapoor. Gina Lollobrigida was also in Berlin for the festival. One evening, the Italian actress got into the same lift as Madhur Jaffrey and Shashi Kapoor, and, according to Merchant, 'fell in love with Shashi'. 'The next morning Gina sent a bouquet of roses to Shashi. But unfortunately she thought Shashi's name was Madhur. Madhur was embarrassed, and Gina was angry that Shashi had ignored her gesture.'

Gina met Shashi at a festival party on the last day of their stay and was 'vexed', according to Merchant. While referring to this incident in his autobiography, *My Passage from India*, he writes that the actress 'whose advances, presumably, were rarely spurned, made a point of confronting Shashi and discovered her mistake...Poor Shashi was terribly disappointed that the confusion had caused him to miss such an opportunity.'

Shakespeare Wallah was critically acclaimed, but Merchant failed to find any distributors. Undaunted and a fount of optimism he hired Baronet Theatre in New York, owned by Walter Reade, and launched the film. He borrowed twenty thousand dollars from Ivory's father and held a benefit show for UNICEF. Merchant and Ivory were on their way—they got a 'profile', as did Shashi Kapoor.

The two Merchant–Ivory films proved to be the actor's launch pad for Hollywood. Impressed by Shashi Kapoor's performance in the two films, director Guy Green, an Oscar winner who had made the much-acclaimed *Patch of Blue* with Sidney Poitier, asked him to play the romantic lead opposite Hayley Mills (daughter of John Mills) in *Pretty Polly*. Green made this film in 1967 for Universal: the American title is *A Matter of Innocence* and the film also has Trevor Howard. Based on a Noel Coward story, it is the coming-of-age tale of a young girl who comes to Singapore with her aunt, and falls in love with their Eurasian guide-gigolo, played by Kapoor. Kapoor recounts an interesting incident that happened on location. 'I was supposed to kiss her on the lips in a scene, and I did it the way I knew. But suddenly the director yelled cut. Hayley's make-up, her lipstick was all over her face and on mine. They had to redo her make-up and shoot the scene again. You have to kiss without spoiling the make-up.' The film was a moderate success, and Shashi now knew how to kiss on-screen.

Director Conrad Rooks had also seen *The Householder* and *Shakespeare Wallah* and cast Kapoor in his film *Siddhartha*. Made in 1972, the film was based on the cult novel of the same name by Herman Hesse. Recalls Shashi: 'After seeing *Shakespeare Wallah*, Rooks approached me. He had made *Chappaqua*. He was one of the flower people, along with Allen Ginsberg—they had been here; all that ganja and the Ganga. He was fond of the Kapoors and wanted to cast the entire Kapoor family in his film. He wanted me as the middle-aged Siddhartha, Randhir Kapoor as the one in his early twenties, Raj Kapoor as the older one, and Prithviraj Kapoor as the oldest. Conrad even wanted a black lady in the film, one who would be stripping the entire time. But his script kept changing. Initially, he even wanted Waheeda Rehman to do this role but I told him that she would neither strip nor kiss. Later he met Simi Garewal socially. At one point he approached Amitabh Bachchan for the role Romesh Sharma eventually played. But I told him that Amitabh would only play the hero. So, they took this new boy from Delhi who fainted when Rooks shouted.'

It was the age of the flower people and hippies: the search for alternative lifestyles had already begun in the late sixties. Widely viewed and commented upon, *Siddhartha* did well at the box office. And Shashi Kapoor graduated to the status of an international movie star.

Meanwhile, the actor had also become a sort of mascot for Merchant–Ivory Productions, moving between Bollywood and quasi-Hollywood. Made in 1970 and written by Jhabvala, *Bombay Talkie* was his third film with the two dream merchants. Kapoor plays a married Bombay film star who has a disastrous affair with an English writer of romantic fiction, played by his wife

Jennifer, while Aparna Sen plays his bored rich wife in the film. Says Ivory: 'In this film his height, charm, good looks helped. By then he was an established star, had his own authority and had developed personal style which had weight.'

Shashi Kapoor and Aparna Sen in Bombay Talkie *(Photo courtesy Merchant–Ivory Films)*

Bombay Talkie failed at the box office. Perhaps it was too melodramatic. A film about European women 'on the prowl in India', as Merchant so evocatively puts it, and the Bombay film world may have been before its time. Irish author Edna O'Brien had come to India as a guest of Merchant–Ivory and saw some of the filming. She was an 'extrovert, flamboyant and bindaas' according to Shashi Kapoor. Merchant–Ivory were inspired by her character but the film itself was not based on her life.

A little known fact is that Amitabh Bachchan was an extra in this film. Shashi Kapoor spotted him on the sets and advised him to leave. Those were Amitabh Bachchan's footpath days, when he was desperately seeking a break as an actor. Recounting the incident, Kapoor says: 'I told him *chup kar*, just go. You will get something better. He knew all about acting and would go far.' Amitabh Bachchan decided to stay on, telling Kapoor that he needed the fifty rupees extras got. Bachchan was one of the extras who carried the funeral bier of the character Shashi Kapoor plays in the film. Fortunately for the future lodestar of Indian cinema, those scenes were cut. Recalls Amitabh Bachchan: 'I approached Shashi for an opportunity to work in a Merchant–Ivory film. I had a walk-on part as a palanquin bearer. I had to earn something. He dissuaded me. There were one or two shots in which I carry the bier to the Benaras ghat but the scenes got cut.'

The film may have floundered at the box office but it remains one of Ivory's favourite films. The protagonist is not the usual sweet Shashi Kapoor: there are metaphorical fangs. The film takes a close look at the Bombay film industry. The Ids of the various characters are close to the surface, and they move easily from passion to violence. The director explores the dark side of the film star. 'Shashi is the seducer here. The long affair drains him: he is obsessed like Richard Burton and Elizabeth Taylor. Shashi draws on his own dark side. We all have our dark sides, and he is able to bring up his,' says Ivory.

The film's opening sequence has one of the most original and comically surreal song and dance numbers, one that would have made Salvador Dali twirl his moustache in delight. Shashi, Helen and extras, clad in yellow flared pants, dance on the keyboard of a giant red typewriter. Their movements on the keys type out fate, and the director in the film says: 'It's very symbolic.' Ivory explains that he had seen many movies with dance numbers inside a champagne glass. 'I saw a typewriter and the glass became a typewriter in the film.' Merchant, however, in his autobiography maintains that the genesis of the typewriter was a dream Ivory had about 'a Busby Berkeley dance routine on the keys of a giant typewriter with Helen…leading the chorus line'.

Bombay Talkie also created a new avatar off-screen for Shashi Kapoor: he became involved in the financial aspects of film-making. According to Merchant, the actor invested some of his own money in the film in exchange for the rights to distribute the film in India. It was the beginning of his own production and distribution company, Filmvalas. There were a few glitches in this arrangement. Shashi had deferred his payment for the films he had done for Merchant and expected to be paid before he began work in *Bombay Talkie*.

Merchant did not have the money at the time. Many actors like Shetty, a popular screen toughie and fight master, had not been paid either. Shashi paid him some money and asked him to 'just keep' the beautiful leather jacket he wore in the film. In his book, Merchant relates how he got out of the embarrassing situation: 'I simply did not have the money to pay him. But Jennifer had a soft spot for me and...lent me the money to pay Shashi. So, in effect, I used Shashi's own money to settle my debt with him. Of course, I returned the money to Jennifer as soon as I was able to, but the whole transaction remained a secret from Shashi.'

Uncannily, a similar scenario had taken place decades earlier with Prithviraj Kapoor. He refused to act in a film until the producer, who was a friend, paid him the five thousand he owed him from a previous film. The producer quietly went to the Kapoor home in Matunga and asked Prithviraj Kapoor's wife to loan him the money. That evening the thespian returned home, triumphant, and handed over the money to his wife.

During the seventies, Shashi Kapoor went into fourth gear in Bollywood, while Merchant and Ivory made a slew of films, many of which were not set in India. In 1982, it was back to India and Kapoor to make *Heat and Dust*, a film that proved to be a turning point for Merchant–Ivory. The film opened and ran for eleven months at the Curzon in London, and in France it was a critical success. It also made money, enabling Merchant to finally buy a charming flat near Portman Place in London. Based on the Booker-prize-winning Jhabvala novel of the same name and made on location in India in 1982, the film catapulted Merchant–Ivory into the big league. It starred Julie Christie and also introduced Italian-British actress Greta Scacchi and musician Zakir Husain as an actor.

Shashi Kapoor acts as a romantic though rather shady nawab who intrigues against the British: they are weary of him and disapprove of his affair with the wife (Scacchi) of a British official (Christopher Cazenove). It is among Kapoor's more complex roles, requiring him to be charming as well as sinister. The nawab had to be charismatic. 'In *Heat and Dust*, Shashi was a decadent prince, a man of the world, a criminal and lover—all four at the same time,' explains Ivory.

The success of the film was heady for even a seasoned actor like Shashi Kapoor, who is not usually given to hyperbole. 'I went on a Universal Studio tour. It was full of posters of *Heat and Dust*. Shashi Kapoor was everywhere. There were premieres in New York, Sydney. I was in India for the premiere of *Utsav* and flew directly to New York. The airlines lost my clothes and I had a new suit made in hours for the reception at the Plaza given by the legendary jeweller Harry Winston. Placido Domingo was there. He knew Foo [Felicity Kendal] and told me he had wanted to marry her. All of us drank a lot. Ismail bought the papers late that night and we sat on the pavement at 3.30 a.m. reading the reviews. It was mind-blowing: this time they were good. Ismail said, "See what I told you [he was referring to the bad reviews for *The Householder*]: when it is bad it does not matter; this does not too."'

Shashi Kapoor had by now become a familiar figure on the international film circuit. 'Shashi could have gone international, like Alain Delon, but he wanted to continue in India,' says Merchant. *Heat and Dust* went to Cannes and other major film festivals. International directors began to show an interest in him. In 1987, he played a major role in *Sammy and Rosie Get Laid*. Directed by Stephen Frears (*Dangerous Liaisons* and *Prick Up Your Ears*) the film—based on a screenplay by Hanif Kureishi—is an apocalyptic portrait of life in Prime Minister Margaret Thatcher's England. Kapoor plays Rafi Rahman, a charming rogue who returns to England from what is presumably Pakistan with a suitcase of ill-gotten money to give to his son, Sammy, played by Ayub Khan Din. Sammy has an open marriage with Rosie (Frances Barber). Rafi, who has been involved with many murky political dealings in Pakistan, wants his son to shift to a better address and provide him a grandchild. He also wants to meet Alice (Claire Bloom), his erstwhile lover whom he abandoned when he left England.

The film was expectedly controversial and got mixed reviews. However, Shashi Kapoor's performance came in for praise from the late Pauline Kael. Writing in the *New Yorker*, the critic who was known to eat film directors for breakfast, was critical of everybody but Kapoor and Bloom: 'Shashi Kapoor is marvellous as a man who adapts to whatever happens (or adapts up to a point). There's no emotional force driving this movie. There isn't even much wit in the film's cleverness. It's there in Kapoor's performance, and in the cunning of Claire Bloom's line readings.'

Shashi Kapoor had made it, and he had even got to act opposite Claire Bloom, an actress he was infatuated with as a young man. Recalls Shashi of his experience working with her: 'We used to call her royalty. The atmosphere changed when she came in. It suddenly felt as if a royal persona had come. It was charged in a different way—the light would seem to change from amber to blue. There was no foul language used. No abruptness.' Not on the sets, but otherwise there was plenty going on in the film, especially towards the end of the film when the screen splits into three, horizontally, and in each layer a couple is making love—simultaneously but separately. Shashi Kapoor and Claire Bloom are one of the three couples in the throes of lovemaking.

Shashi Kapoor acted in two more films—*The Deceivers* and *Muhafiz* (*In Custody*)—under the Merchant–Ivory banner. However, Ivory did not direct either of the films. Merchant directed *In Custody*. And Nicholas Meyer directed the former, which was based on John Masters's novel of the same name. *The Deceivers* was filmed on location in Madhya Pradesh with Pierce Brosnan as William Savage. Savage is a British official with the East India Company who goes in search of thugs, only to be fascinated by their cult—a sort of Conradesque journey into the heart of darkness. The Irish actor was yet to become James Bond but was already a household name in the United States after his successful television series *Remington Steele*. Kapoor plays the wily, portly nobleman with a luxuriant moustache, Chandra Singh, who is actually a thugee.

Kapoor acted in several international productions after *Sammy and Rosie Get Laid*. Some were forgettable, like *Dirty British Boys*, a film made in 1997 by 'a bunch of new people', which also starred Harvey Keitel. 'God, the foul language I had to use in the film,' recalls Shashi. 'The film was shot in Leicester and was quite violent.' Directed by a young graduate from the British Film Institute, the film was about the Asian mafia in Great

Britain. Kapoor plays a mafia boss. Initially honest, he is corrupted by the white mafia, and in turn corrupts other Asians.

Other films he acted in are not widely known. Tony Gerber directed Kapoor in his critically well-received film *Side Streets* (1998). In the film the director takes a close look at the American melting pot through five urban folk tales. Gerber tells parallel stories of five immigrant groups in the five boroughs of New York City on a swelteringly hot summer day. Kapoor plays a fading Bollywood movie idol who overstays his welcome in his cousin's (Art Malik) home on Staten Island. Shabana Azmi acts in the film as well.

Kapoor has a significant role in the controversial film *Jinnah* (1998). Produced by historian Akbar Ahmed and directed by the talented UK-based Jamil Dehlavi (*The Blood of Hussain*, *Immaculate Conception*), the film was almost shelved several times. The Pakistani government was aghast at the idea that Christopher Lee—indelibly etched as the screen face of Dracula—was going to incarnate the Quaid-e-Azam. The producer won this round: Lee bore an uncanny resemblance to Jinnah. The second controversy was sparked by the rumours that Kapoor was acting as the angel Gabreel—a fact that would have introduced a religious element to the film.

The rumours may have had some basis. However, Kapoor eventually appears in the film without wings. He is the narrator of the film—a device used to go back and forth in time, making Jinnah relive his life, to go down the roads not taken, the 'what if' scenario. The film begins with an ambulance carrying a dying Jinnah breaking down in the desert, and soon after you see Jinnah in a library full of computers, with the portly scholar (Kapoor) in its midst. In this scholar's take on Jinnah, James Fox plays Lord Mountbatten and Maria Aitkin Edwina Mountbatten.

Apart from international films, Kapoor has done a few series for BBC radio and has also acted in a popular TV series for NBC: *Gulliver's Travels*. Directed by Charles Sturridge, the widely appreciated series had an impressive international cast: Sir John Gielgud, Geraldine Chaplin, Omar Sharif, Peter O'Toole and Ted Danson.

Actors don't normally fade away: they become producers or directors or get into the nitty-gritty of the film business. Shashi Kapoor did all three, starting with the last. He was an accidental distributor. Strapped for money, Merchant asked him to distribute *Bombay Talkie* to adjust half of what he owed him for *The Householder*. The actor set up his company, Filmvalas, to do this. Later, he distributed a few of Raj Kapoor's films. He took the Delhi territory for *Bobby* and *Satyam Shivam Sundaram*.

It wasn't just whimsy. Shashi Kapoor had a larger game plan: he wanted 'to become a film-maker and distributor like MGM'. He planned to make films and did not want his films to be handled by those who had no clue about cinema or interest in it. 'What do diamond merchants know about films? This way, instead of making a film and waiting for a distributor, I could do both at the same time,' Kapoor tells me.

Shashi Kapoor made his debut as a producer with *Junoon*. Pearl Padamsee had read Ruskin Bond's *A Flight of Pigeons* and suggested he ask Shyam Benegal to direct it. Says Shashi Kapoor: 'We were interested in the British Raj. After reading the script I asked Shyam if he wanted me to act in the film. It was wonderful how he explained the role. Here was this beautiful girl, and the man was not rough on her, didn't touch her at all. The rough Pathan has a wife whom he does not love, and here is this English Flower. Because of her he changed, forgot *jung*, the war, his brother-in-law.' The title is the brainchild of Shabana Azmi and Satyadev Dubey—the two thought of it at the same time and were given five hundred rupees each for the suggestion.

Life on the other side of the screen was not easy. Apart from finding an exhibitor—he had to pay rent in advance for *Junoon*—raising the money for making the films he wanted to was next to impossible. Following in the Raj Kapoor tradition, he sold personal property to make them. The elder brother sold his wife's jewellery; Shashi Kapoor sold 18 acres of land in Shridon, near Panvel on the outskirts of Bombay, to make *36 Chowringhee Lane*.

Critical acclaim came his way, but commercially most of his films did not do well. Shashi Kapoor is convinced that had there been multiplexes when he was making films, it would have been an altogether different scenario. '*Junoon* did all right. In 1979–80, my market was great. But I lost ten lakhs with *Kalyug*, forty with *Vijeta*, twenty-four with *36 Chowringhee Lane*, one-and-a-half crore with *Utsav* and three-and-a-half crore with *Ajooba*,' says Shashi.

Bad luck tripped him as well. Amitabh Bachchan had to pull-out of *Ustav* after he was almost fatally injured during the filming of Manmohan Desai's *Coolie*. Laments Shashi Kapoor: 'Jennifer told me then, "Let's shut shop." It was 1982—*mein sabse maar kha raha tha*.' Eventually, he played the role of the lusty king himself.

Shashi Kapoor turned director with *Ajooba* in 1991. It was the final straw: everything that could go wrong with the film did. The Russians who had funded part of the film withdrew their money towards the end: he could not film the conclusion as planned. Shashi blames it on '*bhagya*, my bad luck'. 'Perestroika and Glasnost had started. The film was almost three-quarters done. The Russians just left me. They packed up and went.' The crew was in Kyrgyzstan at the time and there were fifteen days of filming, including many of the special effects, still to be done. 'Fortunately I had my own action people and cameramen. The damage was about seventy to eighty lakh.'

The costs had also spiralled. The ever-magnanimous Shashi had flown his actors to Moscow first class. 'It was a Hollywood-style production, well-planned and easy on the artists,' explains Amitabh Bachchan who plays the lead role in the film. The film, a light-hearted adventure spectacle with swordplay and magic and dolphins, had Amitabh Bachchan, Dimple Kapadia and Rishi Kapoor. Yet, Shashi Kapoor's directorial debut did not fare well at the box office—suffering the same fate of the two films Shammi Kapoor had directed.

Meanwhile everybody had fun. 'He treated his cast and crew like kings,' recalls Tinnu Anand. Bachchan certainly had a ball: 'There was a wonderful camaraderie on the sets. Shashiji has a great capacity to make friends and build relationships.' He and Shashi Kapoor have always shared an easy camaraderie during their many films together, often behaving like adolescent truants. During their month-long stay in Delhi during the filming of Yash

Chopra's *Trishul*, the two spent their nights dancing up a storm at Tabela, a discotheque in the Oberoi. Recalls Bachchan: 'As a student it was a dream to go there, and I never had the opportunity. Shashi was a good dancer. We would finish by 5 or 6 in the morning, just when Yashji was getting ready for the shoot and we were just finishing the night. We would charge up and change.' At first the director was impressed by his actors' punctuality—till he got wiser.

While no movie moghul has yet usurped Raj Kapoor's title of the greatest showman, his youngest brother was a showman in his own way—but a quiet one. Unlike his brother he never gave himself mammoth birthday parties. Nor did he throw Holi parties. This Kapoor threw parties for his film cast and crew at the end of a film: 'I had seen all the parties. The big sahibs came and not those who made the film: crew, dress, make-up, extras.' If his film was a hit, he gave the workers gifts—'like those small Bush Baron radios which came out in the late sixties with plastic covers'. When the money really came in, the presents were in silver, and he threw a party at the Oberoi or the Taj. The subdued showman carried this habit overseas: after the premiere of *Pretty Polly* in Singapore he gave a party at the legendary Raffles hotel and doled out gifts to all the technicians.

He also played the little showman for the big showman Raj Kapoor. Shashi Kapoor threw a party for the premiere of *Satyam Shivam Sundaram* in Delhi. Raj Kapoor was broke: Though *Bobby* had been a major success, he had not quite recovered from the financial debacle of *Mera Naam Joker*. Shashi Kapoor was the distributor for *Satyam Shivam Sundaram* in Delhi and flew down from Singapore, where he was acting in Manmohan Desai's *Suhaag*, to host the evening. Since it was prohibition time—Morarji Desai was prime minister—the two brothers found a unique solution. Raj Kapoor apparently suggested that Shashi invite an important politician. So Shashi went to Atal Behari Vajpayee, who was foreign minister at the time. He came as the chief guest, and the brothers got all the necessary permissions. The party took place in rooms on two floors of the Maurya Hotel—the doors of the rooms were left open. Shashi Kapoor had been the distributor for *Bobby* in Delhi; hence the big splash at the Oberoi for *Satyam Shivam Sundaram*.

The chivalrous Kapoor also gave parties for broke producers. *Jab Jab Phool Khile* was Shashi Kapoor's first hit. However, since the film's producer had no money, he hosted a party at Juhu Hotel, even paying for the trophy he was given that evening.

Shashi Kapoor is an incorrigible flirt—the sort who can spark far from maternal feelings in a doddering grandmother, and far from platonic infatuation in a nubile young thing. It could be his smile, the crooked canine teeth saving the perfect face from being too beautiful. It could be the easy charm. Or the fact that he comes across as a good human being, an unmacho man with muscle in his brain. Whatever the reason, mention his name and most women confide they have had a crush on him. But quiz Kapoor on the effect he has on women and he is uncomfortable.

On home ground he *was* the fantasy. Even the brides of God succumbed: he must have been the subject of many whispered confessions. Apparently in Goa a nun fell in love with him. The Kapoors often went to Goa, where they had a home on Baga beach. Shashi used to love to swim in the warm Arabian Sea. He had, as he says, 'an okay body. I had on a skimpy swimsuit. She would come and sit next to me and stare, and keep staring, though she never touched me. Jennifer used to tell me that I would ruin the nun's life.' The nun eventually beat a quiet retreat.

Sometimes, these infatuations became uncomfortable. There were several girls—a few as young as fourteen—who ran away from home to Bombay, in the hope of marrying Shashi Kapoor. They came from villages and small towns, from as far as Punjab or Tamil Nadu and Andhra Pradesh. And, they came with their suitcases, occasionally sitting on them for hours while the security men tried to persuade them to leave. Many refused to leave. Recalls Kapoor: 'The security would come up and say that a young girl had been there since four or five in the morning and insisted on meeting me. They said they wanted to marry me. Some of them did not have any money to return home, so we gave them money for their tickets. There were times we had to call the police.'

It wasn't just the women from small towns who succumbed to the Kapoor charm. A besotted novelist–socialite with an acid-dripping pen used to send him her poems. The Kapoor effect was also felt across the oceans: a woman from France and another from Italy—women he had never met—wanted to leave their respective husbands and children and come to India to be with him. A woman in California used to send him clothes for his grandchildren, and offered to look after him: he had never met her either. 'I had old fans, women who wanted to adopt me. Now, young girls come and say that their mothers and grandmothers had crushes on me. In my theatre days there was an old married woman with children my age. She used to send me *dhokla*s and home-cooked food: *tepla*s, *khandavi*,' remembers Shashi. After his wife's death in 1984 he received several marriage proposals from women in India and overseas.

In *White Cargo*, Felicity Kendal describes Kapoor's fatal charm. 'He was funny and glamorous, the most flirtatious man I had ever met. He combined flattery and bullying with such attractive skill that he was almost irresistible. He was too thin, but it made his huge eyes, fringed with thick long lashes, seem even more beguiling. His flashing white teeth and wicked dimple were used to get his own way with both men and women, and the swagger of success was with him long before he became the number one Bollywood superstar.' He'd even flirt with a log of wood.

Bollywood is no different from Hollywood: movie stars are expected to have affairs with their leading ladies. It goes with the job. The affairs of Raj Kapoor and Shammi Kapoor were hardly secrets. Shashi Kapoor, on the other hand, was nothing if not discreet: kiss and tell was not his style. He was the Teflon man for film magazines as far as extramarital affairs were concerned. The only time a rumour about him surfaced was during the making of *Junoon*. There was, for several years, speculation about his relationship with actress Shabana Azmi: she plays the neglected wife in *Junoon*. However, gossip about the two actors did not often cross the threshold of the film industry. Nor was the press in ardent pursuit of his personal life.

Whenever journalists query Shashi Kapoor about his love affairs he has a standard answer: 'Jennifer told me long ago, "Look, I am not an Indian wife."' In other words: don't go down the Kapoor path, or stray on the starry pastures of Bollywood. There would be no looking the other way. It would be pack-up time if he did so.

Their women on-screen may have often been propped up by the Kapoor men, but in life the Kapoor women propped up their men: mothers, wives, lovers and daughters making sure they remained on their feet, and in many instances making sure they got on their feet to begin with. Shashi Kapoor may not have been quite a mama's boy but he certainly is his bhabhis' boy: Krishna Kapoor, Geeta Bali and later Neela Devi have played important roles in his life, as have Jennifer and Sanjana, his daughter.

Jennifer, four years older than him, was central to his existence. 'I was eighteen when I met a girl and she conducted my life ever since,' Kapoor says as if stating a fait accompli. You could say that he placed his life in her hands. She was the biggest influence in his life: she was wife, lover, soul mate, mother of his children and guide, whatever the need of the hour. Like a compass, she guided him, mapping out his life for him. Even today, over two decades after her untimely death from stomach cancer in 1984, Shashi Kapoor still appears to be navigated by her. It almost seems as if a parallel track of the memories of their life together continuously runs in his mind, even as he converses with you. Discuss any subject with him and he inevitably comes up with an apt anecdote concerning her, or something she said, his finger seemingly hovering over the rewind button in his mind.

She nudged him past the important milestones in his life. For example, his first suit. 'I had no party clothes or suit. I bought my first suit in 1958 when I was with Shakespeareana. Jennifer bought the cloth in Calcutta. We paid seventy-five rupees for the charcoal grey cloth, and another seventy-five rupees for the tailoring of the three-button, single-breasted suit.' Before Jennifer, his mother used to buy his clothes, and occasionally his cousin and friend Tiger. Travelling first class was another 'first' due to Jennifer: in their good days members of Shakespeareana travelled first class in trains—and stayed in good hotels. His 'first' trip overseas was to Singapore, when he flew there to act in plays for Shakespeareana.

Shashi Kapoor is convinced that he was destined to marry a foreigner. It was quite a flight of imagination considering the fact that the Kapoor khandaan was conservative. Until Shammi Kapoor, they had married fellow Pathans—Raj Kapoor had even married his father's cousin. Shashi cites two incidents that convinced him that his wife would be a foreigner.

The first inkling was when he was eight. 'I was in my father's play *Deewar*. It was 1945, and I played the son of one of the protagonists. In the play I look at the angrez woman [Zohra Segal] and say I will marry this English woman.' The second: 'My father was fond of astrology and dabbled in it. When I was eleven, Jaigopal Mohla, an astrologer who knew my father from his Peshawar days, told him that I would marry a foreigner. "*Saat samundar paar se pari ayegi aur shadi karega*." (He will marry a girl who will come from across the seven seas.)'

There was yet another reason. Shashi Kapoor happened to meet Jennifer again during the summer of 1956 in Calcutta: Prithvi Theatres were on tour in the region. At the time he was reading Ayn Rand's *Fountainhead*. 'I was fascinated by the character of Dominique Franklin. I could visualize her. I could see a girl with blonde or red hair, and fantasized a lot about her. And then a few days later I see Jennifer, a foreigner—and for twenty-eight years after that...' His voice trails off.

Shashi first spotted Jennifer in the Royal Opera House in Bombay. 'It was during the monsoon and there was a wet angrez girl. I was a hundred yards from the stage. She said, "Kaun hai?" She thought I was the friend she had come with.' Telescoping his life in a sentence he says: 'I spent twelve years at school, joined Prithvi Theatres at fifteen, met Jennifer at eighteen, joined Shakespeareana at nineteen, married at twenty, and had three children between twenty-two and twenty-eight.'

In her book, Felicity gives a more detailed account of the fateful encounter when Jennifer went with her friend Wendy to see the play *Deewar* at the Royal Opera House. Shashi was eighteen, and had a small part in the play. 'Before the performance, Shashi peeped out through the tabs to look at the audience and size them up...He saw sitting in the fourth row of the stalls a young girl with long fair hair. She was dressed in a black and white polka-dotted summer dress with a halter neckline—daring—and she was pretty, laughing with her girlfriend and fanning herself with her programme. Shashi, according to Shashi, fell instantly in love. After the show he raced to the front of the house to introduce himself and asked the girls bashfully if he could offer a guided tour backstage, thinking it would be an unusual treat for Jennifer to meet actors in costume and little imagining that that was how she spent most of her life. But Jennifer and Wendy pretended they knew nothing about the theatre and were overwhelmed and delighted to be taken to meet the cast. The next afternoon I was sitting in a Chinese restaurant, watching Jennifer and Shashi falling in love over their noodles. They would stay together till she died, through thick and sometimes very thin. She never did anything half-heartedly, my sister, it was all or nothing, Love or War. And she had met in Shashi the man she wanted forever.'

Love at first sight may be a bit of cliché. But the two lovers were, in a sense, mirrors of one another. Theatre was their first and abiding love. Both had belonged to the same caste of travelling players and performers. In his days with J. Grant, Prithviraj Kapoor had also performed Shakespeare and Shaw. He had even met Geoffrey Kendal towards the end of the war. The Shakespearean actor enlisted in ENSA, the entertainment wing of the army, and had performed in Bombay. Remembers Shashi: 'Papaji went backstage at one of their plays to congratulate them. My father knew Jennifer's father when he was with J. Grant Company.'

The courtship began immediately, with the teenaged Shashi carefully counting his *paise* (pennies). When they first met he earned just seventy-five rupees a month from Prithvi Theatres, and she three times the amount as the leading lady of Shakespeareana. They often went to Mathura Dairy, a little eatery on Kennedy Bridge, near the Opera House. A plate of puri bhaji cost twenty-five paise, and the two used to share a plate once a month. When they felt a little extravagant they went to Bombellis, famous for its confectionery. 'There was something called a Hawaii pastry. Jennifer and I would go there and order chocolate pastry. It cost one rupee. We could only afford one. She would let me have more than half.'

The fifties were a prudish decade. So, like other young lovers of the time the two often spent their afternoons in darkened movie halls. 'When Jennifer and I were courting we used to sit in the stalls downstairs—a ticket cost Rs 1.50. The balcony was Rs 2.50. After our marriage we went upstairs.' Another favourite canoodling spot was the more isolated China Creek, where many of the fight and romantic sequences of Hindi films were shot.

While their respective parents, the Kendals and the Kapoors, were in the dark about their romance, Shashi's sister-in-law, Geeta Bali, played Cupid. Recalls Shashi: 'During our courtship Geeta bhabhi gave me their car. I would dine Jennifer and take her back. They had three cars—a Buick, Desotto and a Jeep. We would drive to Juhu. Jennifer used to stay in the Church Mission House on Grant Road. It cost me ten rupees: 1.50 for the stalls and then dinner afterwards.'

Even brother Shammi was accessory after the fact. The couple was often apart for long spells: she touring with her father's company and Shashi with his. 'It was terrible. She was in Hyderabad and I was in Bombay. Shammiji saw my long face, and asked me, "*Kyon moo latka raha hai. Kya hua, yaad aa rahi hai*? (Why do you have such a long face? Are you missing her?) Where is she? *Ja*, go to Hyderabad." He took out a hundred rupees from his pocket and gave it to me. In those days it cost about seventy rupees for a ticket. I rushed out and bought an air ticket.' Shammi played a no less important part in Shashi eventually marrying Jennifer. Since Shashi was too diffident to tell his parents that he wanted to marry Jennifer, Shammi did so on his behalf.

The two were inseparable. Jennifer managed to get Shashi to join Shakespeareana in Bangalore. At first it seems Laura Liddell was quite impressed with her daughter's young find. In a letter home she wrote: 'The new boy is going to be brilliant as Laertes and Sergius, and Jane is very happy, she is coaching him on his lines. After all, the poor boy has to learn nine parts in a few weeks! I must say, they make a very attractive couple.'[4]

Describing the giddy days of their courtship, Felicity writes: '"Worship at my feet." Thwack! He hit her shoulder and a fresh bruise joined the little blue cluster already appearing on her bony arms. Jennifer giggled, bent down and touched his sandalled feet in a salaam of obedience. "That's better! You must learn to be respectful to your man...you Blighty memsahib." Shashi took my sister's face in his hands and kissed her hard, paying no attention to me, as I sat on my bed in the room I shared with Jennifer at the Sunny Fields Guesthouse in Bangalore.'

It was a love story quite like the love stories in Hindi movies, with all the melodrama that goes with star-crossed love. Geoffrey Kendal did not chase his daughter's boyfriend with a shotgun. But he was adamantly opposed to their romance and subsequent marriage. Shashi Kapoor came on board Shakespeareana—on and off that is—when he was nineteen because he could not bear to be apart from Jennifer. No doubt his father was not too happy with his son's temporary defection from Prithvi Theatres. And, for a while, their surreptitious meetings (with Felicity playing 'go-between and chaperone') took place without the Kendals finding out.

However, the rift between the two men soon widened. Kendal was inordinately possessive about his eldest daughter. Jennifer had been left behind in England for a few years when the Kendals first came to India during the war with ENSA. She was brought up by her grandaunt, Beaulah Perry. Geoffrey Kendal didn't want to lose her again. Another reason for such possessive behaviour was the fact that Jennifer was not only the leading lady of the company's plays, she did the costumes and was its property manager. Things came to a head when Kapoor joined the company in Singapore. Geoffrey Kendal stopped speaking to him, communicating with him through his younger daughter Felicity. Soon Kendal even stopped looking at Kapoor when both men were acting on stage.

Aware of the fact that her father would never relent, Jennifer announced one morning that Shashi and she were leaving for

Bombay to be married. The previous evening she had told her sister that they had no choice but to leave. 'Daddy has told me that it isn't Shashi he objects to, or the fact that he is Indian, or that he is younger than I am...it is just that he does not want us to leave the company. Shashi has his own country and his own life, and he doesn't want to stay with us for ever, touring Shakespeare.'[5]

The departure of the young lovers probably had more drama than most of the plays staged by the company. Felicity Kendal writes: 'And when we stood on the verandah that morning and Jennifer, red-eyed, threw her arms about his neck, her tiny shoulders shaking with sobs, he stood, stiff and straight, his arms plastered to his sides, looking ahead and silent, until I pulled her away from him and hugged her into the waiting taxi. The look of bewilderment on Shashi's face at this appalling behaviour is something I will never forget. The green Mercedes taxi drove away, Jennifer weeping.'

Leaving Singapore was trying. Penniless and desperate, Shashi Kapoor went to the Air India office in Singapore and 'made a trunk call to Bombay' asking Raj Kapoor to send him money for two tickets to Bombay. Geoffrey Kendal, furious about the relationship between his daughter and Shashi, had refused the actor's passage to India because he did not want him to marry his daughter. Raj Kapoor sent a PTA (prepaid travel advice) for two economy tickets from Singapore to Bombay. Interestingly, many years later, in 1987, Shashi bought a first-class ticket for Raj Kapoor's youngest son, Rajiv, from Moscow to London: he was missing his girlfriend who was in London.

The young couple had to wait until their first son Kunal was born in 1960 to be reconciled with the Kendals. The drama of their departure was, according to Shashi, much ado about nothing. 'When I met her she was twenty-two. They thought that she would never return. My in-laws were afraid to lose their eldest daughter, whom they treated as a son. They did not have a son. We married in 1958, and within five months we were touring with them. What did Shashi Kapoor take away from them?'

Jennifer returned to Shakespeareana, part-time. Meanwhile, Shashi had starting working in films, and joined his wife when he could. Kapoor is too much of a gentleman to express resentment or a sense of hurt. However, it is obvious that prejudice about mixed marriages prevailed at the time. Says Shashi: 'On hearing about Jennifer and I, Laura Liddell's mother had said, "Imagine the black babies." Black! I took Jennifer and Kunal there to show her the baby...I borrowed money to make the trip, taking credit from a travel agency.' Their first-born, Kunal, was a bonny, light-haired boy, and the second child Karan, blonde and fair and lovely as they come in Grand Brittania.

Meanwhile, back in the Kapoor khandaan the family was not exactly overjoyed about their son marrying a foreigner, but there were no serious objections. Ironically, Prithviraj Kapoor's father, who had objected violently to his son going to Bombay to become an actor, was very supportive. 'My grandfather told me, "*Udenal waya kar le* (marry her),"' recalls Shashi. The two had a traditional Arya Samaj marriage in the Kapoor home in Matunga on 2 July 1958. There was no time for a reception. Prithviraj Kapoor flew down that evening from Jaipur, where he was acting in K. Asif's *Mughal-e-Azam*. Determined not to lose a single day of shooting, the director sent his 'Akbar' in a private plane, a Dakota. The three-hour ceremony and dinner over, Prithviraj Kapoor flew back early the next morning, and resumed work without sleeping.

The wedding ceremony took three hours because the Arya Samaj priest insisted on translating everything into English so that Jennifer Kendal—dressed in a red ghagara choli—could understand the significance of the rituals, while the immediate Kapoor family looked on. Geeta Bali did the bridal make-up. She also took photographs of the ceremony and the young couple but none of them came out.

Jennifer Kendal became a Kapoor bahu, and initially lived with the family in Matunga. Hierarchy and family traditions were given great importance here. Perhaps the fact of being displaced from the North West Frontier Province made the Kapoor elders cling on more determinedly to customs and rituals, even inventing some along the way in their quest to give a semblance of solidity and permanence to their existence. The older Kapoor wives, including Mrs Prithviraj Kapoor, were like war wives—holding the home front while their men immersed themselves in work and play. Prithviraj Kapoor was often on the road with his troupe, or on location, acting in films to support his theatre and his family. Raj Kapoor's obsession with his films is legendary—nothing else mattered to him as much, not even his lady-loves. Shammi Kapoor indulged his wild streak, often playing the field.

The youngest bahu took it all in. And when she moved with her husband and Kunal to their new home at Olympus on Altamont Road in the more upscale south Bombay, a new set of rules came into being. She was not the card-playing, kitty-party-going bahu. The home and family became sacrosanct; the over-the-top world of cinema was strictly off limits. A drawbridge came up, keeping the film industry firmly out. 'I had the experience of seeing what was around me,' explains Kapoor. 'I saw others ignoring their families while they were busy at work.' At Olympus, Sundays were off. When Shashi Kapoor first started acting in films he stopped work at eight each evening. He also took six-week holidays, unheard of in the filmi world. 'That was my time. Of course, I had to hear a lot of *taana*s (taunts) from producers and directors and the rest of the film world. They said that I could just as well have done a *babu ki naukri* (been a petty bureaucrat).'

The first years after their marriage were far from easy. The young couple had very little money, and they soon had the added responsibility of a child. Shashi Kapoor worked with his father's theatre group until 1960, when it was disbanded. Jennifer used to join him occasionally when they went on tour. When she fell ill in Mysore neither of the two innocents realized that Jennifer was pregnant. Recalls Shashi: 'Uzraji [Uzra Mumtaz] told me that Jennifer was expecting. She was vomiting, and I did not know. I did not know how to handle it. I was earning seventy-five rupees and so was she. Uzraji gave me ten rupees and told me to take her to a lady doctor. Jennifer was also craving for British food. It was October and hot. In our *langar* (communal eating) all we had was *daal*, *chawal* and *bhaji*. So I bought some cabbage, put in some *maska* (butter) and boiled it. Out came a worm, and she vomited. She told me she wanted nutmeg. I did not know what it was. Years after, our khansama, Abu Mian, told me that nutmeg was *jaiphal*, what you put in cakes.'

It was a modest life in the beginning, after the couple moved to their first home in Olympus apartments. Shashi Kapoor gave his wife two thousand rupees at the beginning of each month to run the house, six hundred of which went towards the rent. 'It was easier for Jennifer because of her touring background. Otherwise, it may not have been possible for a foreigner married to an Indian actor who had become a film star,' explains Kapoor. The reason this Kapoor was different from the rest of the clan—his brothers as well as his nephews, Randhir and Rishi Kapoor—is that he acted in films in order to support his family. It was strictly business. Passion was elsewhere, in theatre, for both Shashi and Jennifer Kapoor. 'I started early, and with a *vilayati* (foreign) wife. We'd go window-shopping. I didn't have enough money to buy a book. Jennifer loved to read, and there were very few libraries. I used to have nightmares about not being able to buy things for her. Or, to give to our children.'

But he had one weakness—cars. Like Shammi Kapoor, Shashi also had a thing about cars. He talks about his early obsession with almost childish glee. His bought his first car, a 46 model MG, with a five-thousand-rupee loan from Shammi Kapoor. But his real love was his second car, a 190 SL Mercedes that he bought in 1962 with a loan from his other brother. Raj Kapoor wrote out a cheque for eighty-four thousand: *Jis Desh Mein Ganga Behti Hai* had been a hit.

Moving uptown and into another world from the one he had grown up in, Shashi's lifestyle underwent a complete metamorphosis. 'My main interest for doing films was that *vilayati biwi ke kharche zyada thay* (the expenses of a foreigner wife were more). My children did not go to the same schools I did. It was all very expensive—horse riding, expensive clubs.' The Kapoors have been regulars at the exclusive Breach Candy Club, and their friends were from the social elite of south Bombay. A room at the far end of the apartment has been christened *chamcha* room. It's a family joke, but this air-conditioned den of sorts—an antechamber if you will—is where visitors who are not part of the inner circle are first ushered in.

The taming of this Kapoor also began in real earnest. The famous Kapoor appetite for food and alcohol was reined in, and moderation entered the family vocabulary. Jennifer could not have been more different from the other Kapoor bahus in regard to food, that all-important pastime of most Kapoors. 'Jennifer used to send *napa tula khana* (diet food) to the studio for Shashi. She made sure that he did not eat fattening food,' remembers publicist and Raj Kapoor's Boswell Bunny Reuben. Shashi Kapoor's weight problems began only after his wife died.

She also steered him away from the Black Label culture that dominates the world of Indian cinema. Whiskey was like holy water for the rest of the Kapoors. Talking about why he stopped drinking whiskey (that is before he stopped drinking altogether), Shashi says: 'You know why I drink vodka. I used to drink whiskey, and that too only Black Label. Jennifer told me that your friends are still in the theatre world. When they invite you they try to serve you Black Label. It is very expensive, and they have to get it in the black market. It is bound to be adulterated, and you will fall sick.'

She was a pacifist and vegetarian. Shashi had to drop his gun: as a young man he had often gone along with Shammi Kapoor on his hunting expeditions. Shashi Kapoor recounts an interesting anecdote when he and his wife went to what was then East Pakistan with Prithvi Theatres. Jennifer was pregnant with Kunal, and the governor of Dacca—who had gone to college with Prithviraj Kapoor—invited him for a duck shoot. 'I got very excited. Jennifer told me: "Just come here. If you shoot any duck, your child will be born dead." I was so petrified. I had said yes and I had to go. It was all very macho. We went in separate pontoons in the lake, and I had a gun. As luck would have it most of the ducks headed towards me. I began to shoot in the air, and Jennifer's words came back to me: "You expect me to create while you destroy." The ducks kept coming towards me. That was the end of shikar for me.'

Jennifer also had exquisite taste, and a taste for the finer things in life. When Shashi Kapoor became a popular film star, and money came pouring in, she could finally indulge in the best the world had to offer, whether it was shoes from Paris, French perfume, or designer scarves and diaries. She was among the early explorers of Chor Bazaar, long before the yuppies discovered this labyrinth of objets d'art in central Bombay. Superb glass paintings of the Company School—dancing girls, nabobs—adorn the walls of their living room. Her collection of old prints, including several striking Daniells, can be found throughout the spacious apartment, one side of which is open to the Arabian Sea. There is a smattering of contemporary Indian art—paintings by Anjolie Ela Menon and drawings by Imtiaz Dharker. A wall of books occupies a substantial area of the living room: all the books are hard bound and several are first editions. Fiction, biographies of theatre and film personalities and books on art dominate the deep mahogany shelves.

The heart of the home is obviously the dining area. One of the irrefutable rules of this Kapoor household was that the family had to have breakfast together, no matter what time anyone came home the night before. A beautiful chandelier of glass and wrought iron hangs from the ceiling above the dining table that has offered many a glorious repast. Breakfast is at eight, and serious business here, served on wooden mats on white damask and very English crockery. It's a pucca English breakfast: freshly squeezed orange juice, oven-fresh home-made brown bread, excellent percolated coffee, cereal, eggs. A tradition which was followed until Shashi moved to Juhu in 2005, even though the white damask may have been dispensed with.

It was the best of both worlds—the East and West—in harmonious equipoise. Jennifer was apparently an agnostic. However, as a Kapoor bahu, she observed the major Hindu religious festivals and rituals for the sake of her in-laws, and was keen that their children imbibe Indian culture. She used to fast with her mother-in-law on *Karva Chauth*: women fast on this day each year for the well-being of their husbands. Interestingly, both Prithviraj Kapoor and Shashi Kapoor also fasted along with their wives. Jennifer kept it until her mother-in-law died. The Kapoors usually spent Christmas in Goa while Jennifer was alive. When they were in Bombay, the rest of the Kapoors were invited to Christmas lunch.

Just as the Kapoor clan mythologized about a Pathan ethos,

giving great importance to hierarchy and traditions (even as the men led a fairly nomadic existence in the illusionary world of theatre and cinema), the Kendals too had imposed a set of rules and rituals to impart a degree of permanence to their gypsy-like existence. Each time the Kendals moved to a new town, or even country, they did so with a caravanserai of trunks and boxes. Laura Liddell insisted on, much to the dismay of her husband, taking along all their belongings. As soon as they settled into a new place she brought out cushions, drapes, rugs, books, framed photographs and other memorabilia to create a sense of home, of roots. Jennifer was 'very much the memsahib' like her mother, according to Sunil Sethi who was friends with Jennifer Kapoor and had interviewed her mother, Laura Liddell. 'There would be tea with sandwiches. The tea would be poured correctly, even if the crockery was broken.'

According to Shashi, the Kendals never had a home. 'I would say that they were the original hippies. Their Bombay address was c/o South East Asian Company. Dhanjiboy was a partner with Kendal's brother, Phillip Brag. Kendal, in fact, was a lovely town in the Lake District. Their only UK address was that of Laura Liddell's sister, and Jennifer's first home was her maternal grandmother's house.'

Home moved centre stage in Jennifer Kapoor's life, becoming all the more important because she had forsaken an acting career to become Mrs Shashi Kapoor. In her case it was her choice, not adherence to the tradition of Kapoor bahus giving up their careers. Perhaps she had tired of the peripatetic existence of her family, of living out of trunks. However, there may have been occasional twinges of regret. In her account in *White Cargo*, about the crucial role Shashi and Jennifer Kapoor played in launching her acting career—from paying her passage to England, getting clothes made for her and paying for her expenses amongst a lot else—Felicity Kendal writes: 'She was helping me to gain something she had wanted for herself...'

Certainly, Jennifer stood out in the company of the Bombay film fraternity. Felicity quotes a telling passage from one of her sister's letters to her: 'Last night at one of Shashi's premieres I wore my long sheath dress and evening gloves. One film star person asked me if I'd forgotten to put the rest of the dress on, and Shashi's heroine asked me if my fingers were cold! Darling, I'm glad you're there.'

However, Jennifer Kapoor did not forsake Jennifer Kendal completely. The great actress in her surfaced from time to time. She acted in several films, including her husband's debut film as producer, *Junoon*, in which she plays Nafisa Ali's Anglo-Indian mother. In Merchant–Ivory's *Heat and Dust*, her cameo role as a gossipy British official's wife was critically appreciated, as was her inspired performance as the English author who has a destructive affair with an Indian matinee idol in *Bombay Talkie*. In the film, Kendal reveals just how versatile she was as an actress. Seductive and melodramatic, she plays havoc with the lives of two Indian men. This was the only film in which Shashi and Jennifer are cast as lovers. According to American author Robert Emmet Long, 'She is a kind of Circe figure who turns men into swine.'[6]

But it was her tour de force performance as Violet Stoneham, a lonely Anglo-Indian spinster in *36 Chowringhee Lane*, a film directed by Aparna Sen and produced by Shashi Kapoor, that is indelibly inked in the memory of film lovers. Kendal won the Evening Standard Best Actress Film Award in 1983 for her performance in this film, and was nominated for the prestigious BAFTA Best Actress Award the same year. (Katherine Hepburn won that year for her role in *On Golden Pond*.) The film won the Grand Prix at the Manila Film Festival in 1982.

This Kapoor bahu was not a hausfrau. Prithvi Theatre, in its second avatar, was her baby. Prithviraj Kapoor had reluctantly brought down the final curtain on Prithvi Theatres in 1960:[7] his voice had gone, and so had his money. It went up again eighteen years later, in 1978. Shashi and Jennifer Kapoor built it on the site of the jhompra where his father had lived during the last ten years of his life. The couple intended it to be an intimate, experimental theatre in Juhu. 'Jennifer and I got it all done—it was my father's vision and our money, and she managed it with twenty lakh rupees of personal money. She wanted a permanent repertory—what Sanjana is now trying to do.'

Strangely enough the lease for the land on which Prithviraj

Kapoor had built his home ran out after ten years, just about the time he died. The land belonged to the Bajaj family. The Urban Land Ceiling Act had come into being. The Bajaj family could not renew the lease. They could, however, sell the property. Rahul Bajaj offered to sell it to Shashi Kapoor, and he bought it for the Prithviraj Kapoor Memorial Trust and Research Foundation. Jennifer and he raised the money to pay for it with a show—Amitabh and Jaya Bachchan, Sanjeev Kumar, Rekha, Shabana Azmi, Mohammad Rafi, Vinod Khanna and Vinod Mehra, amongst others, participated in the show to help him raise the funds.

Prithvi Theatre reopened on 3 November 1978—Prithviraj Kapoor's birth anniversary—with two plays by a few struggling actors from the National School of Drama: Naseeruddin Shah, Om Puri and Ratna Shah. They staged a short Hindi play, *Udvastha Dharmashala*, written by G.P. Deshpande and directed by Om Puri, and a one-act play in English, *The Lesson*.

Prithvi Theatre soon became a watering place for the young and talented of Bombay: aspiring film and theatre actors and directors made this their adda. Jennifer also started Prithvi Café, creating a bit of bohemia in Juhu. The famous Irish coffee (coffee spiked with whiskey) and brownies drew in the hordes, and many plays and films were born here, over endless cups of coffee and discussions on the cane *mora*s (stools). Tea and coffee were cheap. Many an impecunious actor or writer managed to keep body and soul together because of the inexpensive and wholesome food served in the open-air café. Maverick adman Prahlad Kakkar helped Jennifer run the café.

She administered Prithvi Theatre until she fell ill in 1983. Diagnosed with cancer, she died the following year in a London hospital: there had been a series of operations, beginning in Bombay. Kapoor had lost both his parents to cancer. Her parents, sister, husband and children were by her side at the end. Just two days before her death, she wrote 'Readiness is all' on a note and gave it to her father, quoting, as her sister writes in her book, Shakespeare to the last. An agnostic, Jennifer Kapoor was cremated in Golders Green in London. There was no priest at the end. Shashi Kapoor brought her ashes back to Bombay: some were scattered in the Arabian Sea, some buried on the grounds of their Goa home, which she loved greatly. It was to be many years before Shashi Kapoor found the courage to go to Goa.

Ustaad Zakir Husain gives a concert on her birth anniversary every year at Prithvi Theatre. He did so for the first anniversary, and continues to do so.

With Jennifer gone, Shashi Kapoor's world gradually fell apart. At first the signs were not visible. He had already put on a lot of weight for his role in his own production *Utsav*. In the film, Girish Karnad's screen adaptation of the fifth-century Sanskrit play *Mrichakatikka*, Kapoor plays the lecherous and fat brother-in-law of the evil king. The marvellously witty film with a Rabelaisian cast of characters was released in 1985. The kilos, however, stayed put. In fact, he became even fatter as the years went by. Soon, Shashi Kapoor began to resemble a Sumo wrestler. Food, often rich, was gulped down as if there was no tomorrow.

Meanwhile, vodka became a faithful companion. The inner Kapoor surfaced: what Jennifer Kapoor had so successfully put back in the bottle wriggled out. The 'bar' began to open a little before noon: double vodkas flowed until lunch. And then by seven in the evening it was vodka time again. If there was company, well and good, if not, he drank alone.

His career as male lead had wound down by 1984. As a producer he had made some outstanding films. Yet, most of them—perhaps they were before their time—did not fare well at the box office. Lady Luck had obviously abandoned him.

The income tax men came knocking. A notice stuck on the door of his twelfth-floor apartment in Atlas Apartments informed visitors that Shashi Kapoor's home was now in the custody of the income tax department. They had also come calling earlier—in 1982. Shashi Kapoor was in Srinagar at the time, shooting for a film when his wife telephoned him. 'She could not speak. Our children were not allowed to go to school. They searched the place and found nothing. At the time they were scrutinizing the accounts for *Junoon*.'

Financially, Shashi Kapoor was in dire straits for the better part of the nineties. *Ajooba* had taken a heavy toll. Creditors kept knocking on his door, as did the income tax authorities. Shashi Kapoor moved around in a deep rust Ambassador car, his famed white Mercedes just a faint memory. He did so without bitterness, equally at home with very little as he had been with a lot. However, the famed hospitality of the Kapoor home was not given up, nor was his generosity. Actors fondly recall him slipping hundred-rupee notes into their pockets when they were down and out in Bombay.

Eventually, his eldest son Kunal Kapoor, whose career in making advertising films had really taken off, helped the family. Shashi Kapoor also made a huge sacrifice at the time.

One morning I was late for an interview with him at Atlas Apartments. He had left by the time I got there. I hopped into a taxi and went straight to Prithvi Theatre. He was standing outside the theatre, staring at the legendary jhompra which had served as an office for Prithvi Theatre, with evocative blown-up photographs of Prithviraj Kapoor on the walls. This was the morning of the eventful demolition of the bungalow. Kapoor had sold the land to builders to honour his debts—and, ironically, to infuse more money and life into Prithvi Theatre. As the huge demolition ball swung towards the bungalow, Shashi Kapoor's eyes became wet. But the actor in him surfaced: the tears didn't spill, and soon dried up.

The family was financially back on track. Shashi Kapoor, however, slipped further into despondency. On any given morning in the late nineties you could see him sitting in his living room, a large television screen switched on, the day's TV programme clipped from the papers and placed beside him. Earlier, television had been banished to the 'chamcha room'. Kapoor hardly went out. He walked with great difficulty: the knees had given way because of the weight. It's almost as if the actor had put on a body suit to play a fat man and then forgotten to take it off. He had gout and his body was wracked with pain. Osteoporosis had taken a big toll. When asked why he didn't meet friends or go out, he says: 'I have my memories, my thoughts.' A good memory can also be a curse. An ineffable sadness tinged his once mischievous eyes. He had cut himself from many friends, although his childhood friends dropped in. Henry, who was with him in school, used to come and sit silently. He usually brought a basket of different kinds of fish. Vodka became an even more faithful companion.

Shashi Kapoor was in this state when his sister-in-law Neela Devi called to find out how he was. And this set the alarm bells ringing. Recalls Shammi Kapoor: 'My wife spoke to Shashi on the phone. He told her that there was nothing to live for. The next morning I stopped by to see him. I took one look at him and told him what he was doing was a slow death. "Look, why don't you just jump off the twelfth floor, and people will write about you." He said that he didn't want that. "Then," I told him, "I am taking you to the hospital right now." We went to Breach Candy Hospital. Shashi is the baby of the family. I told him how long can you be the baby of the family, you have to grow up. I know he felt isolated, marooned. But it was of its own making. His wife had died. But, I had lost mine too. How long can you go on like this? It becomes boring.' (Coincidences are habitual with the Kapoors. Strangely enough, when Shammi Kapoor fell seriously ill later, it was Shashi Kapoor who took charge and made the arrangements for his care in Breach Candy Hospital.)

Perhaps it was not a death wish that had led Shashi Kapoor to let himself go. Perhaps he just thought his time was up. Sixty-four is a treacherous milestone for the Kapoors: Prithviraj Kapoor died at the age, as did Raj Kapoor. And Shashi Kapoor was convinced that he would not cross it. It was Shammi Kapoor's reasoning with his brother that finally worked. 'If you start believing in this myth—that we are congenitally doomed to die—it becomes one. I told my brother I am sixty-nine. I have crossed the sixty-four barrier,' says Shammi.

After a long spell in Breach Candy, Shashi Kapoor was on his way to recovery and a new life. The doctors slapped prohibition on him—and a strict diet. He lost over twenty-five kilograms. Gradually, he began to resemble his old self; he stopped playing the recluse. Says old friend James Ivory: 'Putting on weight was a form of grieving. He drank and drank, seeking oblivion. I feel that he has come back to us. His sense of fun has survived.'

Shashi Kapoor is now a morning person, presiding over his home from the dining table or from the deep armchair he spends a great deal of time in, like a gentle patriarch who has subsumed the role of the matriarch of the house as well. He is a grandfather five times over. His son Karan, married to an English model, lives in London and has two children; his daughter Sanjana, married to Valmik Thapar, lives in Delhi and has a son. Kunal and his wife Sheena (Ramesh Sippy's daughter) and their two children lived with him for many years before moving to another apartment in the city. So did he, closing yet another chapter in his life. His apartment is too large for one man, and there are too many memories here. 'I like kids because they bring a lot of joy; even their fights bring joy,' says Shashi.

His householder days also seem to be coming to an end. Shashi Kapoor has retrieved his travelling spurs. It took him a while to regain the confidence to travel by himself. The turning point may have been his trip to Cairo to receive a lifetime achievement award during the international film festival there in 2002. Shashi Kapoor travelled alone, something he had not done for a while, charmed the Egyptians and everybody else. Later in the year he flew to Morocco to be part of the jury for the Third International Film Festival of Marrakesh. The travel bug has obviously got to him: he has been to Budapest and spends a fair amount of time in Delhi, often going to Ranthambore with his daughter Sanjana and her family.

He now divides his time between Prithvi Theatre and philanthropy—two of his father's passions. Prithviraj's mantle has fallen on his youngest son. The other two Kapoors were not particularly interested in carrying on the legacy of their father's theatre company, even though both had worked for it.

Not only is Shashi Kapoor carrying on his father's work, he almost appears to be metamorphosing into him. As a young man, he looked exactly like the young Prithviraj. Post middle age his face has filled out the same way, as has his body. His walk also approximates his father's.

Prithviraj Kapoor had started many charities, which Jennifer continued to look after without her husband's knowledge. Shashi discovered after his wife's death the extent to which she had supported charities—and individuals. 'I was thirty-four when my parents died in 1972. I had a busy film life and was unaware of all my father had done,' says Shashi. He took up where they had left off, beginning with setting up the Prithviraj Kapoor Memorial Trust. He sends money orders to about two hundred widows. Among the causes dear to him are cancer awareness and the disabled. Shashi Kapoor is actively involved with the Cancer Society in Pune, Care India and Amar Jyoti in Delhi. Interestingly, Prithviraj Kapoor's initial acts of charities were to help actors who didn't survive the transition from silent films to the talkies.

Nostalgia often takes him by the hand to happier days of the past. Sometimes, he goes to Mathura Dairy where he used to take Jennifer to eat a plate of puri bhaji in their early courtship days. The old manager is no longer alive, but his son brings out a plate: Shashi Kapoor eats in his car because he can't go into the restaurant. Sometimes, he goes back even further in his life to Hollywood Lane in Matunga and the Parsi Colony near Dadar. The golewala around whom he and his friends would gather each evening to chat and slurp down ice balls dipped in lurid pink and orange syrups was still there until a few years ago, 'parked on one side of the garden'.

Those memories no longer remain just his companions. In 2004, he, with journalist Deepa Gahlot, put together a beautiful book—*The Prithviwallahs*—that tells the story of Prithvi Theatre in both its avatars. The book is a homage to his father and to Jennifer Kapoor. Life for him centres increasingly around Prithvi Theatre. He has even moved next to it—into the building where his father's beloved jhompra once stood. He can often be seen in the theatre's outdoor restaurant lunching with his old friends from the theatre, and whoever drops in to see him. He makes the journey across town, back to south Bombay, to swim at the Breach Candy Club. And when he wants to get away from it all, he goes to Mahabaleshwar—to watch the clouds and rain and be by himself.

Life now has structure, and discipline. His day starts early, and ends early as well, with dinner at 6.30 in the evening. In Atlas Apartments he used to play with the children till 7.00, before retiring to his room by 9.30. It's *his* time, usually for reading. Books pile up on his bedside table. Shashi Kapoor has an eclectic taste—they vary from Gulzar's short stories, which have been translated from Urdu into English, to books on cinema and theatre and several tomes written by Valmik Thapar. Biography and fiction also interest him.

As Shashi Kapoor retreats into this bedroom, one feels an invisible 'do not disturb' sign comes up on his door and it's almost as if memories of childhood, old friends and his life with his wife are more real than what is happening around him.

PART 3

The Inheritors

5

Forever Youthful: Rishi Kapoor

Raj Kapoor's middle son was born to act. Barely able to stand on his podgy little legs, Rishi Kapoor would waddle over to a mirror and make faces. One evening, Raj Kapoor gave his toddler son—born on 4 September 1952—a sip from his glass of whiskey. And before he could say, well, Black Label, Rishi began to act like a drunkard in front of the mirror.

Grease paint must have been like mother's milk, stage props his first toys, and the stage and film sets his little world for Rishi Kapoor. This Kapoor made his acting debut early: he had a part in his grandfather's play *Pathan*. 'I was a child asleep on a *khatiya* (string cot). I remember I was very excited about it,' says Rishi. His childhood memories are punctuated with outings in studios. Like his elder brother and sister he had a ball on the sets of *Shree 420*, walking in the studio rain when he was four. More vivid in his mind is playing on the sets of K. Asif's *Mughal-e-Azam* as an eight year old. 'I remember the *Mughal-e-Azam* sets, all that plaster of Paris. It gave me the biggest high to play on the sets with swords.' Equally vivid looms Prithviraj Kapoor in his childhood memories. He was fascinated by his grandfather, and perhaps even more so by his car: 'Papaji had an Opel car. It was kind of yellow-ochre. He used to drive...He was a tall guy in a small car.'

The chubby-cheeked little swashbuckler had to sheath the plaster of Paris swords and return to the real world of school and homework. But it was not an eternally long intermission from the world of cinema. While still a schoolboy, his father used to squirrel him away from Campion School to R.K. to act in *Mera Naam Joker*. The teachers were not amused. He was rusticated. History certainly keeps repeating itself in the Kapoor family: Shammi Kapoor was also hijacked from school to act in *Shakuntala*. Raj Kapoor had to do a lot of explaining to get his son reinstated in school. Recalls Rishi Kapoor: 'Papa came to school. He had to explain that I was not working. So, he only shot on weekends, and had to wait for the vacations. I started practising my autograph signature. I used to stand in front of the mirror to see how I looked while acting.' Rishi Kapoor received the Best Child Actor's Award for *Mera Naam Joker*.

After Dev Anand, the legendary Peter Pan of the Indian screen, Rishi Kapoor has perhaps had the longest innings as a romantic hero. Rishi Kapoor has scored, as he likes to reiterate, a quarter century as a leading man and romantic lover—from *Bobby* in 1973 to *Karobaar* in 1998. And he's obviously not done yet: he plays a middle-aged hero in love in *Pyar Mein Twist* (2005). He went the Kapoor way of all flesh in the eighties. But the audience, especially women, accepted him, double chins and expanding waist notwithstanding. His fans willingly suspended their disbelief in accepting a hero in his mid-forties wooing women half his age, and a quarter his size.

Was it his fair, babyish face? The cast of his fine features configured to spell sweetness and inspire trust? Rishi Kapoor came across as the nice boy who wasn't just led by his raging hormones but loved with his soul as well. He danced like a dream, effortlessly. The star-crossed or tragic lover label fit him well, especially in films like *Laila Majnu*. He also came at a time when screen romance was about love, and not obsession. For schoolgirls and undergraduates in the seventies and early eighties he was a romantic icon, the ultimate ladies man. He symbolized a sense of *masti* and youthful energy, not to forget those magic dancing feet. The Emergency and its aftermath, bringing in its wake cynicism and anger, took place after he was already established. It didn't trip him.

So while Randhir Kapoor and many other actors did not survive the action era or the juggernaut of Amitabh Bachchan, post-*Sholay*, Rishi Kapoor kept going, and going, like the tortoise, past the young teenyboppers with rippling biceps sprinting in short bursts before being pushed off Bollywood Boulevard. He acted in several memorably popular films with Bachchan—from Manmohan Desai blockbusters like *Amar Akbar Anthony*, *Naseeb* and *Coolie* to Shashi Kapoor's *Ajooba*. Like his uncle he, too, was complementary to Amitabh Bachchan, their screen affability and 'niceness' offsetting the lanky actor's edgy intensity. Bachchan weighs his words carefully like a grocer but is surprisingly spontaneous while talking about Rishi Kapoor: 'Chintu is a natural actor. He is one of the finest of our actors and has a certain individuality of his own.'

Raj Kapoor wrote bits of his life into his films, more often than not realizing his fantasies in and perhaps through them. In two of them—*Mera Naam Joker* and *Bobby*—he made his middle son his alter ego. These were Rishi Kapoor's first two films. In both films the character he plays has a name that recalls his father's: Raju in *Mera Naam Joker* and Raja in *Bobby*. The choice of name is particularly significant in the first film, which is Raj Kapoor's most autobiographical one. Interestingly, other directors too have chosen names beginning with the letter R for Rishi Kapoor's screen personae—Rajan, Raja, Rohit, Rajesh and Ravi appear to be favourites.

In *Bobby*, twenty-one-year-old Rishi Kapoor plays a love-besotted teenager. Not only did Raj Kapoor choose a name that resembled his own, he forged a screen persona for his son that would fit him like a glove for over two decades. Love in this film is an end in itself for the irredeemably romantic, often star-crossed, young lover. Love for this baby-faced hero is the highest ideal, worth crashing the barriers of class, caste and religion, and even dying for. In this modern-day Indian avatar of *Romeo and Juliet* with a Kapoorian twist, Rishi is rich, handsome, young and a Hindu. Dimple Kapadia is also young, sensuously beautiful, but poor and Catholic. This new romantic pair who embodied youth and zest captured the imagination of the Indian audience. The duo was like a breath of fresh air because both were acting their ages. Well, almost: Dimple Kapadia was fifteen and Rishi was twenty going on eighteen. Until then, actors well into their twenties and even thirties like Dharmendra and Jeetendra were acting as college boys and dancing around trees.

Mera Naam Joker, which preceded *Bobby*, had been a colossal flop. Raj Kapoor had put all his money and much of himself in what he hoped would be his magnum opus. Its failure hit him and his family hard: the Kapoor coffers emptied and his indomitable spirit hit an all-time low. *Bobby* was a make-or-break film for him. He discarded his old aesthetics, even his grammar of cinema, turning a new chapter with a measure of violence. The film had to be about youth and for the youth. He had to get the young into the cinema halls with something new. 'Modern' became the new mantra. The film had to *look* different. The Kapoor palette changed.

As did Rishi Kapoor. He became, as film journalist Dinesh Raheja writes on Rediffusion.com, a 'male kitsch fashion plate of the 70s Bollywood'. In *Bobby* he wears outsize sunglasses, more appropriate for aviators than teenyboppers. His clothes are incredibly loud and quite over the top: blue, strawberry or wine-coloured bell-bottom trousers, even velvet flares. He sports striped shorts and shirts with blue and lavender stripes. Since Rishi Kapoor was portraying a rebel who defies his arrogant and rich father, he is also fitted out in a black leather jacket and gloves. Zipping up his metallic zipper with a forceful gesture comes across as an act of defiance. Raj Kapoor usually recognized the signposts of change and had an uncanny knack of picking up trends before other cineastes. He also accessorized his son with a motor scooter that had inordinately long metal handles and mirrors on both sides that could reflect his son's face. The revving scooter symbolized youth, energy and modernity—and the macho male.

Bhanu Athaiya, the costume designer who was later awarded an Oscar for her work in Richard Attenborough's *Gandhi*, designed Dimple Kapadia's wardrobe. Bobby (Dimple Kapadia) is a fisherman's daughter but she wears Western clothes that appealed to the emerging middle-class youth culture—blouses tied high above the waist, minis, orange bikinis, her trademark polka-dot Ellie May short blouse and the flowing scarves with which she tied her glorious ponytail (yet to acquire its crowning glory state). Actresses till then did wear trousers and 'modern' dresses but they were more for 'hippy' women like Asha Parekh than for hip youngsters. 'Bhanu Athaiya elevated definitions of style bringing middle-class hipness [sic] to a new level, making youthful sexiness and rebellious looks daringly acceptable.'[1] It was savvy exploitation of nubile flesh draped in occidental clothes, an update from the more indigenous exploration of Padmini's blouse-less sari-draped body in *Mera Naam Joker*.

Was modernity only skin-deep, or dress-deep, in *Bobby*? The film certainly made teenage rebellion fashionable. But ultimately the film is quintessential Raj Kapoor. The Rishi Kapoor character is a rebel, but with a cause. A socialist heart beats here: after all the film is scripted by K.A. Abbas. Rishi Kapoor turns against his capitalist father and wants to marry a girl from the other end of the social spectrum. Her father is a fisherman, marvellously portrayed by a garrulous Premnath. Pran is impressive as Rishi's father, and you can't help thinking of Veronica's father in Archie comics—Raj Kapoor's favourite staple reading material. Photographs of Jawaharlal Nehru and Mahatma Gandhi hang on the walls of Raja's bedroom.

Bobby has more action than Raj Kapoor's earlier films. The two lovers run away on the motorcycle. And after being chased for a long time, finally jump off a cliff into the sea. Had Raj Kapoor gone with his original ending the credits would have begun rolling at this point. But the resemblance to *Romeo and Juliet* ends here. After much prevarication he opted for a happy ending: the pair is rescued by their fathers. In a delicious twist to the tale, Premnath saves Rishi Kapoor and Pran saves Dimple Kapadia. In the end it is love-all and all's well that ends well, like another Shakespearean play.

There was mass hysteria when *Bobby* was first released in 1973, with teenagers sporting shirts with *Bobby* written on them. The actor was mobbed like a rock star. But more importantly, the Raja character in *Bobby* soon became a blueprint for many of Rishi Kapoor's subsequent roles. It wasn't just the fair and lovely babyish face with its pair of lovelorn eyes: unlike his father's famous blue eyes that flashed intensity and passion, his brown eyes radiated puppy-love, warmth and sensitivity. An air of innocence and credibility followed him like a halo. He effortlessly became the character on screen, getting under its skin without the overload of method acting. Baptized as a singing and dancing romantic hero by his director-father, this scion of the Kapoor khandaan had love as his mission in life. Rebellion had to do with reasons of love, not state.

In *Bobby*, Rishi may appear a swaggering persona on the surface, but an aching tenderness and vulnerability come through in this performance, and subsequent ones. It proved to be a durable branding in the age of the angry young man that was lurking around the corner. The Jai Prakash Narayan movement and the Emergency were about to usher in a darker mood in the mid-seventies, paving the way for the action hero. The tall, dark and not screen-conventionally handsome Bachchan soon landed centre stage as the male urban underdog. The Kapoors were generally fair and 'rich looking', not sprung, dhoti-clad, from villages, or from the teeming chawls of the metropolis. Most actors in the romantic mould, including elder brother Randhir Kapoor, were swept away by the avenging screen avatar post Prakash Mehra's *Zanjeer* in 1973.

The happy ending in *Bobby* for the sensational debuting couple was however restricted to the screen. Soon after the film was made, Dimple Kapadia was bundled off to marry the reigning superstar of the time, Rajesh Khanna. It wasn't just a broken young heart she left behind: Rishi Kapoor no longer had a leading lady.

But his next leading lady was right there, under the noses (and ultimately in the family) of the Kapoors: Baby Sonia.[2] Raj Kapoor had even 'signed' her to play the heroine opposite his son in *Bobby*, after taking her screen test. Later he changed his mind because he decided to cast a new face.[3] Raj Kapoor kept Neetu Singh on the R.K. Films payrolls for a year. She was often seen on the sets of the film. Coincidentally, her debut as a lead actress was with Randhir Kapoor in *Rickshawala* in 1973, the same year Rishi Kapoor made his debut as a 'hero' in *Bobby*.

Neetu Singh did eventually become Rishi Kapoor's leading lady (though not in his father's film), and they were to go on to become one of Bollywood's most enduring romantic couples. In 1974, the two were paired together for the first time in *Zehreela Insaan*. The film flopped but a star couple was born. Bouncy, youthful and full of joie de vivre, both actors were natural dancers, the closest the Indian screen has had to American dancing stars Fred Astaire and Ginger Rogers. They looked good together and came across as buddies. A special chemistry bounced off the screen.

The audience loved the new romantic pair, and the two went on to act in nearly a dozen films in quick succession. Most of their films are fun-filled, breezy, romantic comedies—romantic musicals so to speak with, increasingly, a bit of action thrown in as the age of screen violence set in. In 1975, they did *Khel Khel Mein*, *Rafoo Chakkar* and *Zinda Dil*. The following year the young couple held their own in Yash Chopra's rather unusual two-generational love story *Kabhi Kabhie* with the two other romantic pairs: Amitabh Bachchan and Rakhee, and Shashi Kapoor and Rakhee. The two films they did in 1977 couldn't have been more different—Manmohan Desai's *Amar Akbar Anthony*, which had a gaggle of stars and was a phenomenally successful take on the evergreen lost-and-found formula (although it was essentially a platform for Amitabh Bachchan's comic genius), and *Doosra Aadmi*. Directed by Ramesh Talwar, it is a sensitive film about the relationship between a thirty-something woman and a much younger man. Rishi Kapoor and Neetu Singh portray a married couple whose marital bliss is disturbed by the presence of an older woman (Rakhee) who sees her dead husband (played by Shashi Kapoor) in the Rishi character. *Jhoota Kahin Ka* and *Duniya Meri Jeb Mein* followed in 1979. The two also appeared in an eminently forgettable film, *Dhan Daulat*, with Rajendra Kumar and Mala Sinha.

Khel Khel Mein starts with a harmless prank: Rishi Kapoor and Neetu Singh write to a jeweller asking him to place a huge amount of money somewhere. The joke turns sour when the jeweller actually does so and ends up being killed. The police suspect the two. *Rafoo Chakkar* is more than 'inspired' by Billy Wilder's delightful 1959 comedy *Some Like It Hot* in which Tony Curtis and Jack Lemmon spend most of the screen time in drag. In an attempt to escape gangsters after witnessing a gangland murder the two men masquerade as women and join an all women's band, where they meet Marilyn Monroe. Romance gets a bit complicated because she thinks that the two are women. In the Indian take on it, directed by Narendra Bedi, Rishi Kapoor and comedian Paintal are musicians who play for a marriage band. They, too, witness a murder and have to run away from the gangsters by hopping on a train with a woman's group on its way to Srinagar. Neetu Singh's character is running away from a cruel aunt. In this gender-blurring comic farce sprinkled with innuendos, Rishi wears feather boas and kitschy dresses with élan in the cross-dressing scenes. As the young man, he is hardly more subdued: trousers with loud checks, sweaters with a huge heart and bow ties. After *Bobby*, Rishi Kapoor's wardrobe became even more kitsch and outrageous.

Neetu wore tight tops and bell-bottoms, and soon became famous for her minis worn with knee-high boots. Loops dangled from her ears, her two ponytails bounced and her bangs made her look playful. In turn cute and sexy, she also was full of beans. 'Very cheeky, very young' is how film critic Deepa Gahlot describes[4] her while writing about the scene in *Doosra Aadmi* in which she pulls the chain and jumps off the train to join Rishi Kapoor. In what could be described as the 'hotties' of the time, the two were fashion templates for teenagers before the MTV era.

The seventies were also all about guitars and discos—as well as a bit of murder and mayhem. Many of the songs from these films remain popular, as fresh today as they were then. Just as *Bobby*'s eponymous 'Mein shayar to nahin' and 'Hum tum ek kamre mein band hon' came to define young love, so did the drunken number the duo sing in *Khel Khel Mein*: 'Khullam khulla pyaar karenge hum dono'. Nasir Husain's *Hum Kisi Se Kum Nahin* (1977), which has a rather thin and implausible storyline where Rishi Kapoor's character spends most of the film romancing a nondescript Kajol Kiran and looking for his father's killer, was an instant box-office success. It was helped no doubt by R.D. Burman's music (foot-tapping songs like 'Tum kya jaano', 'Bachna ae haseeno' and 'Mil gaya') and Rishi Kapoor's deft footwork. His attire hasn't lost any of its kitschiness in this film. He wears a beret, a locket shaped like a heart and a belt with red hearts. But the pièce de résistance is the white leisure suit with blinding sequins he wears for a song sequence: it reminds one of Elvis Presley's outfits. Or worse: pianist Liberace's camp attire.

The mid- and late seventies belonged to Neetu and Rishi, until they got married in 1980. After their marriage, Rishi Kapoor's popularity took a bit of a dip. He was not a superhero in the mould of Amitabh Bachchan, but the boy next door, the kind you could aspire to marry. Hence, the loss of his bachelor status may have affected his popularity.

The first dimming of applause hurt. His fondness for food and whiskey began to show on him soon enough: gluttony and alcohol are the two cardinal sins of the Kapoors. The career slowdown in the early eighties made his mood swings worse. The Kapoor home on Pali Hill reverberated with arguments over the bottle, and much else.

Insecurity became a clinging companion, like a shadow. Perhaps it was his extreme sensitivity that made him so fragile. He even got actor's block soon after his marriage. Reportedly, one day, while shooting at R.K., he suddenly went cold in front of the camera. His family took him to Loni to recover. Raj Kapoor believed it was a result of exertion since Rishi had been working non-stop for several years. Other actors had also experienced something similar. There was, however, something else bothering him. The actor was worried about being able to fulfil the responsibility of being a married and family man. The breaking point could also have been the initial lukewarm response to his film *Karz*, released in 1980. (The film went on to do amazingly well.) This particular low phase, however, did not last long: the actor bounced back with commercially successful films like *Naseeb* (1981) and *Prem Rog* (1982).

Even though a large number of the films in which he was the

sole male lead did well at the box office, many came and went without a whimper. While his first foray into Muslim socials *Laila Majnu* (1976), directed by H.S. Rawail and co-starring Ranjeeta, was moderately successful, the ones he made later were not. *Deedar-e-Yaar* (1982) with Jeetendra, Rekha, and Tina Munim—also directed by Rawail—was a disaster. The heavy sets, flamboyant moustaches, kurtas, caps and bandgalas did not resonate with the youth: the film looked dated. Not even Rekha as the courtesan with the heart of gold could rescue this one. Obviously, the audience did not warm to Rishi Kapoor in period films.

Yeh Vaada Raha (1982), based on Danielle Steel's novel *The Promise*, directed by Kapil Kapoor, was critically appreciated but commercially a flop. R.D.'s music was popular, particularly 'Tu, tu hai wahi' and 'Jeene ko toh jeetey hain sabhi'. Rishi Kapoor, once again the son of a rich family, falls in love with a poor but beautiful and talented singer (Poonam Dhillon) who lives in a hill station—as did many of the Kapoor heroines. And once again his family (in this case his mother played by Rakhee) forbids him to marry her. So when Dhillon's face is disfigured in an accident, his mother tells him that she is dead. There is an interesting twist in the film. Dhillon has plastic surgery and returns with a new face: Tina Munim's. The face is different. But the voice is similar, and haunts the young hero.

But no matter how ridiculous the plots of the films or how mediocre the directors, Rishi Kapoor was consistently competent. Even in films that fared poorly, he was seldom criticized. In the hands of a good director the actor proved that he was far more than a popular romantic hero with a sweet face. He could be nuanced, impart complexity to his characters and explore the darker sides of man—just as his father had done. In films like *Prem Rog*, *Karz*, *Ek Chadar Maili Si* and *Doosra Aadmi*, the actor has given remarkable performances. Subhash Ghai's immensely successful *Karz* is a fairly unfaithful remake of the American film, *The Reincarnation of Peter Proud*. Rishi Kapoor's sensitive portrayal of the 'reincarnated' rock singer out to avenge his murder by his wife (Simi Garewal in a chilling performance) in his previous life is powerful. And, who can forget the giant gramophone record that was a stage set for Kapoor's spirited song sequence 'Om Shanti Om': the song became quite a rage in discotheques. Or for that matter the insistent and insinuating guitar of 'Ek hasina thi'.

For a long stretch of his career Rishi Kapoor survived without acting in 'multi-starrers' (films with many leading men and women). Apparently, he was even reluctant to act in *Kabhi Kabhie*. Yash Chopra had in fact initially cast Parveen Babi as his love interest, but changed his mind on the day of the mahurat when he realized that 'she did not look good with him'.[5] Eventually, Rishi Kapoor had to share the screen with other heroes. He needn't have worried: the actor had a good long innings in films with multiple heroes. Particularly successful were his films with Amitabh Bachchan. He acted with him in five films, beginning with *Kabhi Kabhie* in 1976, followed by Manmohan Desai's *Amar Akbar Anthony* (1977), *Naseeb* (1981), *Coolie* (1983) and, finally, Shashi Kapoor's *Ajooba* in 1991.

It would have been so easy to be overshadowed by Amitabh Bachchan, or even the macho Vinod Khanna, in *Amar Akbar Anthony*. For once not playing a rich man's son, Rishi Kapoor's screen persona (Akbar) manages to make his presence felt as a rather frisky paan-chewing tapori character brought up by a Muslim tailor: his ticket out from the chawls is his musical talent. In this film, as well as in *Naseeb*, the actor's facility with comedy and his 'golden toes' enabled him to keep up with the superhero, as well as other male stars. In fact, Rishi Kapoor has a flair for comedy and slapstick, and is also quite adept at camping it, just as his uncle Shashi Kapoor was in *Haseena Maan Jayegi*.

Towards the end of the eighties, Rishi Kapoor's luck began to run out. Roles being offered to him were not substantial, and some of his rather indifferent films began to collapse at the box office. Yash Chopra's *Chandni* (1989) brought both the actor and the director back with a bang. Chopra had also hit a bad patch with films. The actor was apparently reluctant to work in *Chandni*: Rishi Kapoor had worked in Chopra's film, *Vijay*, made the year before. The film (in which Anil Kapoor also acted) bombed. Rachel Dwyer, in her book on Yash Chopra, mentions that Chopra had initially asked Anil Kapoor to do the role eventually played by Rishi Kapoor in *Chandni*. Anil declined the film as he found the role 'too weak, too women-oriented'. Besides he did not want to 'sit in a wheelchair'. Rishi Kapoor, too, was worried about acting in a heroine-oriented film: he realized that it would be Sridevi's film. Obviously, this Kapoor never forgot that he was from Bollywood aristocracy. Unlike many of the other stars at the time he was not in awe of movie moghuls. Talking about his reluctance to act in Yash Chopra's film, he told Dwyer, quite tongue in cheek: 'During *Vijay*, he offered me a role in *Chandni*. While shooting in Bangalore I asked him, "Chandni wears white, she is shimmering moonlight. Very poetic, but what's the story?" He said, "It's Chandni." "[Then] what am I there [for]? Am I a star, am I the darkness? There has to be a story."'

Chandni was all about romance with a capital R. Rishi Kapoor's character showers rose petals from a helicopter on Sridevi standing on her terrace to express his love for her. Playing besotted lovers is second nature for the actor. The film, however, also allowed him to imbue love with an obsessive edge. Impressed with the bouquet of contrary emotions (vulnerability, cynicism) Kapoor brought to his role, Chopra offered him the role of the stalker that Shah Rukh Khan finally did in *Darr* in 1993. The actor refused. Particular about his image and standing, he did not want to be directed by Chopra's assistant. (Initially, Chopra's assistant was to direct the film.) Nor did he want to play such a dark character. He told Dwyer: 'I said, "Yashji, do you think I can create terror? I am a romanticist. I have a romantic image. I have a film behind me. I played a negative role...It bombed at the box office. Do you think I can do justice to the role?" He said, "You're a good actor, you'll carry it off." I said, "Carry it off is one thing, but image is a very important thing for a film." He said, "Do the other role." I said, "There's nothing to do in the other role. After working with you in *Chandni*, do you want me to do a subordinate role again? Give me a good role, it need not be a big role, but there must be some meat in it." He probably understood I was not very comfortable and thereafter we never met.'

But Rishi Kapoor proved indestructible. Ironically, his seeming vulnerability became his strength, and he survived on a parallel romantic track. He became known as 'lover boy', and continued with love in the time of sex, violence, and action. His dancing skills continued to help him waltz a succession of nubile starlets on his arms in the beginning of the nineties. And as he grew older (although he wore his years lightly), his leading ladies got younger and younger. Like his other uncle, Shammi Kapoor, Rishi brags about being a star-maker. He was the launch pad for many debutantes and unknown actresses—Dimple Kapadia (*Bobby*), Kajol Kiran (*Hum Kisi Se Kum Nahin*), Shoma Anand (*Barood*), Bhavna (*Naya Daur*), Jaya Prada (*Sargam*), Naseem (*Kabhi Kabhie*), Sonam (*Vijay*), Divya Bharati (*Deewana*), Sangita Bijlani (*Hathiyar*), and Pakistani actress Zeba Bhaktiar (*Henna*). In *Ajooba*, Rishi woos Sonam, still in her teens, while his first screen love Dimple is romantically paired with Amitabh Bachchan. In *Hum Dono* (1995), the actor, then forty-three, danced in a garage with Pooja Bhatt: she would have been about half his age at the time. In jest he once said that he would end up acting with Dimple Kapadia's daughters and perhaps even their daughters.

Reality check finally came for this long-distance runner in 1998, after Rakesh Roshan's *Karobaar*. An 'adaptation' of the American film *Indecent Proposal*, it was finally released in 2000, and promptly fell flat on its dated face. Despite the fact that much of the film is in flashback, the audience could no longer willingly suspend disbelief to accept an ageing hero—though still light on his toes—with bulges in the wrong places wooing Juhi Chawla. The reviews were scathing. Even Neetu Singh is supposed to have said that enough was enough. It was time for her husband to stop playing a leading man and graduate to character roles.

Hemingway said all good writers go to Paris before they die. In a similar vein, all good Indian actors become screen fathers before the final fade-out—sometimes they become middle-aged cops too, like Amitabh Bachchan. After the debacle of *Karobaar*, Rishi Kapoor slipped into playing papa with effortless ease. He draws the line however at donning a policeman's uniform and getting killed in the second scene.

The interlude between playing the romantic lead and the

father of romantic leads was relatively short. Rishi Kapoor began playing papa on-screen with *Raju Chacha* (2000). In this film, Rishi Kapoor plays a middle-aged widower with three children. The film, an uneasy and exorbitantly expensive mix of *The Sound of Music* and *Home Alone*, did badly at the box office. But Rishi Kapoor had finally shed his image of the young romantic hero and was on his way to securing a comfortably large niche in yet another screen avatar: that of the screen father of the leading pairs.

The new millennium proved lucky for him and films followed in quick succession. In 2001 it was Rahul Rawail's *Kuch Khatti Kuch Meethi*. Rishi Kapoor gives a credible performance as an alcoholic father of twin daughters. Separated from his wife, he has custody of one daughter, while his wife has the other. With Kajol playing the twins who are temperamentally poles apart, most screen fathers would have probably been reduced to moving backdrops. But Rishi Kapoor is such a natural and so believable that his portrayal was critically appreciated.

A few months later, in 2002, the actor gave a scene-stealing performance as Salman Khan's reluctant father in David Dhawan's *Yeh Hai Jalwa*. Rishi Kapoor is the richest Indian in the UK, (slyly named Rajesh Mittal) and a model citizen with a perfect family. The only fly in the ointment is this illegitimate son in India who suddenly turns up in England and wants to be acknowledged as his son. In this slapstick comedy, Rishi Kapoor may no longer be playing the leading man but he hogs a lot of screen time and almost walks away with the film with his perfect sense of comic timing. He even wears all those extra kilos with grace.

In Khalid Mohammed's *Tehzeeb* (2003), Rishi Kapoor is the frustrated husband of a successful singer. His role in this film is hardly significant: he appears in a few flashback scenes. The film belongs to Shabana Azmi who plays his widow. The following year, his performance in the popular *Hum Tum*, directed by Kunal Kohli, was appreciated. This time he is cast as Saif Khan's father, and he finally gets his share of romantic frissons—in a sort of romance taking place on a parallel track with his estranged wife, played by Rati Agnihotri. Interestingly, this is the third film (after *Kuch Khatti Kuch Meethi* and *Yeh Hai Jalwa*) in as many years that the two have been paired together as a couple—separated or together.

Rishi Kapoor and romance can't be kept apart for too long. It is back to the future in 2005 with Dimple Kapadia in *Pyar Mein Twist*, a film directed by Hriday Shetty. The *Bobby* team return to the screen as a romantic pair for the third time.[6] In the film they portray a middle-aged couple who plan to marry. In this love story with a 'difference', Dimple Kapadia's screen daughter, who is also on the verge of getting married, is opposed to her mother's second marriage. Indian film-makers have usually lacked the courage to make a mature love story, fearing the audience would laugh at a romantically involved middle-aged pair. Perhaps the unexpected success of Ravi Chopra's *Baghban* (where Amitabh Bachchan and Hema Malini play an autumnal couple—grandparents at that—who romantically pine for each other after their selfish children separate them) made a difference. Shetty is counting on the *Bobby* magic to enhance his film: 'For our generation, Rishi Kapoor and Dimple Kapadia are the ultimate love pair.'[7]

Casting a middle-aged Rishi Kapoor offers an additional bonus to film-makers: it enables them to exploit the lingering appeal of *Bobby*. In both *Yeh Hai Jalwa* and *Hum Tum* there are references to *Bobby*. In *Hum Tum*, Rishi Kapoor and his son Saif Khan sing 'Main shayar to nahin'—almost an anthem of love for the young in the seventies—in a club full of puzzled foreigners. Cannibalizing *Bobby* does not end here. When Rishi Kapoor first meets Saif Khan's girlfriend's mother (played by Kirron Kher), whose name is Bobby, he nonchalantly asks: 'Shall I call you Dimple?' As this book goes to press, Rishi Kapoor is acting in a film being made in English. Shot in Birmingham, it is set in the world of music, and has the singer Apache Indian as part of the cast.

From the time he started acting in lead roles, Rishi Kapoor has made films as if he were on a non-stop treadmill: he has acted in well over 100 films. His career graph has been quite volatile, the lows alternating with the highs. He has given several remarkable and nuanced performances in his long career, trying different images to survive in a cinematic landscape in which action films became more dominant. However, *Bobby* is the most significant milestone in his filmography, a film that still endears him to and defines him for most.

In the nineties, film journalists began to focus on his volatile private life: his marriage, temper, drinking bouts were all fodder for an increasingly intrusive press. Analysing this particularly unhappy junction of his life, he admits that he had hit 'male menopause', fears and insecurities making him irritable and snappy.

Middle age sits uncomfortably on Rishi Kapoor: stubborn youth still clings despite the ravages of time and serious drinking binges. Restlessness lies just beneath his polite exterior. His room at R.K. Films is down the corridor from his elder brother's. The television is on: he likes watching cricket. His table is empty, and cups of tea keep coming. All the while he chews gum. You get the strange feeling that you have to watch what you say. You also get the feeling that this Kapoor is not quite like the others. The gregariousness is missing, as is the garrulousness of his elder brother and two sisters.

Acting may have been second nature for him, but it seems that he wanted to be something more than just a medium for his directors. Rishi Kapoor *did* get to direct a film—*Aa Ab Laut Chalen*. But it was after his father's death. He worked behind the scenes in *Kal Aaj Aur Kal*, and worked, as he says rather wistfully, 'at the fag end of *Mera Naam Joker* in post-production. I used to watch a lot of movies. There were a lot of films I could have directed.' The transition from actor to director was however a bumpy one for Rishi Kapoor, and he was 'disillusioned and dejected', devastated after his directorial debut came and went without even a whimper.

Did he feel that his intelligence was underutilized? According to Tanuja, 'Chintu is intelligent but was kept down.' A past failure still haunts, and because of it an unrealized ambition. Rishi Kapoor failed his English exam in Senior Cambridge for a very stupid reason. 'I was supposed to write a five-hundred-word précis. I thought I would write down the whole thing first and then shorten it later. I wrote sixteen foolscap pages but there wasn't enough time to put it into concise language. Otherwise, I'd done well,' he says with more than a tinge of regret. 'I wanted to do commerce. I wanted to go to London to study in the best college. I was shattered, demoralized.'

Devnar Cottage must have resounded with arguments over his education. His father cast him in *Mera Naam Joker* while he was still at school, but his mother wanted him to study and go on to college. Though none of her children were academic achievers, she sent them to the best schools, even if it meant travelling all the way to town from Chembur. She also did her best to keep the children away from the spotlights. He is also convinced that his mother stayed on with their father—despite a fairly turbulent marriage—because of them. 'My mother is shy. She bore it all because of the children. We were a priority of hers. She did not want us to be teased in school. She did not want us to get a complex.'

The makings of a complex were, however, already underway. Raj Kapoor casts a long shadow. A loving father in his own fashion, he was formidably demanding as a boss. The separation of home and studio was complete. 'From the very first day [on the set] he was Raj sahib or Rajji,' explains Rishi Kapoor, 'and I was an actor.' The dynamics of dynasty seemed to have worked against the successive generations. Rishi Kapoor was terrified of his father, and seldom spoke in front of him. 'Chintu was scared of Papa. He was absolutely mute in front of him. He would just stand and listen to him,' says Neetu Singh.

When Raj Kapoor was angry with an actor or a crew member he tended to take it out on those closest to him. Rishi Kapoor fainted on the sets of *Prem Rog*. Recalls Shashi Kapoor: 'Raj Kapoor worked with anger on the sets of *Prem Rog*.' He pushed his son hard. His previous film *Satyam Shivam Sundaram* had not been a commercial success. It had also provoked critical flak and ridicule: was the maestro losing it with his fixation with Zeenat Aman's breasts? Much rode on *Prem Rog*. Raj Kapoor pulled out all the stops on expenses—a song sequence in the tulip fields near Amsterdam, several scenes shot on location in Mysore Palace and in Loni, mammoth sets erected at R.K. Raj Kapoor needed a hit, and he was tense.

Unfortunately for Rishi Kapoor his father had hit a professional low before *Bobby* as well: *Mera Naam Joker* had been a colossal flop. Says Rishi: 'After the failure of the film we had a financial setback for five or six years. The studio was mortgaged. My father had put every last penny into the film. After the failure he rose to make *Bobby*.' In other words, Raj Kapoor had to push himself hard, and his cast even harder.

Children of celluloid legends generally can't take the weight of the mantles they inherit. It's a Catch-22 situation: if they are not like the famous parent they are considered not good enough; if they are, they are labelled copycats. Satyajit Ray's son Sandeep Ray tried unsuccessfully to follow his father's trail for many years until he found his own cinematic vocabulary. Randhir Kapoor had a genuine flair for comedy but got caught in the trademark Raj Kapoor clownish screen avatar. Critics described him as a bad clone of his father. The youngest Kapoor, Rajiv, was given short shrift for his directorial debut, *Prem Granth*, despite his having acted in his father's last film and incidentally one of R.K.'s biggest hits—*Ram Teri Ganga Maili*.

Rishi Kapoor was the only one to get away. He realized early on that he had to make it outside R.K. Raj Kapoor directed him in only three films: *Mera Naam Joker*, *Bobby* and *Prem Rog*. The rest of the films he acted in were for other producers, and he worked with the biggest banners, including three films for Manmohan Desai, and four for Yash Chopra. After *Bobby*, he became, as he says, 'a busy actor', and the nation's sweetheart. But evidently Papa knew best, no matter how tough a taskmaster he might have been: Rishi Kapoor's more memorable performances have been in his father's films. His sensitive and nuanced portrayal of a plump schoolboy in the first flush of adolescent infatuation in *Mera Naam Joker* has few parallels.

Success came early. It was heady, and destructive. It opened the door for the demons that would plague him for much of his life. In a disarmingly frank interview in the magazine *Filmfare* with film journalist Nina Arora, Rishi Kapoor admits that he was ill equipped to handle it: 'I turned positively obnoxious after *Bobby*. I used to be very arrogant and had lots of attitude thanks to my family lineage, success and fame. I got carried away with all the adulation I received. Naturally, I used to be a bit of a bully and was short on the temper fuse. Since Neetu and I were constantly shooting together, she bore the brunt of it all. And when the flops follow, the frustration makes one a bigger monster.'

The biggest demon was alcohol. The havoc it has played with the lives of the Kapoors has only got worse with successive generations. While the elder Kapoors—Raj, Shammi and Shashi—somehow seemed to know what they were doing even when they had had too much to drink, with Raj Kapoor's three sons the problem ballooned out of control: the liquor consumed them more than they consumed the liquor.

For Rishi Kapoor, alcohol unleashed his darker side. Neetu Singh has in several interviews with film journalists talked about her husband's violent behaviour after a few drinks. In the revealing interview with Arora about her marital life, she talks about how the only person who tried to protect her from her husband's abusive behaviour was her son Ranbir. 'The Kapoors have a cardinal rule: never interfere in each other's lives...I realized that nobody was going to help me, except my son but it wasn't fair to make a child take sides against a father who was a very good father. He did tick his father off a couple of times when Chintu got so high that he smashed everything in sight. But his father could never remember anything the next day. I felt so sorry for poor Ranbir who hated having to confront an innocent-faced father who just stared back in complete amnesia,' says Neetu.

Rishi Kapoor believes alcoholism is an occupational hazard. 'An actor is emoting during the day. He gets drained out and feels like a drink. It is about shedding your inhibitions,' says Rishi. Yet he is refreshingly honest about his infamous drinking binges. Some of it was inevitable, in the genes. 'Food, showmanship and size came from Papaji. From my grandmother's side there was alcohol and light eyes,' he admits. His grandmother's father was a dealer in alcohol, and quite fond of it.

Under the Kapoor braggadocio, this Kapoor admits to being shy. 'When I remove my make-up I am out of the set, and the character I play. I am more reserved. I don't freely mix round. Perhaps I am shy. I don't bask in the glory of any film. Acting is my job, and I do it to the best of my ability.' In some ways he is like his uncle Shashi Kapoor for whom acting was just a way of earning a livelihood: it was not a sacred passion, as it was for Raj Kapoor, or even Prithviraj Kapoor. Nor does he go on about method acting and sweating into a role, like many actors who pick their cues from Hollywood. 'I didn't make a great effort. I just did what I was told. My father used to show me what to do and I did it. He told me to first enact it myself, after which he would correct and fine-tune it.'

'*We marry actresses, don't we*?'

—Randhir Kapoor

Beginning with Shammi Kapoor, many of the male Kapoors have married co-stars. His was the precedent, and after him the deluge of marriages to actresses began. The conservative Kapoors may not have been too pleased with actress bahus, but they had no choice. Yet maintains Randhir: 'Contrary to what people thought, there was no objection to Babita. My father was liberal and broad minded. All of us married actresses. We fall in love and we marry them also. My mother was not an actress but my aunts were.'

When Rishi Kapoor and Neetu Singh decided to marry in 1980, Raj and Krishna Kapoor had no choice but to give their blessings. This marriage was really made in celluloid heaven. The two had played romantic lovers and had danced their way through about a dozen films since 1975 before she hung up her acting gear and married him. She was just twenty-one then, and had been acting since the age of five. Neetu Singh was a natural dancer, with the kind of vivacity that lit up the screen, and a spontaneity that recalled Geeta Bali. Her youthful zest appealed to the young generation.

Neetu met Rishi Kapoor when she was just fourteen. Their romance, as she describes it, could make a good screenplay. 'I got to know Chintu when we used to travel together to studios for four and five years. We were friends. He had affairs, and used to put his girlfriends on the phone to talk to me. Or, I would call them up for him. When I was about seventeen he told me that he missed me when we were not shooting together. I replied, "What rubbish." He took off his shoes and said: "Look, I am not crossing my toes." When I was eighteen, he gave me a key[8] and put it round my neck, saying that this was to lock my heart. He used to accompany me everywhere. Once, after eating at the Taj, he asked me: "Don't you want to get married?" And I said yes, but married to whom? "To me, of course. Who else?" he replied. I told him that I would complete all the movies I had signed before getting married.'

In several interviews Rishi Kapoor iterates that he has never been a romantic. Yet not only does he remember that he first met his future wife on the sets of *Bobby* when he was shooting for the evergreen song 'Hum tum ek kamre mein band hon', he even recalls the exact line of the song at the moment. No bells chimed, nor did violins play. It wasn't love at first sight—the two became friends. According to him, he just got accustomed to her face.

Their engagement was straight out of a Sooraj Barjatya movie. Recalls Neetu: 'Industrialist Anil Nanda was getting engaged to Rajendra Kumar's daughter on 13 April 1979 in Delhi. Ritu [Nanda] had invited me for the engagement. Raj Kapoor and the whole family were waiting for my arrival. Ritu got hold of Rishi and told him, "Now get engaged to her." *Zabardasti*. Ritu managed to find a diamond ring and gave it to me. It was like a fairy tale.' A Cinderella story to begin with. (Ironically, Anil Nanda never married Rajendra Kumar's daughter, or anyone for that matter.) The Kapoors, it seems, did not ask Neetu Singh to stop acting. 'I wanted to rest. I had had enough: three shifts and studies and dancing. I had no friends, no childhood.'

The wedding was like any Kapoor production. The showman and his wife spared no effort, nor money. Apparently, the couple even fainted in all the confusion: perhaps there was nobody to yell cut in the wedding scene! The latest Mrs Kapoor moved into Devnar Cottage, and began playing the role of the perfect bahu. 'From the first day I covered my hair. I wore full sleeves and touched my mother-in-law's feet. I thought this was the right thing to do. I had nothing to go by. My mother was a divorcee. So I followed what I saw in the movies. My mother-in-law told me, "What's wrong with you? *Yeh bilkul nahin karna* (Don't do this). When Rishi goes for shooting, you get your *maalish* (massage) done, and look fresh for him when he comes back from work. Try and look like today's modern girls." So, I began to wear sleeveless kameezes and a nose pin. I had such a different idea about the conservative Kapoor family,' says Neetu.

The husband was more demanding. A tough little master from the beginning, he told her that he did not like 'fat women'. 'Chintu told me on the first day that if I put on weight he will have affairs.' So she immediately bought a Jane Fonda cassette and began going for brisk walks on Pali Hill with Shobha, actor Jeetendra's wife.

Initially, Rishi Kapoor was also very conscious of the Kapoor lineage and concerned whether his young and naïve wife could give parties the way the Kapoors did. It did take a while to get used to being the bahu of Indian cinema's first family. She was, as she says, 'petrified' of Raj Kapoor and his larger-than-life persona. 'I used to shake and shiver when I first met him. He had an overpowering nature, and such an aura, all pink with blue eyes. I was nervous and quiet all the time.' Like the ideal screen daughter-in-law she also tried to cook a perfect Punjabi meal: something she had never had a chance to do before she got married. 'I tried to make *kali daal*. It was a disaster. Papa took one bite, and said it was delicious. It meant so much to me,' she says fondly.

According to her, life at Devnar was a bit like the Italian homes in American films, with everybody 'talking at the same time, and pulling each other's legs. Like the dons, they were loud and would pun all the time. Some would go too far and then say "Oh, sorry".' And of course the emphasis was on food: you talked about what you had eaten, what you were eating and what you wanted to eat next, with the senior Mrs Kapoor ladling out the calories and love with largesse like a good Italian, or for that matter Punjabi, mama.

The younger Mrs Kapoor eventually learned to say no. It wasn't easy to resist the senior Mrs Kapoor's seductions. 'My mother-in-law would take some rice, put ghee on it and *masal, masal ke* add a few potatoes and daal.' The Kapoor favourite dishes were junglee meat (cooked with just pure ghee and kashmiri red pepper), trotters and Goan fish curry. Mistryji, the wizard of the kitchen, was with the family for forty years, and the Kapoor table had no parallel.

Like all Kapoor sons before him, Rishi Kapoor moved out of his parental home two years into his marriage when the couple had their first child: he moved into his wife's mother's home in the more upmarket Pali Hill in Bandra. The R.K. house had to be renovated: there weren't enough bedrooms for all the grandchildren. Pali Hill was the original abode of the screen idols after independence—before the nouveau 'arrivals' began to migrate further north to Juhu. Neetu Singh's mother had a home there, bought with the young actress's earnings.

Neetu Singh had first acted in *Suraj* in 1966. She was just about five then. A year later she acted in *Dus Lakh* and in *Do Kaliyan*, one of the first remakes of *Parent Trap*. There were no breaks for this child star who was her mother's golden goose: she worked right through her teens and stopped working only after she got married.

There is a tinge of bitterness in her otherwise chirpy voice as she talks about her childhood. Or rather, the lack of it. School was not easy: her mother kept pulling her out of school to act in films. 'I was in Madras for eight months while acting in *Do Kaliyan*. I had to study with notes taken by my friends for me, though sometimes my notes were stolen.' She studied at St Joseph's on Peddar Road, but had to leave when she was in the ninth standard to become a full-time actress.

'My spirit had been beaten into submission since childhood,' says Neetu. 'I missed out on a proper upbringing because I was going to the studios when other children went to school. Take it from me, every child artiste, whether here or in Hollywood, is exploited by an ambitious parent. That parent is making money on a child who doesn't know better. No celebrity is entirely normal—there are far too many mood swings.' In her interview with Neetu, Arora says: 'Still, like she [Neetu Singh] says, she was cocooned in blissful ignorance until she was force-fed into "growing up" at fourteen. That horror has never quite left her. If she objected to certain embarrassingly risqué scenes or costumes her protests were silenced with stinging slaps.'

Was Neetu Singh fed hormones to speed the 'growing up' process? Certainly there was talk about her being physically 'mature' well before her time, and well before the age of silicon implants. Like many teenagers whose careers were being steered by ambitious mothers—actress Rekha is among the more well known—her adolescence was bleeped over, killed. Perhaps that explains why she was so ecstatic about marrying into the large Kapoor family, dropping her career like the proverbial hot potato. Even decades later she could not be seduced into acting again: Neetu Singh turned down a role in Karan Johar's *Kal Ho Na Ho*. (Jaya Bachchan eventually took it, playing Preity Zinta's mother in the film.) Home and family are still the centre of her existence.

In the late nineties, Rishi Kapoor and his family moved to a new house built next door to their old one in Pali Hill. Neetu's mother moved with them. Rishi Kapoor asked her to because all of them had lived in her home until then. Contemporary and built on two levels, Krishna Kunj, as the coldly imposing home is named, is decidedly not old world or even remotely rococo, unlike most of the kitschy homes of film stars. There is a great deal of glass and rock and huge sculptures—and corridors. Past the main entrance you can either go up to the more formal, public areas, or downstairs to the glass-enclosed lounge adjacent to the bar where the Kapoors hang out. French windows open out to the lawn. The famous Kapoor hospitality doesn't miss a beat: there is a non-stop relay of snacks and Rishi Kapoor is a generous host. One is uncertain about his 'status': is it his drinking phase or days of abstinence? He gingerly sips his whiskey. The rest of the Kapoors are on Diet Coke and health food. It is a picture of conviviality, like a family portrait, but it appears to be a precarious harmony. Anything could tip the balance, although for the moment everybody is making an effort.

Neetu Singh walked out of her home in the late nineties to a friend's house. And only returned in 2000 when her husband's sister, Rima, was getting married. Earlier Babita had moved out with her two daughters, and stayed away. While Neetu evidently wanted to assert her individuality, she did not want to split the family. The film press went to town on the famous exit of the second Kapoor daughter-in-law. During her days away she also filed an FIR with the Mumbai police, alleging that her husband had physically abused her. Rishi Kapoor at the time was going through a difficult transition—from playing the main lead to character actor, and later to director. The bouts of drinking had become more intense and his mood much darker.

The Neetu Singh who took charge of the keys of their home on her return was a far more confident individual. She has never looked as good; she looks more svelte and well groomed than starlets half her age. Power yoga and her personal trainer, and of course a 180-degree turn away from the Kapoor diet, have brought about her physical metamorphosis. However, the 'inner transformation' she talks of came about with her efforts to find and assert an identity. She read, observed, and most important became Internet savvy.

A new set of rules came into being in the new millennium. Health food, sprouts and diet drinks edged out Peshawari food. Personal trainers and gyms gained importance. A more equitable balance of power was in place, and a mellower Rishi Kapoor. More significantly, a new family mantra reigned: the family that talks together, stays together. Rishi Kapoor had always—like his uncle Shashi Kapoor—refused to work on Sundays. Sunday was family day. However, unlike Shashi, he was an authoritarian father and strict disciplinarian who seldom spoke to his children—just as he himself, as a child and in his youth, barely uttered a word in front of Raj Kapoor. In a sense Rishi Kapoor was just repeating history. 'I did not really see much of my father. In my school days he was busy. Then when I was out of school, I got busy working. I saw very little of him. That is the price that an actor has to pay for stardom,' he admits ruefully.

With the return of the couple's two children from their

respective sojourns abroad, studying, there is a lot more conversation round the table in Krishna Kunj. Says his daughter Riddhima: 'My father is reserved, and orthodox. He is particular about going to family functions and our touching the feet of elders. He used to be more authoritative, but is now changing with us. We did not hang out with him when we were young, now we spend a lot of time talking—about what the day was like and what we will do tomorrow.'

Rishi Kapoor has now tailored his expectations of his children to suit their aspirations. More orthodox than his brothers, he initially wanted his son Ranbir to go to business school in the United States. 'He wanted me to go to Wharton. But I went on the Internet and decided on film school,' says Ranbir who returned home after nearly four years in the States: three at the College of Visual Arts in New York, followed by a year at the Lee Strasberg School of Acting, also in New York.

Both parents then set about grooming him for the screen. Born in 1984, Ranbir Raj Kapoor looks like his mother but has inherited the Kapoor love for food. A plump child, he was nicknamed Gonglu, and talks with great passion about the food in Devnar Cottage. Named after his grandfather, he also inherited his love of caramel custard—the only Kapoor who relishes this relic of the Raj (pun unintended). So, shedding the kilos became his mother's mission, and training him to become an actor his father's new role. Consequently, there is much more dialogue between the two. Says Ranbir: 'I have opened up with him. I never used to utter a word before. I need to bond with Papa. He confides in me about the creative aspects of acting. He has told me to act with my eyes and to underplay my role.'

Unlike many star sons Ranbir did not break the queue and start as a leading man with a gym-toned torso and cosmetically fixed smile. Rishi Kapoor wanted his son to make his way up the hard way, starting as an apprentice before getting in front of the camera—or even working at R.K. He is weary of instant stars, as he is of instant coffee. Consequently, Ranbir became an apprentice, and worked with Sanjay Leela Bhansali on his film *Black*.

Randhir and Rishi Kapoor have plans for him in the family business. This is one Kapoor who has actually gone to film school. Ranbir Kapoor is also keen on direction—his ambition is to make films like his grandfather. 'Raj Kapoor is a demigod; he is my idol. I appreciate him more as a director than actor,' says Ranbir. 'If I become a director, I would like to redo *Jaagte Raho*.'

Riddhima is two years older than her brother, and obviously less tongue-tied in front of her father. Thin as a pencil and sharp-featured she does not share the Kapoorian love for food. Nor are films a passion. She studied fashion design in London, and now wants to open a book café or a boutique gym in their old home on Pali Hill. 'I'm not interested in acting. I am an introvert,' says Riddhima. Of course, she may eventually follow the path taken by her cousins, Karisma and Kareena, although at present acting in films is not part of her plans; marriage is. She is engaged to Bharat Sahni, who is in the textile business, and lives in Delhi. The wedding is expected to take place in early 2006.

Rishi Kapoor has been lucky in his second coming as a character artist: most of his roles have been well-etched and fairly complex unlike many of the stereotypical roles for mothers and fathers in Hindi cinema. Beginning with *Raju Chacha* and through films like *Kuch Khatti Kuch Meethi*, *Yeh Hai Jalwa* and *Hum Tum*, Rishi Kapoor has established himself as a nuanced and mature actor, and not just yet another ageing star. He hasn't lost any of the intensity he brought to his roles as a leading man in films like *Doosra Aadmi*, *Prem Rog*, *Chandni* and *Ek Chadar Maili Si*. It's not for nothing that Lata Mangeshkar once described him as the most talented of the Kapoors. Unlike other middle-aged actors he does not come with a baggage of mannerisms.

Rishi Kapoor may have crossed the half-century mark, but the romantic image he was so possessive about seems to have been rescued from the mothballs, and polished. He is still playing the romantic hero, albeit as a father with grown-up children. On the *Koffee with Karan* show, a refashioned Kapoor with his trim goatee and streaked hair looked all set to romance his first celluloid love. Talking about *Pyar Mein Twist*, he told Johar that his screen couplings with Dimple Kapadia have followed their passages in life: from teenagers in love in *Bobby* to 'mature love' in *Saagar* and finally love in the time when they were both 'getting on'. It's been love in the time of motorcycles as well: riding away into the sunset in *Bobby* in the seventies, in *Saagar* in the eighties and in *Pyar Mein Twist* in the new millennium.

As Rishi Kapoor reinvents himself with each decade, he may yet get a third coming as a thespian, making him the longest surviving Kapoor in the acting arena.

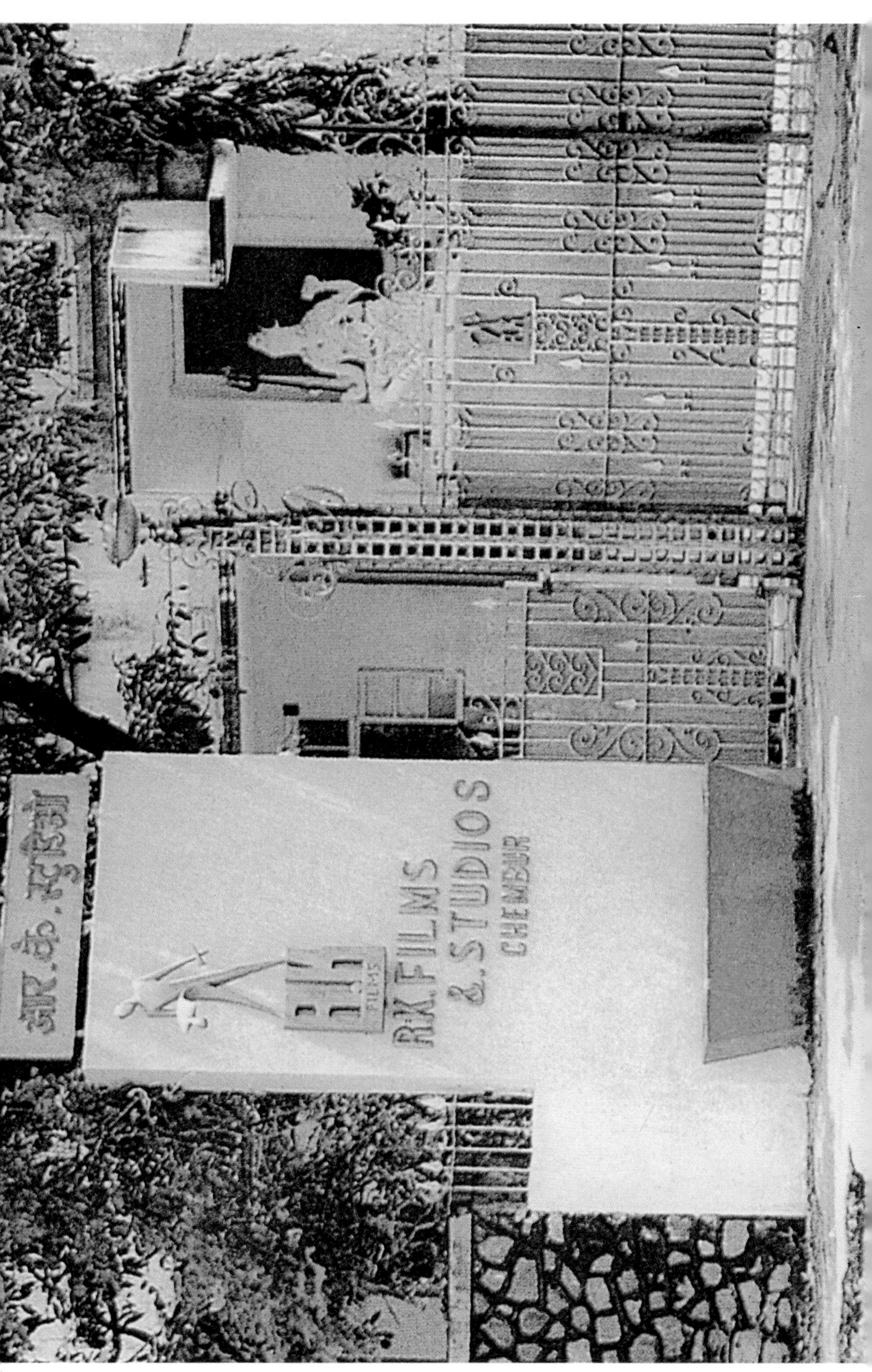

(Photo courtesy Ritu Nanda.)

R. K. FILMS PRESENT

आता है

aag

Produced and Directed by

RAJ KAPOOR

NARGIS, KAMINI KAUSHAL, NIGAR & RAJKAPOOR

Raj Kapoor and Nargis in Russia, 1954. In the wake of *Awara* (1951), which Kapoor described as his 'little contribution to USSR-India friendship', Kapoor became a phenomenon in the erstwhile Soviet Union. (Photo courtesy Ritu Nanda.)

RAJ KAPOOR
NARGIS
RK
RAJ KAPOOR'S
BARSAAT
बरसात
DIRECTED BY
RAJ KAPOOR
MUSIC
SHANKER-JAI KISHAN

Sibling bonding: Urmi, Raj, Shammi and Shashi.
(Photo courtesy Ritu Nanda.)

Prithviraj Kapoor with his grandchildren.

TEENAGERS LOVE STORY FILMED BY RAJ KAPOOR
RISHI KAPOOR
INTRODUCING
DIMPLE KAPADIA
RAJ KAPOOR'S
Bobby
EASTMANCOLOR
PRODUCED, DIRECTED & EDITED BY
RAJ KAPOOR
MUSIC
LAXMIKANT PYARELAL
STORY

Randhir Kapoor with daughters Karisma and Kareena and wife Babita. (Photo courtesy Ritu Nanda.)

Jennifer and Shashi Kapoor waiting for a performance to begin in Prithvi Theatre. Jennifer was largely instrumental in the rebirth of Prithvi Theatres in its new avatar, and always made it a point to buy tickets for every play they saw. (Photo courtesy Roli Books.)

Ritu and Rajan Nanda with son Nikhil, daughter-in-law Shweta, daughter Nitasha and grandchildren Navya Naveli and Agastya. (Photo courtesy Ritu Nanda.)

Rishi Kapoor with wife Neetu and children Riddhima and Ranbir. (Photo courtesy Ritu Nanda.)

6

Lost in the Shadows: Randhir Kapoor and Rajiv Kapoor

RANDHIR KAPOOR

> *'Daboo was talented, and emotional...He was also emotionally disturbed. People put the label of lethargic or careless on him. They were unable to gauge what was happening to him internally.'*
>
> —Lekh Tandon

The title cards of *Awara* roll on the image of a lovely little boy sitting rather forlornly under a gas lamp post. They do so for a fairly long moment in cinematic time. Gradually, almost imperceptibly, the image changes. A street dog moves towards the child: he is obviously looking for food. The young boy shares his roti with the dog. Setting the tone of Nehruvian socialism and the thematic thrust of the film is none other than four-year-old Randhir Kapoor.

Randhir Kapoor was weaned on his father's cinema. Four years later he had a walk-on part in one of the more iconic moments in Indian cinema. In *Shree 420*, three children in raincoats and caps happily prance down the road while Nargis shares her umbrella with Raj Kapoor as studio rain pours down on them. These children are Daboo, his sister Ritu, and brother Rishi Kapoor. Significantly, both Daboo and Ritu cite this little traipse in R.K. as the first recollection of their father. Being Kapoors and congenital foodies the fact that they were taken out for a Chinese meal to Nanking after the shot and got to keep the raincoats may be responsible for the indelible imprint the day has left on their memory. Randhir also remembers his father as being particularly 'affectionate' that day.

Merely twenty-three years separated father and son. Randhir was born on 15 February 1947 in Bombay, less than a year after his parents were married. The same year saw the birth of Raj Kapoor as a director. Just as Prithvi Theatres had been the nursery for Raj Kapoor, R.K. Films was, occasionally, Randhir Kapoor's playground. In one of the photographs in the Kapoor family album a proud father looks on as Randhir (a scrawny, angelic-faced four year old at the time) gapes in wonderment at a huge motion picture camera.

Randhir inherited his father's blue eyes, light hair and fair skin—and his vocation. Randhir Kapoor could not think beyond cinema. No sooner had he graduated from school, he headed for the arc lights, but behind the camera. 'I never thought of anything else. I wanted to both act and direct. It was a typical film background, both paternal and maternal background. And movies were the topic of discussion. Raj Kapoor never spoke about anything else. The only diversion from cinema was food,' recalls Randhir.

In keeping with the history of the Kapoors, college was to elude this Kapoor as well and, initially, Raj Kapoor and his son followed the same career trajectory. When Randhir was seventeen, his father asked Lekh Tandon to take him on as an assistant. Just as Prithviraj Kapoor had requested Kidar Sharma to hire Raj Kapoor as an apprentice 'to learn the ropes' after he failed his school exams.

Raj Kapoor was strong on convention. Says Tandon: 'He told me, "I have been an assistant to Kidar Sharma. He was an assistant to Debaki Bose. You were my assistant and my son will be yours. This is our gharana for four generations."'

Randhir worked on Tandon's films like *Amrapali* (1966) and *Jhuk Gaya Asman* (1968). In a way it was quite an incestuous world, with not more than one degree of separation. *Amrapali* starred Vyjanthimala and Sunil Dutt: the former was his father's heroine in *Sangam*, the latter the man who married and took away his father's muse, Nargis. Tandon in turn was Raj Kapoor's assistant and the son of Prithviraj Kapoor's childhood friend Faqir Chand. Tandon had also directed Shammi Kapoor in *Professor* and *Prince*.

The years of apprenticeship were not easy for Randhir Kapoor. He wasn't exactly a Lord Fauntleroy but he did belong to the first family of cinema. While both his father and grandfather had roughed it the world of third-class train travel and cheap digs during their Prithvi Theatres days, Randhir and his brothers had grown up in relative comfort. They went to more upper-crust public schools in south Bombay: the boys to Campion and the sisters to Walsingham. Culture shock was inevitable. Remembers Tandon: 'Daboo used to have one grudge against me. All the assistants used to travel third class, and I made him do that. He also used to stay where they did. He would cry when his sister came to leave him at the station. But I had to bring them down from royalty.' Tandon did make one concession, and that was to the famous weakness of the Kapoors for good food. He often took him out for a meal. Randhir's love of comfort did not come in the way of hard work. 'Daboo worked like a labourer and mixed with everybody. He liked to play and had a great sense of humour,' says Tandon.

Meanwhile, there was a lull in film-making at R.K.: there was an interlude of over six years between *Sangam* (1964) and *Mera Naam Joker* (1970). During this time Raj Kapoor acted in films for other directors like Mahesh Kaul and Basu Bhattacharya. It was also a long gestation period for what he considered his magnum opus, *Mera Naam Joker*. The failure of the film, a magnificent flop at the time, left him despondent. And it was at this juncture that he handed over the baton to his son to make *Kal Aaj Aur Kal*. The film was made when the Kapoor coffers were fairly empty.

For Randhir Kapoor it was a dream launch and a double debut—both as a director and an actor. It was 1971, and he was twenty-four. The film is significant for other reasons. Three generations of Kapoors act in the film. Prithviraj Kapoor plays the conservative patriarch grandfather, Randhir Kapoor is his rebellious grandson, and Raj Kapoor acts as Randhir's father who is caught in the tussle between the two. Virendra Sinha may have written the script; however, the film, uncannily, perhaps inadvertently, mirrors what was happening in the Kapoor khandaan at the time. The film's bone of contention and leading lady is Babita, who was then Randhir Kapoor's girlfriend and who married him soon after.

It must not have been easy for Randhir Kapoor to direct the other two Kapoors. Legends did not get any bigger than his father and grandfather. Hierarchy was firmly in place: you did not question the elders. Moreover, this Kapoor also had two famous thespian uncles casting their own shadows across his career path: Shammi and Shashi Kapoor had carved out their respective niches in the world of cinema. And Babita was at the zenith of her career when the two fell in love.

The normally outspoken Randhir Kapoor is diplomatic about the trying experience directing his father and grandfather. However, Rishi Kapoor, an assistant to his brother during the making of *Kal Aaj Aur Kal*, is refreshingly frank about what Randhir went through. 'We were all petrified of Papaji. I saw the awe in Daboo. Papaji loved to add lines, even for other actors. Daboo couldn't contain the rhythm of the scene. Nobody could say anything to Papaji, particularly about continuity. He was an institution in himself, and he came from the theatre. He didn't listen to his grandson. He meant well. Yes, there was some strain in Daboo directing Papaji.'

Randhir Kapoor's take is a little different, and perhaps more emotional, in keeping with the Kapoors. 'My grandfather was an obedient and immaculate actor. He didn't force himself as a grandfather, actor or as a star. This was my first venture and even my father did not impose any style. He wanted me to enact scenes for them. Raj Kapoor told me, "A director is the captain of a film and if he does not know his job, he is not a captain." My grandfather was suffering from cancer towards the end of the filming. We had constructed a major set for forty-five days. There was a big hall, and half the film was on that set. He had very high temperature, but he said, go ahead. He was fighting his cancer, and kept saying that the show must go on. He kept telling me, "Don't worry I will complete the film and only then will I die." He did the dubbing under stress. He used to tell me that not only was it his duty as an actor to complete the film and fight the disease, he had a selfish motive: the film was the launch pad of his grandson.'

High on melodrama, and with quite a bit of hamming, the film had its moments. There was humour, and the clash of three generations was interestingly portrayed. However, the film flopped at the box office, partially because of bad timing: the Bangladesh war started, and nightly blackouts drastically reduced cinema audiences. The failure of the film obviously devastated the debuting director: 'I lost interest and heart after *Kal Aaj Aur Kal* and concentrated on running the R.K. empire.' It was to be another four years before Randhir got a chance to wield the director's baton for the second time. In 1975 he directed his father—and himself—once again in *Dharam Karam*. Rekha was his co-star. This time his father was flush with the success of *Bobby*.

Not only was cinema a family business for the Kapoors, the

repertoire of character actors was the same, and the themes they explored often mirrored one another. Both *Awara* and *Dharam Karam* tackle the theme of nature versus nurture. However, the conclusion of the two is quite different. K.A. Abbas, socialist and an integral part of IPTA, obviously discounted heredity. Remember, the eminent judge's natural son is on the other side of the law in *Awara*. In *Dharam Karam*, written by Prayag Raaj, the son of an underworld don is exchanged at birth with the son of a renowned singer. The two revert to type when they grow up, to be exactly what their real fathers are. Environment loses to genes in the younger Kapoor's film.

Underneath the showman garb, Raj Kapoor was a strict disciplinarian and liked to be in total control. Nor did he suffer fools. 'Nobody could have grown under that tree. He wouldn't let anybody make a mistake in his production,' recalls Tandon. 'If I had stayed on at R.K. I would not have been able to make films. He might have assigned others to direct his films but he had his own approach. If one would yell cut, the other would say start.' Other assistants like Ravindra Peepat also left R.K. to make their own films. The Kapoor sons had no choice but to stay.

Randhir Kapoor directed just two films while his father was alive. After *Dharam Karam*, Randhir Kapoor worked for quite a while on a script written by B.B. Bhalla. He was keen to make a film based on it. Raj Kapoor did not warm to the idea. Randhir was disappointed, forced to put his directorial ambitions on hold. Later, impressed by the much-acclaimed television serial *Buniyaad*, he had asked television marathon man Manohar Shyam Joshi to write a script for him. Joshi worked on the script for a film tentatively titled *Ghunghat Ke Pat Khol*. That idea, too, was shelved.

While Raj Kapoor continued to direct and produce films like *Satyam Shivam Sundaram* and *Prem Rog*, Randhir Kapoor took a backseat and was given the responsibility of running the studio. In 1981 he did act in another in-house production, *Biwi O Biwi*. His father produced and Rahul Rawail directed the comedy with Sanjeev Kumar, Rekha and Randhir in the major roles. However, the stamp of Raj Kapoor is unmistakable. Randhir Kapoor finally turned producer, officially that is, with *Ram Teri Ganga Maili* in 1985.

Early on, Randhir Kapoor showed a flair for comedy and timing. Some of his initial films fared well at the box office. *Jawani Diwani*, *Rampur Ka Laxman* and *Chacha Bhatija* were quite popular. He also acted with his uncles: with Shammi Kapoor in *Mama Bhanja* and with Shashi Kapoor in *Heeralal Pannalal* and *Sawaal*. Unfortunately, the label of a comedian clung to him. Unlike Rishi Kapoor he never quite established himself as a leading man, even though he acted in well over forty films for other directors. Since he resembled his father—increasingly so as he grew older—the audience merely saw him as a derivative of his father's comic roles. Randhir Kapoor also put on weight relatively early in his career.

The audience did not quite accept him as a romantic hero even though his father, saddled with lots of extra kilos and baggy eyes, continued playing the love-struck hero into late middle age. Randhir Kapoor is convinced that there was a sharp dip in his acting graph after the advent of the action hero. 'After *Sholay* in the mid-seventies,' says Randhir, 'I was just hanging in there. There were no prime projects. I stopped getting good roles.'

While that may be true, it is equally true that Randhir Kapoor lacked the overweening ambition and grit his father and grandfather possessed. What went wrong? Was Randhir Kapoor a victim of the turbulence in his parents' marriage? Lekh Tandon certainly thinks so. Obviously, the eldest bore most of the brunt of his parents' volatile marriage, and of a largely absentee father. Krishna Kapoor walked out of Devnar Cottage with her children a few times; once for several months at a stretch. Emotionally, it made for a yo-yo existence. Professionally, Raj Kapoor's shadow even crept into the nooks and crannies of R.K. Films: he was omnipresent, even if he didn't want to be.

Just as Raj Kapoor had a complex relationship with his father while growing up so did Randhir. Randhir told me: 'Raj Kapoor was like a great banyan tree, he was Himalayan. His priority was cinema. He was never detached from it, whether he was partying or bathing. It was his life. As a father he was larger than life...You see any normal person cannot become Raj Kapoor.'

This is Daboospeak: Randhir has a unique sense of humour, when he is not being hyperbolic. But the subtext in his remarks about his father reveals that he may have wanted a father more ordinary. This father left behind a mantle that would weigh down the sturdiest of shoulders.

Randhir Kapoor describes himself as a 'south Bombay boy', as distinct from a Chembur boy. An uptown boy is what he means: public schools and English-speaking friends and American movies—and of course loitering with intent in upmarket Bombay, south of Worli. The younger Kapoors were more comfortable in five-star hotels, their natural habitat. Until some of the more ritzy hotels opened in the suburbs in the late nineties, Randhir Kapoor used to head south for his evenings out with the boys—school friends from Campion as well as those from the film industry.

His father chose to be a downtown man, more at home in dhabas and Ravi's Canteen near Chembur where he went for his 5 p.m. south Indian tiffin. The vibrant Bombay of the streets so poignantly brought out in *Shree 420* was his world, and often the catchment area for characters and mannerisms. Recalls Randhir Kapoor: 'Raj Kapoor was not comfortable in five-star hotels. He liked the serenity and calm and quiet here [Chembur], the seclusion. He was a recluse and not a party animal—that was a façade. My mother used to push him to go out to parties. He was obsessed with his work and himself.'

There was another more basic divide, what Randhir Kapoor in his patent witty style refers to as the urban–rural divide. Nostalgia about the North West Frontier did not survive beyond the second generation. Randhir Kapoor believes that his father and grandfather had a romantic notion of the North West Frontier, and lived 'a myth of Peshawar'. 'They talk about it as if it were heaven on earth. But home was in the plains, in backward rural parts of Pakistan,' says Randhir.

When not working or frequenting his favourite addas, Raj Kapoor was happiest in his farm outside Pune: walking through fields of wheat, feeding his chickens or dogs, staring at the sunset over Raj Bagh, cooking yakhni pulao with his cook Sharmaji looking on. The rest of the family, including his wife, did not relish living there, and sold it about fifteen years after his death. Says Randhir: 'His lifestyle included Loni, ours did not. We went there because of him. That was rural India. Our mindset is not. Raj Kapoor was still a Peshawari, and a simpleton who liked sleeping on the floor. We were brought up in the city.' And presumably they slept on beds.

Randhir Kapoor moved to the 'city'—to an apartment on Malabar Hill—soon after he married Babita. Both his uncles lived in that part of town as well. His daughters, Karisma and Kareena, went to the elitist Petit Hall and Cathedral.

Randhir had met his wife on a flight to Hong Kong, and was immediately in awe of her. 'I was a nobody [he was an assistant] and she was a star,' recalls Randhir. The Kapoors are conventional when it comes to customs and may not have been happy with his marrying an actress. But they could not really prevent him from doing so. There was already a precedent: both his uncles had married actresses. And, apparently, Randhir Kapoor told his parents that if he could not marry Babita, he would never marry. He still has not, after years of separation.

However, things started to go wrong after a few years. Film magazines turned their binoculars on their marriage. There were rumours about Babita's affair with popular screen villain Ranjit, as there were about Randhir Kapoor's flings and drinking binges. Reflects Tandon: 'Daboo was very sensitive, and with time became quite withdrawn. He may not have been happy with his marriage, but he had married according to his own choice. This affected his professional life. Raj Kapoor was clear: have your *lafda*s (affairs) but marry into the right families. He was only happy with his daughters' weddings. And, he only respected his wife.'

Randhir Kapoor moved back to Chembur after his father died. He became the keeper of the keys of both Devnar Cottage and R.K. Films. And of the Kapoor traditions, not always willingly: 'As a first-born I do have a moral burden, the family responsibility. I have to do all the dirty work, attend family functions. Others get out of it. I am a very family-minded person.

I may be separated from my wife but I keep calling her up.' Babita and their daughters certainly kept their distance, but there was a rapprochement of sorts when Randhir Kapoor was admitted to Escorts Hospital in Delhi in 2003 for major heart surgery. The daughters cancelled their shooting assignments and moved to Delhi to be with their father.

The young patriarch had an impossible task on the home front as well. 'My mother was dependent on my father. She was not frivolous, and lived in his shadow. She has held us together, but Raj Kapoor was the world for her. Without him she lost interest.' For years the Kapoors carried on, as Randhir Kapoor never tires of saying, on 'autopilot'. Raj Kapoor's bedroom was turned into a mausoleum: his bed, quilt, glasses, shirt and other personal effects were left exactly where they had been when he died. It wasn't until an astrologer advised them—close to a decade after Raj Kapoor's death—to make the bedroom a living space again, did they integrate the bedroom with the rest of the living room. 'The *jyotshi* told us that his spirit was still hovering, and that the rest of us needed to get back to a normal life. He told us that if we started living like normal people we would be more at peace,' remembers Randhir.

Raj Kapoor's huge bedroom was on the ground floor, off the drawing room: the rest of the family had their rooms on the first floor. The walls separating the two rooms have been removed, but the arcs that hold up the walls remain. Photographs of him alone and with the family line the walls. As do paintings of clowns, one of them given to him by Shashi Kapoor.

The long living room, with its sumptuously deep sofas and bay windows, is rather formal today. Life goes on elsewhere, on the first floor where Randhir, his mother and Rajiv Kapoor have their bedrooms. There is an entertainment room on the first floor and another on the second floor. At the turn of the century a new page turned in the life of the ivy-covered bungalow with a sloping roof. The Kapoors almost sold the house: they couldn't at the last minute because of some legal complications.

It was fortuitous, because there was finally a homecoming of sorts. Karisma's wedding to Sanjay Kapur took place here in 2003. It was an R.K. production all right. The showman was missing, but it was a Kapooresque wedding on the extensive lawns of Devnar. All cuisines under the Indian sun and elsewhere were served. Champagne popped and flowed at high tide. After the nuptials were over Randhir Kapoor apparently told his estranged wife that they should get back together again. Recollects Shashi: 'He told his wife, "Karisma is married. Kareena will one day. I am alone, you will be. Why don't we get back together again?"'

In interviews Randhir says that he will never remarry. Babita is his wife and the mother of his children, goes his refrain. The two continue to live apart. Randhir is the good son and the good brother: in an industry full of cynics most people have nice words to say about this affable Kapoor. And, he is a 'buddy' person, often going out on the town with his friends from school and a few from the film industry, like Jeetendra and Rakesh Roshan. Yet, it is not too difficult to discern a hint of loneliness in his existence. The gregariousness and his throwaway wisecracks that even irritated his father may just be his version of the clown persona. He obviously misses his daughters, and it is not easy for them. Asked why he does not move to his wife's home or travel on location with his daughters, he replies: 'Some producer or darzi will keep walking in. It would become too crowded...I'd feel awful, hanging around my daughters' sets waiting for the spot boy to come and say, "*Sa'ab (sic) baby ne mosambi juice bheja hai.*" (Sahib, baby has sent some sweet lime juice [for you]...).'[1]

Back at the studios, the Kapoor brothers are trying to turn the page as well. 'We want to change, to make more youth-oriented and topical films. We want to be more contemporary and content-based. Family socials don't work in these times. Earlier, films were seen by various sections—from rickshawallas to balconywallas. Now with multiplexes you can have a different kind of film.'

The Kapoor brothers have downsized their ambitions. They realize that measuring up to the standards set by Raj Kapoor is an uphill task if not altogether impossible. Randhir plans to produce and direct a film after a hiatus of over a decade. He has also started acting again. In 1998, he acted in Sawan Kumar

Tak's colossal flop *Mother 98* for a lark: the film, based on Shirley Conran's novel *Lace*, revolved around his close friend Rekha and also starred his good pals Jeetendra and Rakesh Roshan. In 2001, he acted in Dev Anand's *Censor* (the cast included Shammi Kapoor). He also had a significant role in Honey Irani's directorial debut *Armaan* in 2003.

So, while Raj Kapoor's films remain money-spinners, acting for other producers allows Randhir Kapoor to indulge his new passion: cruises.

Meanwhile, the three brothers continue to ruminate on whether to make the moribund R.K. into a multiplex and a museum. Few of the old retainers are left. The days of the cottage are also numbered. Randhir Kapoor is refreshingly frank: 'The cottage has been there for sixty years, and is crumbling. There is no point doing it up. Our lifestyles are not the same. My father sat on the floor. I can't sit on the floor. We sit on chairs and sofas.'

Randhir Kapoor is still reluctant to be a Chembur boy. A perennial regret is the wrong turn his father took while reconnoitering for land for his studio: 'If my father had taken a left turn instead of right we would have been in Bandra, sitting on crores—and much closer to south Bombay.'

RAJIV KAPOOR

> *'A week after Raj Kapoor's death Chimpu came to me. He had a bad cut on his head. He was shivering, and appeared completely lost.'*
>
> —Dr Narendra Pandya,
> cosmetic surgeon and friend of Raj Kapoor

While everybody publicly mourned the passing of Raj Kapoor, his youngest son slunk away and went on a three-day drinking binge. His father had left when he needed him most, a few years after *Ram Teri Ganga Maili* (1985). This film was a big one for Raj Kapoor: he had stirred bits of the Ramayana, the Mahabharata, Kalidas's *Shakuntala* and other mythically resonant allusions into this operatic, multi-layered ode to the river Ganga. But the maestro did not live long enough to really savour its stupendous success: the coffers of R.K. Films overflowed after this much-awarded movie. Neither could the film's largely unsung hero Rajiv Kapoor bask in the adulation which follows box-office success: all people could talk about were the caressingly photographed assets of the film's buxom, blue-eyed heroine, Mandakini, under the waterfall—and Raj Kapoor's genius. Alas, *Ram Teri Ganga Maili* did not do for Chimpu what *Bobby* had done for Chintu.

Raj Kapoor's youngest son, Rajiv (Chimpu to his family and friends) was born in 1962. He is almost a spitting image of his uncle Shammi Kapoor. Tall, fair and well built when he started out, he too had a similar hint of insouciance in his lighter-than-brown hazel-specked eyes. Eyes that signalled a swagger, more sexually charged than mushy. A combination of the best of Shashi and Shammi meant that he had the looks of the former and could gyrate with abandon like the latter. This Kapoor was taller than his siblings and better built. The whole world expected Rajiv to take up his uncle's Yahoo persona, and become a dancing star and an action hero. To walk a bit on the wild side. Amongst Raj Kapoor's coterie and habitués at R.K. there was talk about Chimpu being the most talented of his brothers. Lekh Tandon says the thespian told him: 'This boy will make it big. From Prithviraj on he will be the best Kapoor.'[2]

So when his first few films, beginning with *Ek Jaan Hai Hum* in 1983 and *Aasman* in 1984, did not do well, a buzz of disappointment settled around him. One can blame it on those Kapoor genes: being a visual collage of those who have come before him must have made Rajiv's journey treacherous. He reflected in turn his father, uncles and brothers on the screen. Was there then a sense of déjà vu about him which pulled him down? His nieces—Karisma and Kareena—have had it much easier under similar circumstances. Not only were they the first women from Raj Kapoor's branch of the family to act, as women they didn't risk appearing as clones of their ancestors. Being further down the line on the actor-studded Kapoor family tree, Chimpu has had the heaviest cross to bear of all the three sons; it has been incrementally difficult for each generation of Kapoors to establish its identity. Even for Generation Next—it was a long uphill ride before Karisma Kapoor made it past other divas to the top of the heroine marquee, and younger sister Kareena has yet to get there, although she is a sparklingly visible poster girl.

Rajiv had to wait until his father made *Ram Teri Ganga Maili* to experience some success. Raj Kapoor, surprisingly, wasn't in any hurry to cast his son in a film—at least not until after Rajiv had floundered in films made by other banners. After school—college was never an option, just as it hadn't been for his brothers—and between films, Rajiv hung around the sets, assisting his father and doing all the difficult chores. 'Chimpu is being taught the way I learnt, right from scratch...he also sweeps the floors, picks up all the lights, assists, goes to the laboratories, sits up in the editing room, learning the way this craft should be learnt,' says Raj Kapoor.[3] Was Raj Kapoor merely following the Kapoor tradition laid down by his father by making his young son go through what he had gone through himself? But in doing so, did he let the grooming go on too long?

Interestingly, had Rishi Kapoor been a little younger at the time of *Ram Teri...* it is unlikely that Rajiv would have had this chance as well. In his book on Raj Kapoor, Bunny Reuben writes: 'He [Rishi] waits and watches on Pali Hill, reading the trade papers during the weekends and by-hearting the collection figures of all the current releases. But he refuses to pander to the Great Man, knowing his father too well and also not wanting to offend younger brother Chimpu, who is a likely candidate too for the same role in the same film.'

Although the eighties were busy for Rajiv Kapoor, the films he acted in for other banners faltered: not a single one was successful and he could not reap the harvest of being the hero of such a commercially big hit that *Ram Teri*...was. It wasn't that good directors did not want him. In 1985, he acted in Nasir Husain's *Zabardast*. This was the same Husain who had rescued Shammi Kapoor from the 'waiting room' of flop actors and bestowed instant stardom on him with *Tumsa Nahin Dekha*. The director was obviously past his sell-by date, and the presence of veteran actors like Sanjeev Kumar, Jaya Prada, Sunny Deol and Rati Agnihotri didn't help. Perhaps he was unlucky in the kind of films he was offered. Some of the films Chimpu acted in had storylines that had been warmed over several times. In *Aasman*, directed by Tony Ahuja, Rajiv had Tina Munim, Mala Sinha and Divya Rana as his co-stars. He even had a double role (in one role he plays a pilot, just as his father had in *Sangam*). But it is a hackneyed plot of a doppelgänger making his way into the hero's home and into the heart of the girl he wants while the hero is away fighting for his country. Shashi Kapoor and Dev Anand, apart from many others, had been there, done this before. The Kapoors, obviously, can't help running into each other on-screen. Rajiv even acted with cousin Karan Kapoor in *Zalzala*, a film directed by Harish Shah, and starring Dharmendra and Shatrughan Sinha. He played the lead in *Lover Boy* (directed by Shomu Mukherjee), and Ravindra Peepat's *Lava* where he shared screen time with Dimple Kapadia, his brother's first screen love. *Hum To Chale Pardes* and *Shukriya* in 1989 came and went without a buzz. In 1990 he acted in *Zimmedaar*: his two heroines in this film were Kimi Katkar (before she shot to fame in the legendary 'Jumma chumma de de' number with Amitabh Bachchan in *Hum*) and Anita Raj. Rajiv had an encore with Mandakini in *Naag Nagin*, which turned out to be an eminently forgettable film. His acting career was not going anywhere.

This Kapoor did not quite belong in an age of screen violence, presided over by action heroes with switchblade legs and rippling muscles. Romance was a mere backdrop to the action. Rajiv as screen hero was out of sync with the times: he was a throwback to the early seventies, pre-Amitabh Bachchan era, and too early for the romantic family socials spawned after Sooraj Barjatya's *Maine Pyar Kiya*. Sadly, the son said to have Raj Kapoor's flair never really got a chance.

The irony is that Rajiv Kapoor did not even want to be an actor. From the outset he wanted to be behind the camera, and make the kind of films his father did. Rajiv Kapoor is apparently more like his father than his brothers, according to those who have worked closely with Raj Kapoor. Lekh Tandon believes that he has his father's talent and vision and would have probably made films the way Raj did had he been given the chance. Rajiv's approach to cinema is probably very similar to his father's, with music playing a dominant role. Talking about his uncle in glowing terms, Ranbir Kapoor says: 'He is musically inclined. He listens to Aadesh Srivastava's music and then visualizes a film.'

Apart from learning the tricks of the trade while working in R.K., Rajiv also assisted his father in *Prem Rog*. Raj Kapoor however did not hand the director's baton to his youngest son, although he had given Randhir the chance (*Kal Aaj Aur Kal*) fairly early in his career. In fact, he did not let Rajiv direct a film for his friend Ravindra Peepat, who along with Rajiv had been an assistant director for *Satyam Shivam Sundaram* before moving on to make his own films, just as many years earlier he had refused to let Randhir make a film with B.B. Bhalla even after a story-reading session.

Rajiv was obviously disappointed, straining at the leash to do something himself, and could only realize his ambition as late as 1996 with *Prem Granth*, a film inspired by Thomas Hardy's *Tess of the d' Ubervilles*. He was thirty-four at the time, while his father had been just twenty-two when he had directed his first film, *Aag*, and Randhir had not been much older when he made his debut as a director. When asked whether he became a director just because he had failed as an actor, Rajiv admits that he was a 'failure' as an actor but insists that acting was not his first choice. 'I became an actor because I hail from the Kapoor family and secondly, the opportunity to act was offered to me on a platter. I always wanted to be a film-maker.'[4]

The core of Rajiv Kapoor's film may have had a more radical theme—of a 'fallen woman' (read raped) who redeems herself and love triumphs—than those of his father's, but it was made in the Raj Kapoor style, where slickness and stylized shots do not come into the picture. It appeared out of sync in the age of gossamer films shot in Europe or in Australia—old-fashioned stories tarted up in a contemporary 'cool' look. The films of the ruling trinity of film-makers in the mid-nineties—Barjatyas (Sooraj), Chopras (Yash and Aditya) and Johars (Yash and Karan)—were traditional and all about loving the family, where rebellion was short-lived. And their films were stuffed with the latest brands—from clothes to cars and sunglasses. Perhaps, Rajiv should have yoked off the influence of his father, changing both the thematic content of his film as well as his style.

Had *Prem Granth* done well—either critically or commercially—things may have been different for Rajiv Kapoor. His directorial debut was competently made, had wonderful music by Laxmikant Pyarelal and fine acting—especially by Om Puri, Rishi Kapoor and Madhuri Dixit. Unfortunately, his leading actress was lost in transition, and Rishi Kapoor was also getting on in age. Dixit had put on a lot of weight, and was yet to make her glorious second coming (which she did with Yash Chopra's *Dil To Pagal Hai*). The actress has never been a lucky mascot for these Kapoors—as she was for their clansman Anil Kapoor. Her other two films with Rishi Kapoor, *Yaarana* and *Sahibaan*, also did not do well at the box office. Luck was obviously not on Rajiv Kapoor's side. Sanjay Dutt was supposed to act in *Prem Granth*, even though the script was originally written with Rishi Kapoor in mind. But Dutt was in trouble with the police at the time and was forced to stop acting, and Rishi was cast. The Dutt–Dixit chemistry may have altered the fate of the film.

After the debacle of *Prem Granth*, Rajiv's directorial ambitions have taken a backseat. Like his brother Rishi, he too appears to be a victim of the once-bitten-twice-shy syndrome. Rajiv is now involved with the running of R.K. Films, along with his brothers (he was one of the producers of *Aa Ab Laut Chalen*).

Like all the Kapoors, Rajiv has grappled with his personal hell. The curse of the Kapoors has been the most unrelenting with him. Alcohol tripped him early on: the decline, when it began, was steep. His drinking binges are longer and more frequent than those of his brothers. He is known to go off—like a wounded bear—into isolation and drink. His brothers, on the other hand, usually drink with their buddies. The spirit does not make Rajiv Kapoor abusive. It does not unleash his demons. But he does get depressed.

This Kapoor's personal life, especially after his father died, has had the saddest graph. Like his brothers and uncles, Rajiv may have dated actresses—it is reported he was serious about Divya Rana and dated Nagma, amongst others—but unlike them, and like his father, he married outside the world of cinema. It was an arranged marriage with Aarti Sabharwal, a beautiful girl from a Punjabi family in Delhi, who at the time was designing stained glass.

The two were married in Delhi on 11 December 2000. Rajiv lost weight: like all Kapoors he has a fatal attraction for food. It seems the young couple was happy in the beginning: Rajiv was smitten with his wife. He worked hard on scripts, sobered up. But then the old nemesis caught up with him: he soon began to lose the battle of the bottle and the bulge. The fact that his career was not really happening may have triggered the relapse, eventually leading the youngest Kapoor bahu to walk out of the marriage. Initially, she was reluctant to leave. She had even sought the help of Krishna Kapoor. But the cardinal rule with the Chembur Kapoors is not to interfere: Krishna didn't help when Neetu Singh had asked her to either. Just like her in-laws hadn't helped her when Krishna Kapoor had gone through much the same herself. She dealt with her husband's alcoholic excesses in her own way, and by herself. It was part of the baggage of being a Mrs Kapoor.

The youngest Mrs Kapoor moved back to Delhi. And for a while Rajiv Kapoor was on a Mumbai–Delhi shuttle trying to convince his young wife to return. The couple finally divorced in October 2003. It was on one such Delhi 'mission' that I saw Rajiv Kapoor. It was mid-afternoon, and he was at the bar at the Maurya Sheraton. Perched on a stool at the bar he kept talking to the young bartender about life, about the best hotels. When he got up to leave, the barman helped him out, and Rajiv thanked him effusively, saying 'God bless you'—as if he were much older than the bartender.

At the bar his voice sometimes climbed a few decibels, but without any aggression—or swagger. Like the ancient mariner he simply wanted to tell his tale, as if he were seeking a sympathetic ear, a brief respite from his obvious loneliness. It brought to mind what a friend with British Airways told me about Raj Kapoor: the showman occasionally boarded the flight to London alone, drank all the way and 'seemed desperately lonely'. Like his father, Rajiv also seeks out strangers.

Bunny Reuben recounts Raj Kapoor once telling Chimpu: 'I am on one side of the line and you are on the other. Whatever discussions you want to have with me, whatever advice you want from this side of the line, you will get, but always remember that the other side is totally yours. You have to live your life, not me or anyone else.' Perhaps Raj Kapoor should have spent more time as a father—and not as a film-maker—with his youngest son. But then with Raj Kapoor his films were more important to him than his family. In her book, Ritu Nanda quotes her father: 'I'd much rather be a bad father, but I will never compromise my integrity as a film-maker or do anything which belittles that credit-title of mine: directed and produced by Raj Kapoor.'

Rajiv now spends more time in Pune, where he has built a house. There is always talk about his working on scripts for films that he plans to direct. The Kapoor brothers are waiting for the right script. They are in a sort of limbo, a strange twilight zone. They don't want to discard the 'Raj Kapoor style of film-making'. Yet they want to update themselves and make films that appeal to the younger generation. They are three producers in search of a new avatar for R.K., trying to keep up with the new moghuls.

7

Les Girls: Karisma Kapoor and Kareena Kapoor

'Once, Karisma and I were sitting next to each other, and I said to her, "Do you know that I was with your great-grandfather for fourteen years?" There was not a flicker of recognition. She just turned round and said, "Really?" And that was the end of the conversation.'

—Zohra Segal

Karisma Kapoor may just as well have said Prithviraj Kapoor, who? When Babita Kapoor bundled her two school-going daughters, Karisma and Kareena, out of the Malabar Hill apartment she shared with her husband Randhir Kapoor, a branch of the Kapoor family tree snapped, though it didn't quite break. Splintered is a better word. Randhir Kapoor moved back to Devnar Cottage to be with his mother after Raj Kapoor died, while his wife set up a separate home with their daughters and set out on her single-minded, doggedly unrelenting mission to make them screen divas. It was like taking a graft of the old, heavily laden family tree and planting it in new soil.

It has been difficult enough for the Kapoor boys: silver spoons have traditionally been in short supply in the Kapoor khandaan. Even though Prithviraj Kapoor did speak with Kidar Sharma for Raj Kapoor, he made sure that each of his sons made it up the hard and long way. Raj Kapoor may have handed the director's baton to his first-born, Randhir Kapoor, to make *Kal Aaj Aur Kal* for R.K. when he was just twenty-four, but he was never as generous again. Most Kapoor sons have had to fend for themselves, struggling to grab an identity and a life from leftover personas not already used by those Kapoors who had come before them.

For a Kapoor daughter it was mission impossible: girls from this conservative clan get married early, usually arranged, and start families. The boys go into the movies. (Shashi Kapoor's children are the exception. It only happened because the dynasty shifted ground.) This branch of the fourth generation of Kapoors has grown up differently. Les Girls grew up in a quasi-single parent home. They are leaner, tougher and driven. Had Babita not moved out would her daughters have become Bollywood prima donnas, with Karisma straddling the nineties and Kareena catching the bouquet in the millennium? Both are brightly shining stars in celluloid heaven and competent actresses who have flirted with art house cinema, and been praised by the likes of Shyam Benegal, Govind Nihalani and Sudhir Mishra. On Simi Garewal's 'confessional' television show *Rendezvous with Simi Garewal*, Kareena said: 'My parents live separately, we are happy—three independent women. Mom is a wonder woman [who] can take on anyone on this planet...With a mom like that we don't need to go to anyone for advice. She has made a whole empire.'

KARISMA KAPOOR

Karisma (Lolo to friends and family) was set on becoming an actress as a child, and her mother did the rounds of producers and studios while she was still in school, the upscale Cathedral School. At fifteen, Karisma was already on the sets. Before she turned sixteen, her debut film, D. Rama Rao's *Prem Qaidi* (1991), was in the cinema halls, although the first film she acted in was *Danga Fasad* in 1990. Her co-star was the unknown Jeet Upendra and the film bombed miserably.

Karisma may have moved away from the Kapoor house as a child but she didn't leave behind the family's acting genes: she also has her grandfather's blue eyes and his obsessive determination. In her mind, Prithviraj Kapoor may be mired in the realm of myth, somebody too far back in the past to figure in today's scheme of things. However, her grandfather is an important touchstone in her professional life. One could say that her reclamation of the family name begins, and in a way ends, with Raj Kapoor. In several press interviews, both Karisma and Kareena always talk about him as their favourite director—and actor. In 2000, Karisma admitted to the 'bond' between them in a cover story in *Verve* magazine: 'I just loved my grandfather and since I was the first grandchild and [had] inherited his blue eyes, everyone in the family said I had the same way of knitting my eyebrows that he had.' Occasionally, the sisters—the younger much more than the elder—refer to their father but rarely to any of the other talented Kapoors.

R.K. Films was a magical place for Karisma when she was growing up. For a few years, every Sunday from the age of five she used to sit with her grandfather, often on his lap, and watch his old films in the film theatre in the studio. Raj Kapoor has instilled a passion for cinema in many young people. Perhaps Karisma's Bollywood dreams too began here. Karisma recalls her grandfather telling her that he would make a film with her when she grew up. She often talks about watching *Ram Teri Ganga Maili* repeatedly, wishing she were up there on the screen instead of Mandakini. *Sangam* was the other film she watched, particularly the 'Main kya karoon Ram, mujhe budha mil gaya' song.

Did Raj Kapoor really mean what he said to Karisma? One will never know. But had he been the one to launch his granddaughter, her screen debut wouldn't have been such a non-starter. In *Prem Qaidi* she is a gawky teenager with bushy eyebrows and bad make-up. She moves like a puppet being manipulated by an inexperienced puppeteer. Her leading man, Harish, an actor in south Indian films, was an unknown entity in Hindi cinema. Although the film was not a total washout, unfortunately for her the buzz about the film centred around a Kapoor girl wearing a swimsuit and showing a fair amount of flesh—and that too in an insignificant film.

Interestingly, the first film Karisma had signed was Dharmendra's *Barsaat*. (Raj Kapoor's second directorial venture was also called *Barsaat*.) However, she walked out of the project because it was taking too long getting started—despite the fact that Dharmendra was the producer of the film and he wanted to launch his second son, Bobby Deol, with her.

After *Prem Qaidi*, several indifferent films followed in quick succession. The age of coloured lenses and desi bottle blondes had not quite set in. Perhaps people were not ready to accept her blue eyes. Cousin Karan Kapoor's baby blue eyes and blonde hair in the eighties were probably largely responsible for the tepid response to his debut film *Sultanat*. The two did not look desi enough. The lack of success saw this little branch of the Kapoor family shedding tears. In a revealing remark made on Simi Garewal's show, Kareena recalls her sister's despair: 'I have seen Lolo's struggle. Despite the Raj Kapoor name, nobody supported her. My mother had to struggle. Lolo would stay up nights and cry. I used to hide behind the curtain and watch. I have seen a lot with my mother and sister. I lived life through them. The way people would put her down. She would cry and go to sleep. It hurt me and it makes me strong and confident. What makes me? What I learned from them and bundled up into a package of Bebo [Kareena's pet name]. I feel like a man, guy. I am ready for struggle. I can take up anybody.' Brave words because her sister, older by six years, paved the way for her, mowing down the obstacles as she went about signing films.

Before the nineties ended, Karisma had acted in well over fifty films: her father acted in a little over forty films during his entire career. Most of her early films did not require her to be more than an energetic Barbie doll. Fame came with a series of films with Govinda: *Raja Babu*, *Khuddar*, *Coolie No. 1*, *Saajan Chale Sasural*, *Hero No. 1*. The screen twosome clicked because they were bubbly, high on humour and low on emoting.

Fame, however, came with a rider. And, perhaps, an unwanted accolade. With these fun-filled films—several directed by David Dhawan—Karisma was crowned a sex bomb. She also received a lot of flak for her raunchy and suggestive numbers like 'Sexy, sexy, sexy mujhe log bole' (*Khuddar*) and 'Sarkailey khaitya' (*Raja Babu*). The 'Sarkailey khaitya' dance sequence with Govinda was nothing more than simulated sex, but the actress's name became even bigger on the marquee. She had arrived: becoming Heroine No. 1 seemed within reach.

This Kapoor was also a dancing star. But not in the gentler Raj Kapoor–Rishi Kapoor mode. Karisma dances like her grand uncle Shammi Kapoor, with a touch of wildness and an exuberance that makes you feel tired just watching her gyrate. Restraint seems to have been thrown out of the window. But like Shammi Kapoor she too was playing at being the extrovert. For both it had to be success at any cost: both had false starts in their career and lots of failures on their way before finally 'arriving'. You sense that humiliation fuelled their journey up. True grit was at work here for Karisma. Often behind the seeming ease with which she appears to be doing things on the screen is sheer fright—and tears. Recalling an incident on the day of Karisma's wedding, Govinda said: 'David [Dhawan] and I just reminisced about this one shot in *Raja Babu*. Lolo had to climb on top of a wooden plank on a water tank. She cried for an hour, but she did do the shot!'[1]

Until the mid-nineties, Karisma was a saleable star, but not quite A-list: a whiff of B-grade cinema still enveloped her; the word 'class' was not used to describe her. She underwent a dramatic metamorphosis in 1996 with *Raja Hindustani* directed by Dharmesh Darshan. Her 'look' can neatly be divided into a pre- and post-*Raja Hindustani* stage. Overnight, Karisma became hip and cool. The architect of her new, soigné 'look' was fashion designer Manish Malhotra, the modern-day Svengali of Bollywood. Malhotra recalls his 'creation' in an interview with me: 'Karisma had curly hair and bushy eyebrows. I gave her a very different look, one that was very Indian and very modern at the same time. I gave her tight churidars, Sadhana style—what you see in *Waqt*—to highlight her figure, which was very good. I gave her straight hair wigs and brown lenses, and changed the base of her make-up. The first time she put on the brown lens her eyes went completely red, but she carried on. She always had a figure, but it was never highlighted. She used to wear those frilly things. When you are young and first come in, you do not know what to do with yourself. Karisma became a nineties' girl, and more upmarket for everybody. Before the nineties, film costumes were copied by the masses, now the classes were copying them. Mainstream fashion began to respect my work in the movies.

Earlier labelled filmy by the model world, now they were suddenly hip.'

Raja Hindustani is an important turning point in an even more substantial way: with it the star graduated to becoming an actress. Not only was the film a huge commercial success, she won the Filmfare Best Actress Award for it in 1996. The following year brought an embarrassment of riches. Her performance in *Dil To Pagal Hai* earned her two awards for best supporting actress—the National Award as well as the Filmfare Award. The critics sat up and took notice, as did directors of 'other' cinema.

Talking about the importance of *Raja Hindustani* in her career in an interview to Subhash K. Jha for the Indo-Asian News Service (IANS), Karisma said: 'Prior to this I was just a teenager, playing insignificant roles as a college student. I craved to get meaty roles like Madhuri Dixit.' Her craving, ironically enough, was satisfied in *Dil To Pagal Hai*: she got to act with her idol, and didn't fare too badly in comparison. But it was not easy. Apparently, Karisma almost gave up before the scene in which she has to pit her dancing skills against those of Madhuri Dixit for a dance competition. She called her mother, who just said, 'Shut up', and hung up on her. Mother did know best: Lolo danced like never before for that particular scene.

Nor had she ever been as lucky. After *Dil To Pagal Hai* she acted in one blockbuster after another, delivering hits with regularity. Karisma had four major hits in 1999: *Haseena Maan Jaayegi, Biwi No. 1, Hum Saath Saath Hain* and *Jaanwar*. But like all good actresses who start out as little more than bimbettes, she also wanted to do 'serious' cinema. Luckily, she didn't have to wait too long.

Her performance in Khalid Mohammed's *Fiza* (2000), a film in which she plays the sister of a terrorist (Hrithik Roshan), was critically appreciated. It wasn't just the simple act of washing off her make-up and putting on a salwar kameez: her restrained yet expressive performance held the film. She held her own even against a seasoned actress like Jaya Bachchan, and did steal a bit of Roshan's thunder. Karisma, however, could not completely let go of her glamorous screen image in this film. She did an out-of-character disco dance, all dressed in black leather, almost as if she wanted to show she was both the leading lady of the film as well its 'item girl'. Perhaps it was to signal to her fans that underneath the behanji apparel, the sexy Karisma had not quite disappeared. Or was she egged on by Sushmita Sen's 'guest appearance' (often an euphemism in Bollywood for an item number) in the sizzling 'Dilbar, dilbar' song?

Soon after, she got a chance to work with one of the sentinels of art cinema, Shyam Benegal. Karisma's portrayal of the title role in *Zubeida*, the spirited young girl who becomes the second wife of a maharaja, won her the Filmfare Critics Award for Best Performance. Khalid Mohammed scripted the film. Obviously, the journalist–film-maker has played a significant role in her elevation from star to actress. And with this latest laurel, the first Kapoor daughter to become an actress (Sanjana's sojourn in films was brief) made her mark in both mainstream and art house cinema, not willing to let go of either. She is the only actress of her generation who has films with Shyam Benegal and David Dhawan simultaneously. Awards became a habit: she won the Filmfare Award for Best Actress for *Fiza* and the National Award for Best Supporting Actress for *Dil Toh Pagal Hai*. Her later films, including her performance in Boney Kapoor's *Shakti—The Power* ('inspired' by the American film *Not Without My Daughter*), confirmed her arrival as an actress who had delivered on her promise.

Karisma acted in about ten films in the new millennium before she took a small break to marry childhood friend and Delhi industrialist Sanjay Kapur on 29 September 2003. She soon hopped on to the Delhi–Mumbai shuttle to complete her commitments in the behemoth television serial *Karishma—A Miracle of Destiny* and in films.

Shyam Benegal is all praise for this actress, particularly her grit and determination to learn. 'Karisma Kapoor looks like a Renaissance portrait. I would love to take her in another film before she says goodbye.' He needn't worry: film stars don't say goodbye. Karisma certainly hasn't.

Unlike Kareena, Karisma is a very private person and rarely speaks about her personal relationships, other than how much her mother and sister mean to her. Seldom does she speak about her father. Through much of her career, her name has rarely been linked with her co-stars, with the exception of actor Ajay Devgan when they acted in a few films together. The action-hero with the dark brooding looks is said to have rescued her when she had an accident on location. Rescuing young actresses in distress became something of a habit with him: his romance with actress–wife Kajol also began when he saved her life during a film shoot.

Karisma's volatile seven-year-long relationship with actor Abhishek Bachchan guzzled much newsprint in the national press. After all, the two are as blue blood as they come in the kingdom of Indian cinema. Had the marriage taken place it would have been the second alliance between the Kapoors and the Bachchans: Karisma's cousin Nikhil (Ritu Nanda's son) is married to Amitabh and Jaya Bachchan's daughter Shweta. The Karisma–Abhishek engagement announcement came with much fanfare on Amitabh Bachchan's sixtieth birthday celebrations at the JW Marriott Hotel in Mumbai on 11 October 2002. His prospective daughter-in-law touched his feet, and he kissed her forehead.

With an on-again, off-again engagement, their relationship was the stuff television soaps are made of. Karisma is reported to have returned her engagement ring several times, and the last time Abhishek Bachchan just kept it. There was as much drama in this relationship as there was in the television serial *Karishma*. Writer Barbara Taylor Bradford came all the way to Kolkata to sue the producers of the serial, claiming it was based on her novel *A Woman of Substance*. Bradford lost the case, and the serial went on and on, but without much critical acclaim. Meanwhile, the Bachchans and the Kapoors retreated behind a wall of silence about the reasons for the break-up.

The silence spawned all sorts of speculation. Some say Babita and her daughters wanted a court wedding because they did not want Randhir Kapoor to do the *kanyadaan*. Others say Babita wanted to know exactly how much money and property her prospective son-in-law had in his own name, and was not happy with Jaya Bachchan's increasing closeness to Karisma (the two had acted together as mother and daughter in *Fiza*). It seems that she did not want her daughter to repeat the mistake she had made when she married Randhir Kapoor: marrying a less successful actor whose father was a living legend. Abhishek is a little younger than Karisma, and had at the time not been lucky with his films. More speculation: the Bachchans were apparently not too keen about the alliance to begin with and finally put their foot down when Babita insisted on keeping Randhir Kapoor out of the wedding nuptials. It would have complicated matters for their daughter who is married to Randhir Kapoor's nephew.

The final break-up came in February 2003. In September of the same year, Karisma married Sanjay Kapur. And in between there was even more drama. Randhir Kapoor underwent heart surgery in Delhi, and his wife and daughters a change of heart. The two actresses cancelled their respective schedules and flew to Delhi to be with their father. Much emotion flowed. The 'Sicilians', as Randhir Kapoor likes to call his larger clan, closed ranks.

The three prodigal Kapoor women finally returned home—for the wedding. Karisma's *doli* (bridal palanquin) left from her ancestral home. The cream-coloured invitations, letters really, went out from Randhir and Babita Kapoor, and Mrs Krishna Kapoor. Karisma wanted a small wedding ceremony. It was a morning Sikh ceremony at Devnar Cottage, relatively small, elegant and moving, with the bride radiant in a Manish Malhotra light pink ensemble encrusted with crystals. It was also a bit of a designer wedding, with a Rohit Bal sherwani for the groom, and the bride's father in a designer embroidered sherwani.

The sit-down lunch after the ceremony was a Kapoor-style celebration: adjectives can only be incrementally superlative when it comes to the Kapoors. Randhir Kapoor directed this production sparing no cost and underwriting it all. He wanted his daughter's wedding celebrations to be in the best tradition of his father. The 700 guests expanded (as Indian weddings do) to over a 1000 guests comprising family, close friends, film stars and a smattering of politicians. The sprawling lawns of Devnar were transformed into an elegant sheesh mahal with mirrors and mogras—Raj Kapoor's favourite flower. Nearly 200 dishes from over half-a-dozen cuisines of the world—culinary epiphanies from Thailand, Italy, France and from the various regions of India—had the guests in raptures. *La grande Bouffe* as the French would say. Champagne flowed with Kapoorian excess: there are no half-measures for the Pathan bon vivants.

But had Raj Kapoor been looking on he would have undoubtedly let out a slight sigh. Although the party was in the R.K. style all right, the showman's panache and grandeur, and the larger-than-life emotions were missing. What was also missing was some of the family. A turbaned Rishi Kapoor was there, next to his brothers, as were Shammi and Shashi Kapoor—all involved in receiving the guests and playing host. But Rishi's wife Neetu Singh and their two children were conspicuous by their absence. So was Indian cinema's other formidable dynasty, the Bachchans. Nor were their close friends present. It appeared Bollywood was a bit divided that September afternoon.

Karisma moved to Delhi, to live with her husband in his home in Vasant Vihar. The house soon became a fortress. According to neighbours, the walls went higher and all sorts of security systems were installed. And the bride remained elusive. Friends of the Kapur family complain that she didn't make any effort to meet those who were close to her husband, forever running away to mama and Mumbai: the actress was at that time working in *Karishma*. She did accompany her polo-playing husband to polo matches, but remained reticent. Apparently, Karisma was uncomfortable in Delhi society, more snobbish at the core than it is in Mumbai. It could also be her realization that Sanjay's reputation of being a playboy and his alleged addiction to designer drugs may have had more than a whiff of truth to it. The papers talked about his seeing other women.

Real life did not have a happy ending. Karisma returned to Mumbai for the birth of their daughter—and stayed on. Then suddenly in late July 2005 it turned nasty, and public. It became, as a paper put it, Kapur vs. Kapoor. Divorce proceedings began, and a bitter battle for the custody of their baby daughter Samaira ensued. Karisma has reportedly asked for a settlement of Rs 7 crore. What evidently sparked the bitter feud was Karisma getting a passport for their child in Mumbai without informing her husband. In an interesting twist to this marital tale, the court played cupid, asking the couple to consider reconciliation for the sake of their daughter. Bollywood could not have scripted it better: the couple met in Goa for their second wedding anniversary. Things have looked up ever since and the marital problems seem very much a thing of the past. Professionally, Karisma is facing the camera after a two-year hiatus as a judge on the celebrity dance show *Nach Baliye 4*.

KAREENA KAPOOR

> *'Lolo is a hypersensitive girl. She's a lamb. But Kareena's like me. She's willing to take on the world. I keep telling Babs to keep her on a leash. Bebo is going to take this country by storm. Watch her, she's a bomb.'*
>
> —Randhir Kapoor

It's those stubborn Kapoor genes. On the way down this branch of Raj Kapoor's family, they hurried through Karisma, spending just enough time to endow her with her paternal grandfather's blue eyes and grit, but took their time with Kareena, leaving behind a much larger and deeper imprint. In his interview with me, Manish Malhotra, close friend and the architect of Kareena's look, as he was for her sister, said: 'While Karisma is quiet and keeps to her self, Kareena says what she feels and is very outgoing. She is more like a Kapoor—very frank and *bindaas*.'

Incandescent, with almond-shaped tawny eyes that have a splash of green, Kareena Kapoor stands out from her contemporaries who appear to have sprung from identikits. When she started her career, her figure was curvaceous, recalling the amply endowed heroines of her grandfather. A soupçon of plumpness made her look like an Odalisque who has stepped out of an Ingres painting. Today, she is known for her 'size zero' figure and her incredibly toned and gymmed body. Says Shyam Benegal: 'Kareena is extraordinarily beautiful, a true beauty.'

Beyond mannerisms and clowning, she is equally comfortable playing a blonde brat in a micro-mini or a chawl dweller with a single plait. Directors love her. For Govind Nihalani, Kareena is 'restrained and understated like Shashi Kapoor...Her body language changes with the character she plays.' Observes Sudhir Mishra who directed her in *Chameli*: 'She understands the context of the scene, trusts the director and brings something magical of her own into the shot. There is a surprise in the shot—not exactly what you tell her. I think Raj Kapoor is the obvious reference point. Kareena is also like Chintu [Rishi Kapoor], who is an underrated actor.' Karan Johar, on Simi Garewal's show, described her as an inadvertent scene-stealer: 'In a scene in *Kabhi Khushi Kabhie Gham* she is doing nothing, just standing between Shah Rukh and Hrithik, and you are looking at her and not the two stars.'

Kareena is an archetypal Kapoor. She reclaimed her grandfather on Simi Garewal's show: 'If Raj Kapoor would have been alive, he would have been proud of me. He loved me.' She has also grabbed the R.K. legacy—the Kapoor lust for food and life—with both hands. Her father certainly thinks so: 'Kareena is like me, fond of food. She loves good wine, *paaya*, and is a *pataki* (spirited). Ask her directors and they tell you what a foodie she is.' Mishra concurs: 'She is a Kapoor when it comes to food—a carnivore. Loves tandoori chicken and chicken tikka. I always saw her in front of the tandoori stuff.'

What she *didn't* take from her legacy is the name Raj Kapoor gave her when she was born. She and Riddhima, Rishi Kapoor's daughter, were born within a week of each other in September 1980 during the Ganapati puja days. '*Riddhima aur Siddhima aa gayee hain*,' said a delighted grandfather. One kept the name; the other changed hers to Kareena.

The name Kareena Kapoor has an alliterative zing to it. It would certainly look better on a marquee than Siddhima Kapoor. As a four-year-old, Kareena was already dreaming about being an actor: film studios are an early memory for both sisters. Kareena continued to fantasize about being an actress through much of her childhood: 'When I was about nine or ten I used to pick up the phone and say, "I am Bebo and I will be a movie star." For me life's a drama, on- and off-screen. I was always doing my drama off-screen.'[2]

Kareena used to hang around the sets of her sister's films, taking it all in—mugging Karisma's lines and giving her cues. In her mind's eye she was already a star. Once when Karisma was working in a film being made at AVM Studio in Chennai,

Kareena put on the blue sari her sister had worn for a scene, as well as her wig with a fringe. But she didn't stop after this little bit of make-believe. She asked the stills photographer on the sets to take her photograph dressed up as her sister. She was always mixing life and fantasy.

Although this Kapoor was determined to act, she also wanted to prove that she was a brainy Kapoor—a blue stocking babe, like Reese Witherspoon in *Legally Blonde*. So, unlike most of the other Kapoors, she did not say goodbye to books after school. For a while she flirted with the idea of being a normal girl. Kareena briefly attended Government Law College after graduating from Cathedral School. Perhaps she was picking up the trail from her great-grandfather who had studied law. And she, too, abandoned it. Prithviraj Kapoor left because he wanted to do theatre. In her case it was just boredom, a persistent Kapoor malady. Like most yuppie Indians of her generation she also wanted Harvard on her CV. Kareena attended a short course on computer technology at Harvard University. Boredom set in once again. At any rate what mattered was that she came back with a 'Harvard-returned' stamp—in the Age of Brands, Harvard is the best.

It was soon back to the family business. While Karsima had to struggle for nearly eight years, with several reversals of fortunes en route, Kareena made a dramatic entrance with her debut film, J.P. Dutta's *Refugee*, with Abhishek Bachchan as her co-star. Kareena it seems was plotting her career moves according to her own set of rules. To begin with, the choice of *Refugee* as her first film was not an obvious one: she took it on immediately after pulling out of Rakesh Roshan's *Kaho Na Pyaar Hai*—an act of courage, according to Karisma. Karisma is of the opinion that while most other debuting actresses would have chosen a *Kaho Na Pyaar Hai* above *Refugee* at the beginning of their careers, Kareena did exactly the opposite. She, in fact, asks her younger sibling for advice quite often.

Refugee sank, but Kareena had arrived, despite the fact that she played a simple village belle—without make-up or even ersatz rustic clothes that can spell rural chic and sex appeal. And although she acted in several films in quick succession that did not do well commercially, including *Asoka* with Shah Rukh Khan as her co-star, she kept snatching victory out of the jaws of box-office defeat: the movie moghuls still wanted her—Subhash Ghai (*Yaadein*), Karan Johar (*Kabhi Khushi Kabhie Gham*) and the Barjatyas (*Mein Prem Ki Diwani Hoon*).

It wasn't just the Kapoor pedigree. Kareena is that rare kind of actor who devours the camera. After all, she has been rehearsing all her life. Acting began at home, with a 24/7 tutor in her actress–mother. 'Our mother spent a lot of time with us...preparing us both to be professional on and off camera. I would wear my mom's nighties and do Sridevi dance numbers. I would try to pick up Sridevi's expressions. Mom would direct,' recounted Kareena on *Rendezvous with Simi Garewal*. Kareena concentrated on Sridevi's moves in Shekhar Kapur's *Mr India*. She also watched Madhuri Dixit's films to pick up clues about dancing and acting.

Manish Malhotra did not need to overhaul Kareena completely, as he did Karisma. He made the younger sibling more contemporary, and designed a look to go with her more extrovert personality. He says: 'There was too much brown. I gave her more blonde, gave her a trainer and asked her to go on a diet. In *Kabhi Khushi Kabhie Gham* people even noticed her salwar kameezed look. It is a very different look—bolder, the new kind of in-your-face girl. In *Mujhse Dosti Karoge*, she is very la-di-da. She represents Britney Spears in her keds and jeans, and in-your-face glamour. With Karisma it is all very glam-glam and coordinated. With Kareena it is more casual. Like today's girl she is more spirited and confident. Unlike the generation before, this one has an opinion and expresses it.'

Kareena could afford to be more 'in your face' because she had her sister and mother as buffer. The more politically correct Karisma has always been very protective of her. Their career paths have been radically different. Babita Kapoor was a constant chaperone for her elder daughter, the guiding hand who also led her by the hand. In fact, Kareena attended a boarding school in Dehradun for a brief spell during the early days in her sister's career when Babita accompanied Karisma on all her location shoots.

But she stopped when Karisma began to do well. Shyam Benegal recalls that during the making of *Zubeida*, Babita never used to come to the sets. 'She only came during a sequence that had sync sound. Babita wanted to see how the dubbing was done. She is responsible for empowering her two daughters.' Something

Randhir Kapoor also readily acknowledged to me: 'The credit for the girls goes to Babita. She has the drive. My daughters are not party animals. They want to be the best. They carry this mindset from their mother...They have the same drive and determination as Raj Kapoor. They won't cancel a shooting if I want to take them out.'

Kareena usually comes to the sets alone, and is very professional about her work. Her bratty exterior is misleading. She may not be quite the lamb her father considers Karisma to be, but she is still a bit of a lamb albeit in wolf's clothing. On the sets of *Chameli* she spent a lot of time by herself in her make-up van, busy with her SMS, according to Sudhir Mishra. 'She wasn't inhibited, she was rather spontaneous. But somewhere she is very shy. I was told that she was an arrogant brat. However there was a bashful way about her often...She stood in the rain waiting for a shot, and never complained.'

Directors have generally appreciated the professionalism of the Kapoors. 'The Kapoor family is dedicated to their work, they are actors by vocation,' says Benegal, who has worked with two generations of Kapoors. Kareena Kapoor was no exception, just much more ambitious. She was in a hurry to get to the top—and to be the mistress of the universe of both mainstream and offbeat cinema. She wanted to be a star and an actress, something increasingly incompatible in Bollywood. It was she who sought out Govind Nihalani for a role in *Dev* (in which she plays a character based on Zahira, the brave Muslim girl who went to court after the unspeakable atrocities inflicted on Muslim families in Gujarat in the wake of the Godhra incident).[3] Kareena revelled in her role of a prostitute in *Chameli*, even though several actresses had shied away from playing one. On the way from Lucknow to Delhi, after the famous Sahara wedding, Kareena was on the same plane as designer Ritu Kumar. When the topic of conversation turned to Preity Zinta, she said: 'Preity, she's cute. Do you think she could do *Chameli*?'[4]

There is something about Kareena. Directors talk in superlatives about her. Says Sanjay Leela Bhansali, 'Kareena exudes a unique mystery and power in her personality. There's something very striking and untamed. Everything about her is different from the actresses I have worked with before.' She is often compared with Meena Kumari. Bhansali is reminded of 'the pathos of Meena

Kumari and the fire of Nargis' and Mishra believes she has the 'emotional depth of Meena Kumari and the joy of Madhubala'. Is Kareena then a throwback to the stars of the black and white era?

Govind Nihalani observed her rather closely when she worked with him in *Dev*. 'Kareena has an insatiable lust for acting. She surrenders to the character and doesn't apply her personal understanding to the behaviour of a character. This gives an actor the ability to create a character that is different and fresh. She also has her own way of preparing for a character. Kareena has no theatre background; she does not rehearse much. She is one of the few actors who light up when something happens to them. Before a take you call for full lights, the actor goes in front of the mirror and gets ready. But she comes alive once the mirror goes—between the time I say action and cut. There are very few actors like this. Jaya Bachchan is like this. You don't see their preparation. She has a sense of music, and responds to music and melody. It comes across when she delivers her lines. There is a certain melody—*sur me rehti hai*.'

Randhir Kapoor believes that Kareena is a 'typical' Kapoor: '...she loves to shoot her mouth off. Even now when we meet, she'll call for food, we'll have a big feast. She is large-hearted like me.' Perhaps she is out-Kapooring the Kapoors: her father would be happier if she were to rein in some of her brashness. 'She sounds like Shah Rukh Khan in her interviews... She's always making those "I'm the best" statements. I always tell her that she should not blow her own trumpet...She's unnecessarily stepping on others' feet.'[5] Papa does not usually preach, certainly not when it comes to advice about her career. Bebo relies more on her mother's judgement here.

In her short career, Kareena Kapoor has proved that she is a chameleon. It has been quite a sprint from her unforgettable performance as Poo in *Kabhi Khushi Kabhie Gham* to the lower-middle-class girl in *Dev*. There were a string of films which flopped between 2004 and 2006 like *Khushi*, *Main Prem Ki Diwani Hoon*, *Hulchul*, *Bewafa*, *Kyon Ki...*, and *Dosti: Friends Forever*. Yet, she increased her asking price to Rs 1.5–2 crore per film. And did not let the mistakes and scandals, all widely publicized by the press, get her down—whether it was her choice of roles (she refused *Kaho Na Pyaar Hai* and *Kal Ho Na Ho*, immensely successful films by Bollywood moghuls Rakesh Roshan and Karan Johar), photographs of her and boyfriend Shahid Kapur kissing circulated on MMS, or her sister's marital travails. This desi destiny's child is a survivor and Bebo gets what Bebo wants. As she says: 'I'm very moody and just want to be happy. If I want something, I go for it. It can be a film, pizza or Shahid.'[6] The press couldn't seem to get enough of her romance with Shahid Kapur, although the off-screen chemistry was missing on-screen. Her first few movies with Shahid—*Fida*, *36 China Town* and *Chup Chup Ke*—did not do well at the box office.

Ironically, her ascension to superstardom came with the phenomenal success of *Jab We Met* in which Shahid is her co-star, but they had ended their relationship before the movie's release. The effervescence that she brings to Imitaz Ali's endearingly simple tale about a boy, a girl and lots of trains recalls the vivacious spontaneity of Kajol and Preity Zinta, even the screen impishness of her late grand-aunt, Geeta Bali. She became the sweetheart of the nation with her luminous portrayal of the chatterbox persona of Geet, the fun-loving Sikh girl from Bhatinda, who shoots from the heart and is nothing if not honest. Imitiaz Ali says, 'Kareena connected emotionally to the story of *Jab We Met*, to very nook, corner and crevice of the film...I liked the way she listened. She went home secretly knowing what I wanted, not through the intellect or by intellectualizing it, or even by using her brain unnecessarily, but by knowing that the heart connects. Her emotional connect was very high—so strong in fact that her reacting was already a performance.' In an interview on Radio Mirchi, Kareena said: 'Geet is spontaneous, as I am. I also follow my heart. The decision at the end is that I will always stick to my love rather than live with my family. That is the kind of girl I am.' The movie snared her a bumper harvest of awards including the Filmfare, Max Stardust and IIFA Awards for Best Actress. The winning streak continued with the best actress award given by the Apsara Film and TV Producers' Guild.

Equally significant: she hiked her asking price to over Rs 3 crore and she was, to use some of her vocabulary, now 'rocking'.

'It is a love story with the camera. Kareena loves the camera, and the camera loves Kareena.'

—Imtiaz Ali, director, *Jab We Met*

Cut to the Filmfare Awards ceremony, February 2008.

The night belongs to Kareena Kapoor. Of course, she will get the coveted trophy for best actress. And in the audience sits her new beau, actor Saif Ali Khan. Even those illiterate in body language can register the waves of magnetism flowing between the two lovers. But something else is happening here: she seems to have come into her own, both as an individual and as a woman exulting in her sexuality—in her freshly-sculpted size zero figure. The metamorphosis into a star is complete.

It's there in her performance that evening. Kareena does a sort of tap dance number, dressed in a sexy, above-the-thigh, black outfit with a tie and a masculine white collar. She struts about on the stage like a feline dominatrix with a black hat perched insouciantly on her head. And she uses a cane to great and, occasionally, suggestive effect.

It's there in her seduction of the audience. I remember Rajesh Khanna once telling me that each time he looked into the camera he made love to millions of women—all in one go. This was, of course, during the apogee of his matinee idol days when fans sent him portraits drawn with their blood. Kareena may not be so self-delusional, yet. But that evening she is playing the seductress, simultaneously to an audience of many and of just one: her boyfriend. In this display of intimacy magnified she appears to be sharing her love life with the millions who are watching her.

Post *Jab We Met* Kareena has been catapulted to the upper echelons of the celluloid pantheon. She is, arguably, the highest paid actress, with big banners courting her and producers lining up at her door. The advertising world loves her new look: she is the face of many premium advertising campaigns. Nor can the glossies have enough of her with her whittled down, almost waif-like figure hinting at undernourishment on successive covers. Something that has made her an A-list fashion icon. Kareena is thrilled over the fact that she now looks like a 'Hollywood actress', with even the slightest hint of flab exorcised.

Apparently, all the drastic chiselling was done in preparation for *Tashan*, the much-hyped Yash Raj film (April 2008). The media blitzkrieg—shrewdly initiated by the PR machinery—went into overdrive over the bikini Kareena sports in the film. Predictably, Kareena in an eloquent lime green bikini (no frills, clean lines and just about covering the bare necessities) gradually emerges out of the Mediterranean Sea (this bit was filmed in Greece) like a gym-toned goddess, as if she was throwing a gauntlet with the hint of a dare in her eyes. The Kareena–Saif romance that bloomed on location for this film in Ladakh (not to speak of stories about the dejected former boyfriend Shahid Kapur) also consumed miles of newsprint. Her chotte nawab, Saif Ali Khan, wears his love for her literally on his arm—in a bold tattoo in Hindi of her name. Life could not be more beautiful. Her current address, as she keeps telling us, is 'cloud nine'.

The Kapoors have never fought shy of calling themselves entertainers. They are, above all, performers. Kareena doesn't mind being an 'item girl' in some films, and seems to revel in doing sexy item numbers— 'Its Rocking' from the film *Kya Love Story Hai*, 'Yeh Mera Dil' in Farhan Akhtar's *Don* to Shah Rukh Khan's home production, *Billoo Barber*. The ultimate canonization has also been bestowed upon her. When stars grow big even their disembodied voices become marketable commodities. Loaning your voice for animated films is a prerogative of the A-listers in Hollywood. Kareena has now done the voice-over for the female lead (a slinky white poodle) in *Roadside Romeo*, an animation film produced by Yash Raj Films and Walt Disney Company released in October 2008.

Somewhere along the line Kareena began to lead rather than be led—and not just in her lifestyle but in the determined manner in which she began to steer her career. In her obsession with cinema she is more like Raj Kapoor than any other member of the family. Cinema comes first, even before love.

Bebo's grown up fast. No longer mama's baby or little sis, she is moving away from the family nest. Significantly, Kareena is not going from the protective arms of her mother to another set of arms, those of a husband. She apparently plans to move into her own apartment—decorated by former actress Twinkle Khanna—in a building with the delightfully apropos name of Gulab ke Rani in Bandra.

And if she continues to juggle mainstream with slightly off-track films, this new raider of the lost Raj Kapoor legacy could well restore the lustre of the first family of Indian cinema.

8

Dream Boy: Ranbir Kapoor

'Sanjay Sir gave me, or I found the gesture, and connected with Raj Kapoor and his magic world of cinema. It connected me to my legacy.'

—Ranbir Kapoor in an interview with the author

Generation Next of the Kapoor khandaan is revving up its engines, raring to blaze a new trail. Randhir's daughters are unrelenting in their pursuit of fame and fortune. Kareena Kapoor is finally getting into her stride as an actor and as a star. The press can't get enough of her: she has colonized the print and electronic media. Karisma Kapoor may return to the big screen after an interlude of marriage and motherhood, neither having dimmed her zeal for acting. Her troubled marriage and the washing of dirty linen in the courts may have slowed her down but, for her, there is no business like show business.

In keeping with family tradition, the twenty-something Ranbir Raj Kapoor, son of Rishi Kapoor and Neetu Singh, made his debut in 2007 with Sanjay Leela Bhansali's *Saawariya*. (Ranbir was made to cut his teeth outside R.K. when he assisted Sanjay Leela Bhansali in *Black*.) To risk a cliché, a star was born. Although the film fizzled out at the box office, Ranbir snatched victory out of the jaws of defeat, becoming the new 'hottie' in Bollywood, and walking away with the Filmfare award for the best debut actor followed by an 'Apsara' for the best new male face 2008 from the Film and TV Producers' Guild. The new face also parachuted onto the cover of glossies.

A relatively new measure of stardom—star power if you

like—is the profile of advertising campaigns, and Ranbir hit the jackpot with the Pepsi ad, co-starring Shah Rukh Khan and Deepika Padukone.

The first thing Ranbir Kapoor sees when he opens his eyes each morning is the face of Raj Kapoor. This is not the usual photograph of a family member hung on a wall after he or she has died. This 'ancestral' portrait with pride of place in Ranbir's bedroom is actually a cleverly crafted collage of the many faces of Raj Kapoor culled from his films: a pictorial CV of the legendary showman if you like.

Such an awesome legacy may have proved too overwhelming for those higher up on the Kapoor family tree. Shammi Kapoor struggled for five years to carve an identity of his own, which wasn't easy considering the imposing presence of his elder brother. Both Randhir and Rishi Kapoor, to a lesser extent, had to do much the same with the ever-lengthening shadow of their father. GenNow on the other hand wears the RK legacy far more lightly. For the youngest scion of the Kapoor family, being the grandson of Raj Kapoor has proved to be a great calling card: it landed him his first film, *Saawariya*, with a much-sought-after director—and the first Indian film to be produced by Hollywood (Sony Pictures).

Saawariya is Sanjay Leela Bhansali's unabashed homage to Raj Kapoor—from the inception of the film to the recurring images and allusions to the cinema of the maestro. Bhansali based his film on *White Nights*, a short story by nineteenth-century Russian writer Fyodor Dostoevsky. However, the take-off point was, according to Ranbir, the 1959 film *Anari*. In that film, directed by Hrishikesh Mukherjee, Raj Kapoor plays an idealistic, if naïve, painter who comes to a big city where he lodges with a chatty, kind-hearted Christian landlady, Mrs D'Sa (Lalita Pawar).

Bhansali has replaced the painter with a guitar-toting musician—'a dreamer who wants to spread happiness,' as Ranbir Kapoor puts it. The landlady in this fairy-tale film, called Lillian, is a gloriously feisty Zohra Segal. The ever-flirtatious nonagenarian actress insisted on calling the young actor Raj because he reminded her of his grandfather. In fact, the director has even 'borrowed' Raj Kapoor's given name. His protagonist is called Ranbir Raj: Raj Kapoor had dropped his middle name. Bhansali has helped himself unstintingly to Kapooriana celluloid lore—from the RK banner and the iconic umbrella and rain scenes to the quasi-simpleton persona of his outsider-to-the-city hero, who is even referred to as an *awara* or vagabond.

And then there was the much-talked-about towel scene: the will-he-won't-he-drop-it tease of a scene that promises and, yes, fleetingly delivers. In an ironic twist of sorts—poetic justice if you like—the newest Kapoor on Bollywood Boulevard is now at the other end of the probing camera-eye. Bhansali's camera lovingly takes in the contours of Ranbir's well-sculpted, lanky body—doing unto Raj Kapoor's grandson what he did to all the buxom lasses under the waterfall and in the rain. The genesis of this scene is *Bobby*. When Aruna Irani surprises the young, innocent-faced Rishi Kapoor (his son has the same babe-in-the-woods face) in his bedroom, Rishi drops the towel tied around his waist. It was the only thing between him and his manhood. In *Saawariya*, the towel is draped low, hipster style. It becomes almost see-through with the light streaming in from behind. In *Bobby* Raj Kapoor moved the camera away after the nubile Rishi Kapoor drops his towel: we were in the more prudish 1970s then. Besides, the male body was of little consequence then, unlike today when the demand for rippling muscles and gym-toned torsos is from female and male fans alike. Ranbir Kapoor certainly doesn't fight shy of showing his assets. In a free flowing, delightfully candid interview with Khalid Mohammed he said that the 'complicated' towel scene took sixteen takes—and, yes, he was 'wearing nothing beneath it'.

The camera loves this Kapoor. In a finely-judged performance Ranbir manages to stay this side of maudlin in the frequently over-the-top *Saawariya*. He has obviously done a crash course in the films of his grandfather and father. There are moments when this love-struck Majnu is clearly emulating the sad clown Raj Kapoor persona—eyes brimming over with sadness one moment, filled with mirth the next. More metrosexual than macho—even though he does sport rippling muscles—he seems tailor-made for romantic roles.

Unlike his cousins Karisma and Kareena, this Kapoor landed on his feet and began to run after his first film. The epithet 'superstar' attached itself to the young actor even before his second film (Yash Raj Films' *Bachna Ae Haseeno*) went on the floors. *Bachna...* was a little out of sync with the times and Ranbir's second film did not quite live up to expectations, either at the box-office or to critical acclaim. This romantic comedy had its moments but there was a dated feel about Siddharth Anand's directorial take on a young hero and three women in his life. However, once again, this Kapoor emerged victorious. This 'Pappu' can definitely dance—and act. And not just that, he also has a love affair going on with the camera, like cousin Kareena. The camera loves them both. Perhaps he is not as incandescent (or overly narcissistic) as her, but like her, he effortlessly hogs the screen. And like his father, he is equally adept at comedy and romantic posturing.

The stripes that signal Ranbir's 'arrival' are a growing heap of scripts from A-list producers and directors like Feroz Nadiadwala, Karan Johar and Aaamir Khan (although he has apparently opted out of Khan's *Delhi Belly*—a rather raunchy film to be directed by Swedish cineaste Robert Nylund.) Luckily for Ranbir, some directors see a lot of Raj Kapoor in him. Raj Kumar Santoshi, who has cast him in his forthcoming *Ajab Prem Ki Ghazab Kahani* with Katrina Kaif as co-star, was struck by the glimpses of the original R.K. in the character the young actor plays in *Saawariya*. Impressed by Ranbir's thespian skills, Prakash Jha will soon be directing him in *Rajneeti*, a political thriller in which Ranbir's character is based on Rajiv Gandhi.

Moreover, the leading ladies lined up for him are top-drawer: Bipasha Basu and Katrina Kaif. Ranbir has also hogged more than his share of Page 3 visibility, not to speak of film and lifestyle magazine covers. Stars come increasingly as couples. Ranbir's better half is another much-awarded debutant actor, Deepika Padukone. They are the new 'it' couple in celebritydom.

What struck me about Ranbir when I first met him three years ago was how much he resembled his mother. The same droopy eyes with bangs falling into them, similar facial structure—there was barely a trace of the Kapoors in his vulnerable, slightly lost-looking face. For an aspiring young actress to resemble a star mother is probably an advantage. But it is hardly one for a young man. It took Saif Ali Khan a few films and a lot of hard work (and undoubtedly a luxuriant moustache) to come into his own, for people not to dismiss him as a younger male clone of his mother, Sharmila Tagore.

Yet, even then, long before all the plaudits for *Saawariya* had come his way, Ranbir exuded confidence. Underneath the apparent diffidence lay the quiet determination of a long distance runner. Perhaps it had to do with the years he had spent away from home in New York, learning how to make films. He was not just another star brat hanging around for papa to launch him. Life was, as he says, 'sugar-coated' until he went overseas.

During his years at the School of Visual Arts in New York, Ranbir made about half a dozen short films. 'You learn what film making is about—it hits you. Americans are efficient.' It was also coming of age in a tough city. 'I shared an apartment. We would starve, go to McDonald's.' Ranbir also attended the Lee Strasberg Theatre and Film Institute to get a taste of method acting.

Back in Mumbai, homework took on a new meaning. He learnt acting from Rishi Kapoor. 'My father reminded me that acting is not in the genes. People see you as a valid candidate but you can't take it for granted. There is a lot of hard work. It is not about going to the gym and becoming an actor...While giving me tips on dancing he told me that he always danced with his face. It was all about expression. If the mood was on your face, you were in. He also advised me to sing along aloud and not worry too much about the steps...B.R. Chopra had once told him that acting was all about putting in effort and coming across effortless, with a smile on the face. My father tells an amusing story about Shashi uncle. When he was nervous about doing a song, Raj Kapoor told him that he had no reason to be nervous. He said: "You are a Kapoor, just be passionate."'

Mama's lessons had to do with life—and being a good human

being. 'All I am is because of her. She told me to be good to people, be honest to my work and keep no negativity inside me.'

It could well be Neetu Singh's advice that has prevented all the attention, post *Saawariya*, from going to his head. When I met him in the Kapoor home on Pali Hill after the film's release, there wasn't even a hint of a swagger or brashness. The years had brushed away some of the boyishness from his face and his speech was more measured and assured. Yet, a whiff of innocence still clung to him: here was a dreamer who almost appeared to be out of sync with the new breed of actors who speak with American accents, never mind if they have never left these shores. As he tells me: 'I am an old soul, not a New Age man. I would love to be born in the time of Guru Dutt, Bimal Roy, Mehboob Khan and Raj Kapoor.'

The poster over his bed is not only a fount of inspiration but a reminder of the fact that the task of reviving the moribund R.K. banner rests on his broad young shoulders. Perhaps, Prince Charming has finally arrived to awaken the slumbering R.K. Films studio, although there's time yet for this R.K. to pick up the baton. 'The home banner is top priority; it's where I come from. I do want to direct. The minute there's a good story, I will get to work.'

Epilogue

'We are a close-knit mafia. We have our individual personalities, but we are like Sicilians when it comes to a crisis.'

—Randhir Kapoor

Weddings, funerals, near-deaths and annual rites—the Kapoors come together, boisterously, only to go their separate ways afterwards. All three sons of Prithviraj Kapoor were movie stars and directors. Almost all of his grandchildren tried to be. Or, at the very least they have some connection with the entertainment business. They fared badly at school, almost without exception. College, of course, was out of bounds: a stubborn anti-studies Kapoor gene that wriggled in after Prithviraj Kapoor saw to it. Raj Kapoor's three sons—Randhir, Rishi and Rajiv—carried on with the family business in whatever way they could. His daughter Ritu Nanda wrote *Raj Kapoor Speaks*, a book on her father. Shammi Kapoor's son Aditya Kapoor gave up after working as an assistant to his uncle, Raj Kapoor, for five years. He worked in *Bobby*, *Dharam Karam* and *Satyam Shivam Sundaram* before going on to produce video entertainment, and later started his own business. He has now picked up the director's baton after his self-exile from the world of cinema, and is in fact directing cousin Rishi in a film called *Sambar Salsa*. Shammi Kapoor's daughter Kanchan Desai produced a film (*Yeh Hai Jalwa*, starring her cousin Rishi Kapoor) with her husband, Ketan Desai. All three of Shashi Kapoor's children tried to act in films but soon turned to other professions. The eldest son Kunal acted in four films (*Ahista Ahista*, *Trikaal*, *Siddhartha* and *Vijeta* where he plays screen son to his father Shashi in the title role) and then switched to a successful career making advertising films. His former wife, Sheena Sippy, has shot some remarkable photographs of the film world, and held much appreciated shows. Karan Kapoor, Shashi's second son, acted in three films—*Sultanat* (1986), *Loha* (1987) and *Zalzala* (1988)—before hanging up his acting shoes and going behind the camera. Though his screen outings proved forgettable, he created quite a sensation as the incredibly handsome, blue-eyed blond Bombay Dyeing 'dream lover' model who steps out of a billboard and into the bedroom of a woman. He was the John Abraham of his day. Now based in London, he is a photographer and works with several major British papers. Karan also had a small role in the much-acclaimed British television series, *Jewel in the Crown*. Like her siblings, Sanjana, too, cut her teeth in cinema. She appeared in many of her father's films: *Junoon*, *36 Chowringhee Lane* and *Utsav*. And was even the heroine in Ketan Mehta's ill-fated *Hero Hiralal*. She found her calling in theatre, picking up the lost Kapoor theatre gene and taking it forward: she now runs Prithvi Theatre, where brother Kunal is a director on the board. Sanjana has expanded the activities of Prithvi Theatre, taking it beyond Mumbai and widening its scope to include visiting theatre groups, both national and international. In its second coming, Prithvi Theatre has become a pool of talent for film directors—Shyam Benegal, Govind Nihalani, Mahesh Bhatt, among others—to dip into and pick their stars. Prithvi Theatre's workshops for children will undoubtedly produce future actors.

You can almost drive past it. The neighbourhood has closed in, nudging R.K. to forlorn obscurity. Once it dominated the landscape, like a beacon. The studio gates with the iconic R.K. logo opened imperiously. The guard at the helm puffed up with self-importance, perhaps not too unlike the moustached Pathan guard of Imperial Studios who let Prithviraj Kapoor in when he first came to Bombay because he was a fellow Pathan. Indifferent sentinels now let you in, past rusty gates that have seen better days.

Inside, life seems to have moved on, elsewhere. People move about unhurriedly, as if they have all the time in the world. There is a siesta-time feel about the place, as if somebody has just called pack-up. Even nostalgia seems to have taken a sleeping pill. Raj Kapoor's cottage, where his films were conceived and memorable songs sprung to life, looks like a mockery of its previous self. Its lease of life is clearly running out. Logs of wood and useless props are its new occupants, and demolition's axe hangs over it.

Nostalgia, though, hasn't vanished irretrievably. It's been wrapped up and kept away for some rainy day. The studio's dressing room, where Nargis and the heroines who followed her metamorphosed into the objects of fantasy for successive generations, has become a sort of museum for the costumes and accessories from Raj Kapoor's films—a phantom museum-in-waiting. Meanwhile, Mamaji, as pale as the moon and increasingly wispy, wanders about the premises like a ghost from the past. An uncle and constant shadow of Raj Kapoor, Vishwa Mehra is keeper of the flame—and the tired soul of the place. He is the link to the studio's once glorious past, and a living aide-memoire for the inheritors of Raj Kapoor's mantel.

It's a difficult inheritance. The three brothers tried valiantly to continue the 'Raj Kapoor School of film-making' after their father died in 1988. To keep the R.K. flag flying is the new motto. 'We are running on autopilot. We make films the same way, not on a conveyer belt,' declares Randhir Kapoor. In a postscript to their father, each Kapoor made a film: Randhir directed *Henna* in 1990, Rajiv wielded the director's baton for *Prem Granth* in 1996 and Rishi made *Aa Ab Laut Chalen* in 1999. The Kapoors went well over-budget in their last production. Not only did everything have to be the best, 70 per cent of the film was shot in the United States, and for unforeseen reasons the cast had to be flown there twice. 'R.K. has and will always make lavish films,' Randhir told journalist Meena Iyer.[1] The great showman's son is also a showman.

The films were not without merit, but they did not do too well at the box office. Through much of the nineties two floors of the studio were bustling with other producers' films. Towards the end of that decade, however, things began to wind down. The epicentre of Bollywood had definitively moved to Film City in Goregaon, and to studios closer to Juhu. The studio floors have been abandoned: even the admen don't stop here much any more.

Randhir Kapoor sits in his father's office. Raj Kapoor hardly ever entered it, preferring to work in his cottage. 'Raj Kapoor always said that offices are for *dukandar*s (shopkeepers). He believed there was no creativity in an office,' recalls Randhir Kapoor. He rarely uses the term 'my father', preferring to refer to him as 'Raj Kapoor', as if he were an abstract identity, somebody else's father, or a super-size myth. 'Raj Kapoor immortalized himself. A Raj Kapoor will not be born again. We did not see much of him. He was very busy. You see, any normal person cannot become Raj Kapoor unless he is larger than life. We are not as good as Raj Kapoor. We have our own place in the sun. We played our part, a smaller part. It was not about climbing Mount Everest,' says Randhir.[2] The smaller peaks are hard enough.

The three brothers troop into R.K. in the early afternoon. Randhir comes in every day, Rishi Kapoor when he is not out filming, and the youngest when he is in town. All three have their offices on the ground floor of a two-storeyed building: administration and production are carried out here. Lunch begins the day: they congregate in Randhir Kapoor's office. Randhir Kapoor brings the food, packed by their mother, though Rishi brings his tiffin of health food. Continuing a truncated R.K. tradition, departmental heads join the brothers for lunch.

Posters from the more classic R.K. films line the walls of his office. Trophies are stacked behind the huge desk. The studio floors may not be buzzing with activity but the phones keep ringing: there is always some retrospective of his father on somewhere in the world. R.K. films are now ubiquitous on television. Some years ago Sony Classic bought the rights for the R.K. classics for crores of rupees. Raj Kapoor's films still keep the studio and home fires burning. Interestingly, the maestro's biggest flop—*Mera Naam Joker*—now brings in the most money. Astutely, the family kept the rights to the music of their films, with the exception of *Bobby*. The film was shown on Doordarshan after Prime Minister Indira Gandhi requested Raj Kapoor to do so during the Emergency. Today, every time a song sequence from any of the Kapoor films is shown on the small screen or aired on radio, the Kapoor kitty gets that much fuller.

When asked if R.K. would survive after him, Raj Kapoor had said: 'Daboo is a good administrator, Chintu...a good director, and Chimpu will also be a director and a very good one at that. The fate of R.K. Films rests with these three sons of mine.'[3]

The iconic R.K. logo may loom large once again. Randhir Kapoor has announced plans to launch two films under the R.K. banner: one with Kareena, the other with Ranbir. Randhir says, in his inimitably gregarious way: 'Happy days are here again! My father and grandfather must be really proud watching our family from wherever they are!'

Notes

Introduction

1. Manmohan Desai was the director of popular films like *Amar Akbar Anthony*, starring Amitabh Bachchan and Rishi Kapoor. Ramesh Sippy is the director of the blockbuster *Sholay*. Basu Bhattacharya was a well-known middle-of-the-road director of sensitive films like *Anubhav* and *Teesri Kasam*, and Bimal Roy is one of India's greatest directors with films like *Sujata*, *Do Bigha Zamin* and *Devdas* to his credit.
2. Pathan is derived from the Arab word *Fathehan* and means victor.

1. The Socialist from Peshawar: Prithviraj Kapoor

1. Kanjar is a derogatory Punjabi word used to describe prostitutes and eunuchs, and even pimps.
2. Quoted from Urmila Lamba's book *The Thespian: Life and Times of Dilip Kumar*.
3. Quoted from *Indian Film* by Erik Barnouw and S. Krishnaswamy.
4. Ramon Navarro and John Gilbert were heart-throbs of the silent era. Their films were being screened in India, and it is said that Prithviraj took some sartorial tips from their films.
5. Quoted from K.A. Abbas's book *I Am Not an Island: An Experiment in Autobiography*.
6. Vanmala was later to be inducted into *Sikandar* to play the Macedonian's fictitious romantic interest.
7. From *I Go South with Prithviraj and His Prithvi Theatres* by Jai Dyal.
8. Interview with Shankar in Chennai.
9. The correspondence was published in a commemorative booklet brought out to honour Prithviraj Kapoor.
10. Recounted by Yograj Tandon.
11. Quoted from *I Go South with Prithviraj*... by Jai Dyal.
12. Perhaps Raj Kapoor adapted the dacoit's name for the character of Jaggu in *Awara*.

13. Interview with B.M. Vyas.
14. A distant relative of the family, Surinder Kapoor, who assisted Shammi Kapoor for many years, is the father of producer Boney Kapoor and his actor–brother Anil Kapoor.
15. Quoted from *Plain Tales from the Raj* by Charles Allen.
16. Quoted from *Plain Tales from the Raj* by Charles Allen.
17. Red tea: this was a special kind of tea, one that required no milk, and was quite strong. It was particularly good during cold weather.
18. Recounted to me by Colonel Ram Khanna.
19. Manmohan Malhotra was related to Prithviraj Kapoor. He was also Krishna Kapoor's cousin.

2. The Showman and the Joker: Raj Kapoor

1. Prithviraj had put a slip of paper with the name Ranbir Raj under his wife's pillow when she was about to deliver their first-born. The name which had been chosen for him was Srishtinath—that's what the ladies of the house wanted. He was to have several nicknames: Chisto, Gora and Lashkaree.
2. Quoted from *Raj Kapoor Speaks* by Ritu Nanda.
3. Quoted from *Raj Kapoor the Fabulous Showman* by Bunny Reuben.
4. Quoted from *Raj Kapoor Speaks* by Ritu Nanda.
5. Quoted from *Raj Kapoor Speaks* by Ritu Nanda.
6. Quoted from *Raj Kapoor the Fabulous Showman* by Bunny Reuben.
7. Recounted by Ritu Nanda.
8. Recounted by Rashmi Shankar.
9. Mrs Seth has preserved this letter, which was shown to me by Colonel Khanna.
10. Quoted from *Raj Kapoor Speaks* by Ritu Nanda.
11. Shammi Kapoor in *Kehta Hai Joker*, a documentary on Raj Kapoor made by Bobby Bedi.
12. Quoted from *Raj Kapoor Speaks* by Ritu Nanda.
13. Quoted from *Raj Kapoor Speaks* by Ritu Nanda.
14. Quoted from *Raj Kapoor Speaks* by Ritu Nanda.
15. See *The Secret Politics of Our Desires* by Ashis Nandy.
16. Inder Raj Anand wrote *Aag*, *Aah* and *Sangam*; K.A. Abbas wrote *Awara*, *Shree 420*, *Mera Naam Joker* and *Bobby*.
17. Quoted from her article in *The Secret Politics of Our Desires*.
18. Quoted in Rajni Bakshi's essay in *The Secret Politics of Our Desires*.
19. Raj Kapoor behaved like a besotted fan when he met Chaplin. Talking about their encounter with the actor, Dev Anand says: 'We went to see Charles Chaplin in his home in Montreux, Switzerland. His young wife Oona was playing the piano, and their daughter was there. He talked for three hours, all full of wisdom, and Raj sat on the ground. We were in the backyard. Mesmerized, Raj listened to

the man whose persona he took. When we were leaving, Charlie Chaplin came out to see us off. We got on the bus, and Raj kept looking back at the receding figure of Chaplin, which got smaller and smaller. Raj raised his hand and shouted, "Hey, little fellow, bye, bye. We love you." He was meeting his inspiration, his mentor...He took his style.'

20. Quoted from *Raj Kapoor Speaks* by Ritu Nanda.
21. Quoted from *Raj Kapoor Speaks* by Ritu Nanda.
22. Quoted from *Raj Kapoor Speaks* by Ritu Nanda.
23. Quoted from *Raj Kapoor Speaks* by Ritu Nanda.
24. Recounted by Shashi Kapoor.
25. In his book, Reuben quotes sports journalist A.F.S. Tallyarkhan: '...he actually started to work upon the idea to buy up the Cooperabe, including the Western Football Association, and converting the whole complex into something of filmland's football centre.'
26. Rashmi Doraiswami in her paper 'Image and Imagination: Stories of the Nation' presented at a seminar 'Bollywood on Bondi', Sydney, 2002.
27. Quoted from *Raj Kapoor Speaks* by Ritu Nanda.
28. Quoted from *Raj Kapoor Speaks* by Ritu Nanda.
29. On New Year's Eve in 1949, after the success of *Barsaat*, Raj Kapoor tied a mangalsutra around Nargis's neck. Quoting Neelam, Nargis's close friend, T.J.S. George writes in his book *The Life and Times of Nargis*: 'Nargis was deliriously happy that night as she screamed to Neelam, "I am in love with that man." Neelam summed up that extraordinary episode by saying: "I'll never forget that beautiful, unearthly laughter. It lasted for about twenty minutes."'
30. Quoted from *Raj Kapoor Speaks* by Ritu Nanda.
31. Quoted from *The Life and Times of Nargis* by T.J.S. George.
32. Quoted in *The Life and Times of Nargis* by T.J.S. George.
33. Quoted from *Raj Kapoor the Fabulous Showman* by Bunny Reuben.
34. The decision to shoot the romantic sequences in Europe—making *Sangam* the first Indian film to be shot so extensively abroad—was for the sake of convenience. Vyjanthimala was in Karlovy Vary, where *Ganga Jamuna* was being shown, and Rajendra Kumar was in Berlin. So, instead of waiting for them to return to India, Kapoor took his crew there.
35. Quoted from *Raj Kapoor the Fabulous Showman* by Bunny Reuben.

3. The Junglee and the Gent: Shammi Kapoor

1. The film starred his elder brother's *Sangam* heroine Vyjanthimala. Not only is there a distinct lack of chemistry between him and Vyjanthimala, the body language shrieks hostility. Shammi, close to Krishna Kapoor, was perhaps resentful of the actress's spell on Raj

Kapoor. When she wanted to look dishevelled and unglamorous in the forest scene—they have been kidnapped by dacoits—he told her sarcastically: 'Do you think you are a Satyajit Ray heroine?' Obviously, Ray mattered to the brothers Kapoor.

2. Shammi has had his share of awards, and they don't seem to stop coming. He won the Filmfare Award for Best Actor for his remarkable performance in *Andaz* in 1971. In 1995 he was given the Filmfare Lifetime Achievement Award. And in 2005 he received the FICCI Frames Living Legends Award.

4. The Perfect Gentleman: Shashi Kapoor

1. This was the second time he won the President's Award for best actor: the first was in 1962 for *Dharmaputra*, directed by Yash Chopra. He was given a Lifetime Achievement Award at the Cairo International Festival in 2002. And he was chosen best producer by *Filmfare* for three of his films: *Junoon*, *Kalyug* and *36 Chowringhee Lane*.
2. Merchant–Ivory films in which Shashi has acted: *The Householder*, *Shakespeare Wallah*, *Bombay Talkie*, *Heat and Dust*, *The Deceivers* and *Muhafiz*.
3. Pernod is a popular anise-based drink in France.
4. Quoted from *White Cargo* by Felicity Kendal.
5. Quoted from *White Cargo* by Felicity Kendal.
6. Quoted from *James Ivory in Conversation: How Merchant Ivory Makes Its Movies* by Robert Emmet Long.
7. Jennifer, in fact, acted in a couple of her father-in-law's plays—as a mountain belle in *Kalakar* and roles that did not require her to speak.

5. Forever Youthful: Rishi Kapoor

1. Quoted from *<Bollywood 501.com/classic_m_rishi_kapoor>*.
2. Baby Sonia was Neetu Singh's screen name when she was a child star.
3. There is some debate about who first discovered Dimple Kapadia who became the nation's sweetheart and passed into cinema legend after *Bobby*. Some say it was Munni Dhawan, a card-playing friend of Krishna Kapoor, who recommended Dimple to Raj Kapoor. Apparently, Shashi Kapoor had also spotted her in a swimming pool in Juhu and asked his brother to consider her for the role.
4. On *<www.rediff.com>*, February 2002.
5. Quoted from *Yash Chopra: Fifty Years in Indian Cinema* by Rachel Dwyer.
6. The second time was in Ramesh Sippy's *Saagar* (1985) where Rishi Kapoor once again hailed from a rich family and she played the

daughter of a man who runs a tavern in a small fishing village in Goa. The twist in this story is a triangle: actor Kamal Haasan plays a childhood friend of Dimple Kapadia's character.

7. In an interview with Subhash K. Jha for Indo-Asian News Service (IANS), 8 July 2005.
8. You can see the locket in Yash Chopra's *Deewar*. Neetu Singh plays Shashi Kapoor's girlfriend in the film.

6. Lost in the Shadows: Randhir Kapoor and Rajiv Kapoor

1. Quoted in *<www.bollywood501.com/classic_m/randhir_kapoor/>*.
2. Quoted in Bunny Reuben's book *Raj Kapoor the Fabulous Showman.*
3. Quoted from Ritu Nanda's book *Raj Kapoor Speaks.*
4. Quoted from *<www.junglee.org.in/rajiv.html>*.

7. Les Girls: Karisma Kapoor and Kareena Kapoor

1. *Indian Express*, 30 September 2004.
2. Kareena Kapoor in *Rendezvous with Simi Garewal.*
3. It was only later that she changed her stand.
4. Ritu Kumar in a conversation with the author.
5. Randhir Kapoor in an article by Anuradha Choudhary, *Filmfare*, September 2003.
6. *Indian Express*, 21 August 2005.

Epilogue

1. Quoted in *<www.bollywood501.com/classic_m/randhir_kapoor/>*.
2. Quoted in *<www.bollywood501.com/classic_m/randhir_kapoor/>*.
3. Quoted in Ritu Nanda's book *Raj Kapoor Speaks.*

Bibliography

K.A. Abbas, *I Am Not an Island: An Experiment in Autobiography*, Vikas Publishing House, 1977.

Khatija Akbar, *Madhubala: Her Life Her Films*, UBSPD, 1997.

Charles Allen (ed.), *Plain Tales from the Raj*, Macdonald Futura Publishers, 1976.

Ashok Banker, *Bollywood*, Penguin Books India, 2001.

Erik Barnouw and S. Krishnaswamy, *Indian Film*, Columbia University Press, 1963.

Gayatri Chatterjee, *Awara*, Wiley Eastern Limited, 1992, Penguin Books India, 2003.

Chidananda Das Gupta, *The Painted Face: Studies in India's Popular Cinema*, Roli Books, 1991.

Sangeeta Datta, *Shyam Benegal*, Lotus Collection: Roli Books, 2003.

Rachel Dwyer, *Yash Chopra: Fifty Years in Indian Cinema*, Lotus Collection: Roli Books, 2002.

Rachel Dwyer and Divia Patel, *The Visual Culture of Hindi Film*, Oxford University Press, 2002.

Jai Dyal, *I Go South with Prithviraj and His Prithvi Theatres*, Prithvi Theatres, 1950.

B.D. Garga, *So Many Cinemas: The Motion Picture in India*, Eminence Designs Private Limited, 1996.

T.J.S. George, *The Life and Times of Nargis*, HarperCollins Publishers India, 1994.

Lalit Mohan Joshi (ed.), *Bollywood: Popular Indian Cinema*, Dakini Press, 2001.

Nasreen Munni Kabir, *Bollywood: The Indian Cinema Story*, Channel 4 Books, 2001.

Shashi Kapoor (with Deepa Gahlot), *Prithviwallahs*, Roli Books, 2004.

Nikhat Kazmi, *The Dream Merchants of Bollywood*, UBSPD, 1998.

Felicity Kendal, *White Cargo*, Penguin Books UK, 1998.

Geoffrey Kendal, *The Shakespearewallah*, Sidgwick and Jackson, 1986.

Lata Khubchandani, *Raj Kapoor: The Great Showman*, Rupa & Co, 2003.

Urmila Lamba, *The Thespian: Life and Times of Dilip Kumar*, Vision Books Pvt. Ltd, 2002.

Robert Emmet Long, *James Ivory in Conversation: How Merchant Ivory Makes Its Movies*, University of California Press, 2005.

Robert Emmet Long, *The Films of Merchant Ivory*, Henry N. Abrams. Inc., New York, 1997.

Ismail Merchant, *My Passage from India: A Filmmaker's Journey from Bombay to Hollywood and Beyond*, Roli Books, 2002.

Ritu Nanda, *Raj Kapoor Speaks*, Penguin Books India, 2002.

Ashis Nandy (ed.), *The Secret Politics of Our Desires: Innocence, Culpability and Indian Popular Cinema*, Oxford University Press, 1998.

Bunny Reuben, *Raj Kapoor the Fabulous Showman: An Intimate Biography*, National Film Development Corporation, 1988.

Bunny Reuben, *Follywood Flashback: A Collection of Movie Memories*, Indus, 1993.

Sajjan, Sunder and Satya, *Shri Prithvirajji Kapoor Abhinandan Granth*, Triveni Rangmanch Prakashan, 1960.

Zohra Segal (with Joan L. Erdman), *Stages: The Art and Adventures of Zohra Segal*, Kali for Women, 1997.

Yves Thoraval, *The Cinemas of India*, Macmillan India Ltd, 2000.

Selective Filmography

Prithviraj Kapoor

1930: *Cinema Girl*; *Prince Vijaykumar*; *Sher-e-Arab*; 1931: *Namak Haram Kon*; *Bar Ke Pohar*; *Golibar*; *Toofan* (all St); *Alam Ara*; *Draupadi*; 1932: *Dagabaz Ashiq*; 1933: *Rajrani Meera*; 1934: *Daku Mansoor*; *Ramayan*; *Seeta*; 1935: *Inquilab*; *Josh-e-Inteqam*; *Swarg Ki Seedhi*; 1936: *Grihadah/Manzil*; 1937: *Milap*; *President*; *Vidyapati*; *Jeevan Prabhat*; *Anath Ashram*; 1938: *Abhagin*; *Dushman*; 1939: *Adhuri Kahani*; *Sapera*; 1940: *Aaj Ka Hindustan*; *Deepak*; *Chingari*; *Pagal*; *Sajani*; 1941: *Raj Nartaki/Court Dancer*; *Sikandar*; 1942: *Ujala*; *Ek Raat*; 1943: *Aankh Ki Sharam*; *Bhalai*; *Gauri*; *Ishara*; *Vish Kanya*; 1944: *Maharathi Karna*; *Phool*; 1945: *Devadasi*; *Nala Damayanti*; *Shri Krishnarjun Yuddha*; *Vikramaditya*; 1946: *Prithviraj Samyukta*; *Valmiki*; 1947: *Parashuram*; 1948: *Azadi Ki Raah Par*; 1950: *Dahej*; *Hindustan Hamara*; 1951: *Awara*; *Deepak*; 1952: *Anandmath*; *Chhatrapati Shivaji*; *Insaan*; 1953: *Aag Ka Dariya*; 1954: *Ehsan*; 1957: *Paisa*; *Pardesi*; 1958: *Lajwanti*; 1960: *Mughal-e-Azam*; 1961: *Senapati*; 1963: *Harishchandra Taramati*; *Pyar Kiya To Darna Kya*; *Rustom Sohrab*; *Gujree*; 1964: *Ghazal*; *Jahan Ara*; *Rajkumar*; *Zindagi*; 1965: *Asman Mahal*; *Jaanwar*; *Jahan Sati Wahan Bhagwan*; *Khakaan*; *Lutera*; *Shri Ram Bharat Milap*; *Sikandar-e-Azam*; 1966: *Daku Mangal Singh*; *Insaaf*; *Lal Bangla*; *Love And Murder*; *Shankar Khan*; *Sher Afghan*; *Yeh Raat Phir Na Aayegi*; 1967: *Shamsheer*; 1968: *Balaram Shri Krishna*; *Teen Bahuraniyan*; 1969: *Insaaf Ka Mandir*; *Nai Zindagi*; *Sati Sulochana*; *Nanak Naam Jahaaz Hai*; 1970: *Ek Nannhi Munni Ladki Thi*; *Gunah Aur Kanoon*; *Heer Ranjha*; 1971: *Kal Aaj Aur Kal*; *Padosi*; *Sakshatkara*; *Nanak Dukhiya Sab Sansar*; 1972: *Mele Mitran De*; *Bankelal*; *Naag Panchami*; 1973: *Naya Nasha*; 1976: *Bombay By Nite*

Raj Kapoor

1935: *Inquilab*; 1943: *Hamari Baat*; *Gauri*; 1946: *Valmiki* (H); 1947: *Neel Kamal*; *Dil Ki Rani*; *Chittor Vijay*; *Jail Yatra*;

1948: *Gopinath*; *Amar Prem*; *Aag*; 1949: *Barsaat*; *Andaz*; *Sunehre Din*; *Parivartan*; 1950: *Bawra*; *Bawre Nain*; *Dastaan*; *Jaan Pehchan*; *Pyar Sargam*; 1951: *Awara*; 1952: *Amber*; *Ashiana*; *Anhonee*; *Bewafa*; 1953: *Dhun*; *Paapi*; *Aah*: 1954: *Boot Polish*; 1955: *Shri 420*; 1956: *Jaagte Raho/Ek Din Raatre*; *Chori Chori*; 1957: *Sharada*; 1958: *Parvarish*; *Phir Subah Hogi*; 1959: *Anari*; *Char Dil Char Raahein*; *Do Ustad*; *Kanhaiya*; *Main Nashe Mein Hoon*; 1960: *Jis Desh Mein Ganga Behti Hai*; *Chhalia*; *Shriman Satyawadi*; 1961: *Nazrana*; 1962: *Aashiq*; 1963: *Dil Hi To Hai*; *Ek Dil Sau Afsane*; 1964: *Sangam*; *Dulha Dulhan*; 1966: *Teesri Kasam*; 1967: *Around the World*; *Diwana*; 1968: *Sapnon Ka Saudagar*; 1970: *Mera Naam Joker*; 1971: *Kal Aaj Aur Kal*; 1973: *Bobby* (only director); *Mera Desh Mera Dharam*; 1975: *Do Jasoos*; *Dharam Karam*; 1976: *Khan Dost*; 1977: *Chandi Sona*; 1978: *Satyam Shivam Sundaram* (only director); *Naukri*; 1980: *Abdullah*; 1981: *Naseeb*; *Gopichand Jasoos*; *Vakil Babu*; 1982: *Chor Mandli*; *Prem Rog* (only director); 1985: *Ram Teri Ganga Maili* (only director); 1990: *Dhadaka*

Shammi Kapoor

1953: *Gul Sanobar*; *Jeevan Jyoti*; *Laila Majnu*; *Rail Ka Dibba*; *Thokar*; 1954: *Chor Bazaar*; *Ehsan*; *Mehbooba*; *Shama Parwana*; 1955: *Daku*; *Miss Coca Cola*; *Naqab*; *Tangewali*; 1956: *Hum Sub Chor Hain*; *Mem Sahib*; *Rangeen Raatein*; *Sipahsalaar*; 1957: *Coffee House*; *Mirza Sahiban*; *Maharani*; *Tumsa Nahin Dekha*; 1958: *Mujrim*; 1959: *Dil Deke Dekho*; *Mohar*; *Raat Ke Rahi*; *Ujala*; *Char Dil Char Raahein*; *Sahil*; 1960: *Basant*; *College Girl*; *Singapore*; 1961: *Boy Friend*; *Junglee*; 1962: *China Town*; *Dil Tera Diwana*; *Professor*; *Vallah Kya Baat Hai*; 1963: *Bluff Master*; *Pyar Kiya To Darna Kya*; *Shaheed Bhagat Singh*; 1964: *Kashmir Ki Kali*; *Rajkumar*; 1965: *Jaanwar*; 1966: *Badtameez*; *Teesri Manzil*; *Preet Na Jane Reet*; 1967: *An Evening in Paris*; *Laat Saheb*; 1968: *Brahmachari*; 1969: *Prince*; *Sachaai*; *Tumse Achcha Kaun Hai*; 1970: *Pagla Kahin Ka*; 1971: *Andaz*; *Jaane Anjane*; *Preetam*; *Jawan Mohabbat*; 1974: *Manoranjan*; *Chhote Sarkar*; 1975: *Salaakhen*; *Zameer*; 1976: *Bandalbaaz*; 1977: *Mama Bhanja*; *Parvarish*; 1978: *Shalimar*; 1979: *Ahsaas*; *Meera*; 1981: *Ahista Ahista*; *Armaan*; *Harjaai*; *Professor Pyarelal*; *Naseeb*; *Rocky*; *Biwi-o-Biwi*; 1982: *Yeh Vada Raha*; *Desh Premi*; *Prem Rog*; *Vidhata*; 1983: *Betaab*; *Ek Jaan Hain Hum*; *Hero*; *Romance*; *Aan Aur Shaan*; *Wanted*; 1984: *Sohni Mahiwal* (H); 1985: *Badal*; *Balidan*; *Ek Se Bhale Do*; *Ram Tere Kitne Naam*; 1986: *Alla Rakha*; *Kala Dhandha Goray Log*; *Karamdaata*; *Ghar Sansar*; 1987: *Himmat Aur Mehnat*; *Hukumat*; *Ijaazat*; 1989: *Daata*; *Bade Ghar Ki Beti*; *Mohabbat Ka Paigam*; *Batwara*; 1990: *Dhadaka*; 1991: *Ajooba*; *Mast Kalandar*; *Lakshmanrekha*;

1992: *Nischay*; *Humshakal*; *Tahalka*; *Chamatkar* (H); *Heer Ranjha*; *Khule Aam*; *Mahashay*; 1993: *Gardish*; *Aaja Meri Jaan*; *Dosti Ki Saugandh*; *Tum Karo Vaada*; 1994: *Pyar Ka Rog*; *Premyog*; *Rock Dancer*; 1996: *Namak*; *Prem Granth*; *Megha*; *Rajkumar*; 1997: *Aur Pyar Ho Gaya*; 1998: *Kareeb*; *Dhoondhte Reh Jaoge*; 1999: *Jaanam Samjha Karo*; *Sar Ankhon Par*; 2001: *Censor*; 2002: *Waah! Tera Kya Kehna*

Shashi Kapoor

1948: *Aag*; 1950: *Sangram*; *Samadhi*; 1951: *Awara*; 1961: *Char Diwari*; *Dharmaputra*; 1962: *Prem Patra*; *Mehendi Lagi Mere Haath*; 1963: *Holiday In Bombay*; *The Householder*; *Yeh Dil Kisko Doon*; 1964: *Benazir*; 1965: *Jab Jab Phool Khile*; *Mohabbat Isko Kehte Hain*; *Waqt*; *Shakespeare Wallah*; 1966: *Biradari*; *Neend Hamari Khwab Tumhare*; *Pyar Kiye Jaa*; 1967: *Pretty Polly*; *Aamne Samne*; *Dil Ne Pukara*; 1968: *Haseena Maan Jayegi*; *Juari*; *Kanyadaan*; 1969: *Ek Shriman Ek Shrimati*; *Jahan Pyar Mile*; *Pyar Ka Mausam*; *Raja Saab*; 1970: *Bombay Talkie*; *Abhinetri*; *My Love*; *Rootha Na Karo*; *Suhana Safar*; 1971: *Patanga*; *Sharmilee*; 1972: *Jaanwar Aur Insaan*; 1973: *Aa Gale Lag Jaa*; *Chori Chori*; *Naina*; *Mr Romeo*; 1974: *Chor Machaye Shor*; *Insaniyat*; *Jeevan Sangram*; *Paap Aur Punya*; *Vachan*; *Roti Kapda Aur Makaan*; 1975: *Anari*; *Chori Mera Kaam*; *Deewar*; *Prem Kahani*; *Salaakhen*; 1976: *Aap Beeti*; *Deewangee*; *Fakira*; *Koi Jeeta Koi Haara*; *Shankar Dada*; *Naach Utha Sansar*; *Kabhi Kabhie*; 1977: *Chakkar Pe Chakkar*; *Chor Sipahi*; *Doosra Aadmi*; *Farishta Ya Qatil*; *Heera Aur Patthar*; *Imaan Dharam*; *Mukti* (H); 1978: *Ahuti*; *Amar Shakti*; *Apna Khoon*; *Atithi*; *Do Musafir*; *Heeralal Pannalal*; *Muqaddar*; *Phaansi*; *Rahu Ketu*; *Satyam Shivam Sundaram*; *Trishna*; *Trishul*; *Janoon*; *Siddhartha*; 1979: *Ahsaas*; *Kali Ghata*; *Duniya Meri Jeb Mein*; *Gautam Govinda*; *Kala Patthar*; *Suhaag*; 1980: *Do Aur Do Paanch*; *Ganga Aur Suraj*; *Kala Pani*; *Neeyat*; *Shaan*; *Swayamvar*; *Kalyug*; 1981: *Basera*; *Ek Aur Ek Gyarah*; *Kranti* (H); *Krodhi*; *Maan Gaye Ustad*; *Silsila*; *Vakil Babu*; 1982: *Bezubaan*; *Namak Halal*; *Saval* (H); *Vijeta*; 1983: *Bandhan Kachche Dhaagon Ka*; *Ghunghroo*; *Heat And Dust*; 1984: *Pakhandi*; *Ghar Ek Mandir*; *Zameen Aasmaan*; *Swati* (H); *Yaadon Ki Zanjeer*; *Utsav*; *Bandh Honth*; 1985: *Andhi Toofan*; *Alag Alag*; *Bepanah*; *Bhawani Junction*; *Pighalta Aasmaan*; *New Delhi Times*; 1986: *Anjaam*; *Aurat*; *Door Desh*; *Pyar Ki Jeet*; *Karamdata*; *Ek Main Aur Ek Tu*; *Ilzaam*; 1987: *Maa Beti*; *Ijaazat*; *Naam-o-Nishan*; *Sindoor*; *Ghar Ka Sukh*; *Sammy And Rosie Get Laid*; *Chakma*; 1988: *Commando*; *Hum To Chale Pardes*; *Farz Ki Jung*; *The Deceivers*; *Meri Zabaan*; *Aakhri Muqabala*; 1989: *Bandook Dahej Ke Seene Par*; *Apna Ghar*; *Desh Ke Dushman*; *Mera Muqaddar*; *Mera Farz*; *Tauheen*; *Oonch Neech Beech*;

Gair Kanooni; *Clerk*; 1991: *Ajooba* (only director); *Raeeszada*; *Akela*; 1992: *Siyasat*; 1993: *In Custody/Muhafiz*; 1999: *Side Streets*

Randhir Kapoor

1971: *Kal Aaj Aur Kal*; 1972: *Rampur Ka Laxman*; *Jawani Diwani*; *Jeet*; 1973: *Rikshawala*; 1974: *Haath Ki Safai*; *Hawas*; *Humrahi*; *The Cheat*; *Dil Diwana*; 1975: *Lafangey*; *Dafa 302*; *Ponga Pandit*; 1976: *Bhanwar*; *Khalifa*; *Aaj Ka Mahatma*; *Ginny Aur Johny* (guest); *Dharam Karam*; 1977: *Kachcha Chor*; *Chacha Bhatija*; *Dhongee*; *Mama Bhanja*; *Mazdoor Zindabad*; *Ram Bharose*; 1978: *Kasme Vaade*; *Heeralal Pannalal*; *Chor Ke Ghar Chor*; *Aakhri Daku*; 1979: *Bhala Manus*; 1981: *Harjaee*; *Biwi O Biwi*; *Naseeb* (guest); 1982: *Sawaal*; 1983: *Pukar*; *Doosri Dulhan*; *Hum Se Na Jeeta Koi*; 1987: *Khazana*; 1991: *Heena* (only director); 1999: *Mother 98*; 2001: *Censor*; 2003: *Armaan*

Rishi Kapoor

1970: *Mera Naam Joker*; 1973: *Bobby*; 1974: *Zehreela Insaan*; 1975: *Rafoo Chakkar*; *Zinda Dil*; *Khel Khel Mein*; 1976: *Rangila Ratan*; *Laila Majnu*; *Kabhi Kabhie*; *Ginny Aur Johny*; *Barood*; 1977: *Hum Kisi Se Kum Nahin*; *Doosra Aadmi*; *Chala Murari Hero Banne*; *Amar Akbar Anthony*; 1978: *Phool Khile Hain Gulshan Gulshan*; *Naya Daur*; *Badalte Rishte*; *Anjane Mein*; 1979: *Sargam*; *Salaam Memsaab*; *Jhoota Kahin Ka*; *Duniya Meri Jeb Mein*; 1980: *Aap Ke Deewane*; *Do Premee*; *Dhan Daulat*; *Karz*; *Katilon Ke Kaatil*; 1981: *Naseeb*; *Biwi-O-Biwi: The Fun-Film*; *Zamane Ko Dikhana Hai*; 1982: *Yeh Vaada Raha*; *Deedar-E-Yaar*; *Prem Rog*; 1983: *Naukar Biwi Ka*; *Coolie*; *Bade Dil Wala*; 1984: *Duniya*; *Aan Aur Shaan*; *Yeh Ishq Nahin Aasan*; 1985: *Zamana*; *Tawaif*; *Saagar*; *Rahi Badal Gaye*; *Sitamgar*; 1986: *Naseeb Apna Apna*; *Nagina*; *Dosti Dushmani*; *Pahunchey Huwe Log*; *Ek Chadar Maili Si*; 1987: *Khudgarz*; *Pyaar Ke Kabil*; *Hawalaat*; *Sindoor*; 1988: *Vijay*; *Janam Janam*; *Hamara Khandaan*; *Ghar Ghar Ki Kahani*; 1989: *Naqab*; *Khoj*; *Hathyar*; *Gharana*; *Chandni*; *Bade Ghar Ki Beti*; *Paraya Ghar*; 1990: *Sher Dil*; *Azaad Desh Ke Ghulam*; *Amiri Garibi*; 1991: *Ghar Parivar*; *Ajooba*; *Heena*; *Ranbhoomi*; *Banjaran*; 1992: *Kasak*; *Bol Radha Bol*; *Inteha Pyar Ki*; *Deewana*; *Honeymoon*; 1993: *Shreemaan Aashique*; *Sahibaan*; *Gurudev*; *Anmol*; *Damini*; *Dhartiputra*; *Izzat Ki Roti*; 1994: *Mohabbat Ki Arzoo*; *Eena Meena Deeka*; *Saajan Ka Ghar*; *Pehla Pehla Pyaar*; *Prem Yog*; *Ghar Ki Izzat*; 1995: *Saajan Ki Baahon Mein*; *Hum Dono*; *Yaraana*; 1996: *Prem Granth*; *Daraar*; 1997: *Kaun Sachcha Kaun Jhootha*; 1999: *Jai Hind*; *Aa Ab Laut Chalen* (only director); 2000: *Karobaar: The Business of Love*; *Raju Chacha*; 2001: *Kuch Khatti Kuch Meethi*;

2002: *Yeh Hai Jalwa*; 2003: *Kucch To Hai*; *Love At Times Square*; *Tehzeeb*; 2004: *Hum Tum*; 2005: *Pyaar Mein Twist*

Karisma Kapoor

1991: *Prem Qaidi*; 1992: *Sapne Sajan Ke*; *Jigar*; *Police Officer*; *Nishchay*; *Deedar*; 1993: *Sangram*; *Jaagruti*; *Muqabla*; *Anari*; *Shaktimaan*; *Dhanwaan*; 1994: *Khuddar*; *Gopi Kishan*; *Andaz*; *Aatish*; *Raja Babu*; *Dulaara*; *Prem Shakti*; *Andaz Apna Apna*; *Yeh Dillagi* (uncredited); *Suhaag*; 1995: *Jawab*; *Maidan-e-Jung*; *Coolie No. 1*; 1996: *Saajan Chale Sasural*; *Rakshak*; *Papi Gudia*; *Megha*; *Krishna*; *Jeet*; *Bal Bramhachari*; *Sapoot*; *Raja Hindustani*; *Ajay*; 1997: *Mrityudaata*; *Judwaa*; *Hero No. 1*; *Lahu Ke Do Rang*; *Dil To Pagal Hai*; 1999: *Silsila Hai Pyaar Ka*; *Biwi No. 1*; *Haseena Maan Jaayegi*; *Jaanwar*; 2000: *Hum Saath Saath Hain*; *Dulhan Hum Le Jayenge*; *Chal Mere Bhai*; *Hum To Mohabbat Karega*; *Fiza*; *Shikari*; 2001: *Zubeidaa*; *Aashiq*; *Ek Rishtaa: The Bond of Love*; 2002: *Haan Maine Bhi Pyaar Kiya*; *Shakti: The Power*; *Rishtey*; 2003: *Karishma: A Miracle of Destiny* (TV Series); *Baaz: A Bird in Danger*; 2005: *Mere Jeevan Saathi*

Kareena Kapoor

2000: *Refugee*; 2001: *Mujhe Kuch Kehna Hai*; *Yaadein*; *Asoka*; *Ajnabee*; *Kabhi Khushi Kabhie Gham*; 2002: *Mujhse Dosti Karoge*; *Jeena Sirf Mere Liye*; 2003: *Talaash: The Hunt Begins*; *Khushi*; *Main Prem Ki Diwani Hoon*; *LOC Kargil*; 2004: *Chameli*; *Yuva*; *Dev*; *Fida*; *Aitraaz*; *Hulchul*; 2005: *Bewafaa*; *Kyon Ki...*; *Dosti: Friends Forever*; 2006: *36 China Town*; *Chup Chup Ke*; *Omkara*; *Don*; 2007: *Jab We Met*; *Om Shanti Om* (uncredited); 2008: *Tashan*; *Roadside Romeo* (voice); *Golmaal Returns*; *Kambakkht Ishq*; 2009: *Milenge Milenge*; *Main Aur Mrs Khanna*; *Three Idiots* (under filming); *Billo Barber* (special appearance, under filming); Untitled Renzil D'Silva project (pre-production)

Ranbir Kapoor

As actor: 2004: *Karma, India 1964*; 2007: *Saawariya*; 2008: *Bachna Ae Haseeno*; 2009: *Ajab Prem Ki Ghazab Kahani* (filming), *Rajneeti* (pre-production)

As second unit director and assistant director: 1996: *Prem Granth* (assistant director), *Aa Ab Laut Chalen* (assistant director); 2005: *Black* (assistant director)

Index